This collection of essays by distinguished scholars from Britain and North America constitutes a major contribution to the process of remapping the history of early modern British political thought. Based on a seminar held at the Folger Institute's Center for the History of British Political Thought, it takes the union of the Anglo-Scottish crowns in 1603 as its principal focus and examines the background to and consequences of the creation of a British monarchy from a distinctively Scottish viewpoint. In the process, it provides a pioneering study of Scottish political thought from the Reformation of 1560 to the covenanting revolution of the 1640s, shedding new light on the Scots' participation in the invention of Britain and on the collapse of multiple kingship in the mid-seventeenth century.

T0381624

Scots and Britons

Scottish political thought and the union of 1603

Scots and Britons

Scottish political thought and the union of 1603

edited by

Roger A. Mason

University of St Andrews

Published in association with the
Folger Institute, Washington, DC

CAMBRIDGE UNIVERSITY PRESS
Cambridge, New York, Melbourne, Madrid, Cape Town, Singapore, São Paulo

Cambridge University Press
The Edinburgh Building, Cambridge CB2 2RU, UK

Published in the United States of America by Cambridge University Press, New York

www.cambridge.org
Information on this title: www.cambridge.org/9780521420341

First published 1994
This digitally printed first paperback version 2006

A catalogue record for this publication is available from the British Library

Library of Congress Cataloguing in Publication data
Scots and Britons: Scottish political thought and the union of 1603 /
edited by Roger A. Mason.
    p.   cm.
ISBN 0 521 42034 2 (hardback)
1. Political science – Scotland – History – 17th century – Congresses.
2. Scotland – History – 17th century – Congresses.
3. Great Britain – History – Early Stuarts, 1603–1649 – Congresses.
I. Mason, Roger A.
II. Title: Scots and Britons: Scottish political thought and the union of 1603.
JA84.S26S36   1994
620.9411'09'032–dc20   93–32399   CIP

ISBN-13 978-0-521-42034-1 hardback
ISBN-10 0-521-42034-2 hardback

ISBN-13 978-0-521-02620-8 paperback
ISBN-10 0-521-02620-2 paperback

Contents

Part III: Empire and identity

Part IV: The covenanters

Postscript

Contributors

KEITH M. BROWN is a Lecturer in History at the University of Stirling. He is the author of *Bloodfeud in Scotland 1573–1625* (1986) and *Kingdom or province?: Scotland and the regal union 1603–1715* (1992). He is currently working on the aristocracy in late sixteenth- and early seventeenth-century Scotland.

J. H. BURNS is Professor Emeritus of the History of Political Thought, University of London, and Honorary Research Fellow, University College, London. He is the author of *Lordship, kingship and empire: the idea of monarchy 1400–1525* (1992) and editor of *The Cambridge history of medieval political thought* (1988) and *The Cambridge history of political thought 1450–1700* (1991). He is currently writing a book on ideas of kingship in Scotland *c*.1488–*c*.1625.

REBECCA W. BUSHNELL is Associate Professor of English, University of Pennsylvania, Philadelphia. She is the author of *Prophesying tragedy: sign and voice in Sophocles' Theban plays* (1988) and *Tragedies of tyrants: political thought and theater in the English Renaissance* (1990). She is currently writing a book on the ambivalent politics of humanist poetics and the social complexity of humanist education in the sixteenth century.

EDWARD J. COWAN, formerly Professor of History and Chair of Scottish Studies, University of Guelph, Ontario, is now Professor of Scottish History at Glasgow University. He is the author of *Montrose: for covenant and king* (1977) and *The people's past: Scottish folk in Scottish history* (1981). He has contributed to a wide range of books and journals on various aspects of Scottish history and is currently working on Scottish popular culture 1500–1800.

JOHN D. FORD is a Fellow of Gonville and Caius College, Cambridge, and Assistant Lecturer in the Faculty of Law, Cambridge University. He is currently working on a historical study of James Dalrymple, 1st Viscount Stair's *Institutions of the Law of Scotland* in which the foundation text of modern Scots law is located in the context of the presbyterian ideology of Samuel Rutherford and like-minded authors.

MAURICE LEE, JR is Margaret Judson Professor of History at Rutgers University, New Brunswick, New Jersey. His most recent books are *Government by pen: Scotland under James VI and I* (1980); *The road to revolution: Scotland under Charles I 1625–1637* (1985); and *Great Britain's Solomon: James VI and I in his three kingdoms* (1990). His current research is focused on politics in Restoration Scotland.

BRIAN P. LEVACK is Professor of History at the University of Texas at Austin. His publications include *The civil lawyers in England 1603–41* (1973); *The witch-hunt in early modern Europe* (1987); and *The formation of the British state: England, Scotland and the union 1603–1707* (1987). He is currently doing research on witch-hunting in mid-seventeenth-century England and Scotland.

ROGER A. MASON is Lecturer in Scottish History, University of St Andrews. He is the editor of *Scotland and England 1286–1815* (1987) and *John Knox: On rebellion* (1994). He is currently writing a study of sixteenth-century Scottish political culture entitled *Kingship and tyranny: Scotland in the age of reform 1513–1603*.

J. G. A. POCOCK is Harry C. Black Professor of History at The Johns Hopkins University, Baltimore, Maryland, and a founder of the Folger Institute Center for the History of British Political Thought. Among many other titles, he is the author of *The ancient constitution and the feudal law* (1957; 2nd edn 1987); *The Machiavellian moment* (1975); and *Virtue, commerce and history* (1985). He is currently working on a study of Edward Gibbon.

ARTHUR H. WILLIAMSON is Professor of History and Dean of Graduate Studies, California State University, Sacramento. He is the author of *Scottish national consciousness in the age of James VI* (1979) and co-editor with Raymond Waddington of a forthcoming volume of essays, *The expulsion of the Jews: 1492 and after*. He is currently writing a study of Scottish social thought, *Scotland and the European social imagination: from radical nominalism to political economy*.

JENNY WORMALD is Fellow and Tutor in Modern History, St Hilda's College, Oxford. She is the author of *Court, kirk and community: Scotland 1470–1625* (1981); *Lords and men in Scotland: bonds of manrent 1442–1603* (1985); and *Mary Queen of Scots: a study in failure* (1988). She is currently working on a book on James VI and I.

Preface

This collection of essays has its origins in a seminar held under the auspices of the Folger Institute Center for the History of British Political Thought at the Folger Shakespeare Library, Washington, DC, in the autumn of 1990. Taking as its main focus the union of the English and Scottish crowns in 1603, the seminar had three interrelated aims: to explore the range and character of political discourse in Scotland in the period from 1560 to 1650; to analyse the forms of union, federation and empire proposed and debated in contemporary political literature; and to investigate the problems of Scottish self-definition within a British context which the union of 1603 engendered. Over a twelve-week period, a series of distinguished scholars from Britain and North America presented papers addressing these issues. The result was not only a highly successful seminar, but the production of a remarkably coherent body of work which explored areas of Scottish political thought and culture which hitherto have received too little attention from historians. By publishing these papers in a single collection it is hoped to open up a comparatively neglected area of study to a much wider audience and to make a significant contribution to the ongoing process of remapping the history of early modern British political thought.

As published here, the seminar's proceedings fall naturally into four overlapping and interrelated sections. The chapters in Part I are in a sense introductory, providing as they do a broad overview of the background to and consequences of the union of the crowns in both its European and British contexts and highlighting the practical and ideological problems associated with multiple kingship in the early modern period. Part II is more narrowly focused on post-Reformation Scottish political thought in general and the immense influence of George Buchanan in particular; here the papers explore the debates over kingship and sovereignty as these were articulated in the writings of Buchanan and his disciples and critics (including his pupil James VI and I) in the late sixteenth century. This is followed in Part III by chapters which concentrate on the attempts made by the Scots to envisage their place in a united Britain and take as their themes the evolution of an Anglo-British imperial ideology, the contribution of a group of influential Edinburgh mathematicians to the formation of Scottish national consciousness, and the development of distinct forms of legal discourse in Scotland in the reign of James VI and I. Finally, Part IV examines the political thinking of two contrasting figures in the Scottish covenanting movement of the 1640s and relates their ideological concerns and interests to the general development of Scottish political thought since the Reformation. In addition, a brief editor's introduction provides an overview of the period 1560 to 1650 from a Scottish perspective, while a concluding chapter by J. G. A. Pocock reflects on the proceedings of the seminar as a whole and sets it in the broader context of the history of early modern British political thought.

The essays can have no pretensions to being comprehensive in their coverage of the themes explored in the seminar. Meeting for two formal sessions a week over a twelve-week period, and continuing less formally and more convivially outside the confines of the classroom, the seminar inevitably ranged much more widely – and sometimes wildly – than the essays published here suggest. By the same token, it hardly needs saying that the chapters that follow do not amount to a full or definitive account of Scottish political thought from the Reformation to the covenanting revolution. In many respects, the study of Scottish political thought at the time of the union is still in its infancy and this collection can claim to fill only a few of the gaps in our knowledge. I hope, however, that it does go some way towards fulfilling the seminar's original brief and that a fuller appreciation of the problems surrounding the union of 1603 emerges from viewing it through a distinctively Scottish lens. The determination to maintain a Scottish perspective on early modern Britain is what lies behind the otherwise questionable editorial practice of insisting – except on rare occasions – on the Scottish spelling of the Stewart name. In fact, both Mary Queen of Scots and James VI used the form Stuart, as of course did all their seventeenth-century successors. The anachronistic use of the traditional Scottish spelling throughout this volume is intended simply to remind historians of Stewart England that the dynasty which came to the English throne in 1603 ruled over more than one kingdom and possessed more than one crown.

That the seminar on which this book is based took place at all is testimony to the broad-minded approach to their subject displayed by the steering committee of the Folger Institute's Center for the History of British Political Thought. I am very grateful to Lois Schwoerer, Gordon Schochet and John Pocock for making the project possible and for contributing so much to its success. In particular, it is a great pleasure to be able to acknowledge here the immense debt the project owes to John Pocock, whose idea it was to hold the seminar, who contributed energetically to most of its meetings, and who agreed to add a chapter of his own as a postscript to this volume. Without his enthusiastic support the seminar would never have taken place and this collection would never have seen the light of day. A similarly large debt is owed both to the generosity of the National Endowment for the Humanities, which made it possible to bring together scholars from both sides of the Atlantic, and to the staff of the Folger Institute who ensured that the privilege of directing one of their seminars was never less than a pleasure. I am particularly grateful to the Institute's Executive Director, Lena Orlin, to Pat Tatspaugh who stood in for her during a year's sabbatical leave in 1989–90, and to the Program Assistant, Carol Brobeck, for their patient handling of a mass of administrative detail. I would also like to thank Nicholas Phillipson for a great deal of helpful advice when the project was at the planning stage.

The success of such a long-running seminar is as dependent on the responsiveness of its regular participants as it is on the goodwill of those invited week by week to address them. My thanks are obviously due to all the contributors to this collection for their willingness to engage in debate over their papers and for bearing with all the vicissitudes which have accompanied their conversion into print. Equally, however, I would like to thank all those who attended the meetings of the seminar – both the stalwarts who never missed a session and those who dropped in when they could – for responding so readily to the issues which it raised. Their enthusiastic participation made the director's job a hugely enjoyable and stimulating one. While it is impossible to name them all here, I would like to record a special word of thanks to Antonio Feros and Laurie Glover whose companionship and conviviality was an unexpected but very welcome bonus. To my wife, Ellen, I owe a still greater debt: not only for tolerating an absentee husband during the first few months of our marriage, but for her constant support during the lengthy period it has taken to prepare this book for publication. My own understanding of early modern Britain has benefited enormously from having to see it through North American eyes. Finally, I would like to thank Carol Edington for reading over my own contributions to the book with her customary speed and efficiency and Richard Fisher of Cambridge University Press for his customary patience and tact.

Roger A. Mason

Abbreviations

APS	T. Thomson and C. Innes (eds.), *Acts of the parliaments of Scotland* (12 vols., Edinburgh, 1814–75)
BIHR	*Bulletin of the Institute of Historical Research*
BL	British Library
Calderwood	David Calderwood, *The history of the kirk of Scotland* (8 vols., Wodrow Society, 1842–9)
CSP Dom.	*Calendar of state papers, domestic* (London, 1856–97)
CSP Scot.	*Calendar of state papers relating to Scotland and Mary Queen of Scots 1547–1603* (Edinburgh, 1898–1969)
DNB	*Dictionary of National Biography*
DSB	*Dictionary of Scientific Biography*
EHR	*English Historical Review*
EETS	Early English Text Society
HMC	*Historical Manuscripts Commission*
IR	*Innes Review*
Jac. union	Bruce Galloway and Brian Levack (eds.), *The Jacobean union: six tracts of 1604* (SHS, 1985)
McIlwain, *Works*	C. H. McIlwain (ed.), *The political works of James I* (Cambridge, Mass., 1918)
NLS	National Library of Scotland
PRO	Public Record Office
RPC	J. H. Burton *et al.* (eds.), *The register of the privy council of Scotland 1545–1625*, first series (Edinburgh, 1877–98)
SHR	*Scottish Historical Review*
SHS	Scottish History Society
SRO	Scottish Record Office
STS	Scottish Text Society
TRHS	*Transactions of the Royal Historical Society*

Introduction

Imagining Scotland: Scottish political thought and the problem of Britain 1560–1650

Roger A. Mason

Blessed as they are with the benefit of hindsight, historians may legitimately look back on the decade of the 1560s as one of the great watershed moments in Scottish history. These years witnessed a series of interrelated crises – confessional, constitutional and diplomatic – the roots of which certainly lay deep in the past, but which came to a head in the years associated with the personal rule of Mary Queen of Scots. In many respects, the contents of this volume are concerned with the ways in which this 'multiple crisis' resolved itself over the ensuing century and with how the political and clerical elites came to terms with the dramatic changes it wrought. The dates 1560 to 1650 are intended to provide only a rough indication of the book's chronological scope. If one wanted to be precise one might well begin with the outbreak of the Congregation's rebellion in May 1559 and end with the execution of Charles I in January 1649. But the history of political thought and culture is hardly amenable to such exact dating. Inevitably, some of the chapters that follow look back to the period before 1560 and some look forward to the period after 1650 – and some do both. Maurice Lee, Jr, for example, in criticizing the idea of a mid-seventeenth-century 'general crisis', sets Scotland in a broad European context which stretches from the break-up of medieval Christendom to the formation of modern nation-states. Significantly enough, however, he highlights in the process the immense importance of the 1560s as well as the 1640s in the historical development of early modern Scotland (chapter 2). Periodization can, as he suggests, create as many problems as it solves for historians. Nevertheless, there is a great deal to be said for taking the period from 1560 to 1650 as a basic unit of study and for seeing these years as a relatively coherent whole.[1]

---

[1] Standard general works covering the period include Gordon Donaldson, *Scotland: James V–James VII* (Edinburgh, 1965); Jenny Wormald, *Court, kirk and community: Scotland 1470–1625* (London, 1981); Keith M. Brown, *Kingdom or province? Scotland and the regal union 1603–1715* (Basingstoke and London, 1992); and Michael Lynch, *Scotland: a new history* (London, 1991). In addition, Maurice Lee, Jr, *Great Britain's Solomon: James VI and I and his three kingdoms* (Urbana and Chicago, 1990) and Arthur H. Williamson, *Scottish*

For a start, it places the union of the crowns of 1603 at almost the precise mid-point rather than at the end or the beginning of an era. It is all too easy for historians of England to think in terms of a sixteenth-century Tudor age and a seventeenth-century Stuart age. For historians of Scotland there is no such dynastic caesura conveniently coinciding with the turn of the century. Yet they too are inclined, for obvious reasons, to view James VI's accession to the English throne as a major turning-point. In a sense, of course, this perception of 1603 as a significant watershed in both Scotland and England is perfectly justifiable. If nothing else, it created the multiple British monarchy which has aroused so much historical interest in recent years and which gave rise to the seminar on which this collection of essays is based. While this book is certainly intended to address the 'problem of Britain', however, it does so from a specifically Scottish vantage-point. Its purpose is to explore the distinctive nature of Scottish political thought and culture as well as to examine the impact of the union of the crowns upon them. Seen in this perspective, 1603 is not so much the beginning or the end of an era, but a pivotal moment in an ongoing process of Scottish self-definition – and redefinition – which began with the Reformation of 1560 and was to culminate (though not to end) in a second Reformation in the late 1630s and 1640s.

With this extended chronology in mind, it is worth returning to the 1560s to examine in more detail the nature and implications of the critical events of that decade. Most obviously, it was marked by a confessional revolution which saw the Scottish parliament of August 1560 repudiate the authority of Rome, abolish the mass and adopt a Protestant Confession of Faith. While these statutes did not immediately receive royal assent, and while a counter-reformation remained at least a possibility so long as Mary Stewart was on the throne, this rejection of centuries of Catholic tradition proved in the event to be a decisive break with an immensely rich ecclesiastical and cultural heritage.[2] The complex origins of the religious revolution need not detain us here, but the manner in which it was carried through is of crucial importance. For this was not a magisterial reformation initiated and controlled by the crown. On the contrary, it was a reformation from below, fuelled by the changing expectations – if not necessarily the outright com-

---

national consciousness in the age of James VI (Edinburgh, 1979) are both essential reading for the concerns of this volume.
[2] For detailed studies of this and what follows, see Ian Cowan, *The Scottish Reformation: church and society in sixteenth-century Scotland* (London, 1982); Gordon Donaldson, *The Scottish Reformation* (Cambridge, 1960); Gordon Donaldson, *All the queen's men: power and politics in Mary Stewart's Scotland* (London, 1983); David McRoberts (ed.), *Essays on the Scottish Reformation* (Glasgow, 1962); Michael Lynch, *Edinburgh and the Reformation* (Edinburgh, 1981); and James Kirk, *Patterns of reform: continuity and change in the Reformation kirk* (Edinburgh, 1989).

mitment to Protestantism – of a vociferous class of lairds and burgesses and led by a powerful faction of the aristocracy in open defiance of the crown. The long-term consequences of this were manifold. At one level, it gave rise to the strident debate over the crown's place in the reformed kirk which lay at the heart of James VI's clash with the Melvillian presbyterians just as it was central to Charles I's confrontation with the covenanters. Yet a bitterly polarized ecclesiological conflict, large as it looms in the chapters of this book, was by no means the only consequence of the 'popular' character of the Reformation in Scotland.

There was also, as this suggests, a significant social dimension to the revolutionary events of the 1560s which is well worth further comment. In many respects, the term 'popular' is highly misleading, for the critical factor was not so much the role of the common people – about which we know so little – as the unprecedented attendance of over one hundred lairds at the Reformation Parliament of August 1560. This is not to suggest that the revolutionary changes of the 1560s were the direct product of a 'social crisis' precipitated by the increased prosperity of a lairdly class demanding a political voice commensurate with their enhanced economic power. Yet one might plausibly argue that their role in the Reformation was part of a longer-term process of economic and social transformation which began sometime before 1560 and continued through to the 1640s and beyond. The so-called 'rise of the lairds' may or may not constitute a century-long 'silent revolution' the full consequences of which only became manifest in the social dislocation of the covenanting era.[3] Quite clearly, however, the prominence of lairds on the post-Reformation political stage, and not least their displacement of the clergy in government administration and the legal profession, profoundly affected the nature of Scottish political culture and the terms of Scottish political debate. For just as the emergence of a literate, often highly educated, Scottish 'gentry' served to broaden and deepen the social base of the political community, so it encouraged the development of a print culture capable of sustaining sophisticated political discussion characterized by the complex interplay of humanistic, legal and clerical modes of discourse.

Even if it is legitimate to talk of the rise of the lairds, however, it does not necessarily follow that it was accomplished at the expense of the aristocracy.[4]

---

[3] The thesis of Walter Makey's *The church of the covenant 1637–1651* (Edinburgh, 1979), ch. 1. For the social background, see Margaret Sanderson, *Scottish rural society in the sixteenth century* (Edinburgh, 1982). The effects of these changes on the aristocracy are discussed further in two articles by Keith M. Brown: 'Noble indebtedness in Scotland between the Reformation and the Revolution', *Historical Research*, 62 (1989), 260–75, and 'Aristocratic finances and the origins of the Scottish Revolution', *EHR*, 104 (1989), 46–87.

[4] In so far as the lairds considered themselves part of the nobility, the distinction is of dubious relevance. On this and other aspects of contemporary aristocratic culture, see in particular

As we shall see, in the post-Reformation period, a number of new models of noble conduct were devised, to which the aristocracy were urged to aspire. Yet such attempts to persuade the nobility to exercise their authority differently were clearly based on the assumption – whether implicit or explicit – that it was the nobility who remained the key repositories of power within Scottish society. Despite such efforts, moreover, it proved hard to eradicate the traditional feudal–baronial conception of politics which had regulated crown–magnate relations in Scotland since the later middle ages. Aristocratic discontent with the policies of both Mary Queen of Scots and Charles I could be formulated in highly conventional terms as a 'problem of counsel' to be resolved simply by ridding the monarch of evil advisers.[5] In a sense, however, such strategies were no more than an ideological fig-leaf which, if they salved conservative aristocratic consciences, did little to conceal the more profound constitutional issues raised by the events of the 1560s and reformulated in the 1630s. The Reformation was, after all, initiated by a rebellion against royal authority and made safe by the deposition of a queen. The insistence that Mary abdicated voluntarily in 1567 may well be construed as evidence of the instinctive conservatism of an essentially aristocratic political community. But the ensuing debate over the nature and location of sovereignty clearly indicates that the broad ideological consensus which had sustained the Stewart monarchy in Scotland since the late fourteenth century was shattered beyond repair.[6] The emergence of divine right theories of kingship in response to the 'populist' politics of John Knox and George Buchanan polarized Scottish political debate in a manner which was not just unprecedented but which was to resonate profoundly through the constitutional conflicts of the seventeenth century.

If the events of the 1560s destabilized the crown's constitutional position, however, they also raised serious questions about the Stewart dynasty's traditional role as a symbol of the Scottish kingdom's historic and continuing autonomy. For more than a century and a half, between 1371 and 1542, the dynastic interests of the Stewarts were generally perceived to coincide with the 'national' aspirations of the Scottish political community. As a result, the crown became the most potent available symbol of the kingdom's integrity and identity. In 1542, however, the succession of a female monarch, and the prospect of her marriage into a foreign royal house,

---

Jenny Wormald, *Lords and men in Scotland: bonds of manrent 1442–1603* (Edinburgh, 1985) and Keith M. Brown, *Bloodfeud in Scotland 1573–1625* (Edinburgh, 1986).

[5] See Roger A. Mason, 'The aristocracy, episcopacy and the National Covenant of 1638', in Terry Brotherstone (ed.), *Covenant, charter and party* (Aberdeen, 1989), pp. 7–24.

[6] On the basic nature of this consensus, see Roger A. Mason, 'Kingship, tyranny and the right to resist in fifteenth-century Scotland', *SHR*, 66 (1987), 125–51.

set dynasticism and nationalism on a collision course of momentous proportions. Arguably, it was the problem of reconciling the irreconcilable demands of her roles as queen of Scots and European dynast which destroyed Mary Stewart and came close to destroying her kingdom.[7] As it was, by the end of her personal rule, her Scottish subjects had effectively rejected the Auld Alliance with France and thrown in their lot with the Auld Enemy of England. Once again, the origins of this diplomatic revolution, inextricably bound up with the revolution in religion, need not concern us here. More important is the fact that in the event it proved irreversible and that it was finally made secure in 1603 when England resolved her own dynastic crisis by grudgingly accepting the accession of a Scottish king to the English throne. Among the most remarkable – and least well-researched – aspects of this revolutionary break with the past is the speed with which the Scots became reconciled to the prospect of union with England and their reluctance to sever it once it was finally accomplished. As far as the Scots were concerned, the 'problem of Britain' was not a problem with union *per se*, but with the form which that union might take and the way it was perceived in England.[8]

The idea of Britain as a single geo-political entity was not of course a new one. Not only did it have distinguished medieval antecedents, but more pertinently it had been strongly touted in the 1540s in the unionist propaganda orchestrated by Protector Somerset. It is argued here, however, that the vision of Britain which emerged from the 'Edwardian Moment' was loaded with connotations of English hegemony which, stemming from the age-old claim of the English crown to feudal superiority over Scotland, gave rise to what is best characterized as an ideology of Anglo-British imperialism (chapter 7). In their enthusiasm for union, a number of Scots in the late 1540s, and again in the years after 1603, were happy to subscribe to – and develop – this thoroughly Anglocentric idea of Britain. But many others expressed grave misgivings about its implications for Scotland's status and identity within the union. As Jenny Wormald shows, while xenophobia lay behind much of the mutual suspicion and distrust evident in 1603, the situation was aggravated by the difficulty of finding a mutually acceptable solution to the problem of governing a multiple or composite monarchy.

---

[7] For a variety of different perspectives on Mary's reign, see Antonia Fraser, *Mary Queen of Scots* (London, 1969); Gordon Donaldson, *Mary Queen of Scots* (London, 1974); Jenny Wormald, *Mary Queen of Scots: a study in failure* (London, 1988); and Michael Lynch (ed.), *Mary Stewart: queen in three kingdoms* (Oxford, 1988).

[8] See Gordon Donaldson, 'The foundations of Anglo-Scottish union', in his *Scottish church history* (Edinburgh, 1985), pp. 137–63, on the background to union. On the Scots' persistent unionism after 1603, see Brian Levack, *The formation of the British state: England, Scotland and the union 1603–1707* (Oxford, 1987). A number of the essays in Roger A. Mason (ed.), *Scotland and England 1286–1815* (Edinburgh, 1987), also broach the topic.

James himself, whose initial enthusiasm for 'perfect union' proved unpalatable to Scots and English alike, may well have come round to thinking, as many of his Scottish subjects evidently did, in terms of the formula 'king of all and king of each'. But the parity of status which this implied was never likely to sit comfortably with English self-perceptions (chapter 1). Under the circumstances, it is perhaps surprising that the union survived at all. That it did so may well owe something to the fact that, while Scots and Englishmen were acutely conscious of the differences between them, they were also increasingly aware of the common threat they faced from continental Catholicism. Although it is not a theme pursued here, it is at least worth suggesting that, in ideological terms, the vision of Britain as a 'beleaguered isle' menaced by the massed forces of the papal Antichrist did as much as anything to cement the diplomatic revolution of the 1560s, to ensure that union was peacefully realized in 1603 and to prevent its dissolution thereafter.[9]

That said, however, as far as the Scots were concerned, the problem still remained of articulating a vision of Britain which would be something more than England writ large and within which Scotland could continue to be imagined as a distinct community. In fact, in a sense irrespective of union, the revolutionary events of the 1560s had already confronted the Scots with what amounted to an acute crisis of political and cultural identity which forced them to redefine who and what they were. A key figure in the process of reimagining Scotland in terms more appropriate to the post-Reformation world was undoubtedly George Buchanan, and it is no surprise that he figures so prominently in the chapters that follow. Yet, as Arthur Williamson demonstrates, this was an agenda addressed by many contemporary Scottish intellectuals, including a group of distinguished Edinburgh mathematicians – among them Robert Pont and John Napier of Merchiston – whose vernacular writings on prophecy and the apocalypse spoke with urgency to a wide spectrum of Scottish society and testify to the remarkable sophistication of late sixteenth-century Scottish political culture (chapter 8). For the purposes of this introduction, however, it is perhaps more appropriate to concentrate, not on the works of individual writers, but on certain key institutions – the monarchy, the aristocracy, the law and the kirk – which separately and in their interrelatedness provided the means through which the Scots could imagine and define the community to which they belonged. In so far as each of these institutions was a focus of power and authority in Scottish society, each may be said to have generated patterns of

[9] See Carol Z. Weiner, 'The beleaguered isle: a study of Elizabethan and early Jacobean anti-Catholicism', *Past and Present*, 51 (1971), 27–62. Although the 'beleaguered isle' is in this instance purely English, the argument is capable of sustaining a British construction.

thought and discourse in terms of which contemporary Scots could conceptualize their political world. By looking at each of them in turn, therefore, it should be possible to convey some sense of the dynamics of Scottish political thought and culture in the post-Reformation period and the impact of the union upon them.

The most important of these institutions was undoubtedly the monarchy, the traditional focus of the Scottish kingdom's independence and identity. As was suggested above, however, the events of the 1560s, particularly the deposition of Mary in 1567, shattered the ideological consensus which had sustained the Stewart dynasty and initiated a debate on the nature of sovereignty which polarized around 'constitutionalist' and 'absolutist' views of royal authority. The case for elective monarchy and the accountability of kings to their subjects was most influentially stated by George Buchanan, while the counter thesis in the form of a divine right theory of kingship was formulated by no less a person than Buchanan's pupil, James VI himself. Both men were, of course, contributing to a controversy which extended well beyond the borders of Scotland and were doing so in terms applicable to realms other than their own. Nevertheless, it was with Scotland that they were primarily concerned and it was Buchanan's account of the workings of a specifically Scottish 'constitution' which aroused the ire of James VI just as it attracted the attention of the three exiled Catholic critics of Buchanan's theory examined by J. H. Burns. From his analysis of the political ideas of Ninian Winzet, Adam Blackwood and William Barclay, it emerges that their Scottish roots and Marian sympathies led them to develop far less radical – indeed, increasingly conservative – interpretations of Scottish kingship in particular as well as to reflect on the nature of monarchy in general (chapter 6). The extent to which these and other Scots were contributing to a debate of European scope should alert us to the fact that James was able to draw on a wide variety of sources, continental as well as native, in his efforts to relegitimize his rule in the face of his tutor's subversive legacy. It was a task which this most literate and intelligent of kings took very seriously. It was also one which, as Rebecca Bushnell demonstrates, informs much more than his overtly political writings. Her exploration of the influence of literary neo-classicism on both Buchanan and James VI reveals not only the extent to which political and poetic theory interpenetrated in their thinking, but also how different perceptions of the relationship between nature, law and custom gave rise to equally different conceptions of the nature of the Scottish polity and the location of sovereignty within it (chapter 4).

That James VI felt deeply threatened by Buchanan's political ideas is beyond dispute. But it was not in fact his tutor's influence alone which drove the king to assert the 'free' and 'absolute' nature of his authority. It was Buchanan as interpreted by the radical presbyterians. For just as

Buchanan's republican politics were quickly internalized by presbyterian clerics such as Andrew Melville, so James's development of a divine right theory of kingship was intimately related to his efforts to establish an English-style royal supremacy over the Scottish kirk (chapter 5). James, in short, responded to the inherent anti-imperialism of presbyterian thought by embracing whole-heartedly the imperial ideology developed in England to underwrite the Tudor monarchy's assertions of supreme authority over both church and state. In the late 1540s, and again after 1603, this essentially English ideology, validated by appeals to English historical precedents, was reinterpreted in explicitly British terms. Yet the result, as already suggested, was a vision of an Anglo-British imperial monarchy to which the Scots could subscribe only by repudiating their own kingdom's historic autonomy and identity (chapter 7). In the later middle ages, the crown's role as a symbol of Scotland's freedom from English overlordship had generated an elaborate historical mythology, which located the foundation of the kingdom by Fergus I in 330 BC and traced a continuous line of over one hundred kings down to the reigning monarch himself.[10] After 1603, the Scots continued to cling to this *mythistoire* as the linchpin of their historic and continuing identity. Its effective abandonment by the monarchy, however, divested it of much of the meaning and authority which it had previously possessed. In the seventeenth century, such interest as the Stewarts displayed in their fabled Scottish ancestry was as occasional and opportunistic as their visits to their ancient Scottish patrimony. Indeed, as Keith Brown shows, the successors of James VI and I proved increasingly indifferent to maintaining even the illusion of Britishness which he had fought so hard to foster. Gradually, in the course of the century, crown and court alike became identified – and identified themselves – as essentially English institutions (chapter 3).

An absentee and increasingly Anglicized monarchy was hardly an ideal symbol of Scotland's uniqueness and integrity. The aristocracy, however, who had traditionally played a disproportionately important role in Scotland's decentralized political culture, appeared to offer more promising material.[11] During the sixteenth century, the conventional feudal–baronial image of the nobility, compounded of the martial ethos of the chivalric code and the feudal obligation of service to the crown, was challenged by the emergence of two alternative models of noble conduct and, by extension,

---

[10] On this, see Roger A. Mason, 'Scotching the Brut: politics, history and national myth in sixteenth-century Britain', in Mason (ed.), *Scotland and England*, pp. 60–84.

[11] The works of Wormald and Brown cited in note 4 above provide essential background to what follows in this and the next paragraph. In addition, see Jenny Wormald, 'Bloodfeud, kindred and government in early modern Scotland', *Past and Present*, 87 (1980), 54–97, and

two alternative conceptions of the community they dominated. Firstly, the writings of Hector Boece, George Buchanan and David Hume of Godscroft presented an ever more classicized picture of Scotland as an aristocratic republic founded on civic humanist principles. In this case, the nobility, schooled in Ciceronian virtue, were charged with preserving the welfare of the community as a whole and, where necessary, with restraining a vicious monarch's abuse of royal power. The image this conjures up of the Scottish nobility striding across the heather in tartan togas clutching well-thumbed copies of Cicero in their hands, while certainly a caricature, is still highly suggestive. If instead of Cicero, however, they were carrying well-thumbed copies of the Bible, a rather different image of the aristocracy – and of Scotland – emerges: that is, of a godly magistracy ruling a godly common-wealth according to the law of God. For Scots, the *locus classicus* of this Calvinist model of an inferior magistracy was the writings of John Knox where noblemen are repeatedly reminded that their office and authority derives from God and that they are duty bound to protect the 'true religion' from the tyranny of ungodly rulers. It was a paradigm of aristocratic conduct which was not only espoused by the reformed ministry in Scotland, but which could also, as E. J. Cowan makes plain, inform and legitimize the behaviour of even the greatest of noblemen. His study of *MacCailein Mor*, the first and only marquis of Argyll, shows that while the 'covenanting earl' could draw on native Gaelic sources to justify his opposition to Charles I's regime, he was equally well aware of his duties and responsibilities as an inferior magistrate of the realm (chapter 10).

To these three images of the aristocracy – feudal–baronial, civic humanist and Calvinist – it is as well to add a fourth one – and one which was a good deal less flattering to noble self-esteem. For whereas the three discussed so far were predicated on the relative independence of the nobility from crown control, the fourth in its most extreme form saw them as little more than functionaries of a centralized royal administration with powers and privi-leges wholly dependent on the will of an absolute monarch. The extent to which James VI's attitude to the aristocracy was informed by the ambition to fashion an absolutist Scottish state is a matter of some debate.[12] Never-theless, his efforts to 'civilize' their behaviour – to uproot the feud, for example, with all that this implied in terms of the exercise of independent

Keith M. Brown, 'In search of the godly magistrate in Reformation Scotland', *Journal of Ecclesiastical History*, 40 (1989), 553–81.

[12] Sparked initially by Maurice Lee, Jr's *John Maitland of Thirlestane and the foundations of Stewart despotism in Scotland* (Princeton, 1959), and rumbling through a good deal of the literature on the king's relations with the nobility already cited. The most recent contri-bution is Julian Goodare, 'The nobility and the absolutist state in Scotland 1584–1638', *History*, 78 (1993), 161–82, where further references to the debate can be traced.

local lordship – can certainly be construed as part of a broader campaign to create a social and political elite amenable to the bidding of the crown and answerable to the public justice of the royal courts. In this respect, the emergence in late sixteenth-century Scotland of a centrally organized cadre of professional lay lawyers was of crucial ideological as well as practical significance. For as Brian Levack shows, leading members of the profession such as Sir Thomas Craig and John Russell were prepared to lend legal weight to James VI's self-image as a sovereign law-maker. Their absolutism, however, like their unionism, was heavily qualified by their concern to preserve and protect the ancient laws and liberties of the realm (chapter 9). It would clearly be unwise, therefore, to think of the legal profession as simply the tool of a burgeoning absolutist state. After all, it was a lawyer, Archibald Johnston of Wariston, who framed in the National Covenant the grievances of a noble elite alienated by their provincialization within Charles I's Anglo-British empire and deeply perturbed by his erosion of the same – ill-defined – laws and liberties which had in the past guaranteed their privileged position in the Scottish political community.[13]

The study of contemporary Scottish legal culture is still in its infancy and, while further research is unlikely to uncover a Scottish equivalent of the English 'common law mind', the extent to which it was possible to imagine Scotland in terms of a distinctive body of law remains to be determined. The same can hardly be said of the kirk, the fourth and last of the institutions to be examined here, whose ability to generate visions and revisions of Scotland has attracted a good deal of attention from historians.[14] Yet here too there are many gaps in our knowledge. There is still much to be learned, for example, about the intellectual formation of leading covenanting ministers such as Alexander Henderson and Samuel Rutherford, while the social and cultural environment which nurtured the likes of Johnston of Wariston remains largely unexplored. In terms of imagining Scotland, however, one can say with some certainty that the fundamental objective of the Scottish kirk was the creation of a godly commonwealth ruled by a godly prince in accordance with the law of God. Of course, simple as it may sound, this ambitious project was not without its ideological as well as practical problems. John Ford's analysis of Samuel Rutherford's

---

[13] Essential reading here includes Allan I. Macinnes, *Charles I and the making of the covenanting movement 1625–41* (Edinburgh, 1991); Maurice Lee Jr, *The road to revolution: Scotland under Charles I 1625–1637* (Urbana and Chicago, 1985); and David Stevenson, *The Scottish Revolution 1637–1644: the triumph of the covenanters* (Newton Abbot, 1973).

[14] Williamson's *Scottish national consciousness* is a key text here, but see also D. G. Mullan, *Episcopacy in Scotland: the history of an idea 1560–1638* (Edinburgh, 1986), and Leigh Eric Schmidt, *Holy fairs: Scottish communions and American revivals in the early modern period* (Princeton, 1989). John Morrill (ed.), *The Scottish National Covenant in its British context 1638–51* (Edinburgh, 1990), also contains a number of essays relevant to what follows here.

political thought, for example, highlights the acute tensions in the presbyterian mind between humanist accounts of civil society such as George Buchanan had propounded and the powerful strain of biblical literalism associated with Scottish Protestantism since the time of John Knox (chapter 11). Ultimately, it was this intense biblicism which lay behind the National Covenant. It was, after all, perfectly possible to find precedents for a godly Scottish commonwealth in the Scottish past itself. But the pristine – and proto-presbyterian – glories of the Culdees were as nothing compared to the example of God's chosen people of Israel. Such legitimacy as the covenanters required was to be found in the fact that in 1560 the Scots had entered into a covenant with God which bound them, as it had bound the commonwealth of Israel, to fulfil the imperatives of the divine will. 'Now, O Scotland, God be thanked', wrote Rutherford in 1634, 'thy name is in the Bible.'[15] Over the next two decades, the consequences, not only of attempting to realize this vision of a covenanted nation, but of trying to do so within a British framework, would become all too apparent.

In many respects, the drawing up of the National Covenant in 1638 is the ideal moment at which to end this introductory survey. For in so far as it succeeded in adumbrating a wide range of Scottish self-perceptions, it also embodied the Scots' frustration at their failure to find legitimate means of realizing them. Ultimately, as they would find, the problem went much deeper than the policies and personality of Charles I. It was the more fundamental one of the regal union itself and of devising a form of composite monarchy capable of accommodating the aspirations of its several parts. Unfortunately for the Scots, however, the 'problem of Britain' was not one which greatly exercised the minds of the English. Whereas the endeavour to be both Scots and Britons was a genuine challenge north of the border, in the south the idea of being both English and British was simply tautological. What follows in this book might well be characterized as an extended exploration of the roots and implications of this tautology.

[15] Quoted in S. A. Burrell, 'The covenant idea as a revolutionary symbol: Scotland 1596–1637', *Church History*, 27 (1958), 338–50, at p. 348.

Part I

Perspectives on union

1   The union of 1603

Jenny Wormald

There were the Scots
Who kept the Sabbath
And everything else
   they could lay their hands on

Then there were the Welsh
Who prayed on their knees
   and their neighbours

Thirdly there were the Irish
Who never knew what they wanted
But were willing to fight for it anyway

Lastly there were the English
Who considered themselves a self-made nation
Thus relieving the Almighty
   of a dreadful responsibility

This jingle graces a tea-towel currently on sale in the Edinburgh tourist shops. 'As Others See Us' appears at the top, the word 'UNION' at the foot. It is as good an introduction as any to that moment on 25 March 1603 when these four peoples came together in 'union' under a single king, James VI of Scotland and now I of England, Wales and Ireland. It is certainly a better clue to contemporary attitudes than the official statement of that union, the king's proclamation of 20 October 1604. James confidently laid a dreadful responsibility on the Almighty's shoulders. It was because of His providence that there now existed 'the blessed Union, or rather Reuniting of these two mightie, famous and ancient Kingdomes of England and Scotland, under one Imperiall Crowne'. Thus 'it is our dutie, to doe our uttermost endeavour, for the advancement and perfection of that ... which

I have two particular debts to record. The first is to the editor, not only for his helpful efficiency, but for patience in waiting for this paper which was beyond the call of duty – and blessedly cheerful patience at that. The other is to Patrick Wormald, for his marvellous evocation of the creation of God's Chosen People, and the thousand-year background to an early-modern Scottish problem.

God hath put together ... an uniformitie of constitutions both of body and minde ... A communitie of Language, the principall meanes of Civil societie, An unitie of Religion, the chiefest band of heartie Union, and the surest knot of lasting Peace.' And in the furtherance of God's work, the king would 'discontinue the divided names of England and Scotland ... and take the Name and Stile of KING OF GREAT BRITTAINE'. But under the sonorous assurances lay only stupendous difficulties – the difficulties still reflected in the modern doggerel.[1]

Contemporary creators of symbol naturally reinforced the king's confidence rather than his awareness of these difficulties. Poets extolled the king of Britain. Samuel Daniel rushed to welcome the king on his way south to London in 1603, urging his new kingdom of England to

> Shake hands with Union, O thou mighty State!
> Now thou art all Great Britain and no more;
> No Scot, no English now, nor no debate;
> No borders, but the Ocean and the Shore;
> No Wall of Adrian serves to separate
> Our mutual love, nor our obedience;
> Being subjects all to one Imperial Prince.

In his verse 'Two famous kingdomes separate thus long', the English poet Michael Drayton wrote of James as the king who would bring unity to warring realms, and bade him

> O now revive that noble Britaines name
> From which at first our ancient honours came
> Which with both nations fitly doth agree
> That Scotch and English without difference be
> And in that place where feuds were wont to spring
> Let us light jigs and joyfull Paeans sing.

That itself has a certain air of doggerel. But even the mighty pen of Shakespeare was turned to this theme; the 'twofold balls and treble scepters' in *Macbeth* seem to have referred first to England and Scotland, and second to James's three kingdoms, which were not, as one might expect, England, Scotland and Ireland, but Britain, Ireland and France. And *Cymbeline*, written in 1608 when sadly James's union project was dead, still extolled Britain, with a wealth of imperial imagery.[2]

---

[1] J. F. Larkin and L. P. Hughes (eds.), *Stuart royal proclamations I: royal proclamations of King James I, 1603–1625* (Oxford, 1973), pp. 95–6.

[2] John Nichols (ed.), *The progresses, processions and magnificent festivities of King James the First, his royal consort, family and court* (4 vols., London, 1828), vol. I, p. 121; J. William Hebel (ed.), *The works of Michael Drayton* (5 vols., Oxford, 1961), vol. I, p. 474, lines 137, 143–8; Emily B. Lyle, 'The "Twofold balls and treble scepters" in *Macbeth*', *Shakespeare Quarterly*, 28 (1977), 516–19.

Inevitably, Scottish poets also added their voices. Robert Ayton addressed the river Tweed as

> Fair famous flood, which sometyme did devyde
> But now conjoyns, two Diadems in one.

And for Alexander Craig, one of that distinguished band of court poets who came south with James, and equally happy with his self-styled roles as 'Scoto-Banfa' and 'Scoto-Britane', James was

> a father and a famous prince
> Great are the bounds which are, great king, thine owne,
> and like a sacred scilure in this fence
> Keepes Britaine whole, least it be over throwne.[3]

One poet did more than write. The first of the seven magnificent arches under which James passed in his ceremonial entry into London in March 1604 was designed by Ben Jonson. It showed a figure representing the monarchy of Britain, seated beneath the crowns of England and Scotland, and bearing an orb carrying the motto 'Orbis Britannicus, Divisus ab orbe', 'to shew', as Jonson said, 'that this empire is a world divided from the world'. He was referring not to the English channel, nor even to the already notorious English xenophobia, but to the special destiny for Britain heralded by Virgil and now realized by James, the new Augustus.[4]

Yet barely concealed beneath the panegyrics were writings of a very different sort. Jonson himself, just as he was establishing himself as the leading poet of the court and beginning a literary relationship with a literary king which would offer him far more than Elizabeth had ever done, wrote his masque *Hymenai* in 1606 partly in praise of union. But he had already almost thrown away all his new opportunities when they had scarcely begun. The risk he took, in collaborating with Chapman and Marston in writing *Eastward Ho* is, in these terms, inexplicable, and later he was to try to insist that it was not he who was responsible for the offending passages. But who could miss the allusion in the line 'I ken the man weel, hee's one of my thirty pound knights'? The censor's pen might partially mitigate another offending passage; but although the full version has not survived, enough was left in the speech

Now (Ladyes my comfort) what a prophane Ape's here! Tailer, *Poldavis*, prethee fit it, fit it: is this a right Scot? Does it clip close? and beare up round?

---

[3] C. B. Gullans (ed.), *The English and Latin poems of Sir Robert Ayton* (STS, 1963), p. 24, lines 1–2; D. Laing (ed.), *The poetical works of Alexander Craig of Rosecraig* (Hunterian Club, 1873), p. 25, lines 9–12.

[4] Graham Parry, *The golden age restor'd: the culture of the Stuart court 1603–42* (New York and Manchester, 1981), p. 4.

to let an English audience laugh at the miserliness of the Scots come among them. And 1605, with James already bruised by his first encounter with an English parliament which did not share his vision of Britain, was not the time to write an open satire on the union, in the famous passage enthusing about the delights of Virginia, which got through in the first printing of the play and was only expunged in the second:

And then you shal live freely there, without Sergeants, or Courtiers, or Lawyers, or Intelligencers – onely a few industrious Scots perhaps, who indeed are disperst over the face of the whole earth. But as for them, there are no greater friends to English-men and *England*, when they are out an't, in the world, then they are. And for my part, I would a hundred thousand of 'hem were there, for wee are all one Countreymen now, yee know; and wee shoulde finde ten times more comfort of them there, then wee do heere.[5]

Jonson survived the huge censorial row which this produced; he did not suffer the penalty for libel of having his ears and nose slit, as first proposed, and he was only briefly imprisoned. He had powerful voices to speak for him; and James, now and later, had the wisdom to see that making too much fuss about what appeared on the London stage might only stir worse tensions. It had not, after all, been the union-conscious king, but one of his new 'thirty pound knights', Sir James Murray, who first complained about the play. The king lost his temper – and regained it.

There was little else he could do, then or later. At the end of his reign in England, as at the beginning, criticism of the policies of the king of England were linked to the king of Scotland and his Scottish subjects. Nationalist doggerel was by no means confined to the late twentieth century. The jingling anti-Scottish verse recorded by Sir Francis Osborne is well known:

> They beg our goods, our lands, and our lives,
> They whip our Nobles, and lie with our Wives,
> They pinch our Gentry, and send for our Benchers,
> They stab our Serjeants, and pistol our Fencers.
> Leave off, proud Scots, thus to undo us,
> Lest we make you as poor as when you came to us.[6]

In 1621, an anonymous poem attacking Sir Giles Mompesson and his fellow patentees, the Catholics, the Spaniards, the pope, and English criminals, summed up each item to be redressed on this fairly comprehensive list with the refrain 'God a mercy good Scott'. And a Cambridge ballad satirizing the

---

[5] C. H. Herford and P. and E. Simpson, *Ben Jonson* (11 vols., Oxford, 1925–53), vol. IV, pp. 582, 532, 570; Janet Clare, *'Art made tongue-tied by authority': Elizabethan and Jacobean dramatic censorship* (Manchester, 1990), pp. 118–24.

[6] Nichols (ed.), *Progresses*, vol. II, p. 449; Walter Scott (ed.), *The secret history of the court of James I* (2 vols., Edinburgh, 1811), vol. I, p. 217.

visit of the ambassadors of Spain and Brussels to the university in 1623, and complaining bitterly about the granting of degrees to them and their companions, on the grounds that none had sufficient intellectual merit and all got them free (which was more objectionable to the university being left an open question), included in its list Lisby and Shaw who

> did the king on draw
> to give them leave to commence
> And marvill not that it was beg'd by [a] Scott
> since it will save an expence

while

> Seton the scott must not be forgott
> though of his degree he did miss
> A child is gott better than his Ma[ties] letter
> for such a commencement as his.

The ballad is wildly inaccurate; the king was not present, nor were the French, as it claimed. What matter, when it was 'to bee sold in the Cambridge Exchange at the signe of the schollers head, [and sung] to the tune of Hoop doe me no harme goodman'; publicity seems to have been assured.[7]

Clarendon was later to write that after James's death, 'many scandalous and libellous discourses were raised, without the least colour or ground … long after, in time of license, when nobody was afraid of offending majesty, and when prosecuting the highest reproaches and contumelies against the royal family was held very meritorious', and that was certainly true of these choleric critics and future parliamentarians Osborne, Anthony Weldon and Edward Peyton.[8] But it does not explain Bishop Goodman, relatively favourable to the king and yet provoked to rage by the 'number of Hangbies [at court], whole families of poor people, especially Scots. This made the [English] courtiers in fear of infection and dangerous diseases. They were nasty for want of clean linen. There was much stealing, filching and robbery; it was not safe for a man to walk in the night. Thus, as poor people do always flock to a common, so did they flock only for diet.' Indeed, only one English person had reason to thank the Scots; it was the 'hate and detestation of them' which caused Elizabeth's reputation, at a very low ebb by 1603, to revive, as Goodman pointed out.[9] He and Jonson stand in a

---

7 Folger Shakespeare Library, MS x.d.232; Loseley MS L.b.676; Nichols (ed.), *Progresses*, vol. IV, p. 812–3.
8 W. D. Macray (ed.), *Clarendon's history of the rebellion* (6 vols., Oxford, 1888), vol. I, pp. 29–30. The tracts by Osborne, Weldon and Peyton are in Scott (ed.), *Secret history*, vol. I, pp. 1–298, 299–482, and vol. II, pp. 1–90, 301–466.
9 Godfrey Goodman, *The court of King James*, ed. J. S. Brewer (2 vols., London, 1839), vol. I, pp. 320–1, 98.

different tradition. They could recognize merit in the Scottish king. But they shared his critics' distaste for his Scots. Weldon might go further than Goodman in seeing, among the dirty, backward, uncivilized and parasitic crew who came swarming south after the union of the crowns, a king who was the laziest and dirtiest of the lot: effectively, the most offensive of colonials seeking a better life not as hospital porter or garbage collector, but as king of England. But as far as union and the king's Scottish subjects were concerned, friend and foe alike in England had the same message. Eventually even James had to listen to it.

No doubt, in the hands of these writers of drama, doggerel and documentary, the message was muted. But even before 1603, there was a much more public statement of it. The English hijacked the 'empire of Britain'. The famous preamble to Henry VIII's Act in Restraint of Appeals in 1533 had claimed only that 'this realm of England is an empire'; this invocation of the Roman imperial past thus revived in England a fashion which had appeared only briefly in the reign of Richard II, but had been used by the French since the thirteenth and the Scots since the fifteenth centuries. But it was a limited invocation. The French and the Scots alike used the term not to signify a universal empire, but an enclosed one, in which the kingdom itself was the empire, and even Henry VIII, despite his sporadic and sometimes bloody ruminations on Scotland as a vassal state, was primarily concerned in 1533 to assert that England, being an empire, was subject to no outside – that is, papal – power: *rex in regno suo est imperator*.[10] When the wider concept of the empire of Britain appeared, it did so, legitimately enough, to describe an empire created by two equal partners, England and Scotland. Protector Somerset might use force to bring about the partnership, but he was exceedingly careful to propose 'ung empire quy sera dict et nommé tousjours l'empire de la Grande Bretaigne et le prince dominateur d'icelluy empereur de la Grand Bretagne'; and if 'le prince dominateur' was to be the English Edward VI, he was to rule over 'twoo brethren of one Islande of greate Britayn'.[11] By the later sixteenth century, however, possibly because the future of the empire of England was now distinctly uncertain, there was

[10] G. R. Elton (ed.), *The Tudor constitution: documents and commentary* (2nd edn, Cambridge, 1982), p. 353; Walter Ullmann, '"This realm of England is an empire"', *Journal of Ecclesiastical History*, 30 (1979), 175–203; *APS*, vol. II, p. 95, c. 6; Norman Macdougall, *James III* (Edinburgh, 1982), p. 98; Ian Stewart, *The Scottish coinage* (London, 1955), pp. 65–7. Cf. below, ch. 7.

[11] S. T. Bindoff, 'The Stuarts and their style', *EHR*, 60 (1945), 192–216, especially pp. 200–1. For discussion of what Arthur Williamson has aptly called 'the Edwardian Moment', see Williamson, 'Scotland, Antichrist and the invention of Great Britain', in John Dwyer *et al.* (eds.), *New perspectives on the politics and culture of early modern Scotland* (Edinburgh, 1982), pp. 34–58; and Marcus Merriman, 'James Henrisoun and "Great Britain": British

something of a pre-emptive strike. Nervous Tudor Englishmen were busy reminding themselves of their version of Anglo–Scottish history, painting onto the tomb of Edward I the inscription 'malleus Scottorum'. Meanwhile the Welsh antiquary Humphrey Lhuyd coined the phrase 'British Empire'. It was taken up by his much more influential contemporary John Dee, who used it to describe English imperial power and the sovereignty of the sea. Dee's view of where such power lay was made even more startlingly clear in his advice to Elizabeth to revive the homage done by kings of Scotland to her ancestors, and actually produced a form of oath which James VI should take to 'the Noble and Superior Lady of the kingdome of Scotland'. Astraea was the British empress; her empire had broadened out from Henry VIII's kingdom entire unto itself to an imperial power with at least one province – Scotland.[12] All that was wrong was that it was the flimsiest of wishful thinking.

This was the background, however, to the casual and slap-happy way the word was used in the context of the union of the crowns. James naturally took up the Somerset line; his accession medal described him as 'Emperor of the whole island of Britain'. In 1604, Dee duly addressed him as monarch of 'this Britysh Empire', but in view of his earlier use of the phrase, his meaning was to say the least ambiguous. And already in 1600 Thomas Wilson had returned to the Henrician meaning, writing of the 'absolute Imperiall Monarchy' of England.[13] In such an absolute empire, the Scots could have no part. Understandably, they responded either with an equally exclusive interpretation, or by avoiding the word altogether. John Russell wrote his 'treatise of the happie and blissed Unioun betuixt the tua ancienne realmes of Scotland and Ingland ... presently undir the gratious monarchie and impyir of our dread soverane, King James the Sixt of Scotland, First of Ingland, France and Ireland' in 1604, with a revision in late 1604–5. 'Impyir' here might initially seem to refer to countries brought together by the union. But Russell added a second brief treatise to his major work, setting out the duties of a Christian prince, and this time he made his

union and the Scottish commonweal', in Roger A. Mason (ed.), *Scotland and England, 1286–1815* (Edinburgh, 1987), pp. 85–112.

12 B. W. Henry, 'John Dee, Humphrey Llwyd, and the name "British Empire"', *Huntington Library Quarterly*, 35 (1971–2), 189–90, points out that Lhuyd used the phrase in his *Commentarioli Britannicae descriptionis fragmentum*, written in 1568 and published in 1572, just beating Dee to it. On Dee, I am very grateful to Dr W. H. Sherman for letting me read his path-breaking thesis, '"A Living Library": The readings and writings of John Dee' (unpubl. Ph.D. thesis, Cambridge, 1992), and to quote from it: the advice to Elizabeth is on p. 294. Frances Yates, *Astraea: the imperial theme in the sixteenth century* (London, 1975), pp. 29–87.

13 C. H. Firth, '"The British Empire"', *SHR*, 15 (1918), p. 186; Sir Thomas Wilson, *The state of England (1600)*, ed. F. J. Fisher, in *Camden Miscellany 16* (Camden Society, 1936), p. 1.

meaning clearer. This *speculum principis* was intended to aid the king 'in the administration of his Imperiall Crounes'. In his valedictory letter to James, however, Russell was already showing the unease creeping in to mar Scottish enthusiasm, and there he took his point about two crowns further, adjuring the king to

> Lett it not begyne with ane comœdie, and end in ane tragœdie; to be ane verball unioun in disparitie nor reall in conformity ... thairby, to advance the ane kingdome, to great honor and become forzetfull of the uther, and sua to mak the samyn altogidder solitat and desolat, qhilk cannot stand vith zour M. honor. As god hes heichlie advanceit zour M. lett Scotland qhilk is zour auldest impyir be partakeris of zour blissingis. Inlykmaner with thankfulnes to god, and visdome to zour impyr, remember s^r the six royal qualities, requisit in ane gude prince.

By this stage, it almost looks as though the particular purpose of discussing princely virtues was to remind James of his duty to his empire of Scotland. And this supporter of union returned to the point at the end of his letter: 'as zour M. loves zour avin standing, vith zour posteritie, and veill of this haill Ile: be nevir unmyndfull of this zour first and auldest impyir of Scotland, and of zour gude subiectis heir.'[14] He had reason to worry. The careful listing of the king's titles in the heading to his main tract was forced on him by the refusal of the English house of commons to accept the style 'King of Great Britain'. Its use in the second version of the tract reflects another source of tension: James had unilaterally adopted it, by royal proclamation and not with parliamentary agreement. This was not only threatening and offensive. It is also a reminder of just how far early seventeenth-century Englishmen and Scotsmen alike were from thinking out the full implications of what happened in 1603; despite the king's insistence on himself as 'King of Great Britain', there was never any suggestion, let alone rumpus such as happened in 1952 at the accession of Elizabeth II (and I), that his new position made him simply and entirely the first James, a title used only by subsequent generations of Anglocentric historians.

Russell's worries were shared by the members of the Scottish parliament. In setting up the Scottish part of the commission to discuss the union in 1604, parliament referred to James's 'maist Ancient and Native kingdome', where the king, though physically absent, was 'zit present by his princelie power, fatherlie cair and prudent commandementis'. What had been created by the union of the crowns was 'a constant and freindlie coniuncioun with thair nichbour cuntrey of England Now united by alledgeance

---

[14] Russell's 'A treatise of the happie and blissed Unioun' is printed in *Jac. union*, pp. 75–142. The second, unprinted treatise and the valedictory letter are in NLS Adv. MS 31.4.7, ff. 21 r–26 v and f. 27 r–27 v, following on the 'happie and blissed Unioun'. The quotations are on f. 21 r, and f. 27 r and 27 v. For further discussion of Russell's treatise, see below, ch. 9.

and loyall subiectioun in his Maiesties maist Royall persone'; but MPs were confident that his plans for union in no way would 'prejudge or hurt the fundamentall lawes Ancient privilegeis offices and liberteis of this kingdome quhairby ... the Princelie Authoritie of his maist Royall discent haith bene thair mony aiges mantened', for any such hurt would mean that 'it culd no moir be a frie monarchie'. James's intentions, they announced, were no more than to reform indifferent and temporal statutes and particular customs, so that the present peace and amity between England and Scotland could be assured for the future.[15] It was a very limited view; and 1607 found them reacting with considerable touchiness to a report that the English house of commons believed them to be intent on maintaining separation, precisely because they had excepted the fundamental laws of the kingdom from the subjects to be discussed by the Anglo-Scottish commissioners. They hastened to explain that they had never intended the phrase to cover particular acts and statutes or other laws and customs which might stand in the way of conformity, but only 'these fundamentall lawis wherby your Majestie, efter so long a discent, dois most happelie injoy the crown'. But the commons had also objected to their insistence that Scotland should remain a 'free monarchie'. This phrase, they said,

we can nevir better interprete then your Majestie hes alreddy done; for we nevir meant thairby to except aganis onie counfounding as it wer of these two befoir separated kingdomes in one glorious monarche and impyre of the whole Yle, bot onlie that this your Majesteis antient and native kingdome sould not be so disordourit and maid confusit by turneing of it, in place of a trew and freindlie Unioun, into a conquered and slavishe province.

James had, in fact, dealt with these points four months earlier, in his speech of 31 March 1607 to the English parliament, where he denied the 'alleadged ... aversenesse' of the Scots.[16] But the tone of the king's speech was very different from that of the letter from his Scottish parliament. James had sought to be wholly reassuring to the hostile English. The Scots sought to reassure the king – but only up to a point. They would use the word 'impyre', provided it meant the enclosed empire of the whole island. But they were also aware that 'empire' might mean centre and slavish province. Hence, while the English stressed the English/British empire, the Scots infinitely preferred to emphasize their free monarchy, and remind James that theirs was his ancient kingdom.

If both sides preferred to define concepts of monarchy and empire according to immediate political needs, it is hardly surprising that appeals to history were of no help in establishing a *modus vivendi* for the Great Britain

[15] *APS*, vol. IV, pp. 263–4.   [16] *RPC*, vol. VII, pp. 535–6; McIlwain, *Works*, p. 300.

of which James dreamed. James's use of history was not in any case one which calmed the fears of his English subjects; he had an unfortunate tendency to invoke it to prove the superiority of king over parliament and law. As far as the union was concerned, the one point on which everyone agreed, or at least paid lip-service to, was that two ancient kingdoms had long been at war, and were now at peace; the union was thus a very Good Thing. The king himself referred in his proclamation of October 1604 to 'two mightie nations, having bene ever from their first separation continually in blood against each other'. But he was not the first Scotsman to do so. It was a message heralded almost a century earlier by that most impressive and tough-minded scholar John Mair, in his *Historia Maioris Britanniae*. In a work produced eight years after the disastrous defeat of the Scots at Flodden, it was enterprising, to say the least, of this Scottish theologian to argue not for the Auld Alliance with France, but for the benefits which would accrue from Anglo-Scottish friendship, and the reasons why such friendship would make sense. The point was forcibly restated by the great lawyer Sir Thomas Craig of Riccarton, a man very close to the king, and one of the Scottish commissioners for union in 1604, who opened his treatise *De unione regnorum Britanniae* with a chapter entitled 'The separation of the crowns of the island is the cause of all the calamities that have befallen Britain'. This went further than the king in arguing that there never had been a time when the island was united. Now, therefore, men should undoubtedly rejoice; for, as he said at the beginning of his second chapter, 'our most sapient and invincible Prince James, now king of all Britain, has formed a resolve whose praise shall resound to posterity, to unite indissolubly the two kingdoms of Scotland and England. The catastrophes of the past would never have so vexed the island had the whole of it been controlled by a single powerful monarchy.'[17]

This was no doubt true – from the Scottish point of view. But the 'catastrophes of the past' had been caused by precisely the desire to establish a 'single powerful monarchy': an English one. The Scots naturally preferred peace to the horrors of invading English armies moving north. The English perspective was much more limited. Only recently had they become inclined to value peace with Scotland, because of shared Protestant religion and the advantages of their traditional enemy becoming a friendly neighbour now that the new enemy was Spain. The careful arguments put forward by James, or Craig, or Sir Robert Cotton, setting early seventeenth-century Scotland and England into a historical pattern in which the small

---

[17] Larkin and Hughes (eds.), *Stuart proclamations*, vol. I, p. 95; John Mair, *A history of Greater Britain*, ed. and trans. A. Constable (SHS, 1892); Thomas Craig of Riccarton, *De unione regnorum Britanniae*, ed. and trans. C. S. Terry (SHS, 1909), pp. 207, 227.

and warring kingdoms of France, of Spain, indeed of England and Scotland
themselves, had gradually come together into greater units which ensured
strength and peace, were not likely to move the English.[18] Their history, as
far as Scotland was concerned, had been starkly and aggressively imperialist.[19] Now they had to redefine 'imperial' in the Henrician sense of exclusion
rather than the medieval Edwardian one of conquest, precisely to protect
their own historical past in which Scotland had been a vassal state. In that
context, a unity of equal partners had no appeal. Far more powerful were
the arguments used against the name of Britain in the parliament of 1604.
Only a few years earlier, Elizabeth's Welsh ancestry had been extremely
useful in establishing her role as British empress. Now, 'Britain' appeared in
a very different light; and James's references, in his proclamation, to 'the
true and ancient Name, which God and Time have imposed upon this Isle,
extant, and received in Histories, in all Mappes and Cartes' failed to
impress, while the fact that it was now used 'in Ordinary Letters to Our selfe
from divers Forraine Princes' was positively objectionable. The 'assumption of a name though antient, yet peculier to the weakest part of our Nation,
and those conquered by the great charge and much expense of English
bloud, and by this conquest united unto us' would be a matter of dishonour.
Foreign nations might 'hould it as a mark of conquest of servitude branded
on us'. Moreover, it would cause unnecessary confusion. Travellers abroad
would find that they were not recognized by the new name; and the state
would become endlessly engaged in renewing all treaties made 'by the
Antient name of England, & Kinges and Queenes of England'. It was all so
burdensome, and so horrible to contemplate. A contemporary Scottish
writer might respond with the acid comment that 'I wish it [the name] were
such as they do esteme of it', but his was a very lone voice in the general
enthusiasm for Englishness.[20]

Secular history was a double-edged weapon, therefore. The veneer of
religious unity was, if anything, even less helpful. James was in no doubt
that what God wanted was Great Britain. Half a century earlier, even some
Englishmen had contemplated the idea of Britain as divinely ordained by
God. It was a very different matter in 1603, when a Scottish king would
become British monarch; and it was only the Scottish tracts which took up

---

[18] McIlwain, *Works*, pp. 272–3; Craig, *De unione*, pp. 208–27; Robert Cotton, 'A Discourse of
the Descent of the K's Mty from the Saxons', 26 March 1603: PRO SP 14/1/3.

[19] On 'British' history as 'a process of conquest and forcible anglicisation', see Gerald Aylmer,
'The peculiarities of the English state', *Journal of Historical Sociology*, 3 (1990), 91–108, and
John Gillingham, 'The beginnings of English imperialism', *ibid.*, 5 (1992), 392–409. Gillingham traces the 'cultural images which provided the moral energy for English imperialism' back to the twelfth century. The Scots had a long history of resistance by 1603.

[20] Larkin and Hughes (eds.), *Stuart proclamations*, vol. I, p. 97; PRO SP 14/7/59; Bruce
Galloway, *The union of England and Scotland, 1603–1608* (Edinburgh, 1986), p. 37.

the concept of Britain as God's elect nation, so strongly emphasized in the king's own proclamation of October 1604. The English, by then nourished on a diet of Foxe and Jewel, naturally took a profoundly different view of the Almighty's responsibility and intentions. Elizabeth, the new Constantine, had fulfilled His purpose in saving His church and people of England. Indeed, they did not stop at considering England as the elect nation. In a marginal note to a book written in 1559 by John Aylmer, future bishop of London, *An harborowe for faithfull and trewe subiectes*, the position was made quite clear. GOD IS ENGLISH was the rubric for that part of the text which read 'Play not the milk-sops . . . Show yourselves true Englishmen in readiness, courage and boldness: and be ashamed to be the last. Fear neither French nor Scot. For first you have God and all his army of angels on your side.'[21] God is English. Even the most extreme of Scottish covenanters, at the height of their confidence in the seventeenth century, never quite made such a direct claim. The Scots, with great pride in their post-Reformation church, could describe it in 1616 as 'through the abundant grace of our Lord . . . one of the most pure Kirks under heaven this day'.[22] They believed passionately in that church as a part of the universal reformed church, united with the reformed churches of Europe, and serving God with missionary zeal – as indeed even the English discovered to their horror when, during the chaos of the mid-seventeenth-century civil war, the Scots tried to impose their faith, the faith of Geneva, on their erring Anglican brethren, thereby challenging English certainty that their church alone was the true heir of the erring church of Rome. The Scots might well have insisted that God was certainly not English. But if He had to be given honorary national identity, then He was not Scottish either; He was European.

---

[21] Galloway, *Union*, pp. 33–4. For the texts of the Scottish tracts by Robert Pont and John Russell and the anonymous 'Treatise about the Union of England and Scotland', and notes on those by other Scottish writers, *Jac. union*, pp. 1–142, 241–4. For excellent and subtle discussion of Scottish attitudes, see Arthur H. Williamson, *Scottish national consciousness in the age of James VI* (Edinburgh, 1979), especially chs. 3 and 4. Aylmer is quoted by Patrick Collinson, *The birthpangs of Protestant England* (London, 1988), p. 4.

[22] *The booke of the universall kirk. Acts and proceedings of the general assemblies of the kirk of Scotland, 1560–1618* (4 vols., Maitland Club, 1839–45), vol. III, p. 1139. Dr Roger Mason has drawn my attention to the assertion of Samuel Rutherford, 'Now O Scotland, God be thanked, thy name is in the Bible', and Archibald Johnston of Wariston's description of the 'glorious marriage day of the kingdom with God', and suggested a chauvinism very similar to Aylmer's. I do not think that, even in these writers, it is quite so extreme. But I would certainly accept that the more universalist attitudes of the late sixteenth and early seventeenth centuries changed, as the fears and strains of the mid-seventeenth century focused Scottish minds on their Scottish God, for reasons very similar to those which caused worried Englishmen to cling to their English God. See *The diary of Sir Archibald Johnston of Wariston 1632–39*, ed. G. M. Paul (SHS, 1911), pp. 400–1, and, on Rutherford, S. A. Burrell, 'The covenant idea as a revolutionary symbol: Scotland 1596–1637', *Church History*, 27 (1958), 338–50, at p. 348.

Again, we are being forcibly reminded of the profound differences between the two countries being pressed into union by dynastic accident. The Scots, in religious as much as secular matters, showed an outgoing, confident sense of being part of a wider whole; their European vision had been their *raison d'être* since the end of the thirteenth century, when the veneer of Anglo-Scottish friendship of the twelfth and thirteenth centuries had been violently torn away by the imperialist ambitions of Edward I. The English belief in themselves as God's chosen people, their land flowing with milk and honey, shown particular divine favour, which in 1559 toppled over into Aylmer's spectacular claim, had a far longer pedigree. It was the creation of Bede.[23] But in the course of the middle ages, other nations had caught up with, and overtaken, this early English perception. In the thirteenth century, Louis IX and, to an even greater extent, Philip the Fair, took unto themselves the title 'rex christianissimus', and used it to great effect to create the concept of the French as a holy people, governed by the special representative of God. The Spanish position was even more astonishing. From the fourteenth century the Castilian monarchy had turned its back on the normal rituals of sacral kingship. Instead, it put almost all the emphasis on secular power: the royal horse which the king alone could ride; the knighting by a mechanical statue of St James; the election and acclamation by his subjects. By the sixteenth century, it was combining this with the extension of Ferdinand and Isabella's propagandist use of the title 'Very Catholic Kings' as a means of asserting particular divine favour within Spain into the Hapsburg claim to have been marked out by God as the preservers of the true faith against the infidel and the heretic. It was a universal mission. 'The principal foundation of this high edifice', wrote Fray Juan de Salazar in his *Politica Española* of 1619, 'the hinges and axles on which this great machine turns, lies not in the rules of the impious Machiavelli, which atheists call "reasons of state" ... but in

---

[23] Patrick Wormald, 'Bede, the *Bretwaldas* and the origins of the *Gens Anglorum*', in P. Wormald (ed.), *Ideal and reality in Frankish and Anglo–Saxon society: studies presented to J. M. Wallace-Hadrill* (Oxford, 1983), pp. 99–129; and 'The Venerable Bede and the "Church of the English"', in Geoffrey Rowell (ed.), *The English religious tradition and the genius of Anglicanism* (Oxford, 1992), pp. 13–32. For later medieval English claims, John W. McKenna, 'How God became an Englishman ', in D. J. Guth and J. W. McKenna (eds.), *Tudor rule and revolution: essays for G. R. Elton from his American friends* (Cambridge, 1982), pp. 25–43. Professor Collinson has convincingly modified the extreme views of England as *the* elect nation advanced by W. Haller, *Foxe's 'Book of martyrs' and the elect nation* (London, 1963), and emphasized the universalist and providentialist approach of Foxe: *Birthpangs of Protestant England*, ch. 1. Nevertheless, he himself points out that Aylmer's claim, though it 'still has the capacity to shock as well as to amuse', was a 'commonplace' (p. 4). And certainly, even if England was 'an' elect nation rather than 'the' elect nation, a tradition running strongly from Bede to Milton is, whatever the competition, peculiarly powerful and adamantine.

religion and the service and honour of God.'[24] The English, manifestly not favoured by God in either their foreign ambitions or their domestic affairs by the fifteenth century, had fallen behind. No wonder the 'Edwardian Moment', with its concept of Britain as elect, was so brief. No wonder, when it was succeeded not by a moment but by a quinquennium when it looked as though England would be swallowed up by God's Catholic Hapsburgs, the relief of Elizabeth's succession pushed Aylmer over the top. In stark contrast to the outward-looking and missionary approach of the Spaniards – or the Scots – rival claims and political events had forced the kingdom with the oldest claim by centuries to be God's chosen people into the straitjacket of total insularity. They were hardly likely to welcome the suggestion, within half a century, that the union of the crowns of 1603 demonstrated that God's purpose for them was to make them a part of the elect nation of Britain.

Antiquity, present symbolism, royal will and divine intention might all be invoked to legitimize the recreation of what Cotton called 'this glorious Empier ... of Great Brittane'. But behind the pageantry and the triumph and the glory of that heady moment when at last one king reigned over the kingdoms of Scotland and England lay the harsh reality that the name of Britain might be on at least some men's lips, but the concept of Britain was repugnant to their minds, and 'Rex Britanniae' would mean no more within the British Isles than 'Rex Hispaniae' did when in the 1620s Olivares tried and failed to bring the kingdoms of the Iberian peninsula into the Union of Arms.

Nor did other models help. The tracts written about union, its nature and its problems naturally turned to the other unions of the period for analysis and example. There were plenty to draw on. There was none which could be regarded as completely successful. Indeed, at least one, in the very recent past, had been short-lived farce.[25] When the Poles elected Henri de Valois, the future Henri III, as their king in 1573, the would-be union lasted eighteen months, breaking at the moment when Henri succeeded his brother Charles IX; changing from royal to travelling clothes behind the curtains of his bed in the Wawel palace in Kracow, he slipped out and headed posthaste for the border, leaving his unwanted kingdom to the

---

[24] Joseph R. Strayer, 'France: the holy land, the chosen people, and the Most Christian King', in T. K. Rabb and J. E Seigel (eds.), *Action and conviction in early modern Europe* (Princeton, 1971), pp. 3–16; Teofilo F. Ruiz, 'Unsacred monarchy: the kings of Castile in the late middle ages' in Sean Wilentz (ed.), *Rites of power: symbolism, ritual and politics since the middle ages* (Philadelphia, 1985), pp. 109–44; and J. H. Elliott, 'Power and propaganda in the Spain of Philip IV', *ibid.*, pp. 145–73, quoting Salazar on p. 148.

[25] For this and what follows on Poland and its unions, Norman Davies, *God's playground: a history of Poland* (2 vols., New York, 1982), vol. I, pp. 115–55, 322–3, 413–20, 433–7.

accompaniment of cries of 'Sire, why do you desert us?' from a Polish nobleman frantically swimming up the Vistula. Even this remarkable physical feat did not endear his Polish subjects to their French king. Nor was the Polish–Swedish union successful. Sweden itself had already experienced the problems of union, extricating itself from the Union of Kalmar with the dominating powers of Norway and Denmark in 1523; but, weak kingdom though it was, it managed to sustain its union with Finland. In 1587, Sigismund Vasa, heir to the Swedish throne, was elected king of Poland. Again, the potential union broke when he succeeded to his other kingdom; but this time, it was the second kingdom which rejected him. His attempt to establish himself as king of Sweden in 1593 lasted five months, although it was not until 1599 that he was formally deposed. The main issue was religious; Protestant Sweden would not accept a proselytizing Catholic. The underlying problem was how to create a union.

A third Polish experiment did work. In 1386 Jogaila, or Jagiello, grand duke of Lithuania, married the Polish child-queen Jadwiga, and founded a dynasty which was to maintain a personal union of Poland and Lithuania for almost two centuries. In 1569, three years before the death of the last Jagiellonian king, this became an incorporating union, on lines which anticipated the Anglo–Scottish union of 1707, by the Treaty of Lublin. It was achieved in the teeth of considerable opposition. Within twenty years, in 1588, Lithuanian hostility produced the Third Lithuanian Statute, which asserted the separate sovereignty of the duchy. This entirely conflicting constitutional position remained unresolved until 1791 – two years before the Second Partition of Poland, which made the resolution entirely redundant.

What this unusually successful and long-lasting union underlined, therefore, was the virtual impossibility of resolving the clash between national and supra-national interests. Poland and Lithuania somehow managed to survive together by having both represented, however mutually exclusively, on their statute book. Perhaps it was the very refusal to insist on clarity which was the key to success; but that was never going to work in any union involving early-modern Englishmen, with their obsessional, and fruitless, search for constitutional clarity. Certainly it underlines the crucial importance of national perceptions and susceptibilities; and it was on these that the attempt by the Spanish Monarchy to move first towards increased centralization based on Castile, and second towards a closer union of the Iberian kingdoms appeared to founder. After 1561, the Spanish Monarchy ceased to be peripatetic. Philip II ruled from Madrid. In stark contrast to his father Charles V, Philip held only two Cortes in Aragon; the effort involved, it seemed, was no longer justified by the return from the poorer nation which could offer him nothing compared with the silver flooding into Castile from the New World. Yet it was a fundamental mistake. The very fact that the union of Aragon and Castile had begun under two rulers meant that even when the crowns were united in one person, the concept of 'king of all and king of each' could be sustained. Philip not only significantly undermined it, but did so while maintaining the propaganda of the Hapsburg monarchy's world mission. Now, that all-embracing perception became a Castilian one, and Aragon, in the fifteenth century the more successful kingdom, was shown all too forcibly its irrelevance. What made it all the worse was that the king who could treat part of his inheritance in this way showed a very different face to his acquired kingdom of Portugal in 1580. Admittedly, the presence of Spanish troops on their border did much to persuade the highly reluctant Portuguese to accept the ruler of the Spanish kingdoms. Yet Philip took great care to preserve their independent constitutional rights and privileges; and in 1581–2, he was in Lisbon. Virtual Portuguese autonomy was not, in the long run, enough; Portugal took advantage of Spanish weakness in 1640 to disentangle itself. In the rather shorter run, the neglect of Aragon in the late sixteenth century ensured that when the dreadful truth became apparent in the early seventeenth, after Philip's death, that Castile could not sustain single-handed the burden of Hapsburg religious and secular imperialism, Olivares was doomed to fail when he tried to involve Aragon and Catalonia in the great Spanish enterprise.

Underlying these problems was the fundamental difficulty that there was as yet no acceptable ideology which might weld disparate kingdoms together. In the course of the seventeenth century it became clear that, despite all its problems, the Spanish solution of 'king of all and king of each' was remarkably durable, in the Old World and the New.[26] But to the English and Scotsmen of 1603, Philip's actions, and indeed a century of Spanish history, made Spain the most unacceptable of all models of composite kingship or empire; for Charles V and Philip II raised the peculiarly terrifying spectre of universal monarchy. And although the Spaniards themselves never talked about empire, but rather *Monarchia*, it was the perception of Spanish imperial power which haunted the Scots who, in 1607, refused to contemplate being a 'slavishe province, to be governed by a

---

[26] This discussion obviously relies heavily on the works of J. H. Elliott, especially *Imperial Spain* (London, 1963); *The count-duke of Olivares: the statesman in an age of decline* (New Haven, 1986); *Spain and its world* (New Haven, 1989); and 'A Europe of composite monarchies', *Past and Present*, 137 (1992), 48–71. I also learned much from a lecture by Anthony Pagden, 'The comparative character of British and Spanish empires in America', given to the seminar directed by Professor John Pocock on 'Empire, confederation and republic: from Atlantic dominion to American union', Folger Shakespeare Library, 1992.

Viceroy or Deputye, lyke suche of the King of Spaynes provinceis'.[27] It equally haunted the English, threatened as they had been in the 1550s with losing their independence and becoming part of the Spanish hegemony. In fact, the inhabitants of Britain missed a crucial point about the subjects of the Spanish Monarchy, assuming that its viceroys were the agents of a colonializing imperial power, when in fact they were the representatives of the 'king of each'. It was profoundly paradoxical; for what Scotland and England in practice came to adopt, in a distinctly haphazard manner, was exactly the Spanish model, without its ideology. James never did become in any real sense king of Britain. In so far as his role can be defined, he was king of all, and king of each.

The difficulty in 1603 was that the English were not particularly interested in 'king of each', infinitely preferring that James should now be king of England. Not only was this not the king's view, but it was not the view of the Scots who came with him either; and these unwelcome incomers simply could not be ignored. By the end of May 1603, a commission of two Scots and two Englishmen had met; and as a result of their deliberations, into the king's household, the cellar, the buttery, the pantry, the larder, the bakehouse, the kitchen, came the Scots, often to have 'the like wages' to those of English yeomen and grooms and serjeants. And to add insult to injury, lesser Scots fry could not always be relied upon to stay put and show proper appreciation for their new positions; as early as 20 June 1603, Alexander Douglas petitioned to be released from the job he had been given a mere five weeks earlier, as one of the keepers of the council chamber, 'forasmuch as I am presently to return to Scotland upon special occasions'.[28] Inside that council chamber, there now sat not only the solid phalanx of the old Elizabethan councillors, but the new king's additions. How far was his attempt to widen the political spectrum by bringing in new Englishmen – the earls of Northumberland and Cumberland, the former Essex supporter Lord Mountjoy, Lord Henry Howard and others – appreciated, even by the beneficiaries, when the price to be paid was that five of the thirteen new men, Lennox, Mar, Hume, Elphinstone and Kinloss, spoke with Scottish accents? Sir George Hume, later earl of Dunbar and the most influential of all the Scots, in both England and Scotland, until his death in 1611, became for a short time chancellor of the exchequer, and began the Scottish hold on the office of master of the wardrobe, in which he was followed up by that most remarkable of Jacobean spendthrifts, James Lord Hay; both ran up debts far greater than the English masters of the reign, notably – of course – the reforming Lionel Cranfield. Lennox became lord steward of the household. And of course the noise and bustle of these inner sanctums, the privy

[27] *RPC*, vol. VII, p. 536.   [28] PRO, LS 13/168, ff. 71, 74–6. SP 14/2/10, f. 14 r.

and bedchamber, immediately became Anglo-Scottish; indeed, in the bed-chamber – even more offensively – almost exclusively Scottish. The king, according to the French ambassador de Beaumont, naively thought that if he had seven of each nation in the bedchamber, both sides would come to like and esteem one another. On the contrary, said the ambassador, the result was to create even greater animosity, and scandalize the rest of the court. James quickly realized the truth. When, seven years later, Sir John Holles moaned about the Scots 'standing like mountains betwixt the beams of his grace and us', and wistfully suggested that 'we must humbly beseech his majesty that his bedchamber be shared as well to those of our nation as to them', he was referring to an exclusion of the English which went right back to the summer of 1603.[29] The Scots were indeed perceived as grabbing 'everything they could lay their hands on'.

There was, therefore, a social as well as a political problem. It was one which went out beyond the world of the court. For to poverty, dirt and greed, the Scots added the sin of aggressiveness and ready violence. Con-temporary accounts leave no doubt that free-born and, one is asked to believe, peace-loving Englishmen no longer felt safe; and neither did the Scots. In June 1603, the duke of Lennox and the earls of Shrewsbury and Cumberland mounted an Anglo-Scottish resistance to the Anglo-Scottish disorder in Queen Anne's court. In April 1604, Lord Chief Justice Popham was ordered to arrest 'certain loose people commonly called swagerers and of the damned crew [who] raised manie quareles against some of our subjects and servants of our nation of Scotland'; but the king's perspective was hardly that of the English. Guy Fawkes could invoke hatred of the brawling, grasping Scots – and the king who took their part – in his last-ditch appeal to Spain for help against the Stewart succession in July 1603.[30] It was a thread which ran right through the reign. That invaluable correspondent John Chamberlain recorded a rumpus at a race at Croydon in 1611 between the Scot William Ramsay and the earl of Montgomery, pacified only 'for want of weapons'. A year later, London was witnessing 'two or three accidents of late, very unlucky, that make some boyling twixt

[29] Neil Cuddy, 'The revival of the entourage: the bedchamber of James I, 1603–1625', in David Starkey (ed.), *The English court from the Wars of the Roses to the Civil War* (London, 1987), pp. 173–225; Galloway, *Union*, pp. 17–18; BL, Add. MS 30640, f. 97 v. Holles, linking James's munificence to the Scots with the problem of English parliamentary supply, claimed that 'the King's equal affection to us as them would help us all' and pointedly asserted that equality would mean that 'this fearfull term of grievance shall no more be remembered and we hereafter shall live most happy subjects under a far more happy sovereign': *HMC, Portland MSS*, vol. IX, p. 113.

[30] PRO, SP 14/2/9, f. 13 r. SP 14/7/29, f. 63 r. A. J. Loomie, 'Guy Fawkes in Spain: the "Spanish Treason" in Spanish documents', *BIHR*, special supplement 9 (London, 1971),

the Scottes and our nation', one of which was a row between James
Maxwell, gentleman usher, and James Hawley, gentleman of the Temple,
which lasted for two months, and took the combined efforts of the king, the
Temple benchers, the lord chamberlain, the duke of Lennox, and the earls
of Pembroke, Suffolk, Northampton and Worcester to bring to an end.
Hawley's contribution included turning up to one unsuccessful recon-
ciliation with forty gentlemen to support him, and more generally the Scots
took fright; they kept away from the theatres and all parts of the town except
Charing Cross, where they huddled together 'for that they find unruly
youths apt to quarrell and redy to offer yll measure', and indeed it was
reported that 'the Scottishmen were bodilie afraide for we heard of above
three hundred that passed through Ware towards Scotland within ten days'
of the final outcome. It was a nasty moment – nastier, but not fundamentally
different from the trouble which flared up in the house of lords in 1621 and
deeply upset the king, because just when he was getting on to easier terms
with the commons, 'the wind should thus come about into a corner of the
upper house', when a group of younger English lords chose to take offence
on the issue of Scottish and Irish precedence.[31]

Such tensions spilled out beyond the confines even of London and the
court. Dee's grandiose claims about the sovereignty of the sea ran into two
problems in James's reign. The first arose from a direct challenge to English
perceptions, when Grotius claimed the *Mare liberum* on behalf of the
Dutch, and the king replied by invoking John Selden, who responded with
his *Mare clausum* in 1618.[32] Much more prosaically, however, the sea under
English sovereignty was not closed only to the Dutch. The masters of the
Trinity House sent in to parliament a lengthy list of considerations why
Scottish ships should not be counted as one with English ships, mainly
because they would be far more employed because of their ability to
undercut the English, for all sorts of unworthy reasons: they victualled
much more cheaply in Scotland, being prepared to fare more hardily, and
their mariners used 'a kind of Trade of Marchandiz, by which they make
their Waiges; in Scotland they bie Knitt Wastecotts knitt Hose, Scotche
Cappes ... and Scotche Coles for Ballist, and sutch other like, for the which
they paye not Custome nor imposition in or out'.[33] And if that was enough

---

especially pp. 22–4, 61–3. Jenny Wormald, 'Gunpowder, treason, and Scots', *Journal of British Studies*, 24 (1985), 157–64.

[31] N. E. McClure (ed.), *The letters of John Chamberlain* (2 vols., Philadelphia, 1939), vol. I, pp. 340, 348, 352–3, 355; vol. II, pp. 346–8.

[32] David Armitage, 'The Cromwellian Protectorate and the languages of empire', *Historical Journal*, 35 (1992), 533–4; Richard Tuck, *Natural rights theories: their origin and development* (Cambridge, 1979), pp. 86–90, and *Philosophy and government, 1572–1651* (Cam-
bridge, 1993), pp. 212–14.

[33] BL, Harl. MS 158, ff. 165 r–166 r.

to make English seamen ashamed of their would-be partners, even worse for the English government was the irresponsible way in which individual Scotsmen used the benefits of union to enjoy themselves abroad. Salisbury was sorely tried in 1604–5 by the activities of one Sir James Lindsay, who had acted as a papal agent before 1603, and now turned up in Rome, apparently – so it was widely rumoured in England – with the king's commission, to whisper sweet nothings into the papal ear about James's desire to convert, and discuss a positive influx of cardinal-visitors to England.[34] Even more dramatic was the entirely unscrupulous Scots Catholic rogue Thomas Douglas. Taking advantage of his brother being in the service of the Scottish Secretary Sir James Elphinstone, Douglas stole the signet, and went off with it to an impoverished Frenchman lodging in an alehouse at Blackfriars, who obligingly wrote him six letters of credence to foreign princes, the archbishops of Mainz and Triers and others. His trip abroad appears to have been a riotous success, until he made the mistake of arriving on the elector palatine's doorstep in the archbishop of Mainz's own coach, with a letter of credence to the duke of Cleves in his pocket. The puritan palatine, deeply suspicious and wholly failing to see the joke, sent him back to the Tower in chains.[35] More generally, the Scots complicated foreign policy. Cornwallis felt it necessary to please James in 1614 by telling him that, as ambassador to Spain, he cared for the Scots 'as he did those of his owne countrey'; and fears of the Auld Alliance between Scotland and France lay behind the unease Abbot felt about proposals for a French match in the same year, proposals which indeed were thought to emanate from the Scots.[36]

And so this ramshackle 'union' lurched on, satisfying neither ideologically nor practically. It was, of course, impossible to break as long as James lived; his vision of a perfect union might be blocked by its opponents, but in his reign at least the English and the Scots had to live out their marriage of distaste and distrust, in the higher echelons of society, at court and in government, with the additional burden of having to behave for at least part of the time as if the marriage was welcome. Yet it would be wrong to think that only James's existence or, indeed, the fact that his only viable successor was heir to both kingdoms and hardly likely to give up either, prevented the union from falling apart. In large measure, the union had come to be an accepted fact of life by 1625, sufficiently inoffensive to most people on either side of the border to be tolerated and maintained. James

[34] PRO, SP 14/14/41*, f. 99 r; SP 15/15/26, ff. 42 r–44 r; SP 85/bundle 3, ff. 36 r, 42 r, 46 r, 48 r–v.

[35] PRO, SP 14/14/50, ff. 112 r–113 r.

[36] PRO, SP 14/77/43(i), f. 73 r; PRO 31/3/47, ff. 245 v–246 r, 249 v. I am grateful to Professor Conrad Russell for these references.

may have failed to secure what he wanted; but the credit for keeping any sort of union in being was very much his.

To his uncertain subjects, he gave out conflicting signals. His promise, before his departure from Scotland, to return every three years was, of course, not kept, and was to be a major grievance by 1607. The English were more immediately worried. His letter from Holyrood to the mayor and aldermen of London might soothe them with tact and flattery, but it took only six words to disturb; London, said the king, was 'the chamber of our imperiall crowne', and no one can have believed that he conceived that crown in Elizabethan terms. By the time he got to Newcastle on 11 April 1603, he was designing a new British coinage.[37] The whole nature of his accession was, indeed, disruptive and disturbing. Elizabeth's fear of wrapping her own winding sheet went back to the last days of her sister's life, when she watched Mary's councillors and servants stream down the road to Hatfield. But Holyrood and the north of England were a great deal less accessible; men had to travel far to fix their interest with their new sovereign, and some – notably Cecil – could not leave London and travel at all.[38] And when the king did arrive in his 'chamber', it became all too horribly apparent that union was not a hidden agenda; it was at the top of the open one.

English fear of James as the divine-right monarch who made awesome claims for himself which broke all accepted English rules and conventions surely arose directly out of their agony over union. Certainly James's Scottish writings, *Basilikon doron* and *The trew lawe of free monarchies*, encouraged the idea that the new king arrived with a dangerous concept of his power already intact. But as there is some doubt about how widely his books were actually read, as opposed – especially in the case of the first – to being bought, it seems reasonable to argue that what terrified the English, and especially those lawyers who sat in the house of commons, was the king's actions in creating his British kingdom.[39] His proclamation of

---

[37] BL, Stowe MS 574, f. 3 r; Bodleian MS Ashmole 1729, f. 78 r.

[38] On the day after Elizabeth's death, 25 March 1603, Cecil rushed off a letter to James, in which he told the king that 'I shall not rest till myne eyes have sene that blessing which this kingdome hath long desired', but – making a virtue out of necessity – explained that he would not make an 'untymely intrusion' like other men, but stay in London on the king's behalf, for a few days. The days lengthened; and on 10 April, Egerton, Buckhurst, Nottingham and Cecil showed their mounting concern about those who, having nothing to do in London, would flock to the king, 'where they would both with infinite importunitys cumber his Majesty, some for one thing, some for another . . . ': PRO, SP 14/1/2 and SP 14/1/18.

[39] J. Craigie (ed.), *Basilikon doron of King James VI* (2 vols., STS, 1944–50), and *Minor prose works of King James VI and I* (STS, 1982): *The trew lawe* is on pp. 57–82; Jenny Wormald, '*Basilikon doron* and *The trew lawe of free monarchies*: the Scottish context and the English

October 1604 was his immediate response to their refusal, entirely justified from their point of view, to underwrite 'Britain' by parliamentary statute. It was a horrifying assertion of uncontrolled royal power. The older view which saw Henry VIII's Statute of Proclamations of 1539 as making such an assertion is no longer accepted, even if a question-mark remains over an act which ran into considerable trouble in parliament, lords and commons, whose life was short, and which was associated with a monarch of increasingly autocratic tendencies. What is not in doubt is that by the early seventeenth century the statute was certainly seen as an unacceptable statement of arbitrary royal will. But no Tudor proclamation ever threatened the kingdom of England as James's did in 1604; and it is difficult to avoid making a connection between new fears of a long-dead act and James's actions. Ironically, the king himself attacked his Tudor predecessor who had 'sought by parliament to make his proclamation a law' and whose 'seeking in that point was tyranical'; and it is hardly coincidence that he dragged this reference into his exchange in 1610 with Henry Yelverton who had been too outspoken on the issues of subsidy and, worse, the hated Scots. But this unexceptionable comment can have done little to reassure, when both English constitutional procedure and English self-perception had been suddenly shattered by a proclamation from a Scottish king.[40]

All this created an atmosphere where it was all too easy for James's remarkably conciliatory approach to be obscured. Yet conciliatory it was. This 'cradle king' took endless pains to remind his English subjects that his long experience of rule in Scotland did not mean that he had nothing to learn in England. In 1616, he described in his speech in the star chamber how 'When I came into England, although I was an old King, past middle aage, and practised in government ever sithence I was twelve yeeres old, yet being heere a stranger in governement . . . I resolved therefore with Pythagoras to keepe silence seven yeeres, and learne myself the lawes of this Kingdome.' On the issue of union, where he had manifestly not kept silent, he was prepared to admit the mistake. 'When I first propounded the Union',

---

translation', in Linda Levy Peck (ed.), *The mental world of the Jacobean court* (Cambridge, 1991), pp. 51–4.

[40] On the 1539 statute, G. R. Elton, 'Henry VIII's Act of Proclamations', in Elton, *Studies in Tudor and Stuart politics and government* (4 vols., Cambridge, 1974–92), vol. I, pp. 339–54; R. W. Heinze, *The proclamations of the Tudor kings* (Cambridge, 1976), pp. 153–77. For the row between James and Yelverton, 'Narrative of Henry Yelverton', *Archaeologia*, 15 (1806), 27–52; the king's remark is on p. 43. Proclamations were a matter for particular concern in the 1610 parliament, the immediate issue being the fear that the publication of the *Booke of proclamations* in February 1610 was designed to make proclamations equal with law: Elizabeth Read Foster (ed.), *Proceedings in parliament, 1610* (2 vols., New Haven, 1966), vol. II, p. 22. It is a good example of mutual distrust – and misunderstanding.

he said in 1607, 'I then thought there could have bene no more question of it, then of your declaration and acknowledgement of my right unto this Crowne, and that as two Twinnes, they would have growne up together. The errour was my mistaking; I knew mine owne ende, but not others feares ... Neither can I condemne you ... having not yet had so great experience of my behaviour and inclination in these few yeeres past, as ye may peradventure have in a longer time hereafter.'[41]

It was not the only mistake he admitted. As early as November 1604, he had come to appreciate the particular offence caused by giving Scotsmen place in England. Somewhat disingenuously, he wrote to Cecil saying that he had never intended to do so in any case until 'tyme had begone to weare awaie that opynion of different Nations'; he himself had left very little time indeed when he first came south. But he was tactful and circumspect in his assurances that he would always prefer an Englishman to a Scotsman, even though 'I knew a Scottishman for a miracle that were more capable for any such place, then any Englishman in England', and he cited *Basilikon doron* in defence of his contention.[42] It is all too well known that he did continue to favour his Scots, especially in his lavish gifts of money. But this letter does indicate the flexibility of a king who would listen to his English subjects even if he would not forget his Scottish ones; the clash came between the balance he was trying to create and profound English reluctance to admit that the Scots had a continuing claim on him, even English surprise that he should agree that they did.

Efforts to reassure went further than his letter. His speech to the English parliament in 1607 was, in effect, a list of points designed to allay English fears. Thus he argued that it was paranoid – 'devilish' was his word – to suspect that he would give the Scots more attention than the English; using the example that he would fear the plague more in London than Northampton or Berwick, he asked 'thinke you that I will preferre them that be absent, lesse powerfull, and farther off to doe me good or hurt, before you, with whom my security and living must be, and where I desire to plant my posterity?' He was taking a considerable risk; this was not a message which would do anything to mitigate rising fears of neglect in Scotland. Nor did he succeed in convincing his English audience. Yet he battled on with his line. In 1616, speaking in the star chamber, he made an astonishingly explicit reference to his priorities, asserting that in proposing his union he had desired to unite Scottish to English law, and not the other way round, and

[41] James described himself as a 'cradle king' in his very bitter poem 'The answere to the Libell called the Comons teares', written in 1623: J. Craigie (ed.), *The poems of James VI of Scotland* (2 vols., STS, 1955–8), vol. II, pp. 183–91, line 134. McIlwain, *Works*, pp. 328, 291.
[42] PRO, SP 14/10A/40.

went on to insist that 'my intention was alwayes to effect union by uniting Scotland to England, and not England to Scotland'.[43]

This was very blunt. It was also, strictly speaking, politically irrelevant; the perfect union had been killed nine years earlier. Indeed, even in 1607, or 1604, it had already been too late for James to persuade his English subjects that initial excessive enthusiasm could give way to steady advance. Neither patience nor enthusiasm, when offered by a king with the wrong accent, would count against English history or English fears of loss of pride and place. But the Jacobean Muhammad did go to that relentlessly immoveable object, the English mountain, and painfully try to climb it. It was a dangerous sport. He never did scale it; and the Scottish pitfalls were potentially immense. But perhaps the real surprise is that he clung on as successfully as he did. His policies over union could be ill-timed and devious; he did show the face of neglect as well as favour to his Scottish subjects, while imposing these subjects and their interests too ruthlessly on his English ones. Yet his dawning recognition of political reality did persuade him to move from the early demands of equality to a greater emphasis on the fact that Henry VII's prophecy about the greater drawing the lesser was not only correct but acceptable to him. This meant offering the Scots less than he had promised, while still demanding from the English more than they actually wanted to give. But at the same time Scottish fears were never allowed to become too intense, while English ones were soothed and reduced. It was a highly intelligent approach; indeed, it was probably the only approach which would bring any kind of achievement. By adopting it, he created a union which perhaps only he had really wanted in 1603. By 1625, he had done much to ensure that others saw its advantages, and in so doing, had given it hope for the future.

[43] McIlwain, *Works*, pp. 298–9, 329.

2   Scotland, the union and the idea of a 'General Crisis'

Maurice Lee, Jr

The nature of what historians, over the last thirty years or so, have agreed to call the 'General Crisis' of the seventeenth century has prompted a certain amount of sporadic and genteel debate. It is a subject that has aroused interest but not passion, unlike the gentry controversy and, more recently, the 'revisionist' version of the causes of the English civil war. My own previous contribution to the debate, an article published in 1984 called 'Scotland and the "General Crisis" of the seventeenth century', argued that 'general crisis' as a way of explaining what happened in Europe in those years, though appealing, was unsound.[1] The article demonstrated, at least to its author's satisfaction, that the Scottish case was an exception to all of the many hypotheses that scholars had floated as to the nature of that supposed crisis, and therefore, since events in Scotland precipitated what happened in England, clearly 'Exhibit A' in any crisis theory, the whole idea was fatally flawed. It goes without saying that what transpired in Scotland and England, and Ireland too, would not have happened as it did, or perhaps at all, had it not been for the Anglo-Scottish union of 1603. Alas for authorial pride, however: the idea of a 'general crisis' still seems to be alive and well, though rather less written about in the last few years. So what follows is a reconsideration of the nature of the seventeenth-century 'crisis', if that is the proper word, once again from the Scottish vantage-point, and some suggestions which may provide a new starting-place for discussion.

One of the impediments to thought weighing upon historians, especially political historians, is our agreed-upon chronology. We all accept the existence of something called the seventeenth century, which is in one sense true and in another profoundly false. The crisis theorists have told us that the general crisis, whatever it was, happened in that century, although some argue that it began earlier. This has led to narrow, rather tunnel-minded thinking about it, focused on two major phenomena, the domestic upheavals of the 1640s and 1650s, and the international-cum-domestic unpleasantness in central Europe which we call the Thirty Years' War. (This tidy label is

---

[1] *SHR*, 63 (1984), 136–54.

another impediment to thought: if the Peace of Westphalia had been signed a little sooner, or a little later, we might realize more clearly than we now do that the German tragedy was one facet of a much larger phenomenon.) The obvious difficulty with this double focus is that the major domestic upheaval, and the only successful one, that in Charles I's three kingdoms, had only tenuous connections with the continental conflicts that were so obvious a factor in the revolts elsewhere. So R. B. Merriman's six contemporaneous revolutions[2] remain just that, without a satisfactory common explanation.

It may seem presumptuous for a nit-picking scholar to accuse other historians of not thinking big, but in this case the charge seems justified. Of all those who have grappled with this intractable problem the one who has come nearest to a solution is T. K. Rabb. In his elegant little book on the 'general crisis'[3] he has asked one of the right questions: why did stability return to Europe in the last third of the seventeenth century? And he has gone on, in passing, to suggest the right answer, though unfortunately he does not follow it up. Had he done so, this essay probably would not have been written.

Rabb is certainly right in saying that Europe in 1700 was vastly different from Europe in 1600. One can say that about any of those hundred-year periods we agree to call centuries, to be sure. But the difference between 1600 and 1700 is arguably greater than that between any other such hundred-year interval before or since in the history of western civilization. The case, briefly, is this. Western civilization began in Europe with the collapse of Roman authority in the west – a standard textbook observation. In the fifteen-hundred years of its existence our civilization has had two organizing principles – two paradigms, to use a fashionable word – within which we have operated. The first was the idea of Christendom. The second is the idea of the omnicompetent, centralized, bureaucratic state. In 1600 the old idea was still alive, though in its death throes. In 1700 it was dead and the current organizing principle had triumphed, though there were still patches of instability in areas as widely separate as England and Russia.

In its first phase this newly triumphant organizing principle most commonly took a dynastic form, typified by that devout prince, Louis XIV, the self-proclaimed embodiment of the state. The French Revolution, an event whose significance has sometimes been exaggerated, made two major changes in it. In the first place the Revolution undermined – some might say, destroyed – the principle's dynastic component. (The Americans, to be sure, had already rejected dynasticism, but they, like the Scots, were on the fringes of the civilized world. What happened there was not decisive.) After

---

[2] R. B. Merriman, *Six contemporaneous revolutions* (Oxford, 1938).
[3] T. K. Rabb, *The struggle for stability in early modern Europe* (Oxford, 1975).

1793 a king was no longer necessary, or even desirable, as a symbol of the state. In the place of the crown there arose other symbols: Marianne, John Bull, Uncle Sam, the flag, whose burning has become such an unspeakably depraved action to some people in the United States. Second, and more important, the French Revolution added a fourth necessary qualifying adjective. The omnicompetent, centralized, bureaucratic state must now also be the national state. So over the course of the last two hundred years fragmented nationalities have come together, as in Italy and Germany, and multi-national empires have come unglued, whether based on dynastic principle such as those of the Hapsburgs and Romanovs (whose policies in this respect the various Soviet autocrats from Lenin to Gorbachev did not change in any significant way), or on racial superiority and the 'White Man's Burden', such as the British. And from Ottawa to Belgrade to Moscow the problem is still very much with us.

The other two great principles of the French Revolution, liberty and equality, have tended to cut in opposite directions in their impact on the state, with the result that one has often been sacrificed to the other. In 1789 equality was a new idea, born of the Enlightenment; its enforcement depended upon the power of the omnicompetent state, whose power was always greatly enhanced thereby. One need look no further than the history of the United States since the presidency of Abraham Lincoln for an illustration of the truth of that statement. Liberty was a much older idea, stemming from the contractual nature of medieval government and the rights, mostly property rights, of the privileged and unequal: their 'liberties'. It is an idea that is potentially highly subversive of the organizing principle of the omnicompetent state, particularly in our own time, when it is indissolubly associated with the principle of democratic elections. So in many states liberty was, and is, suppressed, sometimes in the name of equality, sometimes in the name of inequality. In others, such as the United Kingdom, ingenious ways have been found to get around it, by arranging for the periodic election of an autocrat who, once installed in power, can behave in much the same way as Frederick the Great. In still other places, thanks very often to the principle of proportional representation, liberty has produced a replication of the Polish diet. In the United States yet another pattern obtains. Its founding fathers were concerned to preserve liberty; so they wrote a constitution designed to prevent the erection of an omnicompetent, centralized, bureaucratic state. Their success has been only partial. The government of the United States is indeed omnicompetent, centralized, bureaucratic, and at the same time subject to periodic fits of deadlock and paralysis, like the England of Charles II. Since the electorate is able to put an end to this situation if it wishes to do so, however, Americans have not yet had to call upon a Dutch saviour other than Franklin D. Roosevelt.

The all-powerful state was a matter of slow growth. The government of Louis XIV was not born in the crucible of the wars of the earlier part of the century; its roots go back at least to the days of Louis XI, or even to those of Philip the Fair, when the first signs of the weakening of the idea of Christendom began to appear. Significantly, the French government's attack upon the papacy in the person of Boniface VIII was formulated by the new men, lawyer–bureaucrats such as Guillaume de Nogaret. While the papacy was undergoing first, assault, and then virtual subordination at the hands of the French monarchy, Dante was eloquently expounding his Gelasian vision of pope and emperor together leading mankind to spiritual and temporal felicity. Coming from a man who was himself the victim of the strife of Guelf and Ghibelline in his beloved Florence, it was a vision more Utopian than Thomas More's. Yet behind it lay the reality of belief. It would be a daring person indeed in the Western Europe of Dante's time who would deny that, in the words of Pope Boniface in 1302, 'it is altogether necessary to salvation for every human creature to be subject to the Roman Pontiff'.[4] The men and women of Western Europe thought of themselves as Christians; they believed in the all-encompassing nature of the Christian message; they believed that outside the church there was no salvation.

The erosion of the grip of the church on the minds and imaginations of the faithful over the next two centuries is a familiar story that need not be repeated here. Yet the ideal of a united Christendom remained, as deeply held by Luther and Calvin as by Erasmus and More and Loyola, yet corresponding less and less to reality. The great turning-point was the Schism, a disaster which in no way could be fitted in with any conceivable version of God's plan for the universe and which could only be ended by the action of secular governments. From that moment the balance began irrevo- cably to shift. Hus was burned in 1415; the heresiarchs of the next century died in their beds. Universalists though they were, self-proclaimed reformers rather than revolutionaries, Luther and Calvin had shattered the unity of Christendom beyond recall.

In the middle of the sixteenth century, however, almost no one was prepared to accept the finality of that break-up. Nor, as it turned out, were large numbers of people prepared to accept the mounting power of the dynastic state, its growing centralization, its bureaucracy's steady assaults upon localism and the independence and liberties of the privileged, its increasing interference in and regulation of economic life, its more frequent and more extensive forays into people's pocketbooks, forays made more necessary and more grievous by inflation and war. What resulted was a

---

[4] The bull *Unam sanctam*, in Columbia University, *Introduction to contemporary civilization in the west*, 2nd edn (2 vols., New York, 1954), vol. I, pp. 322–3.

century of conflict on two fronts, which frequently intertwined with each other: throughout all of western civilization, intermittent attempts to restore the unity of Christendom through the elimination of papists or heretics, depending on one's point of view, and, almost everywhere, attempts to check the steadily growing power of the centralizing bureaucratic state before it achieved omnicompetence. 'Crisis', as Rabb has pointed out, is not an entirely satisfactory word for what happened, since it usually implies intensity and brevity, followed by resolution.[5] So the title of the first collection of essays on the problem, *Crisis in Europe 1560–1660*, is something of a contradiction in terms.[6] (Ironically, whoever invented the title of this collection got the dates pretty much right, though none of the essays discusses the significance of that hundred-year period as a whole.) Rabb's own title, however, conjures up an incomplete vision, since the two struggles envisaged two different sorts of stability that were incompatible with each other – or rather, those who struggled against the encroaching state wanted to preserve the sort of instability that their view of liberty entailed and that the dynasts were determined to wipe out. Both struggles failed, and the result was caesaropapism, exemplified in all sorts of different ways, from the revocation of the Edict of Nantes to the first amendment to the constitution of the United States. The organizing principle within which western civilization had operated since its inception was dead, on earth and in heaven too. One of the ornaments of the new age was Sir Isaac Newton, appropriately enough master of the mint to King William III and II, the Calvinist king who, having ousted his Catholic father-in-law from the thrones of his three kingdoms, made an ally of the pope in his long and ultimately successful effort to thwart the ambitions of the Most Christian King of France.

The so-called 'General Crisis', then, was of a rather larger order of magnitude than those who have previously grappled with it have indicated, save Rabb, who wrote of the 'larger development' into which his analysis fits as 'the glacial disintegration of medieval society'.[7] This is almost right, though, as is sketchily indicated in the preceding pages, it was more than a society that was dying. Where, then, does Scotland fit into this large scheme of things? At the beginning it played a prominent part, far more prominent than one might expect of a kingdom whose role in the affairs of western civilization had always been peripheral at best. Historians like to date the beginnings of the wars of religion in 1560 with the tumult of Amboise. There were the Schmalkaldic wars, to be sure, but they were a sort of

[5] Rabb, *Struggle for stability*, pp. 29–33.
[6] Trevor Aston (ed.), *Crisis in Europe 1560–1660* (New York, 1967).
[7] Rabb, *Struggle for stability*, p. 35.

curtain-raiser, quickly overshadowed by the last instalment of the Hapsburg–Valois conflict, which ended with the Treaty of Câteau-Cambré-sis in March 1559. In fact the wars of religion began with the riots that took place in Perth in May 1559, when the Protestant opponents of the Catholic regent, Mary of Guise, responded with violence to what they regarded as her violation of a promise not to outlaw certain Protestant preachers. Indeed one might argue that the greatest significance of the tumult of Amboise was that it, and a Protestant wind which scattered a relieving force, kept the distracted French government from coming to the aid of the beleaguered regent, who was the mother of its own, and Scotland's, queen. So the Protestant party won its provisional triumph in Scotland in 1560, a triumph that became permanent thirteen years later with the surrender of Edinburgh Castle, the stronghold of the last armed supporters of the now deposed and fugitive Mary Queen of Scots.

The Scotland of Queen Mary was hardly the model of a centralized, omnicompetent, bureaucratic state. The great aristocrats were petty kings in their own regalities, they and their followers controlled local government in both town and country, there was no bureaucracy – though a nucleus of legal talent, the essential element of a bureaucracy, was beginning to collect in Edinburgh – and the crown's military and financial resources were meagre. Scottish monarchs were not without assets, however.[8] The dynasty was an old one and commanded loyalty, as its ability to weather the difficulties created by repeated minorities demonstrated. A king who knew how to lead would be obeyed: English invasions, often threatened and frequently suffered, reminded almost every generation of Scots of the awful consequences of being without a king. The very lack of central govern-mental institutions that could apply any legal check to royal authority was in fact a potential asset to a king if – and it was a big *if* – he could find a way of making himself independent of the magnates. James IV did not try. He was a magnates' king despite his destruction of the greatest of them, the lord of the Isles, and a Crusader who wore an iron chain to atone for his sins, sexual and other. James V, who wore no iron chain to atone for his incessant womanizing and was anything but a magnates' king, did try. His instrument was the church, from which he extorted large sums of money. But the patron of the anticlerical poet–dramatist Sir David Lindsay did nothing for the church in return, and he self-indulgently spent the money mostly on buildings. Unlike his father, he had no vision of the unity of Christendom – he was too much of a Tudor. His one permanent governmental legacy was

---

[8] On this point, see especially the works of Jenny Wormald: *Court, kirk and community: Scotland 1470–1625* (London, 1981); *Lords and men in Scotland: bonds of manrent 1442–1603*

a professional court, the college of justice. His hapless daughter, absorbed in her dynastic calculations and confronted by a religious situation unique in Europe, with the papal church the church *de jure*, and the new dispensation actually in control and financed in large measure by a tax on the legal church, not only could not solve her problems, she could not even provide leadership. So she went under, and the old church went under with her.

The deposition of Mary had repercussions far beyond the borders of Scotland. It was a major event in the century-long 'crisis' that was gripping western civilization, because it meant the end of the possibility of the restoration of the authority of the old church in the British Isles from within; after 1573 that could be accomplished only by foreign invasion. Had the Catholic queen of Scots succeeded or displaced her cousin on the English throne, to which, in Catholic eyes, she was already entitled, had English support for Dutch and Huguenot rebels never materialized, there would have been no need for the Invincible Armada, and we might all be writing of the triumphs of that new Constantine, King Philip the Great, the reunifier of Christendom.

But Mary failed, and eventually paid for her plotting with her life. Her execution brought the possibility of peaceful dynastic union between Scotland and England, which seemed utterly remote when James IV married Margaret Tudor, ever closer as Elizabeth continued to dwell in single blessedness. (It should be remembered that James IV was far from being the first Scottish king to marry an English princess. Like his father-in-law, James IV was a descendant of John of Gaunt, and arguably had as good a claim to the English throne as did Henry VII.) So James VI, when he came to govern for himself, faced a set of circumstances unique in the annals of Scottish kingship. The English throne might one day be his, ought to be his when Elizabeth died by the rules of primogeniture; it became the great object of his life to sit upon it. At the same time he was confronted by a church with a mission, a church that had a covenant with God. Of all of God's reformed churches it was the purest. It had won through against great odds thanks to God's special favour. If it maintained its purity, if indeed it became purer still, then, with God's help, it could and would carry its message through Christendom. The Scots were a blessed people, the Lord's chosen instruments – an idea that can be found, arguably, as early as the Declaration of Arbroath.[9] Their prince must be godly too, that is, he must listen to, and obey, the spokesmen of the Lord. James believed in himself as

(Edinburgh, 1985); *Mary Queen of Scots: a study in failure* (London, 1988); and many articles, especially 'James VI and I: two kings or one?', *History*, 68 (1983), 187–209.

[9] Gordon Donaldson, *The faith of the Scots* (London, 1990), p. 88.

a godly prince, and the vision of a unified Christendom caught his imagination also, provided that it took place under his auspices. In his early years on the English throne he and his publicists conjured up the image of James as the new Constantine who would preside over an ecumenical council to achieve reunification. While he was still only James VI, however, he had to deal with the kirk's overarching vision of the kingdom of Christ Jesus, in which he was only a member. So he created a vision of his own, that of the free monarch, God's vicegerent, answerable only to Him and not to those who imagined themselves to be God's privy councillors. Furthermore he had the resources to help him implement his vision, resources in men, the educated laymen, mostly lawyers, to create a bureaucracy, and resources in wealth, in the form of church lands annexed to the crown in 1587, to reward them. He was also mercifully free of institutional checks on his authority. Scotland, as Arthur Williamson accurately remarks, had no 'ancient constitution',[10] and its parliament was amenable to royal control thanks to that peculiar institution known as the committee of the articles. The checks on royal authority were political and economic: the entrenched power of the magnates, especially at the local level, the intransigence of God's privy councillors, Andrew Melville and his ilk, the limited, though growing, national wealth available for taxation, and the political dangers inherent in James's attempting to tax too heavily or too often in his delicate circumstances. There is no need to repeat the familiar story of James's success in dealing with his problems.[11] By 1603 the outlines of the all-powerful state that was to be the wave of the future were visible in Scotland. There was a modern theory of monarchy and a central bureaucracy in place, though hardly as yet a centralized or omnicompetent regime. But the lineaments of the latter could be perceived.

The union transformed the Scottish scene, and the circumstances of King James. It put at his disposal the resources of a far wealthier kingdom which he might use to complete the implementation of his vision of free monarchy in Scotland, and it insulated him from clerical and aristocratic backlash. At the same time, as James I of England, he found himself having to deal with a polity that, by comparison with Scotland's, was medieval and decidedly backward. The benevolent (for a monarch) principles of Roman law were unavailable in England. Parliament was a medieval anachronism which his

---

[10] Arthur H. Williamson, *Scottish national consciousness in the age of James VI* (Edinburgh, 1979), p. 146.

[11] See the works of Wormald cited in note 8 above, and also Gordon Donaldson, *Scotland: James V–James VII* (Edinburgh, 1965), chs. 8–15; Maurice Lee, Jr, *John Maitland of Thirlestane and the foundations of Stewart despotism in Scotland* (Princeton, 1959) and *Government by pen: Scotland under James VI and I* (Urbana, 1980); and Keith Brown, *Bloodfeud in Scotland 1573–1625* (Edinburgh, 1986).

Tudor predecessors had failed to emasculate when they had the chance. Henry VIII might have done so had he used the wealth of the monasteries as Thomas Cromwell had evidently wished him to. Cromwell was the man who represented the future: a centralizing bureaucrat whose fingers reached into every aspect of English life, a thoroughly secular-minded politician who had no use for the idea of Christendom and stressed the ancient (and quite mythical) autonomy of the *ecclesia Anglicana* in his anti-papal propaganda. But Henry foolishly dispensed with Cromwell, plunged headlong into continental war once again (thus demonstrating that he had learned nothing from the military failures of the 1520s), sold monastic lands to pay for these wars, which gained him nothing, and in so doing threw away the chance to rid the English monarchy of its medieval incubus, parliament, this 'rotten seed of Egypt', as James called it after seven years of unsatisfactory experience with it. But James was not about to undertake the task that Henry had failed to perform. As he remarked to the Spanish ambassador, the count of Gondomar, 'I . . . found it here when I arrived, so that I am obliged to put up with what I cannot get rid of'.[12] He did not wish to provoke constitutional confrontation. On the two major constitutional issues between James and parliament, James was in the right: the judges upheld his right to levy impositions, and foreign policy had always been the province of the crown.

The political bigamy that the union entailed was bound to cause trouble sooner or later. James avoided it. He continued to consolidate the power of the 'new' monarchy in Scotland, executing even his own cousin, Earl Patrick of Orkney, when that ruffianly and self-willed magnate carried his defiance too far. He drew back from his one major misstep, the five articles of Perth; the damage that blunder caused need not have been permanent. The creation of the omnicompetent, centralized, bureaucratic state would take time; the process was further advanced in Scotland than in England when James died. Charles had no patience with obstacles, and no sense that patience was a necessary monarchical virtue. The tale of his unwisdom need not be retold.[13] But the nature of the backlash he provoked must be spelled out; it is crucial to the larger analysis of this essay.

In Scotland Charles behaved like a modern king, a 'new' monarch. He forced annual and increasing taxes through meetings of the convention of estates and his one pre-1637 meeting of parliament. He put an end to the *de*

---

[12] Quoted in Maurice Lee, Jr, *Great Britain's Solomon: James VI and I and his three kingdoms* (Urbana and Chicago, 1990), p. 93.

[13] See Rosalind Mitchison, *Lordship to patronage: Scotland 1603–1745* (London, 1983); Maurice Lee, Jr, *The road to revolution: Scotland under Charles I 1625–1637* (Urbana and Chicago, 1985); Donaldson, *Scotland: James V–James VII*, ch. 16; and Allan I. Macinnes, *Charles I and the making of the covenanting movement 1625–1641* (Edinburgh, 1991).

facto autonomy of the privy council that had obtained in the last fifteen years of James's reign, and weakened its influence by excluding members of the college of justice from it. His Act of Revocation, itself of questionable legality, threatened the grip of most magnates and many lairds on property rights and superiorities in so far as these had been acquired from crown or church. Men feared, wrote Archbishop Spottiswoode, that the revocation would 'call in question all men's rights since King Fergus'.[14] Charles tolerated no opposition, and tried a member of the nobility, Lord Balmerino, on a capital charge for allegedly circulating a paper critical of his policies. He behaved like the foreigner he was: his foreign and economic policies were perceived as damaging to Scotland's welfare. His principal agent after 1633, the earl of Traquair, was a self-made bureaucrat with no constituency among the people who counted. And, of course, Charles attempted to impose a religious change that was deeply offensive to the vast majority of the Scottish people.

The upheaval, when it came, took place under aristocratic leadership. It was, wrote the disapproving clerk of the Aberdeen city council, 'the nobility's covenant'[15] – though of course not all of the nobility turned against the king. Scottish aristocrats as a class had good reason to worry about their position. The union threatened Scottish national identity, a matter of concern for many Scots besides nobles, of course. It also greatly reduced most aristocrats' political influence and their expectations of favour at the hands of a now-distant monarch. King James's political skills had disguised many of these harsh realities and kept discontent in check; the very different policy and behaviour of his son made the noblemen's new situation painfully apparent.

There is also the question of the aristocracy's economic position. Walter Makey's analysis of the 'silent revolution' – a combination of inflation, fixed monetary rentals from feued lands, and the threat posed by Charles's Act of Revocation to the nobility's possession of the teinds, which, when paid in kind, were inflation proof – has given rise to the hypothesis that this was a revolt of downwardly mobile 'mere' aristocrats for whom debt was more alarming than royal absolutism or religious radicalism and who, in Keith Brown's words, 'following a long hard look at their accounts', rode off to Greyfriars Kirk to sign the covenant and join the revolution.[16] Brown's own

---

[14] 13 July 1627, Spottiswoode to the earl of Annandale, in J. F. S. Gordon, *Ecclesiastical chronicle for Scotland* (3 vols., London, 1875), vol. I, pp. 487–88.

[15] John Stuart (ed.), *Extracts from the council register of the burgh of Aberdeen 1625–1642* (Edinburgh, 1871), p. 157.

[16] Brown's analysis is contained in two articles, 'Noble indebtedness in Scotland between the Reformation and the Revolution', *Historical Research*, 62 (1989), 260–75, and 'Aristocratic finances and the origins of the Scottish revolution', *EHR*, 104 (1989), 46–87. The quoted

researches demonstrate, however, that although aristocratic indebtedness was indeed a fact of life, nobles were frequently able to stave off their creditors for long periods of time. Furthermore they, like their English counterparts whom Lawrence Stone analysed in his famous book,[17] were worse off in the years between 1590 and 1610 than they were thereafter, though the later 1630s were difficult owing to a combination of bad harvests, heavy taxation and Lord Treasurer Traquair's policies of retrenchment. Yet some of the nobles in dire financial straits, like the earl of Morton, were royalists, while one of the richest of all, the young earl of Buccleuch, was an enthusiastic covenanter who in 1642 bought the lands and lordship of Dalkeith from the bankrupt Morton for the enormous sum of £320,000.[18] The extent to which a landed man, whether noble or laird, was impelled to ride off to sign the covenant after an inspection of his account books remains unknown and, given the state of the records, is likely to remain so.[19]

It is clear enough, however, that when 'Laud's liturgy', as the new prayer book was called, touched off the explosion in July 1637, the powder keg had much in it besides fear of popery. Indeed, it had to contain more; religious discontent by itself would not have provoked the alliance among the people who counted in Scotland that was the necessary preliminary to successful resistance to the king's policies. This was true in England as well, though Caroline Hibbard has persuasively demonstrated how significant a factor fear of popery was in precipitating the upheaval there.[20] To the extent that this was a war of religion, however, it was a very peculiar one, quite unlike those on the continent or the wars of the Congregation, analogous only to what was going on in Muscovy, in that in both England and Scotland it was a war in defence of the existing system of belief against innovation on the part of the crown. The same observation applies to most of the other aspects of the opposition to Charles on both sides of the Tweed. The king was the modernizer, the innovator, the man moving, however ineptly and clumsily, along the road travelled by all the 'new' monarchs of the continent. His opponents, covenanters and parliamentarians alike – and, one might add, like Catalans and defenestrators and Frondeurs in other contexts – were defenders of the old ways, of their liberties in the medieval sense. The power and privilege of the medieval ruling class was at stake. (Let no one be fooled by the leadership of King Pym and, later, of Oliver Cromwell, those quintessential country gentlemen, south of the Tweed. The eclipse of

---

phrase is on p. 87 of the latter article. Walter Makey's discussion occurs in the first chapter of his *The church of the covenant 1637–1651* (Edinburgh, 1979).

17 Lawrence Stone, *The crisis of the aristocracy* (Oxford, 1965).
18 Sir William Fraser, *The Scotts of Buccleuch* (2 vols., Edinburgh, 1878), vol. I, p. 279.
19 Brown makes this point: 'Aristocratic finances', pp. 48–9.
20 Caroline Hibbard, *Charles I and the Popish plot* (Chapel Hill, 1983).

aristocratic leadership in England was a temporary condition. The ultimate triumph of parliament there meant the triumph of the aristocracy, whose grip on government in the eighteenth century was as tight as ever it was in the days of the feeble house of Lancaster.) The twin crises of the breakup of the medieval, and the imposition of the modern, organizing principle, which in Scotland had flared briefly into violence under Mary and been quieted by the skills of James VI, and so long deferred in England by the conservatism and inertia of Elizabeth and James I, now erupted in full force.

There was an eruption in Ireland as well, of a rather different kind, which considerations of space preclude discussing here. It was precipitated by events in the larger island, and had a profound impact on what happened there, from its outbreak in October 1641 until Cromwell brutally ended it almost a decade later. The 1640s saw a war of three kingdoms, not merely a civil war in each. We are all greatly in the debt of, among others, J. G. A. Pocock, Conrad Russell and David Stevenson for their valuable work on what is now called, properly, the 'British' problem (shorthand for 'British Isles', not 'Great Britain').[21]

The rapid collapse of royal authority in Scotland sparked the revival of covenanting enthusiasm. The prompt sweeping away of the episcopal structure, and the apparently united religious zeal of the triumphant covenanting party gave rise, in some quarters at least, to the vision of the Scots as God's chosen people, carrying their crusade out of Scotland to – who knew where?: the Day of the Lord might well be at hand. The Solemn League and Covenant spoke grandiloquently of encouraging other Christian churches 'groaning under, or in danger of, the yoke of anti-Christian tyranny' to follow the island kingdoms' example.[22] David Stevenson, whose work constitutes the standard account of the Scottish revolution,[23] has persuasively argued that the motives of most of those who made the alliance with the English parliamentary leadership in 1643 were defensive. This was especially true of the aristocratic politicians who were concerned primarily with retaining what they had already won by the parliamentary legislation of 1641. But if they were preoccupied with their medieval liberties, some of

---

[21] J. G. A. Pocock, 'The limits and divisions of British history: in search of the unknown subject', *American Historical Review*, 87 (1982), 311–36; Conrad Russell, *The causes of the English civil war* (Oxford, 1990), *The fall of the British monarchies 1637–1642* (Oxford, 1991), and many articles, especially 'The British background to the Irish rebellion of 1641', *Historical Research*, 61 (1988), 166–82; David Stevenson, *Alasdair MacColla and the Highland problem in the seventeenth century* (Edinburgh, 1980), and *Scottish covenanters and Irish confederates* (Belfast, 1981).

[22] E. J. Cowan, 'The Solemn League and Covenant', in Roger A. Mason (ed.), *Scotland and England 1286–1815* (Edinburgh, 1987), p. 193.

[23] David Stevenson, *The Scottish revolution 1637–1644* (Newton Abbot, 1973), and *Revolution and counter-revolution in Scotland 1644–1651* (London, 1977).

their apocalyptically minded allies fed on the equally medieval vision of a Christendom reunited under the aegis of that best of all the best-reformed churches, their own. No such vision existed in England. God might speak first to His Englishmen, but since He said such different things to different individuals amongst them, the religious vision that triumphed there was the appalling one (to the covenanters) of Independency. The idea of a united Christendom had died in England at the hands of Henry VIII and Cromwell, who sent its spokesman, Thomas More, to the block. It is paradoxical that the same king who shattered the medieval organizing principle in England also greatly deferred the creation of the modern one there by following policies that necessitated the retention of a powerful parliament.

One of the remarkable aspects of the upheaval in Scotland was that it produced no separatist movement among the king's enemies. Nor, by contrast with England, did it spawn any republican sentiment. The covenanters believed in union with England, a federal union which would limit the power of the royal executive and thus produce all the advantages brought about by the great event of 1603 and mitigate its disadvantages. The marquis of Argyll, that hard-bitten pragmatist, pleaded eloquently for continuance of the union 'so happily established betwixt us' in a speech to the house of lords in 1646.[24] And when Charles I was executed, those then in power in Scotland, the most radical elements amongst the king's opponents, at once proclaimed his son king of England and Ireland as well as Scotland. This fateful decision, which precipitated the Cromwellian conquest, was taken without any consideration of possible alternatives, such as proclaiming Charles II king of Scotland only, or not proclaiming him at all.

The radical wing of the covenanting movement was in power in 1649 on account of the disastrous failure of the Engagement of 1647. The Engagement, which represented the effort of many of the great magnates still in opposition to the king to rescue him from his English captors and at the same time preserve their own authority, was ruinous in every respect. It was the decisive step in the shattering both of the vision of a reunified Christendom and of the aristocratic polity enshrined in the legislation of 1641. It split the aristocracy, already weakened by the defection of the now-defeated Montrose and his associates, between the Engager majority and the sizeable minority headed by Argyll. The defeat of the Engager army broke the aristocracy's grip on the government, which for two years fell into the hands of the radical leadership in the kirk and its cowed aristocratic spokesmen, until its army in turn was routed at Dunbar. The kirk party itself then split apart, between Resolutioners and Protesters; the final result

---

[24] E. J. Cowan, 'The union of the crowns and the crisis of the constitution in seventeenth-century Scotland', in S. Dyrvik et al. (eds.), The satellite state (Bergen, 1979), p. 133.

was effective English military conquest and occupation. Oliver Cromwell accomplished what neither Edward I nor any of his successors down through Edward VI's Lord Protector Somerset had been able to achieve.

The four years between the signing of the Engagement and the battle of Worcester marked the end of medieval Scotland. Gone was the vision of a united Christendom. Gone was the vision of the Scots as a chosen people, especially dear to God. Gone too was the willingness of the aristocracy to defy the king in defence of their liberties. The awful years between 1649 and 1651 showed them where rebellion led: to humiliation before their inferiors, and to the real possibility that major financial exactions would be added to that humiliation. Lay patronage was abolished, royal grants of superiorities of kirklands were cancelled, the committee of estates could tax the heritors of a parish or presbytery if voluntary contributions to succour the poor were inadequate, with heritors who gouged their tenants paying extra, ministers' stipends were to be augmented, and a parliamentary committee was set up to look into the sufferings of all oppressed tenants, whose troubles were owing to 'the guiltiness and sins of your Lordships and such as rule in the land'.[25] Even after the weakening of its influence after Dunbar the kirk was still powerful enough to compel Engager nobles such as Lauderdale to do public penance for the iniquity of their past behaviour before it would consent to their readmission to public service. The aristocracy had learned that 'No bishop, no king' was only part of the truth; the rest of the truth was 'no nobility either'. And there followed nine years of alien military dictatorship, during which the magnates were, if lucky, merely reduced to helplessness and bootlicking if they wanted a favour; if unlucky, they were heavily fined or imprisoned or in exile. Small wonder that as a class the Scottish aristocracy embraced the returned Charles II with such fervent enthusiasm in 1660. The despotism of an absentee king, a vastly unattractive prospect in 1637, now seemed to them far preferable to any repetition of the ghastly indignities they had undergone since the destruction of the Engager army at Cromwell's hands twelve years before.

For Scotland, then, Rabb's 'struggle for stability' was over after 1660. The covenanters' vision was dead. The polity of the kingdom was recognizably modern in many ways, with a government that rested to a very substantial degree on military force. The burden of taxation was heavy and permanent, and soldiers were employed to make life unpleasant for delinquents. The magnates did not venture to oppose the king's will. They often intrigued viciously against one another, but the purpose of the intrigues was invariably to persuade Charles either to retain or dismiss those who governed in his name. Parliament, when it met, carried out his wishes and

[25] Stevenson, *Revolution and counter-revolution*, pp. 137–40.

was usually very active – given the amount of legislation the parliament of 1661–3 enacted, and its heavy work schedule, it is difficult to understand how it could have been so steeped in alcohol as the opponents of the re-established episcopal church claimed. Judges were equally subservient; when Sir John Gilmour, president of the court of session, expressed an opinion on the law of entail displeasing to the king, it was thought that Charles might dismiss him.[26] The south-west was disaffected in religion and was the scene of the two rebellions against Charles's government. Both were minor affairs and easily put down. The aristocracy took no part in them, and some of their members were frightened out of all proportion to the danger they presented – Lord Treasurer Rothes, for instance, was in a state of panic in the aftermath of Rullion Green. There was still lawlessness in Scotland, but much less than before, even in the Highlands, where magnates' quarrels over jurisdiction were often the cause of the trouble. Magnates' power in their local areas was still great – there were no *intendants* sent out from Edinburgh – but with the lessons of 1649–51 fresh in their minds, they did not disobey the king. Lauderdale's frequently quoted comment to Charles in November 1669 that 'never was king so absolute as you are in poor old Scotland' was an accurate assessment.[27] The aristocracy was content to acquiesce, provided that its own position of superiority over everybody else in Scotland was not endangered.

By contrast England after 1660 remained governmentally medieval – there had been nothing like the experience of 1649–51 in Scotland to frighten the English landed classes. The struggle for stability there was very far from over. None of the issues that had precipitated the uprising against Charles I was settled in 1660 save for fiscal feudalism and prerogative courts; the consequence was potential deadlock between the demands of an executive that needed the wherewithal to govern according to the new organizing principle and a medieval-minded legislature, whose only real weapon was fiscal strangulation. Toward the end of his life Charles II found a way out of the deadlock by reconstructing parliament and rendering it subservient by a combination of ideology and patronage and a government paid for by the expansion of the hereditary excise and customs duties. His foolish brother threw it all away, and the result was the triumph of that medieval anachronism, parliament. What this meant was further delay in the creation of the omnicompetent, centralized, bureaucratic state, and the necessity for the invention of a new principle on which it could operate, since the medieval instrument of resistance had triumphed over the modern dynastic absolutist.

---

[26] 29 September 1663, Thomas Ross to the countess of Wemyss, in Fraser, *Scotts*, vol. II, pp. 390–1.
[27] O. Airy (ed.), *The Lauderdale papers II* (Camden Society, 1885), p. 164.

The victory of the English landed classes in their long contest with the crown had a bizarre consequence in Scotland, in the form of the creation of an unprecedented and artificial medievalism. That hitherto docile tool of those in power, the Scottish parliament, was completely changed in character by the abolition of the committee of the articles. Parliament promptly became a new arena, a most desirable arena, in which the magnates could intrigue against one another. Parliamentary debate was vigorous, and sessions were often dramatic. But the real game was the same as it had been before 1688: the favour of the crown, or, with Queen Anne, of those who wielded the power of the crown. The English government was not pleased: present circumstances – the war to contain the ambitions of Louis XIV – made the game too dangerous to allow it to continue. So, after seventeen years, it was ended. The magnates acquiesced in the abolition of their new playing field in the hope and expectation that they – and perhaps the country as well, but certainly they – would benefit. The union of 1707 made little difference for a generation, and the disappointment in Scotland was correspondingly great. But many of the magnates flourished under the new rules. They learned to intrigue in the antechambers of the Harleys and Walpoles and Newcastles as they had in those of Charles II, and those who were disappointed and became Jacobites paid for it. The state north of the Tweed was indeed omnicompetent, centralized, bureaucratic, and sufficiently Scottish, with its distinctive church and legal system, to keep the vast majority of the patriotic from rebellion.

In due course the new organizing principle took hold south of the Tweed as well. Parliament, that medieval anomaly, gradually worked out the mechanism by which to transform itself into an engine of modern government: the cabinet. If any one man can lay claim to being the progenitor of the cabinet system, it is that untrustworthy Machiavellian, ever fertile in expedients, Robert Spencer, earl of Sunderland, the last chief minister of the last would-be absolutist king. Thomas Cromwell and he stand at the beginning and the end of the English story, as William and John Maitland and the latter's grandson Lauderdale stand at the beginning and the end of the Scottish. The man who implemented Sunderland's vision was his fellow Chit, Sidney Godolphin. The fierce factional struggles of Anne's reign deceived J. H. Plumb, among others, into imagining that stability had not yet been achieved, but it had: these were the quarrels of the victors over the spoils, resembling the behaviour of the Scottish magnates after 1660.[28] Eventually one faction triumphed, on both sides of the Tweed: the 'Venetian oligarchy' of Walpole in the south and the voracious Campbells in the north. The political marriage they ultimately consummated was blessed, not

---

[28] J. H. Plumb, *The growth of political stability in England 1675–1725* (Baltimore, 1969).

in St Paul's, but in the new cathedral in Threadneedle Street. Walpole and Islay were the heirs of Godolphin and Lauderdale. The government ran in the name of the sovereign, and recent research has rescued both Anne and her Hanoverian successors from the caricature of incompetence and incomprehension once drawn by Whig historiography.[29] The leadership in parliament nevertheless became the executive; it gradually transformed the royal bureaucracy into its bureaucracy, and reached its hand into every facet of British life: omnicompetent and centralized.

There was, then, no 'general crisis', as usually defined, in the Europe of the seventeenth century. What there was was the death of one organizing principle and the triumph of another. The whole process took a very long time, and Scotland, like every other state in Christendom, was involved. The timetable in Scotland approximated the dates in the Aston book: 1560–1660. The union of 1603 both accelerated the process and created circumstances which made possible a sharp backlash. In due course the backlash came, and brought about further acceleration. At the same time the union tied Scotland to a far wealthier and more powerful kingdom where the process began sooner, in the 1530s, ended later, early in the eighteenth century, and created a new and different form of modern state that, after 1707, encompassed both. From that time on the consolidation of ministerial authority has proceeded, not without its ups and downs. It is now possible for a prime minister to govern like Frederick the Great. If he or she shows signs of turning into Charles I, however, it is, happily, still possible for the Jenny Geddeses on the back benches to bring about an overturn without hurling anything more damaging than epithets.

---

[29] For example, Edward Gregg, *Queen Anne* (London, 1980); Ragnhild Hatton, *George I: elector and king* (Cambridge, Mass., 1978); and the many works of Jeremy Black on foreign policy which stress the crucial role of George II.

3 The vanishing emperor: British kingship and its decline 1603–1707

Keith M. Brown

> The kingdom of Scotland generally had been long jealous that by the King's continued absence from them they should by degrees be reduced to but as a province of England and subject to their laws and government, which it would never admit to.[1]

Edward Hyde, earl of Clarendon's observation on the Scottish reaction to the regal union of the early seventeenth century was made by a man who tried, unsuccessfully, to persuade Charles II that the provincialization of Scotland was exactly what was required to ensure that that kingdom never again acted as a catalyst to rebellion throughout Britain. More than most, Clarendon understood that British kingship made complex demands on a monarch over and above those of a mere king of England, but Charles I was not the only king to run into difficulties in interpreting his role as a multiple monarch. Multiple monarchy, and the absentee kingship which invariably attended it, was experienced by many European states and their monarchs during the course of the seventeenth century. It undid Sigismund Vasa who found it impossible to rule Poland and Sweden and was deposed as king of the latter in 1599; it cost Philip IV of Spain his Portuguese throne in 1640; and it shook the Austrian Hapsburgs' rule in Bohemia in 1618 and in Hungary in 1705. However, no one in 1603 imagined multiple monarchy would be so self-destructive, and instead James VI's accession to the English throne was seen to herald a new golden age for Protestant Britain. In 1630 Sir Robert Gordon, a Sutherland nobleman, wrote:

This Succession drew towards it the eyes of all men, being one of the most memorable accidents that had happened a long tyme in the Christian world; for the Kingdome of France haveing been reunited in aige before, in all the Provinces therof formerlie dismembered, and the Kingdome of Spain being of more fresh memory united and maid intyre, by the annexing of Portugal in the person of Philip the Second, there remained bot this third and last union for the counterposing of the

---

[1] W. D. Macray (ed.), *Clarendon's history of the rebellion* (6 vols., Oxford, 1888), vol. I, p. 113.

power of these monarchies, and the disposing of the affairs of Europe therby to a more sure and universall peace and accord.[2]

Here at the northerly edge of Europe spoke an internationalist with an eye to the balance of power, a British enthusiast who made a successful career at the London court, and a Scot, proud of his native dynasty. Sir Robert Gordon was one of those courtiers who epitomized the integrationist process which James VI and I believed would create a new British people. Yet in 1642 Sir Robert set his face against the imperial monarchy, abandoned the court and his property in Salisbury, and joined the covenanters in the struggle against Charles I. Among the covenanters' grievances were the shortcomings of absentee kingship, which was, for the Scots at least, what British kingship became.

In James Hodges's 1706 edition of *The rights and interests of the two British monarchies* he reported on the failure of early proposals for 'melting down the two crowns and making one out of both', indicating in a symbolic way the constitutional limitations on the regal union. There was no single crown, no common laws of inheritance, and the king's political capacities differed in the three kingdoms. Sharing a king was not the same as being subject to the same imperial monarchy, an idea largely discredited by the eighteenth century, except among a chauvinist English lobby whose opportunist claims sparked off a round of mutual book-burning by the two parliaments.[3] Yet whether he had one crown or two, or even three, a British king had only one head, and the practical question of British kingship had to be faced. It has been argued that it is absurd to treat James VI and I as 'two separate individuals', but centuries of English arrogance and Scottish parochialism have colluded in preventing a debate on British kingship.[4] Overwhelmingly, biographies of Britain's seventeenth-century kings discuss their success or failure solely on their performance as English kings. To take one remarkable example, Charles II has been described as a successful politician because he 'saved England from the fate of contemporary

[2] Sir Robert Gordon, *A genealogical history of the earldom of Sutherland* (Edinburgh, 1813), p. 249.

[3] William Ferguson, 'Imperial crowns: a neglected facet of the background to the treaty of union', *SHR*, 53 (1974), 22–44; Brian P. Levack, *The formation of the British state: England, Scotland and the union 1603–1707* (Oxford, 1987), pp. 51–9; J. A. Lovat-Fraser, 'The constitutional position of the Scottish monarch prior to the union', *Law Quarterly Review*, 17 (1901), 252–7; W. S. Mackenzie, 'The constitutional necessity for the union of 1707', *SHR*, 5 (1908), 52–66.

[4] Jenny Wormald, 'James VI and I: two kings or one?', *History*, 68 (1983), 187–209. Maurice Lee, Jr, *Great Britain's Solomon: James VI and I and his three kingdoms* (Urbana and Chicago, 1990) also demonstrates a healthy move in the direction of a British approach to James's reign.

Scotland', a conclusion which is reasonable for a king of England but not a king of Great Britain.[5]

Both the Tudors and the Stewarts of the sixteenth century drew on a long-established native tradition defining good kingship, but there were no precedents or mirrors-of-princes for a British king, and from the start James VI and I had to find his own way. Dual monarchy had been thought about before by that pseudo-Welshman, Henry VII, who in marrying his daughter to James IV in 1503 dismissed the risk of bequeathing his kingdom to a Scot, commenting that the greater kingdom inevitably would draw the lesser. Dynastic union with Scotland was postponed for a century, during which the Tudors identified themselves with the English nation, while their Welsh origins served to arouse Welsh enthusiasm.[6] These Welsh roots also opened up a means of subordinating the so-called British History to the needs of an imperial English monarchy, and from the 1540s British propaganda was projected north towards Scotland and given added impetus in the portrayal of England as an elect nation.[7] Scottish hostility towards a British empire, expressed in the Brut and Constantinian traditions, was exemplified by historians such as John Fordun, Hector Boece and George Buchanan who undermined the imperial mythology.[8] Under Queen Elizabeth, the

---

[5] J. R. Jones, *Charles II: royal politician* (London, 1987), p. 190. By contrast, a good example of how to write about a British king is Ronald Hutton, *Charles II: king of England, Scotland and Ireland* (Oxford, 1989). Countless examples of this Anglocentric approach can be cited for seventeenth-century British monarchs. John Miller, *James II: a study in kingship* (Hove, 1977), is right to observe that James was 'an Englishman ... [who] ... put English interests first', p. 217, but this does not excuse his very brief treatment of Scottish and Irish affairs, pp. 210–19. J. Baxter, *William III* (London, 1964), pp. 269–81, describes William's system of ruling in which Scotland and Ireland were treated as minor departments of government, but his ignorance of Scottish affairs appears even greater than that of William himself. Edward Gregg, *Queen Anne* (London, 1984), ignores Scotland except where it impinges on English affairs, and in examining 'The role of the monarch' discusses the issues only in an English context.

[6] Peter Roberts, 'The Welshness of the Tudors', *History Today*, 36 (January 1986), 6–13; M. A. Nash, 'A Welsh family on the English throne', *Contemporary Review*, 248 (1986), 142–9; D. Williams, 'The Welsh Tudors: the family of Henry VII', *History Today*, 4 (1954), 77–84.

[7] T. D. Kendrick, *British antiquity* (London, 1950), pp. 34–41; S. Anglo, 'The British History in early Tudor propaganda', *Bulletin of the John Rylands Library*, 54 (1961), 17–48; Frances Yates, *Astraea: the imperial theme in the sixteenth century* (London, 1975), pp. 29–87; William Haller, *Foxe's 'Book of martyrs' and the elect nation* (London, 1967); Patrick Collinson, 'A chosen people? The English church and the reformation', *History Today*, 36 (March 1986), 14–20.

[8] For the application of such ideas to Scotland and resistance to them, see Roger A. Mason, 'Kingship, nobility and Anglo-Scottish union: John Mair's *History of Greater Britain* (1521)', *IR*, 41 (1990), 182–222; Marcus Merriman, 'James Henrisoun and "Great Britain": British union and the Scottish commonweal', in Roger A. Mason (ed.), *Scotland and England 1286–1815* (Edinburgh, 1987), pp. 85–112; Roger A. Mason, 'Scotching the Brut: politics, history and national myth in sixteenth-century Britain' in *ibid.*, pp. 60–84; Arthur

mid-century British ideology was displaced by a more overt English nationalism, but as a Scottish succession loomed in the last decade of the century,
dramatists reflected English nervousness at domination by foreigners.[9]
Those fears appeared to be justified in 1604 when James VI and I addressed
his English parliament on the subject of dual monarchy:

What God hath conjoyned then, let no man separate. I am the Husband, and all the
whole Isle is my lawful Wife; I am the Head, and it is my Body; I am the Shepherd,
and it is my flocke; I hope therefore no man will be so unreasonable as to thinke that
I that am a Christian King under the Gospel, should be a Polygamist and husband to
two wives; that I being the Head, should have a divided and monstrous Body.[10]

James's mystical concept of union failed to inspire an English audience
deeply suspicious of British ideology, and already prepared to accept the
doctrine of the king's two bodies. Following the failure to achieve a union of
parliaments in 1604, British kings for the remainder of the century ruled
over a body politic which was indeed 'monstrous'.[11] Among the Scots too
there were doubts about the royal strategy, but James VI and I was able to
ameliorate the disadvantages of absentee kingship because of his long
experience of ruling in Scotland.[12] Yet by the early eighteenth century
Henry VII's prediction had been fulfilled. Queen Anne was also an enthusiast for Anglo-Scottish union, but described the Scots as 'strange people',
and is commonly, and approvingly, quoted as telling her first English
parliament that 'As I know my own heart to be entirely English, I can
entirely assure you there is not anything you can expect or desire from me
which I shall not be ready to do for the happiness and prosperity of

---

H. Williamson, *Scottish national consciousness in the age of James VI* (Edinburgh, 1979). See
also below chapter 7.

[9] Margaret Axton, *The queen's two bodies: drama and the Elizabethan succession* (London,
1977), pp. 76–130. English self-doubt is evident in plays such as the collaborative *Misfor-
tunes of Arthur* (1588), Robert Green's *The Scottish history of James the fourth slaine at
Flodden* (1598), and possibly William Shakespeare's *Henry V* (1599), and in *Love's martyr:
or Rosalind's complaint*, a collection of poems on similar themes. Submerged English hostility to a foreign dynasty re-emerged in the 1640s in, for example, E. Peyton, *The divine
catastrophe of the kingly family of the house of Stuart*, in Walter Scott (ed.), *Secret history of
the court of James the first* (2 vols., Edinburgh, 1811), vol. II, p. 310.

[10] McIlwain, *Works*, p. 272. For a discussion of the Scoto-Irish roots of this view of kingship,
see M. J. Enright, 'King James and his island: an archaic kingship belief?', *SHR*, 55 (1976),
29–40. The relationship between marriage and union was exploited by Ben Jonson in the
1606 masque *Hymenai*, see D. J. Gordon, '*Hymenai*: Ben Jonson's masque of union', in
S. Orgel (ed.), *The Renaissance imagination* (Berkeley, 1980), pp. 157–84.

[11] Ernest H. Kantorowicz, *The king's two bodies: a study in medieval political theology* (Princeton, 1957), pp. 445–6, note 425.

[12] Praise for James's handling of multiple monarchy is found in Maurice Lee, Jr, *Government
by pen: Scotland under James VI and I* (Urbana, 1980), and Wormald, 'Two kings or one?'.
For a more critical interpretation, see Keith M. Brown, *Kingdom or province? Scotland and
the regal union, 1603–1715* (Basingstoke and London, 1992), pp. 86–99.

England'.[13] Not until the latter half of the eighteenth century did George III recapture something of James VI and I's pride 'in the name of Britain', much to the disgust of the English.[14]

Increasingly, historians are coming to a more holistic understanding of kingship in which pomp, ceremony and ritual are seen as aspects of power and not mere presentational gimmicks.[15] Even after the aura of divine-right monarchy had faded, Queen Anne so valued the power of ceremony and was 'so exact an observor of forms, that she seemed to have made it her study'.[16] In England the Tudor monarchy established a range of icons and images many of which were understood and appreciated even by the illiterate masses.[17] In Scotland less attention was paid to visual imagery, although James VI's baptism in 1566 demonstrated that the Scots were able to mount a sophisticated show when cash was available and the occasion demanded it.[18] From 1603 James threw a vast array of resources behind his image-building in England, but he could not simply appropriate for himself the Elizabethan legacy, much of which was offensive to the Scots, including himself.[19]

---

[13] William Ferguson, *Scotland's relations with England: a survey to 1707* (Edinburgh, 1977), p. 200; J. R. S. Whiting, *Commemorative medals: a medallic history of Britain from Tudor times to the present day* (Newton Abbot, 1972), p. 103.

[14] Lewis Namier, *The structure of politics at the accession of George III* (London, 1963), p. 14, note 1.

[15] Clifford Geertz, 'Centres, kings and charisma: reflections on the symbolics of power', in J. Ben-David and T. N. Clarke (eds.), *Culture and its creators: essays in honor of E. Shils* (Chicago and London, 1977), pp. 150–71; D. Cannadine, 'Introduction', in D. Cannadine and S. Price (eds.), *Rituals of royalty: power and ceremonial in traditional society* (Cambridge, 1987), pp. 1–19. Kevin Sharpe, *Criticism and compliment: the politics of literature in the England of Charles I* (London, 1986), pp. 3–4, makes the point that 'The ceremonies and rituals of courtly and monarchical life were – to the Monarch no less than to his subjects – the rituals of divine kingship'. A not altogether satisfactory attempt to investigate some aspects of image is Richard Ollard, *The image of the king* (London, 1979). Cynthia Herrup's review article 'Beyond personality and pomp: recent works on early modern monarchies', *Journal of British Studies*, 28 (1989), 175–80, urges a holistic approach to the study of kingship, but betrays the usual Anglocentrism: 'A sitting king was the center of the English structure of power'. He was, but this is rather like saying that Philip II sat at the centre of a Castilian power structure.

[16] R. D. Bucholz, 'The court in the reign of Queen Anne' (unpubl. D. Phil. thesis, Oxford, 1987), p. 278. By contrast William III and II was the least image-conscious king of the period, delegating much of the ceremonial side of monarchy to his wife until her death in 1694: Baxter, *William III*, p. 279.

[17] John N. King, *Tudor royal iconography: literature and art in an age of religious crisis* (Princeton, 1989); S. Anglo, *Spectacle, pageantry and early Tudor policy* (Oxford, 1969); Roy Strong, *The English icon* (London, 1969); Roy Strong, *The cult of Elizabeth: Elizabethan portraiture and pageantry* (London, 1977); D. M. Bergeron, *English civic pageantry 1588–1642* (London, 1971). See too Yates, *Astraea*, pp. 29–87, for the imperial theme.

[18] Michael Lynch, 'Queen Mary's triumph: the baptismal celebration at Stirling in December 1566', *SHR*, 66 (1990), 1–21.

[19] Graham Parry, *The seventeenth century: the intellectual and cultural context of English literature, 1603–1700* (Harlow, 1989), p. 14, where he claims James outdid Elizabeth in the scale of his propaganda campaign.

Instead he and his advisers had to invent a new dynastic tradition.[20] The desire to put down roots in England was evident in the change of name from Stewart to Stuart, the deliberate linking of the dynasty with the Tudors (begun even before 1603 in the naming of Princess Elizabeth and Prince Henry), royal residence in London, the intended new palace at Whitehall, the appropriation of Tudor pageantry and ceremonial, and the propaganda of court masques.

King James also acquired a new title. In 1603 he assumed the style 'King of England, Scotland, France and Ireland' (the order was reversed in Scotland), but there were problems in such an arrangement, and quarrels over precedence were common at court. When at Princess Elizabeth's wedding in 1613 the Scottish lyon king wore the Scottish arms before those of England, one offended Englishman wrote 'it is thought a strange affront offered at such a time, in such a place, to such a people'.[21] Compromise on the royal style proved impossible, and in October 1604 James signalled his determination to force recognition that he had 'attained the monarchy of the whole of Great Britain' by altering his title by royal prerogative to 'King of Great Britain, France and Ireland'. Yet while English courtiers such as Sir Edward Coke cultivated favour by devising a British coat of arms, and Scots such as William Drummond of Hawthornden referred to 'the King of Great Britain (for so I must now, for distinction of two Kings in one Island, call him)', few subjects shared the king's enthusiasm for an imperial British monarchy.[22] On the issue of the king's title the English were more successful in ignoring James's view, and while in Scotland the new British style was adopted officially, even here there was no rush to recognize the change. In 1616 James himself had to remind an unenthusiastic Scottish treasurer-depute that he had ordered all seals to 'have engraved theron the arms of all his majesty's kingdoms', and to have a new quarter-seal made since the old and worn pre-1603 seals still were being

---

[20] On this theme, see D. Cannadine, 'The context, performance and making of ritual: the British monarchy and the "invention of tradition" c. 1820–1977', in E. Hobsbawm and T. Ranger (eds.), *The invention of tradition* (London, 1983), pp. 101–64. Also useful is I. Hayden, *Symbol and privilege. The ritual context of British monarchy* (Tucson, Ariz., 1987). Hayden describes how the monarchy became an 'autochthonic institution' in the twentieth century. (p. 60).

[21] John Nichols (ed.), *The progresses, processions and magnificent festivities of King James the first, his royal consort, family and court* (4 vols., London, 1828), vol. II, pp. 604–5, and see note on p. 606 for James giving priority to the Scottish arms elsewhere. From 1654 the Protectorate coat of arms included the Irish harp and the St Andrew's Cross: R. E. Sherwood, *The court of Oliver Cromwell* (London, 1977), pp. 54, 97.

[22] Nichols (ed.), *Progresses*, vol. II, p. 53; Conrad Russell, 'The British background to the Irish rebellion of 1641', *Historical Research*, 61 (1988), 171. Correspondents appear to have used either style. Thus Mr Chamberlain referred to James both as king of Great Britain and

used.[23] By 1630 the Scots were protesting against the imposition of the British style, and during the revolution a decade later they reverted to 'King of Scotland, England, France and Ireland'. Surprisingly, and provocatively, in a rush of royalist enthusiasm in 1651, they crowned Charles II king of Great Britain, and it was this style that was used in the oath of allegiance by Scottish privy councillors in 1661. However, after 1660 the British style was unfashionable, and only made a brief reappearance in Scotland during the duke of York's visit in 1679–81. English resistance remained, and it was only after the parliamentary union in 1707 that Queen Anne unequivocally adopted the British style in her title.[24]

At his English coronation in 1603 James VI and I's principal objective was to win over his English public by projecting an image of a king following in the footsteps of his Tudor predecessors. The coronation service preserved intact the entire medieval *liber regalia* (although it was performed in English for the first time), while the Scots were given a low profile in the ceremony.[25] Yet the occasion was exploited to underline the king's expectations for the future Great Britain. James's frantic dubbing of knights before the coronation made sense when viewed in the light of a comment by a Roman observer who believed that to date 700 knights had been created, but that 'He [James] has also the intention of bringing up the number to a thousand, as King Arthur had when he had conquered the Kingdom'.[26] When the royal procession arrived at the Tower of London the king was treated to a unionist oration:

The partition-wall betweene these two Kingdomes by the finger of God at your coming to the crowne is gone. He hath made Israel and Juda one in you; no more two Kingdomes, nor two Kings; nor two pastors, nor two flockes; nor two kindes, nor two

king of England; Nichols (ed.), *Progresses*, vol. III, pp. 14 and 16. James himself often dated his letters 'in the yeare of our raigne of Great Britaine'; *ibid.*, vol. II, p. 371.

[23] H. Paton (ed.), *Report of the historical manuscript commission on the manuscripts of the earl of Mar and Kellie* (2 vols., London, 1904, 1930), vol. II, p. 70.

[24] S. T. Bindoff, 'The Stuarts and their style', *EHR*, 60 (1945), 192–216; Ferguson, 'Imperial crowns'; Levack, *British state*, pp. 1–2.

[25] C. Wordsworth (ed.), *The manner of the coronation of King Charles the first of England*, Henry Bradshaw Society 2 (London, 1892), pp. 79–83, which also deals with James I; J. W. Legg (ed.), *Three coronation orders*, Henry Bradshaw Society 19 (London, 1900), pp. xv–xxx, 19; J. W. Legg (ed.), *The coronation order of King James I* (London, 1902); P. E. Schramm, *A history of the English coronation* (Oxford, 1937); Nichols (ed.), *Progresses*, vol. I, pp. 229–34. Even in 1953 prominent sociologists could write that 'The Coronation is exactly this kind of ceremonial in which the society reaffirms the moral values which constitute it as a society and renews its devotion to those values by an act of communion': E. Shils and M. Young, 'The making of the coronation', *Sociological Review*, new series 1 (1953), 67. Naturally such an establishment view was challenged immediately: N. Birnbaum, 'Monarchies and sociologists?: a reply to Professor Shils and Mr Young', *ibid.*, 3 (1955), 5–23.

[26] Legg (ed.), *Coronation order of James I*, p. lxviii.

mindes; nor two regions, nor two religions. One King, one people, one law, and, as it was in the beginning, one land of Albion. Al things in one Heavenly God one; al things in one earthly God, ('for I have stiled you Gods,' as the Scripture speaketh,) one![27]

The accession and coronation were celebrated by writers and hacks falling over one another to get into print with similar ideas.[28] James's English coronation ceremony was stage-managed to present him as king of England, but the supporting propaganda was heavily British in tone. Later English coronations were more Anglocentric.[29] In 1661, at Charles II's English coronation, held on St George's Day, little British iconography was deployed; a Roman conquerer, Old Testament figures, Neptune, the sun, Christ and the messiah of Isaiah were the most recognizable. Most of these were commonplace among the European monarchies of the period. The Roman imperial theme was popular with James VI and I who saw himself as the new Caesar ruling a British empire, but after the Restoration it was employed in an English context. John Dryden cast Charles II as another Augustus, and this was the inspiration behind Aurelian Cook's best-selling biography of the king, *Titus Britannicus* (1685). However, this title was less attractive to the English public than a pirated and abridged version which was published as *Augustus Anglicus*. The Neptune theme had its roots in Elizabethan iconography, but as the father of Albion and the god of the sea which formed the natural limits of James VI and I's empire, it was adapted to suit a British audience (although James dropped the martial dimension). Charles I, in similar vein, had a medal struck in 1630, demonstrating his dominion over the seas. The idea had not been lost at the Restoration when James Howell, the royal historiographer, wrote of Charles's unrivalled naval power, derived from the fact that he was 'the King of Great Britain ... for he commands no less than four Seas, which are circumfluent about his Territories'. Yet these strands connecting Charles II's coronation with James VI and I's British ideology were implicit; there was no attempt in 1661, or at later English coronations, to repeat the explicit British references of 1603.[30]

[27] Nichols (ed.), *Progresses*, vol. I, p. 331.
[28] 'The very Poets, with their idle pamphlets, promise themselves great part in his favour', *ibid.*, vol. I, pp. xxxvii–xlvi, 235–44, 408–19.
[29] Wordsworth (ed.), *Coronation of Charles the first*; Legg (ed.), *Three coronation orders*; Schramm, *English coronation*; Sir E. Walker, *A circumstantial account of the preparations for the coronation of his majesty King Charles the second* (London, 1820); F. Stanford, *The history of the coronation of King James II and Queen Mary* (London, 1687).
[30] Walker, *Coronation of Charles the second*; G. Reedy, 'Mystical politics: the imagery of Charles II's coronation', in P. J. Korshin (ed.), *Studies in change and revolution: aspects of English intellectual history 1640–1800* (Menston, 1972), pp. 19–42; Parry, *Seventeenth century*, pp. 110–12; Whiting, *Commemorative medals*, p. 40; Graham Parry, *The golden age restor'd: the culture of the Stuart court 1603–42* (Manchester and New York, 1981), p. 65.

English sovereigns were crowned for 'this Kingdom of England, and the Dominions thereto belonging', but those 'Dominions' (Ireland and any colonial possessions) did not embrace Scotland. In 1625 it was rumoured that Charles I intended having the Scottish regalia sent south, and while at his trial in 1644 Archbishop Laud was cleared of the accusation of attempting to embrace Scotland within the text of the English coronation oath, Laud did exert some editorial influence on the proceedings, which were gaudier and more extravagant than they might otherwise have been. Charles indicated his desire to go to Scotland to be crowned as early as 1625, but it was 1628 before he asked Archbishop Spottiswoode 'to prepare for our consecratione according to the antient forme of that kingdom, making use of what you ever remember to have seen at our consecratione heir, soe farr as it salbe found expedient'. It was the privy council that discouraged his visit on account of the anticipated cost, and Charles did not make the journey north to be crowned until 1633. The coronation was intended as a stage-managed exercise in presenting a Scottish king to his public. The English were kept out of view, with only the English royal heralds, and the captains of the Gentlemen Pensioners and the Yeomen of the Guard riding in the coronation procession through Edinburgh, while Bishop Laud was left to engage in undignified pushing to establish for himself some minor role in the proceedings.[31] However, it was typical of Charles I that the elements of English ceremonial and the evidences of authoritarian kingship merely antagonized the Scots. By contrast, the other Scottish coronation of the century, that of Charles II at Scone in 1651, was manipulated by the covenanters to authenticate contractual monarchy, to emphasize the country's attachment to the crown following its rejection in England, and to express native pride in a Scottish dynasty. This last point was conveyed forcefully in the resurrection of the ancient tradition of reciting the names of over a hundred of Charles's predecessors. Yet the logic of the Solemn League and Covenant drove the Scots to crown Charles II 'King of Great Britain, France and Ireland'.[32] This provocative action, and Charles's

---

[31] R. J. Lyall, 'The medieval coronation service: some seventeenth century evidence', *IR*, 28 (1977), 3; Wordsworth (ed.), *Coronation of Charles the first*, pp. lvii–lxiii, 18–24, 93–106; J. Stuart, *Scottish coronations* (London, 1902), pp. 63–140; D. Masson and P. H. Brown (eds.), *Register of the privy council of Scotland*, second series (8 vols., Edinburgh, 1899–1908), vol. I, p. 151; vol. II, pp. 367, 381. For a detailed description of the ceremonies, James Haig (ed.), *The historical works of Sir James Balfour* (4 vols., Edinburgh, 1824–5), vol. IV, pp. 383–403. Gilbert Burnet later dismissed it all as 'entertainment and shew', Gilbert Burnet, *History of my own time*, ed. O. Airy (3 vols., Oxford, 1877), vol. I, p. 31.

[32] There was no anointing, Charles swore to uphold the covenants, and the centrepiece of the proceedings was a long sermon by Rev. Robert Douglas; Stuart, *Scottish coronations*, pp. 141–219. Charles I had been anointed, but James VI had the greatest of difficulty in persuading the clergy to anoint Queen Anne in 1590. For some useful discussion of the coronations of 1633 and 1651, see John Morrill, 'The National Covenant in its British

subsequent invasion of England at the head of a Scottish army, created a propaganda coup for the English republicans who derided the 'young bonny Scotch King'.[33] Hence Oliver Cromwell's play on deep-felt English prejudices when he addressed his countrymen at the outset of the invasion in 1651: 'Now that should awaken all Englishmen, who perhaps are willing enough he should have come in upon accomodation, but not he must come from Ireland or Scotland'.[34]

Charles II was the last king to be crowned in Scotland, and James VII and II failed even to take the coronation oath, a lapse that made the legality of his deposition in 1689 all the easier.[35] His English coronation allowed no formal role for the Scots, and the presence of John Drummond, the Scottish secretary of state, was by right as an English privy councillor, while the scrupulousness in excluding non-English subjects extended to the Scottish horse troop and foot guards being left in their barracks. Nevertheless, this English affair was recognized in Scotland, where the privy council ordered bonfires to be lit in Edinburgh.[36] William III and II established a new precedent with the administration of the Scottish coronation oath to the sovereign in Whitehall. On 11 May 1689 the commissioners of the estates and those noblemen present in London attended on William and Mary in the banqueting hall where

they presented to his majestie a letter from the estates; then the instrument of government; then a paper concerning the grievances which they desired might be redressed; and, lastly, an addresse to his majestie for turning the said estates into a parliament; all signed by duke Hamilton, as president of the meeting: then their majesties took the coronation oath, which they both also signed; after which the commissioners and several of the Scotch nobility kissed thair majesties hands.[37]

This furtive ceremony contrasted with the orchestrated public theatre which had surrounded William and Mary's acceptance of the English Declaration of Rights in February of that year.[38] There was even less publicity when

context', in John Morrill (ed.), *The Scottish National Covenant in its British context 1638–51* (Edinburgh, 1990), pp. 1–30.

[33] L. Potter, 'The plays and the playwrights: 1642–60', in P. Edwards *et al.* (eds.), *The revels history of drama, 1613–1660* (London, 1981), pp. 290, 303.

[34] W. C. Abbot (ed.), *The writings and speeches of Oliver Cromwell* (4 vols., Cambridge, Mass., 1937–47), vol. II, p. 39.

[35] William Ferguson, *Scotland: 1689 to the present* (Edinburgh, 1975), p. 5.

[36] Stanford, *History of the coronation of King James II*; Lyall, 'Medieval coronation service', p. 3; H. Oakes-Jones, 'The king: his ancient royal body guards, horse and foot', *Journal for the Society of Army Historical Research*, 16 (1937), 63–86; *RPC*, second series, vol. XI, p. 281.

[37] For William, see N. Luttrell, *A brief historical relation of state affairs from September 1678 to April 1714* (6 vols., Oxford, 1857), vol. I, p. 533.

[38] Lois G. Schwoerer, 'The Glorious Revolution as spectacle: a new perspective' in S. B. Baxter (ed.), *England's rise to greatness 1660–1763* (Berkeley, 1983), pp. 109–49.

Secretary Seafield privately administered the coronation oath to Queen Anne on 8 March 1702, the same day on which she took the English accession oath. An English coronation followed on St George's Day, but there was no Scottish coronation.[39]

Seventeenth-century governments recognized that popular identification with the monarch was important, and varying efforts were made to observe a royal calendar.[40] In Scotland the anniversary of the king's accession was ignored before 1603, probably because of the circumstances in which it took place, but also because of James VI's distaste for public ritual. In England some popular aspects of the Elizabethan accession day survived into his reign, but James did not stage an accession-day tilt until 1624.[41] Similarly, the king's birthday in Scotland was not a public occasion, and James's lack of interest ensured that 19 June never acquired the significance of Queen Elizabeth's birthday, which gained a new vitality in England in the 1620s as a means of expressing support for a militant Protestant foreign policy.[42] Charles I abandoned the public ritual of the accession day, but in England in the 1630s the birthdays of King Charles and Henrietta Maria attracted a growing interest. Once the conflict with the covenanters had begun the king's birthday celebrations acquired new significance for royalists, but when Charles's birthday was marked by the beleaguered garrison in Edinburgh Castle on 19 November 1639 the salvo from the guns ominously caused a large portion of the castle walls to collapse.[43] In the post-Restoration era observance of the king's birthday continued to be a litmus test of loyalty. In England, Royal Oak Day (29 May) combined the king's birthday, his formal accession and the beginning of the Restoration itself, and proved to be a popular spring festival which survived into the reign of King William. Scottish observance of Charles II's birthday was made statutory in

[39] Gregg, *Queen Anne*, p. 151.

[40] David Cressy, *Bonfires and bells: national memory and the Protestant calendar in Elizabethan and Stuart England* (London, 1989).

[41] Steven Orgel and Roy Strong (eds.), *Inigo Jones: the theatre of the Stuart court* (2 vols., London, 1973), vol. I, pp. 179–81. On Elizabeth's accession-day festivities, see Strong, *Cult of Elizabeth*, pp. 129–62; Roy Strong, 'The popular celebration of the accession day of Queen Elizabeth', *Journal of the Warburg and Courtauld Institute*, 21 (1958), 86–103; Yates, *Astraea*, pp. 88–111; all show the importance of a revived chivalry in acting as a vehicle for expressing national ambitions and fears. The inauguration of Henry as prince of Wales anticipated the next reign with similar Elizabethan themes, Nichols (ed.), *Progresses*, vol. II, pp. 324–45; Roy Strong, *Henry, prince of Wales and England's lost Renaissance* (London, 1986). The chivalric revival came to an end in the early years of Charles's reign: Alan Young, *Tudor and Jacobean tournaments* (London, 1987), pp. 37–42.

[42] Queen Elizabeth's birthday continued to be recognized even in the late seventeenth century, Luttrell, *Relation*, vol. I, p. 388, for 1686, and vol. II, p. 618, for 1692. King Charles's Day also outlived Charles II, e.g. 28 May was celebrated in 1692, *ibid.*, vol. II, p. 467.

[43] David Stevenson, *The Scottish revolution 1637–44: the triumph of the covenanters* (Newton Abbot, 1973), p. 178.

the first session of the restored parliament, but initially there was resistance.[44] Gilbert Burnet recorded disapprovingly that 'Under the colour of drinking the king's health, there were great disorders and much riot every where', and it was this potential for disorder which made the king's birthday something of a double-edged weapon.[45] In London, James VII and II's birthday (which was also a celebration to mark the defeat of Monmouth and Argyll) was marked by the customary 'publick demonstration of joy, as singing of bells, store of bonfires, etc'. Enthused by James's earlier residence in Edinburgh the Scots too celebrated, encouraged by a privy council that more than most understood the need for royal festivals. The privy council paid for the cost of bonfires at Holyroodhouse and on Arthur's Seat, and met the expenses of the burgh's magistrates 'for glasses and bottles broken at the solemnity'.[46] Post-Restoration monarchs also marked their accessions with displays of bells and bonfires in London and provincial towns, but while Scottish towns sent their quota of loyal addresses to James VII and II in 1685, the accession day did not acquire the fixed status it enjoyed in England.[47] The post-Revolution government of William III and II nervously tried to impose a more sombre mood on public ritual, ordering that 4 November 1690 (King William's birthday and anniversary of the Torbay landing) be observed in Edinburgh

with all solemnity and tokens of joy and particularly with puting on of bonfires and ringing of bells and fyring of guns from their Majesties castles and forts. And the Lords of Councill doe unanimously declair they will meet in this place the said day and that they with the magistrats and councill of this citie will walk in solemne order to the cross and their give publict testimony of their great joy for his Majesties happy birth.[48]

By the late seventeenth century the king's birthday had become one of the few recognized symbols of unity and loyalty to the monarchy throughout Britain, but it also provided an occasion for marking discontent with the regime and the king's birthday riots were to become a feature of eighteenth-century political life.

After 1603 royal births and marriages took place in London, and it was there the events were most likely to be publicly recognized. Princess Mary,

[44] P. H. Brown et al., (eds.), Register of the privy council of Scotland, third series (16 vols., Edinburgh, 1908–70), vol. III, pp. 345, 347; vol. IV, pp. 57–8, 71–2, 83, 101. In 1680 Luttrell recorded that 'We are advised from Edinburgh in Scotland, from Wigan in Lancashire, and other places, of the great joy and solemnity the 29th of May, his majesties birth day, was kept', Relation, vol. I, p. 46.

[45] Burnet, History, vol. I, p. 166.

[46] RPC, third series, vol. XI, pp. 166, 183–4; vol. XII, p. xxv.

[47] Luttrell, Relation, vol. I, pp. 330, 340, 390, 401.

[48] RPC, third series, vol. XIV, p. 449; vol. XV, p. 511. By 1691 the celebrations were even more elaborate; ibid., vol. XVI, pp. 576–7.

born in April 1605, was the first Stewart to be born in England, giving Londoners their first opportunity to celebrate a royal birth since October 1537. There was genuine joy at the arrival of this English-born princess, and 'the Citizens of London made bonfires throughout London, and the bells continued ringing all the whole day'.[49] The marriage of Princess Elizabeth to Frederick, elector palatine, in 1613 was also a London event, but much of the intended propaganda accompanying the marriage sought to emphasize Britain's position at the centre of a European Protestant alliance. Nevertheless it was St George who was depicted slaying a Catholic dragon.[50] The marriage in 1624 of Charles and the French Catholic princess, Henrietta Maria, saw official encouragement of popular enthusiasm so that bonfires were lit in London, bells rang out, the cannon in the Tower fired salvoes, and the organ in St Paul's Cathedral was played as loud as possible for two hours.[51] Edinburgh appears to have ignored this event, but when the lyon king of arms arrived with the news of the birth of Prince Charles on 1 June 1630 the Scots did celebrate:

ther was grate joy and triumphe made by shoutting of canon, ringing of bells, bonfyres and the lyke. The magistrates of Edinburghe made a grate banquett one the Heigh Street to the Lordes of his Maiesties privey counsaill, and others of the nobility and judges. The table stood below the crosse towards the Trone and did containe some 200 persons; they were waitted one by the herauldes in ther coattes, and his Maiesties trumpetts.[52]

After the Restoration official thanksgiving celebrations throughout Britain were more organized. For example, in May 1661 the Irish parliament sent an address to Charles II congratulating him on his decision to marry Catherine of Braganza, and in Dublin 'Bells, bonefires and ordinance' marked Irish approval of the forthcoming marriage.[53] The popular Protestant marriage of William of Orange and Princess Mary on 4 November 1677 led to jubilant celebrations throughout England which embarrassed King Charles,

---

[49] Nichols (ed.), *Progresses*, vol. I, p. 505. At the princess's baptism in Greenwich Palace, performed according to English rites (unlike those of Prince Henry and Prince Charles), the only non-English personnel taking part were the Danish duke of Holstein and the Franco-Scottish duke of Lennox; the godmothers were Lady Arabella and the countess of Northumberland; *ibid.*, vol. I, pp. 512–13.

[50] Nichols (ed.), *Progresses*, vol. II, pp. 536–53; Parry, *Golden age*, pp. 95–107. Imperialism was a major theme in the intended entertainments, e.g., *The Lord's masque* sponsored by the English earls of Salisbury and Montgomery and the Scottish Lord Hay – 'Let the British strength be added to the German: can anything equal it? One minde, one faith, will join two peoples, and one religion, and simple love.' The masque was never performed.

[51] Charles Carlton, *Charles I: the personal monarch* (London, 1984), p. 56.

[52] Balfour, *Works*, vol. II, pp. 178–9.

[53] C. W. Russell *et al.* (eds.), *Calendar of state papers relating to Ireland* (13 vols., London, 1872–1910), vol. X [1660–2], p. 338.

although the Scots again were less vociferous.[54] In fact the Scots were more likely to keep to the prepared script, and when James VII and II's son was born, the privy council orchestrated the public response. Bonfires were lit in Edinburgh on 29 January 1688 'in commemoration of the thanksgiving for her Royal Majesties being with child and emploring the Divine Majestie for the preservation of the Royal Race'.[55]

National saints' days provided a useful opportunity for linking the crown with popular festivities. James VI and I was unenthusiastic about the cult of St George, but saw the potential of the Order of the Garter to act as an integrative organization, rewarding eight of his Scottish friends with membership of this exclusive English order. His sons were interested in Garter ideology and ritual, and both Henry and Charles sought identification with St George. Charles II's English coronation on St George's Day was a clear statement of Englishness, as was that of Queen Anne who took an interest and pride in the Order of the Garter in which the Scots had been reduced to two knights. Of course the visual potential of St George was more attractive than St Andrew – one cannot imagine Charles I depicted as St Andrew hanging upside down on a cross, but kingly dignity could bear Rubens portraying him as St George. The tangible ceremonial of the Order of the Garter with its annual feast, medals and robes contributed towards making the relationship between the monarchy and the cult of St George a close one. The Scottish equivalent, the Order of the Thistle, had been defunct since the death of James V in 1542. It was revived by James VII and II, only to be neglected again until Anne restored the order in 1703, and she wore the combined Orders of the Garter and Thistle at the thanksgiving service for the union of the parliaments at St Paul's Cathedral on 1 May 1707.[56] In contrast to the festival of St George, St Andrew's Day on 30 November received little crown patronage. Samuel Pepys recorded in 1666 that while some in Whitehall wore St Andrew's crosses, 'most did make a mockery at it', and the Pentland rising gave the English parliament an excuse to sit that day, 'people having no mind to observe that Scotch saint's day till they hear better knews from Scotland'.[57] In 1669 an Irish official wrote from Dublin that 'this being St Andrews' Day the Scothmen [sic] about the town here are as drunk as beggers'.[58] St Andrew's Day was an excuse for Scots to drink and indulge in patriotic sentiment; it had little connection with the British crown.

[54] The council did organize some 'solemnities' in Edinburgh, *RPC* third series, vol. V, pp. 271–2.
[55] *RPC*, third series, vol. XIII, p. xliii.   [56] Gregg, *Queen Anne*, p. 240.
[57] R. Latham and W. Mathews (eds.), *The diary of Samuel Pepys* (10 vols., London, 1970–83), vol. VII, p. 391.
[58] *CSP Ireland 1669–1670*, p. 29.

The monarch's role as a focus around which the British peoples gathered to fight their enemies offered a potentially unifying symbol. However, the absence of military victories under James VI and I and Charles I discouraged the growth of pride in British arms, while the wars of the 1640s threw the three nations into conflict with one another. When the English parliament resolved that 3 September should be celebrated as a day of public thanksgiving it was in recognition of Oliver Cromwell's victories over the Scots at Dunbar and Worcester.[59] Yet while James VI and I was no warlord, he succeeded in identifying threats to his person with an attack on the state itself. For James the Gowrie conspiracy of 5 August 1600 was the most traumatic experience of his life, and he insisted that the English celebrate the official Scottish version of his deliverance. The highlight of his 1617 visit to Scotland was showing English courtiers around the scene at Perth of his great escape seventeen years before.[60] The 5 August celebrations disappeared from the calendar after James's death, but the Gunpowder plot of 5 November 1605 became a permanent fixture throughout England where it had threatened the entire political establishment. The Scots joined in the official marking of an event aimed as much at them as at Protestants, but it never acquired the mass appeal to Protestant militancy which emerged in England in the 1630s, and more dangerously in the 1670s and 1680s. Even the merging of Gunpowder Day with King William's birthday and the Torbay landing on 4 November failed to stir up the passion so noticeable in London and many English provincial towns. By comparison the Scottish privy council's preparations for 5 November 1689 were dull and stately.[61] The popish plot of 1678 was another occasion for British Protestants to join together in thanking God, and the Scots marked the crushing of the plotters with a dour general fast on 18 December.[62] English naval victories against the Dutch in the summer of 1665 sparked off victory celebrations in London on 14 August, but in Scotland the war was unpopular. Charles II had to instruct the privy council in Edinburgh that 'because wee think it fitt that

---

[59] Frances Dow, *Cromwellian Scotland 1651–1660* (Edinburgh, 1979), p. 30.

[60] The Gowrie remembrance was turned into another occasion to publicize the king's view of monarchy. Thus in 1608 Bishop Andrews preached on 1 Samuel 26.9: 'And David said to Abishai, destroy him not; for who can stand against the Lord's anointed and be guiltless'; Nichols (ed.), *Progresses*, vol. I, p. 203. For the 1617 visit to Perth, see Scott (ed.), *Secret history*, vol. II, pp. 116–17. In 1615 the poet Fennor recited 'A Speech Concerning the Gowrie treason and the Gunpowder Plot' before the king in the bishop's palace in Salisbury; Nichols (ed.), *Progresses*, vol. III, p. 97.

[61] *RPC*, third series, vol. XIV, p. 449. The connection between Gunpowder Day celebrations and popular Protestantism was not always appreciated by the crown. For example in 1685 London parish officers were ordered to 'make no bonefires nor throw any squibs'; Luttrell, *Relation*, vol. I, p. 362.

[62] *RPC*, third series, vol. VI, pp. 59, 62–3. Charles II's deliverance from a supposed plot in 1683 was celebrated throughout Britain; Luttrell, *Relation*, vol. I, pp. 274, 279.

our kingdom of Scotland doe also shew their thankfulnes to Almighty, who is the giver of victory', then the Scots too were to hold celebrations throughout the country.[63] It was only with the duke of Marlborough's great victories over the French with multi-national armies that the military dimension of the British crown began to act as a unifying concept. Thus the service of thanksgiving which Queen Anne attended at St Paul's on 27 June 1706 to mark the victory at Ramillies was repeated throughout all three kingdoms.[64]

More pervasive than any of these events, which tended to be concentrated in major cities and towns, were prayers for the royal family. These were said weekly from every pulpit in the three kingdoms. Hence in 1603 ordinary English people quickly became familiar with the identity of their new Scottish sovereign and his family. That this was a political undertaking was widely recognized, and in the 1640s the saying of prayers for Charles I became a hotly divisive issue in England. North of the border the covenanters, with their ingrained sense of royalism, clung even more tenaciously to their prayers, and it was 1657 before the English military government persuaded the majority Resolutioner wing of the church to abandon praying for Charles II.[65] After 1660 Charles insisted that every parish church in Scotland pray for him, the queen, his mother, the duke of York and the rest of the royal family.[66] Those ministers who refused, the Protesters, were evicted from their parishes. Much the same happened in England and Ireland, and the process was repeated throughout Britain after 1688–9 when the clergy were required to pray for William and Mary. Sunday by Sunday the British peoples stood, sat or knelt in churches throughout the three kingdoms and prayed to the same God for the welfare of their common king.

Many of James VI and I's servants left instructions for their corpses to be returned to Scotland for burial, but James chose to lie alongside his English ancestors in Westminster Abbey, and the precedent he established was followed by all his successors. James began the process of Anglicizing the death rituals of his dynasty long before 1625. His daughters Sophia and Mary, his mother, Mary Queen of Scots (transferred to Westminster from Peterborough in 1612), Prince Henry, Arabella Stewart, Queen Anne and the duke of Lennox all preceded James into the Westminster vault between 1606 and 1624. In death, as in life, the Stewarts were becoming an English family. Nevertheless, the death of Prince Henry in 1612 was an occasion for sorrow throughout Britain. English poets such as John Taylor in his 'Great

---

[63] *RPC*, third series, vol. II, pp. 56–7, 187–8.
[64] Gregg, *Queen Anne*, p. 216. On the theme of military integration, see Keith M. Brown, 'From Scottish lords to British officers: state building, elite integration and the army in the seventeenth century', in Norman Macdougall (ed.), *Scotland and war AD 79–1918* (Edinburgh, 1991), pp. 133–69.
[65] Dow, *Cromwellian Scotland*, p. 196.   [66] *RPC*, third series, vol. I, pp. 88, 95–6.

Britain all in Black' joined with the Scot, William Drummond, whose 'Tears on the death of Meliades' was perhaps the most accomplished literary product of this sad event. The funeral itself was staged in London, but the English were not allowed to hijack the occasion. Carried in the procession alongside the standard of the prince of Wales and the banners of the dukedom of Cornwall and earldom of Chester were the banners of the principality of Scotland, the dukedom of Rothesay, the earldom of Carrick, and 'The great embrodered banner of the Union' held aloft by the English earl of Montgomery and the Scottish earl of Argyll. James's own funeral was equally British in the outpouring of epitaphs and in the staging of the event. One English poet reminded his readers:

> Deaths iron hand hath clos'd those eyes
> Which were at once three kingdoms eyes.[67]

When James's corpse was transported from Denmark House to Westminster he was attended by 'the most pairt of the nobility of both his kingdomes'. James would have approved of this coming together of English and Scots, as he would have been flattered by Sir James Balfour's observation that 'The lyke number of mourners cannot be said to have beine seine at once in Brittane heirtofor'. In Westminster, John Williams, bishop of Lincoln, preached a sermon entitled *Great Britain's Solomon*, a description which the late king had cultivated since his youth, but which also had been used by Elizabethan image-makers. Unfortunately, the event was not entirely without national tension. A dispute broke out between the archbishops of Canterbury and St Andrews over precedence, and this was exacerbated by Charles's insistence that John Spottiswoode wear English vestments. Rather than comply, Spottiswoode 'refused to be a murner and appeared not', a stand which elicited a good deal of surprised admiration in Scotland.[68] But in 1625 mourning for the king was not confined to London. In Edinburgh

his Majesties grate chamber and chapell at Holyrudhousse wer hung with blacke clothe, his chamber of presence, privey chalmber, and bed-chalmber with black velvet, fitted with clothes of estait, and with stoules and cusheons conforme. His majesties seat in the grate church of St Geilles at Edinburgh was lykwayes covered with blacke.[69]

The special nature of Charles I's death led after the Restoration to a general fast being observed on 30 January which became the day of the Royal Martyr. However, while the Irish government set aside 30 January as an

---

[67] Nichols (ed.), *Progresses*, vol. II, pp. 493–504; Strong, *Henry*, pp. 220–5; Parry, *Golden age*, pp. 86–91.

[68] Balfour, *Works*, vol. II, pp. 116–17; *RPC*, second series, vol. I, pp. xii–xiii.

[69] *RPC*, second series, vol. I, p. 11.

official day of solemn mourning and fasting, the Scottish privy council does not appear to have bothered.[70] Mourning for the Royal Martyr was allowed to fade away in England during the reign of King William and was not revived by Anne. In Scotland, the burgh of Aberdeen chose to mark Charles II's death in 1685 with a show of civic grief, but the Scottish government was remarkably unmoved by the death of this sovereign or his successors.[71] Of course, the most intense aspects of the official mourning for a dead monarch were experienced by the court and the citizens of London who could view the funeral procession carrying the wax effigies of the deceased. Efforts were made to widen the sense of national identification with the mourning process through the distribution and sale of funeral medals, popular funeral prints, poetry and the pulpit. Among the thirty-six medals struck in 1694 following the death of Queen Mary, one bore the inscription 'Mary, the delight and comfort of our British world, lamented', while *Great Britain's lamentation for her deceased princess* was one of 110 printed sermons and tracts. More important than the attempt to appeal to a British market is the fact that the medals and publications were available throughout Great Britain.[72] In the case of James VII and II something of the Renaissance ideology of mystical kingship was revived, and the king's own corpse was dismembered and distributed among a number of English and Scottish Catholic foundations on the continent.[73]

By 1603 the days of itinerant monarchy were long over, but in early seventeenth-century England a king was expected to show himself to his people. James VI and I was criticized for his obvious distaste for the public progresses and pageants Elizabeth I had so enjoyed – he 'would bid a pox or plague on such as flocked to see him' – although he saw more of England than any Tudor monarch, and in his younger days travelled throughout Scotland from Dumfries to Inverness.[74] Nevertheless, James was contemptuous of the general public, and Gilbert Dugdale warned Londoners in 1604 that

---

70 *CSP Ireland 1660–1662*, pp. 190–1.
71 Bruce P. Lenman, *The Jacobite risings in Britain 1689–1746* (London, 1984), p. 42.
72 Lois G. Schwoerer, 'Images of Queen Mary II, 1689–95', *Renaissance Quarterly*, 42 (1989), 741–8; P. S. Fritz, 'The trade in death: the royal funerals in England, 1685–1830', *Eighteenth Century Studies*, 15 (1982), 291–316. At Cromwell's funeral six banners were carried in the procession representing England, Scotland, Ireland, Wales, the union and the late protector himself; Sherwood, *Court of Cromwell*, p. 58.
73 Miller, *James II*, p. 240. On this subject, see too W. Arens, 'The demise of kings and the meaning of kingship: royal funerary ceremony in the contemporary Southern Sudan and Renaissance France', *Anthropos*, 79 (1984), 355–67; Ralph E. Giesey, *The royal funeral ceremony in Renaissance France* (Geneva, 1960).
74 Nichols (ed.), *Progresses*, vol. IV, p. 650. Geertz, 'Centres, kings and charisma', p. 153, argues that 'royal progresses (of which, where it exists, coronation is but the first) locate the society's center and affirm its connection with transcendent things by stamping a territory with ritual signs of dominance'.

'your Soveraigne perchance may mistake your love, and punnish it as an offence', advising them to keep their distance and 'doe as they doe in Scotland, stand still, see all, and use silence, so shall you cherish his visitation'.[75] This dour reaction to the king's presence was underlined by 'an honest Scotsman' who prophetically warned in 1603 that 'the applause of the people [of England] is so obsequious and submissive [they] will spoil a gud king'.[76] However, civic leaders were keen to impress the new ruler. When the opportunity arose for a civic pageant, such as on his visit to Southampton in September 1603, James was pleased to be greeted with 'the assured hope of a perpetuall Union of your Realme of Scotland into this Kingdome'.[77] It was London which was most indulgent of the king's British aspirations. The royal entry in 1604 was a magnificent extravaganza, the first event of its kind since 1559, and an opportunity for James to adopt publicly the symbolism of the Elizabethan monarchy. The opening encounter between St George and St Andrew was abandoned due to the general lack of organization, but elsewhere the imperial British message was visible. At the first of seven elaborate arches, the Fenchurch arch, James was presented as emperor of Britain with London, the new Troy, as his capital. Against this backdrop Monarchia Britannica was dressed to represent the united kingdoms, holding in her lap a little globe with the inscription 'ORBIS BRITANNICUS', and beneath this the Virgilian text 'DIVISUS AB ORBE', showing 'that this Empire is a world divided from the world'. Elsewhere Brutus imagery, Trojan imperial themes and Astraean mythology were all prevalent, but these essentially English myths now were employed to claim the restoration of a British golden age brimming with imperial possibilities. A chorister of St Paul's lauded James as the

> Great Monarch of the West, whose glorious stem
> Doth now support a triple diadem
> Weying more than that of thy grand-grandsire Brute.[78]

At the lord mayor's show of 1605 *The triumph of re-united Britannia* was performed, and British kingship again was celebrated. 'England, Wales and Scotland, by the first Brute severed and divided, are in our second Brute

[75] See Axton, *Queen's two bodies*, pp. 145–7; Nichols (ed.), *Progresses*, vol. I, p. 414; A. Wilson, *The history of Great Britain, being the life and reign of King James the first* (London, 1953), p. 3.

[76] Quoted in Wormald, 'Two kings or one?', p. 190.

[77] Nichols (ed.), *Progresses*, vol. I, p. 227.

[78] Bergeron, *English civic pageantry*, pp. 65–104; Nichols (ed.), *Progresses*, vol. I, pp. 329–99, 341, 357, 378, 417; Parry, *Seventeenth century*, pp. 12–14; Parry, *Golden age*, pp. 1–21. Parry recognized in this a deliberate attempt 'to invest James with the symbolism of the old Queen, just as the coronation had invested him with the traditional regalia. Thus Thomas Dekker, who wrote much of the 1604 entry text, worked hard to ensure that James was integrated into the established state mythology'. *Ibid.*, p. 16.

re-united and made our happy Britannia again'. London revelled in its role as 'Brute's Troy', and in the 1607 show the theme was repeated with James being addressed in a speech entitled *Magno, maximo Britanniae regis*.[79] That Englishmen responded to such ideas was due, however, to the superficial British coating added to the existing English national myth. In 1610, for example, Prince Henry's civic reception at Chester took place on St George's Day. There was praise for the Anglo-Scottish peace as the basis for imperial greatness, and all the usual figures of Brutus, Cambria and Neptune were trotted out, but the Chester authorities felt less need to pander to Prince Henry's Scottish birth than London did to King James, and the pretence was abandoned.

> So Britaines, when they fight with cheere, they say,
> 'God and Saint George for England' to this day.

Henry, an enthusiast for all things English, would not have been offended.[80] Charles I travelled in a slightly wider circle around London than his father in the years before the British wars, but he too placed privacy before public spectacle, even refusing to make an entry into the English capital in 1625. The Scottish background of the dynasty, changing fashions and sheer cost all played their part in this retreat from public view, a retreat which cost the dynasty dearly in popularity.[81]

In Scotland absenteeism also affected public perceptions of the monarchy. James promised to return to Scotland every three years, but in 1607 he told the English parliament that the Scots, other than those coming to court, 'will be seldom seen and saluted by their king, and that as it were but in a posting or hunting journey'.[82] James did return in 1617, when the Scottish burghs kept civic pageantry to a minimum, concentrating on the short, learned addresses they knew appealed to their cerebral king. A number of these addresses referred dutifully to the union, but at Perth on 5 July the burgh gloried in the defeat of a catalogue of foreign invaders (although in a remarkable display of polite restraint the English were not named), and the king was pertinently reminded that 'The ancient nation of Scots, decended of the victorious Greeks and learned Egyptians ... was in the chyldhood of her rysing empyre greatlie obliged to the goodnesse of

[79] Nichols (ed.), *Progresses*, vol. I, pp. 564–76; vol. II, pp. 155–7.
[80] *Ibid.*, vol. II, pp. 296–306. Also see *ibid.*, vol. II, pp. 319–22, for the 1610 'London's Love to Prince Henry'. Henry's devotion to all things English is argued in Strong, *Henry*, p. 8. Of course St George had Arthurian connections which had been exploited by the Elizabethans; Yates, *Astraea*, p. 109.
[81] R. Malcolm Smuts, 'Public ceremony and royal charisma: the English royal entry in London, 1485–1642', in A. L. Beir *et al.* (eds.), *The first modern society: essays on English history in honour of Lawrence Stone* (Cambridge, 1989), pp. 65–93.
[82] Levack, *British state*, p. 28.

God'. There was no British imperialism here, and certainly no Trojans! Of course, by 1617 many Scots regretted that their king had abandoned them for London. The magistrates at Stirling made this clear in their critical compliments, and one Sir Thomas Craig (not the unionist lawyer) wrote nostalgically:

> Live *Nestor's* dayes King James but live among us
> By blood and birth thou do'st alone belong us,
> Stay then at home, to *Thames* make no returne,
> Sleip with thy fathers in thy fathers urn.[83]

Yet the most noted media event of Charles's reign was the 1633 Scottish progress when Clarendon admitted that 'the King appeared with no less lustre at Edinburgh than at Whitehall', and Sir James Balfour proudly recorded that 'For many ages this kingdome had not seine a more glorious and staitley entrey'.[84] The Edinburgh civic pageant allowed the Scots to indulge in their royalist tradition, and one triumphal arch showed 'the haill number of the Kings that ever rang in Scotland from fergus the first to his awin Majestie whiche will exceid to the number of ane hundreth and sevin'.[85] Twenty-nine years earlier the English needed to be impressed by James VI and I's Tudor ancestry, now it was the Scots who were asked to see this *émigré* king as the descendant of an ancient Scottish royal lineage. Charles returned again in 1641, but as a defeated king come to make concessions and to consider demands that he spend more time in Scotland.

The Restoration monarchs rarely strayed outside the home counties. Charles II had a depressing stay in Scotland in 1650–1, vowing never to return, and after 1660 confined his progresses to nearby race-courses such as Newmarket and the occasional outing to Winchester. James VII and II was less insular, having spent most of 1679–81 in Scotland, albeit as an exile, and he conducted a Scottish progress in the autumn of 1681. During his short reign he made a progress of the English west country and the Welsh border in 1687, but he never returned to Scotland, and only an unsuccessful dynastic war took him to Ireland in 1690.[86] His rival, William III and II, was the first reigning king to set foot in Ireland since Richard II, and was the first king of Scotland never to visit the country at all. In fact no reigning monarch went there between 1651 and 1822. Yet it was the English who complained of being abandoned as William annually set out for the continental war theatres, and in the context of debating Anglo-Scottish union in 1700 Sir

[83] C. V. Wedgwood, *Poetry and politics under the Stuarts* (Cambridge, 1960), p. 13.
[84] Clarendon, *History*, vol. I, p. 107; Balfour, *Works*, vol. II, pp. 193–204; vol. III, pp. 354–82.
[85] Bergeron, *English civic pageantry*, pp. 105–21; Balfour, *Works*, vol. II, pp. 194–204.
[86] Miller, *James II*, pp. 210–16; Luttrell, *Relation*, vol. I, pp. 138, 411–12.

Bartholomew Shower declared that the English had as much right to complain of absentee kingship as the Scots.[87] In the autumn of 1695 William did conduct a short English progress, in reality a disappointing electioneering trip in which he did his best to avoid the crowds towards which he displayed the same uncomfortable disdain as that other foreign king, James VI and I.[88] In Anne the English again had a monarch who ruled from her London court, rarely leaving the capital, especially after 1708 when ill-health took its toll. She never contemplated visiting her other kingdoms, although she had been in Scotland with her father in 1681. The 1701 Act of Succession ensured that the Hanoverian dynasty would not rule England as absentee monarchs, but nothing was said about residence in Scotland.

Few subjects ever saw the king, but all encountered his image on the coinage and on medallions. A silver accession medal of 1603 portrayed James VI and I's untypically armoured bust with a Latin inscription which translates 'James I, Emperor of the whole island of Britain and King of France and Ireland'. The silver coronation medal of 1604, produced for the popular market, built on this early imperial theme with an obverse inscription 'James I, Caesar Augustus of Britain, Caesar the heir of the Caesars, presents this medal'. From 1604 the common coinage of both kingdoms featured the new title 'king of Great Britain'. The five shilling sterling, or sixty shilling Scots, distinguished by a rose or thistle on the housings of the royal charger which James was portrayed riding, carried what became a common seventeenth-century inscription, 'QVAE DEUS CONIVNXIT NEMO SEPARET' ('What God has joined together let no man separate'). The 1604 coinage also saw the appearance of the short-lived 'Thistle Crown' with its reverse motto taken from Ezekiel 37.22: 'FACIAM EOS IN GENTEM VNAM' ('I will make them one nation in the land, on the mountains of Israel. There will be one king over all of them and they will never again be two nations or be divided into two kingdoms'). Yet by 1611 the Scots had altered the quartering of the royal arms to show the Scottish royal arms in the first and fourth quarters with the English now relegated to the second.[89] At Charles I's English coronation in 1626 an unusually martial gold coronation medal was issued with the inscription 'Charles I by the grace of God, King of Great Britain and Ireland', while the 1633 Scottish coronation was commemorated

---

[87] Henry Horowitz, *Parliament, policy and politics in the reign of William III* (Manchester, 1977), p. 269.
[88] S. van Raaij and P. Spies, *The royal progress of William and Mary* (Amsterdam, 1988), pp. 133–43.
[89] Whiting, *Commemorative medals*, pp. 36–40; C. Oman, *The coinage of England* (London, 1967), pp. 289–99; A. B. Richardson, *Scottish coins* (London, 1977), pp. 267–8; C. H. V. Sutherland, *English coinage 600–1900* (London, 1973), pp. 157–63; and see too the introduction to J. D. Bateson and N. J. Mayhew, *Sylloge of coins of the British Isles*, vol. XXXV (Oxford, 1987).

in a medal the reverse of which showed the thistle and rose entwined with the date. There were few later innovations with the coinage, although a 1637 issue portrayed Charles wearing his English crown on the obverse and his Scottish crown on the reverse.[90]

Charles II's Scottish coronation medals of 1651 used the Scotland, England, France and Ireland title rather than following his coronation service in the use of Great Britain. However, it was during Charles II's reign that the Britannia figure was popularized. After making its first appearance in a Protectorate medal of 1654, Britannia was employed in most Restoration medals. It was the 1667 medal which first depicted Britannia seated on the sea-shore, holding a spear and shield, and watching the navy. The figure of Britannia appeared on the English coinage from 1665 holding the old Union Jack (the combined St George and St Andrew crosses), and after 1672 'BRITANNIA' commonly appeared as an inscription, surviving into the reign of Queen Anne, who was often portrayed in the role herself. Many of the medals and coins of the Restoration and post-Revolution period also make some allusion to the triple monarchy, such as in the form of linked crowns or three sceptres.[91] The Torbay landing in 1688 was commemorated in a medal proclaiming the 'liberty of England', but on the reverse is Britannia wearing three crowns, one on top of the other. A 1691 medal marking William's departure for the continent shows him as a lion, and Queen Mary as a lioness trampling on snakes threatening her three cubs, the three kingdoms. The gold union medal of 1707 gave prominence to the English Garter parapher-nalia, but a union of equals is reflected in the English and Scottish shields pictured side by side on the reverse. After 1707 Anne appeared on Scottish coins wearing the English crown, but the heraldry of the coinage placed the English and Scottish arms 'party per pale', that is together in the first and fourth quarters.[92]

Royal portraiture produced for popular distribution as well as formal state portraits was predominantly Anglocentric. There were no George IV-type portraits of a king resplendent in phoney Highland garb. The Daniel Mytens portrait of James VI and I emphasized that he was king of England with the king dressed in his Garter robes and sitting on a throne below the Tudor rose. Yet the British dimension was not entirely neglected, and appropriate

---

[90] Whiting, *Commemorative medals*, pp. 40–2; Oman, *Coinage of England*, pp. 300–7; Richard-son, *Scottish coins*, pp. 276–8; Sutherland, *English coinage*, pp. 163–71; Stuart, *Scottish coronations*, pp. 143–5. Charles's coinage used both royal styles, employed roses and thistles and showed him wearing both crowns.

[91] Whiting, *Commemorative medals*, pp. 48–80; Oman, *Coinage of England*, pp. 326, 329–36; Sutherland, *English coinage*, pp. 171–8. The model for Britannia was a Scottish mistress of Charles II, Frances Stuart, later duchess of Richmond.

[92] Whiting, *Commemorative medals*, pp. 80–115; Oman, *Coinage of England*, pp. 337–47; Rich-ardson, *Scottish coins*, pp. 326ff.

imagery illustrated books such as Henry Peacham's *Minerva Britannia* (1612), or James's own *Workes* (1616). The decoration of the banqueting hall at Whitehall by Rubens is an overtly British work, and 'Britannia Triumphans' encapsulates King James's imperial ideology even if the famous 'Judgement of Solomon' panel depicts a still incomplete vision of Anglo-Scottish union.[93] That image of a British emperor remained potent in the artistic representation of kings throughout the century. William III and II was painted by at least thirty different artists during his lifetime (most commonly as Hercules, Alexander the Great or Caesar), but it was Sir Godfrey Kneller's portrait of William as king of Great Britain that was the favoured official portrait, and this was copied for foreign princes, government buildings, colonial governments and friends of the king.[94] On 3 November 1689 the Scottish privy council wrote to the secretary of state in London indicating that

it is requisit their Majesties portraitures should be drawn at leanth upon on board to be put up at the head of the Councill board, according to custome, and that his Majestie may give ordors for drawing the samen to be put up ther after the usuall maner.[95]

There was little difference here from the state of Maryland which commissioned Kneller to paint a portrait of the king in 1695. While royal imagemakers paid little attention to the Scottish origins of the Stewarts, the century did produce one notable achievement on this theme. The most significant dynastic paintings of the century were commissioned in 1684 and hung in Holyrood Palace. The depictions of the 111 predecessors of Charles II are poor works of art, but they demonstrated the monarchy's enduring links with Scotland and contributed to the revival of royalist sentiments in the 1680s.[96]

Prior to the union of 1603 the Stewarts made their most impressive statements of power in the form of architecture, but James VI lacked the

---

[93] Parry, *Golden age*, pp. 1–39, 218–23, and Parry, *Seventeenth century*, pp. 33–4, discusses a range of visual iconography. Roy Strong, *Tudor and Jacobean portraits* (2 vols, London, 1969), vol. I, pp. 161–5, 175–80; vol. II, pp. 315–25, 341–56; Roy Strong, *Britannia triumphans: Inigo Jones, Rubens and Whitehall palace* (London, 1980), pp. 16–34; D. J. Gordon, 'Rubens and the Whitehall ceiling', in Orgel (ed.), *Renaissance imagination*, pp. 24–50; R. Toynbee, 'Some early portraits of Charles I', *Burlington Magazine*, 91 (1949), 4–9.

[94] Raaij and Spies, *Royal progress*, pp. 40–1, 69–73, 159–60; Luttrell, *Relation*, vol. I, p. 547.

[95] *RPC*, third series, vol. XIV, p. 519.

[96] S. Bruce and S. Yearly, 'The social construction of tradition: the Restoration portraits and the kings of Scotland', in D. McCrone *et al.* (eds.), *The making of Scotland: nation, culture and social change* (Edinburgh, 1989), pp. 175–88. For the political and cultural context in which these paintings were commissioned, see Hugh Ouston, 'York in Edinburgh: James VII and the patronage of learning', in John Dwyer *et al.* (eds.), *New perspectives on the politics and culture of early modern Scotland* (Edinburgh, 1982), pp. 133–55.

resources to emulate his ancestors in building. He showed a superficial interest in building in England after the union, but in Scotland crown buildings were allowed to delapidate, necessitating a hurried renovation in 1617 for the king's visit. Like Inigo Jones's masque sets the architecture of Caroline England sought to express Charles I's obsession with form and order. It was this belief that art could be employed to civilize the nation which encouraged Charles to plan a remodelling of Edinburgh, and the new parliament house, built between 1633 and 1639 at great cost to the burgesses of Edinburgh, was only the first stage of this scheme. There was more than a touch of irony in the fact that the imperial monarchy's two greatest architectural legacies, the parliament house in Edinburgh and the banqueting hall at Whitehall, were the scenes of its greatest humiliations.[97] Even before the duke of York's visit in 1679, Charles II refurbished and added to Holyrood Palace, extensively damaged by Cromwell's soldiers, in an effort to complete his father's vision for the city.[98] Elsewhere the ruins of Falkland Palace, accidentally burned down by English troops, the rotting timbers at Linlithgow, and the empty halls of James V's great palace at Stirling told another story. Queen Mary took some interest in the furnishings of Holyrood, but the dual monarchs were more concerned with their English properties, at Hampton Court or Kensington House, or in the Netherlands. Queen Anne made a modest contribution to the crown's buildings in England, but ignored Scotland. It was not until Prince Albert had the idea of a royal retreat at Balmoral in the nineteenth century that the monarchy again left a statement in stone on the Scottish landscape.

It is very easy to exaggerate the effectiveness of cultural patronage by the crown in this period.[99] In no area was its failure to form opinion more spectacular than in those Jacobean and Caroline court masques advocating a peaceful and prosperous united Great Britain, ruled by a divinely ordained emperor who claimed to be the inheritor of a tradition reaching back to classical antiquity and pre-Roman Christianity.[100] In the early years of the union, royal patronage ensured that British themes were given a high profile by a range of artists and writers. Sir William Cornwallis's *The miraculous and happie union of England and Scotland*, Anthony Munday's 1605 pageant *The triumphs of re-united Britain*, and John Speed's *Theatre of Great*

---

[97] R. Malcolm Smuts, *Court, culture and the origins of a royalist tradition in early Stuart England* (Philadelphia, 1987), pp. 98–101.

[98] Hubert Fenwick, *Architect royal. The life and works of Sir William Bruce 1630–1710* (Kineton, 1970), p. 32.

[99] R. Malcolm Smuts, 'The political failure of Stuart cultural patronage', in G. Lytle and S. Orgel (eds.), *Patronage and the Renaissance* (Princeton, 1981), pp. 165–87.

[100] May McKisack, *Medieval history in the Tudor age* (Oxford, 1971), p. 121.

Britanie (1612) all met with royal approval.[101] Of course, there was the problem of which Britain men had in mind. The Anglocentric imperial mythology surrounding figures such as Brutus, Constantine and Arthur had to be manipulated carefully in a court filled with many powerful Scots. Michael Drayton and Sackville Norton continued to peddle their old-fashioned English version of British origins in the face of criticism from fellow countrymen such as Samuel Daniel who dismissed the notion of a once-united Britain – 'a multitude of pettie regiments' – but embraced a forward-looking vision of union based on imperial monarchy. This was something another court poet, Sir William Alexander, the Scottish tutor to Prince Henry and Prince Charles, eulogized as he anticipated a colonial empire stretching out from Britain to Ireland and America and in which the Scots would have a fair share.[102] Yet the relative ease with which British ideas were accepted at court conceals the extent to which Elizabethan imagery was being disguised. For example, the 'Fortunate Isles' was a description of Britain very much in vogue at the Jacobean and Caroline court and in 1606 a number of English and Scottish noblemen formed themselves into a fellowship they called 'The errant knights of the fortunate isles'.[103] Yet this already had been a powerful English metaphor during the reign of Elizabeth, embracing classical ideas about English distinctiveness, a kind of Spenserian mysteriousness, and an element of Protestant apocalypticism.[104] In *The masque of blackness*, Ben Jonson's first court masque (performed in 1605), unionist ideology was expressed within this frame of reference:

> With that great name Britannia, this blessed isle
> Hath won her ancient dignity and style,
> A world divided from the world, and tried
> The abstract of it in his general pride.

In 1610 in *Prince Henry's barriers* the same idea turned up again alongside Arthurian imagery depicting the court as a second Camelot presided over by a peace-loving second Arthur. Prince Henry himself appeared in the role of Meliades, lord of the Isles (an ancient Scottish title) in the company of three English and three Scottish knights drawn from 'the fortunate isle of Great

---

101 Parry, *Golden age*, p. 69. However, James did not give blanket approval to anyone who showed an interest in British ideas: P. Styles, 'Politics and historical research in the early seventeenth century', in L. Fox (ed.), *English historical scholarship in the sixteenth and seventeenth centuries* (Oxford, 1956), pp. 51–2.

102 Kendrick, *British antiquity*, pp. 102–11; Axton, *Queen's two bodies*, pp. 135–43; Nichols (ed.), *Progresses*, vol. I, pp. xliii–xlvi, 121–34; Wedgwood, *Poetry and politics*, pp. 8–12; Arthur H. Williamson, 'Scotland, Antichrist and the invention of Great Britain', in Dwyer *et al.* (eds.), *New perspectives*, pp. 50–2.

103 Nichols (ed.), *Progresses*, vol. I, p. 431.

104 J. W. Bennett, 'Britain among the Fortunate Isles', *Studies in Philology*, 3 (1956), 114–40; Yates, *Astraea*, pp. 63–70.

Britain'. Over the succeeding years these British references reappear in the culture of the court. The Arthurian element is again present in *Oberon, the fairy prince* and *For the honor of Wales*; Jonson made use of a huge floating island in the 1624 *Neptune's triumph*; and the last masque of the reign was entitled *The fortunate isles and their union*.[105] Yet a scratch on the surface of court life reveals a steady seam of English triumphalism which received welcome patronage from Prince Henry and was to break out again in the 1620s in association with Charles.[106] Inigo Jones carried the British message over into the next reign, although the explicitness of the Jacobean masques was missing, reflecting Charles's less dogmatic interest and the reduced topicality of the idea of British kingship. Scots poets such as Sir William Alexander and William Drummond of Hawthornden – 'a Scots Elizabethan' – offered little in response.[107] Britain gradually was subsumed into an English view of monarchy, but lingered there as a sub-theme into the 1630s in masques such as the 1632 *Tempe restored* (or *Albion's triumph*) and Thomas Carew's 1634 *Coelum Britannicum*, in which the masquers themselves were a mixture of English and Scottish peers in a production celebrating the unification of Britain and the restoration of ancient British values. Union itself was less important to Charles than his role in presiding over, and actively pushing forward, the final chapter in the process which transformed the barbaric Britons and Picts into civilized subjects of the imperial monarchy. Yet Inigo Jones's last masque, the 1637 *Britannia triumphans*, was something of an ironic swansong for a Britain already beginning to crack at the seams.[108]

---

[105] Steven Orgel (ed.), *Ben Jonson: the complete masques* (New Haven and London, 1975), pp. 47–60, lines 211–12, 216–24; pp. 142–58, lines 20–4, 74–6, 171–4. In the *Barriers*, Jonson heaped praise on a succession of English rulers who are superseded in their achievements by James:

> Henry but joined the roses that ensigned
> Particular families, but this has joined
> The rose and thistle, and in them combined
> A union that shall never be declined.

See too C. Williams, 'Merlin and the prince: the speeches at Prince Henry's barriers', *Renaissance Drama*, new series 8 (1977), 221–30; Strong, *Henry*, pp. 141–51, 160–74; Nichols (ed.), *Progresses*, vol. II, pp. 266, 270. For further Arthurian imagery, Orgel, *Ben Jonson*, pp. 159–73, 277–91, 481. James himself had made use of Arthurian imagery in Scotland in 1588 at a masque in Holyrood Palace (below Arthur's Seat).

[106] Smuts, *Court, culture and origins*, pp. 15–50; King, *Tudor royal iconography*; Strong, *Henry*, pp. 29–32; Parry, *Golden age*, pp. 64–94.

[107] David Reid, 'Royalty and self-absorption in Drummond's poetry', *Studies in Scottish Literature*, 22 (1987), 115–31.

[108] Orgel and Strong (eds.), *Inigo Jones*, vol. II, pp. 480–3, lines 356–60; vol. II, pp. 567–80, 661–7. In *Coelum Britannicum* the visual centrepiece of the masque was one of the most spectacular of Jones's career. A mountain appeared out of the centre of the stage on top of which were seated England, Scotland and Ireland 'all richly attired in regal habits appro-

In the 1640s and 1650s that Elizabethan nationalism which had been subsumed in a British myth by the crown broke loose. In large part this was because Britain itself was the creation of the mystical and divine kingship destroyed forever outside the banqueting hall in January 1649. To Abraham Cowley, the new Britain forged by Cromwell's Ironsides had been transformed from the 'Fortunate Isles' to 'Albion's stubborn isle', no longer happy and blessed by a British king, but 'chang'd and curst', and only the return of a British king could restore the health of the island.[109] The Restoration did see some revival in British ideas by English antiquarians, and John Aubrey's painstaking collection, *Monumenta Britannica or a miscellanie of British antiquities*, was inspired by Charles II's passing interest in the ancient ruins at Avebury. There were resonances here with James VI and I's encouragement of Inigo Jones to write his account of Stonehenge demonstrating that it was built by the Romans to impress the Britons with the merits of civilization.[110] Andrew Marvell also looked back at the lost opportunity for union in the 1650s, appealing for 'No more discourse of Scotch or English race'.[111] Instead England and Scotland were recognized as distinct, union was unfashionable and Britain was associated with the hated Protectorate. John Dryden made use of Arthurian iconography in his *Albion and Albanicus* and co-operated with Henry Purcell in *King Arthur*, but this is an English Arthur and in his *Annus mirabilis* it is English naval, military and commercial power which is heralded. This new English empire was formed by the Navigation Acts and the city of London, it was not a British empire founded on the mysteries of the personal union.[112] Furthermore, financial restraints increasingly meant that the court's influence in dictating, or even stimulating, cultural and artistic trends declined from the 1670s. By the reign of Queen Anne the court had lost the initiative in artistic patronage to the English aristocracy in their country houses, or in political clubs such as the Kit Kat with its wholly English membership.[113] The Scottish aristocracy found themselves torn between preserving a native, provincial culture, or

priate to the several nations, with crowns on their heads, and each of them bearing the ancient arms of the kingdom they represented'. *Ibid.*, vol. II, pp. 661–7.

109 Sherwood, *Court of Cromwell*, pp. 135–47; Parry, *Seventeenth century*, pp. 101–5.
110 Stuart J. Piggott, *Ancient Britons and the antiquarian tradition. Ideas from the Renaissance to the Regency* (London, 1989), pp. 103, 113. The Restoration also saw a new bout of British history being written by English writers; Kendrick, *British antiquity*, pp. 100–2.
111 E. S. Donno (ed.), *Andrew Marvell: the complete poems* (Harmondsworth, 1972), pp. 85, 189.
112 P. Hammond, 'Dryden's *Albion and Albanicus*: the apotheosis of Charles II', in D. Lindley (ed.), *The court masque* (Manchester, 1984), p. 170; Parry, *Seventeenth century*, pp. 107–126; M. Foss, *The age of patronage: the arts in England 1660–1750* (New York, 1971), pp. 25, 29–30.
113 Raaij and Spies, *Royal progress*, pp. 67–90; Bucholz, 'Court of Queen Anne', pp. 275–326; R. J. Allan, 'The Kit Kat Club and the theatre', *Review of English Studies*, 7 (1931), 56–61.

assimilating the Anglocentric ideology which dominated the elite culture of eighteenth-century Britain. The crown's long wars with France did create something of a martial imperial ideology, and Joseph Addison again evoked the island spirit:

> Tis liberty that crown's Britannia's isle,
> And makes her barren rocks and her bleak mountains smile.

Here was a new whig myth, founded on the apparently unique freedoms enjoyed under a constitutional monarchy, and sustained by the pretence of equal nations fighting together against the tyrants of continental Europe.[114]

Perhaps British kingship would have thrived more successfully outside London. There is evidence of an appetite for complementary courts in Edinburgh and even in Dublin where in only a few years prior to 1641 the earl of Strafford created a 'vigorous theatre-life' around his vice-regal court.[115] Kings were much more wary of allowing a powerful focus of competing loyalty to evolve in Scotland, permitting the king's commissioner only a very narrowly defined role.[116] Besides, successful Scottish courtiers would have been outraged had they been relegated to a proconsular court in Edinburgh. Yet when something like this did appear during the duke of York's brief residence in Scotland there was an explosion of enthusiasm for the royal family and a renewed determination to underline its Scottish origins. Scottish noblemen deserted London – 'I do not hear of one that stays', wrote Lord Wharton[117] – and Edinburgh became the centre of a thriving court culture with an unmistakably Scottish flavour. The impetus carried on into James's own reign, by which time the Holyrood paintings were completed, the Order of the Thistle was revived in 1687, and the public was eagerly buying a published account of Prince Henry's baptism in 1594 in which 'the Genius, Wit, Learning and Delicacy of the Scots court, at so great a distance in Time, is epitomised'.[118] In the early seventeenth century Englishmen had looked back at the reign of Queen Elizabeth for symbols of national pride at a time when a British monarch threatened their national identity, now it was the Scots who wistfully conjured up memories of those days before union deprived them of their kings.

The 1679 departure of so many Scots for Edinburgh contrasted sharply

---

[114] Foss, *Age of patronage*, pp. 145, 198–9.
[115] Edwards, 'Society and the theatre', pp. 23–4.
[116] In Scotland the crown operated something like the 'underdeveloped concept of delegation' identified in early Tudor England; David Starkey, 'Representation through intimacy: a study in the symbolism of monarchy and court office in early-modern England', in I. Lewis (ed.), *Symbols and sentiments: cross-cultural studies in symbolism* (London, 1977), p. 195.
[117] C. H. Jones, *Charles Middleton. The life and times of a Restoration politician* (Chicago, 1967), p. 46.
[118] Ouston, 'York in Edinburgh', in Dwyer *et al.* (eds.), *New perspectives*, pp. 133–55.

with the exodus south in 1603. During James VI and I's reign over two-fifths of the more important court offices were held by Scots, and the crucial bedchamber was virtually a Scottish domain until the last few years of the reign. Even under Charles I Scots enjoyed a high court profile.[119] After 1660 no Scot held a major court office, and in 1677 Edward Chamberlayne wrote in *Angliae notitiae* that 'the Gentlemen of the Bedchamber, consist usually of the prime Nobility of England', a telling comment on a department that began its life staffed by the Scottish body-servants of a Scottish king only a generation earlier.[120] By the reign of Queen Anne the only Scots to hold court office were two doctors, and it was little wonder that Lord Godolphin wrote to the earl of Seafield that 'As to the argument of English influence, how can the Queen but bee influenced by her English servants when she has no Scots servants near her person'.[121] This English queen was very different indeed from James VI and I surrounded by his Scottish cronies, or even Charles I whom Clarendon thought 'in his nature too much inclined to the Scots nation, having been born among them, and as jealous as any one of them could be that their liberties and privileges might be invaded by the English, who, he knew, had no reverance for them'.[122] Yet even under James and Charles the Anglicizing of the monarchy outpaced the efforts to create a truly British institution. After 1660 Scotland's connections with the monarchy were reduced to sporadic and unenthusiastic outbursts of bells and bonfires, prayers for the royal family, a scattering of portraits and medals held by noblemen in their houses, and a coinage which increasingly served to remind Scots of their relative poverty. The regal union began with a king-emperor, striving to create a new identity for the monarchy, and presiding over a court in which national elites rubbed shoulders and were confronted with an idea of Britain which suited neither stereotype. It ended with a little Englander queen, presiding over a dull, insular court staffed by English tory families, an ornament at the heart of a new English colonial empire in which the North Britons were promised the gleanings. The emperor had vanished, and with him his new clothes.

---

[119] Neil Cuddy, 'The revival of the entourage: the bedchamber of James I, 1603–25', in David Starkey (ed.), *The English court from the Wars of the Roses to the Civil War* (London, 1987), pp. 173–225; Keith M. Brown, 'Aristocracy, Anglicisation and the court 1603–38', *Historical Journal*, 36 (1993), 543–76; Keith M. Brown, 'Courtiers and cavaliers: service, Anglicisation and loyalty among the royalist nobility', in Morrill (ed.), *The Scottish National Covenant*, pp. 155–92.

[120] E. Chamberlayne, *Angliae notitiae* (London, 1677), p. 154.

[121] Bucholz, 'Court of Queen Anne', pp. 124–31.

[122] Clarendon, *History*, vol. I, p. 114.

Part II

George Buchanan

4 George Buchanan, James VI and neo-classicism

Rebecca W. Bushnell

Just as twentieth-century historians have debated whether Renaissance humanism was revolutionary or conservative, sixteenth-century writers disagreed about whether literary neo-classicism was liberating or constricting, capable of fashioning a new national poetry or interested only in aping an alien past. In so far as the Renaissance argument about neo-classicism was articulated in terms of freedom versus servility, innovation versus tradition, and patriotism versus cosmopolitanism, this conflict can be correlated with significant developments in early modern European political thought: specifically, the formation of national consciousness, the rethinking of the relationship between present law and past custom, and the conceptualizing of political autonomy and sovereignty.

This chapter explores the neo-classical poetics of George Buchanan and James VI of Scotland in the light of their political thought, especially with regard to the issues of Scottish nationalism, the role of tradition in Scottish politics, and sixteenth-century formulations of authority and law. Such an exercise may help us understand what the humanist scholarly and literary enterprises contributed to both literary culture and political thought in sixteenth-century Scotland. It also reveals the political flexibility of humanism and neo-classicism: after all, James and Buchanan shared many assumptions about culture and its role in reforming Scotland (and informing its kings), even when they thought and wrote so differently and to opposite political ends. Buchanan's literary neo-classicism and humanist scholarship, as manifested in both his plays and tracts, made him aware of his isolation in the present while he was also seeking continuity with the Scottish past. When James VI sketched out a neo-classical poetics in his early *Essayes of a prentise in the divine arte of poesie*, his own interpretation of neo-classicism, which celebrated 'invention' and rejected precedent, in turn allowed the king to fashion himself as the reformer of Scottish culture and the 'inventor' of its laws, who would break free of the past.

With the exception of Gavin Douglas's preface to his *Aeneid* translation and James VI's 'Schort treatise, conteining some reulis and cautelis to be observit and eschewit in Scottis poesie', published in 1585 as part of the

Essayes of a prentise, sixteenth-century Scottish literature initially shows little direct evidence of a great concern over the issues involved in imitation, invention and the cultivation of a vernacular language which are endemic to the continental literary culture of the sixteenth century. The neo-classicists of sixteenth-century France and England assumed that imitating ancient models would improve both the writer's own character and his native language. Many of the neo-classical theorists, most notoriously Joachim Du Bellay, saw themselves as defending their native language and country when they rejected crude native or 'barbarous' practices and adapted classical models; for them, 'forward' or new thinking was 'backward' thinking.[1] Jean Dorat's Greek epigraph for Du Bellay's *La deffence et illustration de la langue françoyse* names the author a patriot for defending the language of France,[2] even though – or because – Du Bellay vilified 'ces vieilles poesies Francoyses: ... comme rondeaux, ballades, vyrelaiz, chantz royaulx, chansons, & autres telles episseries, qui corrumpent le goust de nostre Langue, & ne servent si non a porter temoingnaige de notre ignorance'.[3] As several scholars have noted, the theory and practice of neo-classical imitation thus brought to the surface conflicts in humanist historiography. Nancy Struever argues that in the Italian Renaissance imitation entailed a productive sense of anachronism, stimulating 'fresh speculation on general historical premises', and establishing that 'one must accept discontinuity as true and comprehend time as a limitation of personal choice'.[4] Ideally, imitation nurtured an awareness of the past and one's difference from it at the same time as it assumed a continuity between past and present.[5] In practice, however, imitation more often generated conflict between those who assumed that 'the ancients had discovered the basic features of the various possible poetic genres and that these should inform

---

[1] See Nancy S. Struever, *The language of history in the Renaissance: rhetoric and historical consciousness in Florentine humanism* (Princeton, 1970), p. 95, on how 'the "Moderns" thus become those who still cling to the recent barbaric past; the "Ancients" are the party of renewal and illumination'.

[2] Joachim Du Bellay, *La deffence et illustration de la langue françoyse* (1549), ed. Henri Chamard (Paris, 1948), p. 10.

[3] *Ibid.*, pp. 108–9.

[4] Struever, *Language of history*, p. 96. In *The light in Troy: imitation and discovery in Renaissance poetry* (New Haven, 1982), p. 33, Thomas M. Greene writes of France and England that 'the advent of humanism conferred a keener historical consciousness upon the literary mind and created an etiological problem: the task of constructing retrospectively a past from which a literary work could visibly emerge without damaging anachronism. For a humanist literature, this past was most commonly ancient and the etiological solution was embraced by the term *imitation*'.

[5] See Struever, *Language of history*, p. 193, for example: 'Rhetorical *imitatio*, with its concept of virtuosity as both a command of past techniques which possess continuous sanctions and a sensitivity to the unique demands of the present situation, provides a model of continuity in change'.

all poetry for all time'[6] and those who saw that poetic form might change over time in different cultures.

Literary neo-classicism came relatively late to Scotland, and the circumstances it encountered there differed from those in France and England. In Scotland humanism and neo-classicism confronted uniquely Scottish constructions of language and national identity. In particular, unlike England or France, sixteenth-century Scotland was a multi-lingual culture, with Middle Scots, English, Latin and Gaelic all in current use and the identity of the 'Scottish' language still in flux.[7] In Gavin Douglas's case, the indeterminacy of the vernacular seems to have reduced rather than magnified any anxiety about the difference between his and Virgil's language. While he acknowledged his own vast poetic inferiority to Virgil and admitted that 'besyde Latyn our langage is imperfite',[8] he was determined to work at improving what he called his 'rurall wlgar gros' and 'lewit barbour tong' by borrowing terms from Latin, French and English 'quhar scant was Scottis'.[9] Similarly, Douglas's sense of difference from the past was less marked than Du Bellay's. While his preface does touch on the problem of cultural difference in discussing how to treat the gods and other supernatural phenomena,[10] Douglas's ancient Italy is still essentially a medieval world.

Even in a time of growing national consciousness in Scotland, Douglas's overt discussion of the need to write in the vernacular as opposed to Latin was unusual. As in the rest of Europe in the middle ages, in sixteenth-century Scotland Latin was the primary language of state and education. Scotland also strongly supported the writing of Latin verse concurrently with vernacular composition. Two explanations can be offered for the fact that 'from 1500 to 1650 the Scots far outnumber the English' in writing Latin verse:[11] first, because the linguistic situation in Scotland was

---

[6] Marvin Carlson, *Theories of the theatre: a historical and critical survey, from the Greeks to the present* (Ithaca, N.Y., 1984), pp. 54–55.

[7] Roderick Watson, *The literature of Scotland* (New York, 1985), p. 79. See also Agnes Mure Mackenzie, 'The Renaissance poets (1): Scots and English', in James Kinsley (ed.), *Scottish poetry: a critical survey* (London, 1973), pp. 33–67, at p. 35; and Alex Agutter, 'Middle Scots as a literary language', in R. D. S. Jack (ed.), *The history of Scottish literature: vol. I, origins to 1660* (Aberdeen, 1988), pp. 13–25.

[8] *The Aeneid of Virgil, translated into Scottish verse by Gawin Douglas, bishop of Dunkeld* (2 vols., Bannatyne Club, 1839; repr. New York, 1971), vol. I, p. 15.

[9] *Ibid.*, vol. I, pp. 3–7.

[10] First, he takes the medieval approach of assuming that one must see these phenomena as allegorical or 'in similitudes, and undir quent figuris'; he then suggests, however, that in those days 'war ma illisionys,/ By dewillich warkis and coniurationis,/ Than now thar beyn, so doith clerkis determ' (*ibid.*, vol. I, pp. 9–10).

[11] J. W. L. Adams, 'The Renaissance poets (2): Latin', in Kinsley (ed.), *Scottish poetry*, pp. 68–98, at p. 70. See also R. D. S. Jack's 'Introduction', in Jack (ed.), *History of Scottish literature*, p. 2.

unstable, 'Scottis' did not dominate the culture as English did in England; second, Scottish literary and intellectual culture was far more international and Latinate than English culture.[12] Humanism and Renaissance culture did not hit Scotland like a shock wave: rather, it dispersed gradually through the education of Scottish scholars abroad, who found on their return some opposition from the schoolmen and divines but acceptance at court and in some educational circles.[13]

George Buchanan's career shows clearly how, in both its philosophical and literary manifestations, European humanism could be assimilated into Scottish culture and political thought. As he had spent his early career primarily in France, Buchanan's prodigious literary efforts were all composed in Latin. At the same time, he was most distinctly a Scot, engaged in Scottish politics – and polemics – and writing a patriotic history of Scotland.[14] Buchanan freely admitted his lack of interest in the vernacular, professing that he would

perceive, without regret, the gradual extinction of the ancient Scottish language, and cheerfully allow its harsh sounds to die away, and give place to the softer and more harmonious tones of the Latin. For if, in this transmigration into another language, it is necessary that we yield up one thing or other, let us pass from rusticity and barbarism to culture and civilization, and let our choice and judgment repair the infelicity of our birth.[15]

From the point of view of historians of political thought, however, Buchanan was a Scot whose political writings specifically addressed Scottish controversies, and whose political thinking influenced the Anglo-American tradition.

---

[12] Adams, 'Renaissance poets', p. 70. Adams also notes that 'the Renaissance, with its emphasis on *imitatio veterum*, seems indeed to have penetrated the Arts curriculum in Scotland before it succeeded in displacing the schoolmen in the "higher" studies of philosophy and theology' (*ibid.*, p. 71). According to Durkan, Scottish scholars mostly wandered to Paris and other continental centres of learning; few Scottish students were to be found, however, at Oxford and Cambridge: John Durkan, 'The cultural background in sixteenth-century Scotland', in David McRoberts (ed.), *Essays on the Scottish Reformation 1513–1625* (Glasgow, 1962), pp. 274–331, at p. 278. But cf. Jenny Wormald, *Court, kirk and community: Scotland 1470–1625* (London, 1981), pp. 102–103, on the importance of England in the 1530s as a 'haven' for Scots 'of unorthodox views'.

[13] See John Durkan, 'The beginnings of humanism in Scotland', *IR*, 4 (1954), 5–24. Cf. Wormald, *Court, kirk and community*, pp. 181–5, on the impact of Melville's educational reforms on the universities in the 1570s. See, for a broad account, John MacQueen (ed.), *Humanism in Renaissance Scotland* (Edinburgh, 1990).

[14] Because Buchanan was a neo-Latinist and spent so much time in France, scholars of French rather than British literature usually claim the literary Buchanan. See the introduction to P. Sharratt and P. G. Walsh (eds.), *George Buchanan: tragedies* (Edinburgh, 1983), p. 1. All citations of Buchanan's plays will be from this edition.

[15] George Buchanan, *The history of Scotland, from the earliest period to the regency of the earl of Moray*, trans. James Aikman (2 vols., Glasgow, 1845), vol. I, p. 9. For the Latin text (as Buchanan would wish), see *Rerum Scoticarum historia* (Utrecht: Elzevier, 1668), p. 6.

For Buchanan, the Scottish and neo-Latin identities intersected, particularly when he was writing classical tragedy, which brought to the surface tensions in his own conception of history, law, custom and time. Like the writers of the Pléiade, Buchanan seems to have believed generally in the possibility of renewing modern culture through a return to the old (just as he thought civilization's coming to Scotland would be marked by the country's conversion to Latin). Yet his political writings take contradictory positions on the relationship between the past and present: at some points, his texts show the writer's acute awareness of historical and cultural difference, when he rejects the tyranny of custom; at other points, however, Buchanan's polemics emphasize the continuity between the past and present. It is in the classical tragedies that such contradictions are expressed formally and aesthetically as well as discursively. Buchanan's neo-classical insistence on dramatic verisimilitude, restricting dramatic time to twenty-four hours and thus compressing events into an oppressively truncated moment in time, in effect cuts off the play's action from its own history. In *Baptistes*, in particular, this formal compression of time becomes a central theme, when the characters debate the role of tradition in shaping the present and future, while they themselves feel the acute pressure of time.

In both the *De jure regni apud Scotos* and the *Rerum Scoticarum historia*, Buchanan characteristically appealed to ancient Scottish custom, which he identified with natural law, as a way of defending current political practices. As he tells the story in *De jure*, in defending the deposition of Mary Stewart, the fact that Scottish kings were originally granted a limited authority by the people is confirmed by the evidence of long-held usage and beliefs which have never been publicly contradicted ('accessit praeterea longi temporis confirmatio, & perpetui iuris a populo vsurpatio, nullo vnquam decreto publico reprehensa').[16] This tradition was not the same as the common law in England; rather, in a country where law was largely underdeveloped, people respected 'a body of unwritten traditions which were neither feudal in origin nor in any sense the law of the land', a body of traditions which primarily described the reciprocal responsibilities of the nobility and monarch.[17] Most importantly, Buchanan held that tradition to be consonant with a kind of divine or 'eternal law', which was the basis of his political theory. At the end of the *History*, for example, in Buchanan's version of a speech delivered by the Regent Morton, the opponents of Mary's deposition are upbraided because they 'do not reflect upon what they owe to the

---

[16] George Buchanan, *De jure regni apud Scotos, dialogus* (Edinburgh, 1579; facsimile edn, Amsterdam, 1969), p. 66. For a translation, see Charles Flinn Arrowood, *The powers of the crown in Scotland* (Austin, Tex., 1949), p. 107.

[17] Arthur H. Williamson, *Scottish national consciousness in the age of James VI* (Edinburgh, 1979), pp. 6–7.

examples of their forefathers; and forget those eternal laws, which have been held sacred since the foundation of the monarchy, and enforced by the illustrious nobles, who set bounds to the despotism of the crown'.[18] For Buchanan, divine law and the law of reason dictated the sole injunction that we love God and our neighbours as ourselves;[19] this rule, in turn, underwrote the Scottish traditions of elective monarchy and the responsibility of the ruler to the electors.[20] In effect, then, Buchanan's drawing on custom privileged the past at the same time that he assumed that history itself illustrates timeless principles.[21]

While it identifies tradition with natural law and the law of reason, the *De jure regni* at key moments demonstrates a keen consciousness of the present tense of the dialogue, its unique situation in time and space. At such moments, Buchanan often opposed reason to custom rather than assuming that the first underlies the second. In response to Maitland's claim that custom has the force of law, and people customarily suffer the government of tyrants, the Buchanan of the *De jure regni* condemns the 'tyranny' of custom or precedent (*consuetudinis tyrannis*) evident in both the present and antiquity, and reminds Maitland of the matters in which he follows reason rather than ancient custom ('cogita tecum quot sint res, nec hae exiguae, in quibus rationem secutus ab inveterata tot seculis consuetudine desciveris').[22] Just as he thus rejected an appeal to a custom he disliked, Buchanan was careful to historicize his interpretation of texts when it suited him. In particular, when confronted by the traditional objection raised by citing St Paul's enjoining the Romans to obey their magistrates, the *De jure regni's* Buchanan cautions that we must read that statement in its context, considering when, for whom, and why it was written ('non enim verba solum examinare oportet: sed quibus temporibus, ad quos, & cur scripserit').[23] Similarly, in response to Maitland's citation of the passage from 1 Samuel 8,

[18] Buchanan, *History*, vol. II, p. 550. In his article, 'George Buchanan and the ancient Scottish constitution', *EHR*, supplement 3 (1966), H. R. Trevor-Roper argues that Buchanan also composed the surviving manuscript version of this speech.

[19] Buchanan, *De jure regni*, p. 11; Arrowood, *Powers*, p. 48.

[20] See Trevor-Roper, 'Ancient constitution', pp. 12–13, on the two cardinal principles of Buchanan's political writing: that Scotland had always had an elective monarchy, and that 'this system is no mere Caledonian freak but has its roots in the laws of nature'.

[21] See Roger A. Mason, '*Rex stoicus*: George Buchanan, James VI and the Scottish polity', in John Dwyer *et al.* (eds.), *New perspectives on the politics and culture of early modern Scotland* (Edinburgh, 1982), pp. 9–33. Mason points out that 'as Buchanan himself implies, Scotland did not possess anything remotely akin to a common law enshrining the rights of the subject and delimiting the sphere of governmental authority ... Patently, his conception of the legal framework of the state is neither rooted in nor guaranteed by positive law. He is, on the contrary, appealing solely to divine or natural laws which he believes the ancient Scottish polity to have embodied and exemplified' (*ibid.*, p. 26).

[22] Buchanan, *De jure regni*, p. 69; Arrowood, *Powers*, p. 110.

[23] Buchanan, *De jure regni*, p. 71; Arrowood, *Powers*, p. 112.

in which God offers the people a tyrant when they beg for a king, Buchanan replies that the passage is irrelevant, because history does not mention any legitimate monarchies in Asia ('neque usquam, quod sciam ab historicis mentio fit legitimi regis in Asia').[24] Thus, although elsewhere it appeals to the force of custom and ancient tradition, the *De jure regni* criticizes the tyranny of custom: further, while it posits that divine and natural law underlies Scotland's ancient constitution, the *De jure regni* draws attention to the relativism of cultures and political institutions, which reason can differentiate.[25]

Buchanan's own writing of the history of Scotland similarly lacks a coherent historiography, faithfully following Boece's legendary lists while vilifying other myths of British history. Commentators have reacted accordingly. H. R. Trevor-Roper separates Buchanan from 'modern' historians such as Machiavelli and Guicciardini, grouping him with the 'humanist historians', by which he means historians who 'believed in texts' and whose 'only originality ... was to purge their chosen text of barbarous solecisms' and rewrite it in fine Latin.[26] James E. Phillips, however, sees Buchanan as 'unreservedly on the side of the "moderns"' in historiography, and capable of 'critical scepticism'.[27] Such disagreement is the natural product of a symptomatic contradictoriness in Buchanan's uses of Scottish history. As McFarlane points out, sometimes Buchanan did not practise what he preached: he notes how, even though Buchanan retained Boece's forty kings because they served his political purposes, 'he shows, in theory, a reasonably critical attitude'.[28] More fundamentally, his works demonstrate a conflict between the critical consciousness of the humanist philologist and historian who recognized the difference between past and present and subjected the tyranny of custom to the light of reason, and the polemicist who knew the power of the argument of tradition and the usefulness of the myth of Scottish history in Scottish political discourse.[29]

[24] Buchanan, *De jure regni*, p. 70; Arrowood, *Powers*, p. 111.
[25] See Williamson, *Scottish national consciousness*, p. 111, on Buchanan's perception of the uniqueness of the Scottish situation.
[26] Trevor-Roper, 'Ancient constitution', p. 21.
[27] James E. Phillips, 'George Buchanan and the Sidney circle', *Huntington Library Quarterly*, 12 (1948–9), 23–55, at p. 50. Cf. I. D. McFarlane's final judgement of Buchanan in *Buchanan* (London, 1981), p. 440.
[28] McFarlane, *Buchanan*, p. 426: 'He talks of the need to rely as far as possible on first-hand information, and to discard "vain fables"; he points to the need for establishing just how documents were transmitted and particularly at a time when script was virtually unknown; he fights shy of poetic traditions and warns the reader against undue reliance on bards, though one might feel that his own failings were similar to theirs – memory defects, adulation born of patronage, prejudice and passion.'
[29] In his essay 'Scotching the Brut: politics, history and national myth in sixteenth-century Britain', in Roger A. Mason (ed.), *Scotland and England 1286–1815* (Edinburgh, 1987),

When Buchanan set out to write a play, rather than a political dialogue, pamphlet or prose history, the conventions of the form itself brought to the surface these tensions in his historical thinking.[30] The appearance of the *De jure regni* is often linked with the publication of *Baptistes*: although he published the tract in 1579 (two years after *Baptistes*), Buchanan probably began it in the late 1560s, and scholars think that Buchanan rewrote and published *Baptistes* in 1577 to reflect his current political thinking.[31] When Buchanan chose to dramatize an episode from biblical history to make a political point about tyranny and resistance, the form which he adapted was that of neo-classical tragedy.

Among the early humanist dramatists in France, Buchanan was unique in his fidelity to the example of Greek drama, which he imitated directly (having already translated Euripides).[32] Buchanan must have known that he was doing something unusual in imitating Greek tragedy, rather than Seneca or the moralities, by compressing the action to a single event in a narrowly defined time and space. The representation of time in Greek tragedy (however distorted by the neo-Aristotelians) is based on a conflict between the present and past, contrasting 'heroic values and ancient religious representations with the new modes of thought that characterise the advent of law within the city-state'.[33] On the surface, tragedy shows us the quintessentially present time of enactment, what Jean-Pierre Vernant calls 'a human, opaque time made up of successive and limited present moments';[34] this is a time which the audience experiences as the present in its enactment. In this brief duration of time, tragedy evokes both the values of a mythic past, increasingly inaccessible to the understanding of the

pp. 60–84, Roger Mason argues that as far as Buchanan's political theory was concerned 'the mythical kings were a convenience, not a necessity. They *were* a necessity, however, if the antiquity and autonomy of the Scottish kingdom were not finally to fall victim to the blandishments of the British History' (pp. 73–4). See also Anthony Grafton, *Defenders of the text: the traditions of scholarship in an age of science, 1450–1800* (Cambridge, Mass., 1991), p. 26, on the way in which Renaissance humanist scholarship was, in general, divided between historical and ahistorical modes of reading.

[30] Both of Buchanan's scriptural tragedies were probably written in the early 1540s when he was in Paris and then Bordeaux, although *Jephthes* was not published until 1554, and *Baptistes* not until 1577. Although he first composed the plays some time before the *De jure regni* and *History* were written and published, when Buchanan was in Paris in the late 1520s and early 1530s McFarlane suggests that 'he moved in circles where historiography was very much in evidence'; Buchanan was probably thinking about writing a patriotic history of Scotland in the earlier part of his career (McFarlane, *Buchanan*, p. 416).

[31] *Ibid.*, p. 385; see also Sharratt and Walsh, *Tragedies*, p. 13.

[32] See Raymond Lebègue, *La tragédie religieuse en France: les débuts (1514–1573)* (Paris, 1929), p. 467; see also pp. 460, 463, 465.

[33] Jean-Pierre Vernant and Pierre Vidal-Naquet, *Tragedy and myth in ancient Greece*, trans. Janet Lloyd (Paris, 1972; Brighton, 1981), p. 4.

[34] *Ibid.*, p. 19.

present, and the scheme of 'divine time', which is incomprehensible to the human mind.[35] Greek tragedy plays out the horror of living in this circumscribed time of experience, where the future is mysterious and the past oppressive.[36]

As Sidney suggested in his *Defence of poetry*, Renaissance poets could see this tragic time as a liberation from the constraints of historical time. In anticipating objections to his strictures about tragic time and place, Sidney attributed to such critics ignorance of the difference between history and art: 'And do they not know that a tragedy is tied to the laws of poesy, and not of history; not bound to follow the story, but having liberty either to feign a quite new matter or to frame the history to the most tragical conveniency?'[37] The tragic poet is liberated from history, which is bound merely 'to tell things as things were';[38] he is freed both from history's unedifying immorality and from the conventional rules of time itself. 'Representing' foregrounds the present moment, obscuring the sequence of events which led up to it. In tragedy, this past may be reported, but not represented: in not being enacted on the stage, the beginnings and causes of events are thus distanced and suppressed outright.[39]

Such a temporal construction, as Sidney suggested, ran counter to the conceptual bases of early modern historiography, and especially for polemical writers such as Buchanan, who were concerned to connect past and present in an unbroken chain. The *agon* in Greek tragedy reflects the institution of new law for the city state; in his political writings, however, Buchanan wrote of Scotland as governed by ancient and 'natural' law which had never changed.[40] Whereas Greek tragedy represents a division between the ideology of past and present, Buchanan's history and polemics envision

---

[35] Pierre Vidal-Naquet, 'Temps des dieux et temps des hommes: essai sur quelques aspects de l'experience temporelle chez les grècs', *Révue de l'histoire des religions*, 157 (1960), 58. See also Vernant and Vidal-Naquet, *Tragedy*, p. 19.

[36] See Jacqueline de Romilly, *Time in Greek tragedy* (Ithaca, N.Y., 1968), chs. 1 and 2. See also Rebecca W. Bushnell, 'Time and history in early English classical drama', in Gordon J. Schochet (ed.), *Law, literature and the settlement of regimes*, Proceedings of the Folger Institute Center for the History of British Political Thought, vol. II (Washington, D.C., 1990), pp. 73–86, from which some short parts of this essay are borrowed.

[37] Sir Philip Sidney, *A defence of poetry*, ed. J. A. Van Dorsten (Oxford, 1966), p. 66.

[38] *Ibid.*, p. 36.

[39] Sidney's image of the poet in the *Defence* is to be distinguished from his own later practice and beliefs: see Arthur F. Kinney, 'Sir Philip Sidney and the uses of history', in Richard Strier and Heather Dubrow (eds.), *The historical Renaissance: new essays on Tudor and Stuart literature and culture* (Chicago, 1988), pp. 293–314.

[40] Cf. J. G. A. Pocock, *Politics, language and time: essays on political thought and history* (New York, 1971), p. 240, on how English thinking was dominated by common law, which was never 'new', where 'law was conceived as custom, and the activity of law-making was conceived as the conversion into written precedents of unwritten usages whose sole authority was that of immemorial antiquity'.

the present as part of the past. Yet, influenced by humanist scholarship and its insistence on the historical specificity of language and custom, Buchanan was himself aware of living in a specific place and time, even when he appealed to both natural law and tradition. His classical plays' evocation of a moment caught between past and future plays out these conflicts about time through the characters' own anxiety about the brevity of their own experience of history.

Although it is generally considered to be aesthetically inferior to *Jephthes*, *Baptistes* best exemplifies this clash between tradition and historical consciousness both formally and discursively. In the preface, Buchanan himself described the play as linking past and present: the event may be old (*veteres*) because it happened centuries before, 'but if we consider as new what is fresh from recent recollection (*recenti memoria*), this will certainly be new', for the human race continues to practise fraud and calumny, and the wicked oppress the good (lines 48–51).[41] Buchanan thus suggested that the story of the past is also the story of the present, whether he referred to specific events or the general condition of humankind. However, the action of the play is itself compressed, involving the last hours of the Baptist's life, which is sensed as a time of imminent danger. The temporality of crisis is thus set against the rhythm of a repeatable history.

Baptistes both opposes and identifies the eternal realm of God and the temporal world of Herod, in playing out the story of the martyr's defiance of a tyrant. The following exchange expresses the initial opposition concisely:

> HER. Cum in astra venies, loquere tum caelestia;
> terrena iura patere dum terram coles.
> IO. Terrena vereor regna, pareo regibus;
> aeterna patriam regna puto, regem colo.   (lines 508–11)[42]

From Herod's point of view, the conflict is a purely political one, an issue of placating the people or self-protection (lines 542–4). At the play's end, too, Herod's decision is based on his immediate concerns, when he apparently gives in (although in fact he had already decided to do so) in response to the Queen's urging that he affirm his own authority. From John's point of view, however, the events are enacted before the all-seeing eyes of God. While at first it appears as though John opposes the two kings of heaven and earth, he tells himself and the Chorus that in fact both kings want the same thing; it is the will of Herod and the will of God that he should die. Where

---

[41] Sharratt and Walsh, *Tragedies*, p. 134.
[42] *Ibid.*, p. 145: '*Herod*: Speak of matters heavenly when you reach the stars. As long as you dwell on earth, bear with earthly laws. *John*: I respect earthly kingdoms and I obey their kings; but the eternal kingdom I consider my native land, and its king I worship'.

there seems to be opposition, God's will encompasses Herod's wicked intentions: His eternal time, in turn, enfolds the present moment of Herod's power.

Thus correlated with the realms of God and Herod are two kinds of temporality. The unenlightened characters do not see a continuity or relationship between past, present and future, whereas John the prophet links himself to both past and future. Even at the very beginning, when the rabbi Gamaliel recalls to Malchus the precedent of their forebears' actions in such a crisis, the ambitious Malchus retorts that old things belong to the old, while 'our own ways suit us' ('vetusta veteres nostra nos magis decent', line 175). The Chorus, too, is conscious of the difference between the splendid exploits of an earlier age ('aevi splendida facta prioris', line 580) and the present world which God seems to have deserted. In general in *Baptistes* such temporal constriction in the present is a mark of corruption. Herod, the Queen, Malchus, and the Chorus all seem beset by the pressure of time. The Queen attacks Herod for moving too slowly, insisting that something must be done *now*, lest John become too powerful and his authority should weaken ('tu lentus usque auctoritatem regiam / labare nondum sentis', lines 345–6). The Queen's attitude functions as a sign of both political and spiritual blindness: these characters recognize neither the relationship between the political tradition and the present nor the meaning of their actions beyond the present moment of crisis and its secular consequences.[43]

In *Baptistes*, John the Baptist, like the Priest, establishes continuity between past, present and future both politically and spiritually. For many humanist historians, the past and present dovetailed with Christian or eschatological time, beginning with the creation and fall of man, and ending in apocalypse.[44] Using typology or the symbolic language of prophecy,

---

[43] In *Jephthes*, such blindness is also implicitly criticized in Jephtha and the Priest's debate over whether to obey custom or present exigencies. The Priest invokes paternal affection as a natural law, according to which the sacrifice of a child is 'what our sacred mother nature forbids, what our love of kin struggles against, and what God loathes' (Sharratt and Walsh, *Tragedies*, p. 82). More important than any single human utterance is God's eternal law: as the Priest puts it, 'God's voice is the single, simple, self-consistent truth. What he has once ordained continues fixed and implanted on its unchangeable course, and cannot diverge in the slightest degree to left or right' (*ibid.*, p. 83). Jephtha himself connects this divine law with what 'our fathers' customs approve' (*ibid.*, p. 82); the Priest does so explicitly in claiming that God 'rejoices in being worshipped not according to your decree but by the law, rite and customs which he approves' (*ibid.*, p. 84): 'True religion, true piety is not to worship God by a practice which you have self-deceivingly established for yourself, and not to slaughter any victims whatsoever in sacrifice, but those which the decrees of laws sent from heaven demand, and which ancestral custom approves' (*ibid.*, p. 85). Here custom and tradition are seen to be consonant with divine or eternal law: Jephtha understands only the significance of his own utterance in a single moment from which he cannot detach himself.

[44] See J. G. A. Pocock, *The Machiavellian moment: Florentine political thought and the Atlantic republican tradition* (Princeton, 1975), p. 31: 'All these propositions denoted temporal

Christian historians struggled to situate individual human actions in this eternal time.[45] So *Baptistes'* John is careful to claim that he only upholds precedent and ancient rites ('sacra quam pie colam / et instituta vetera', lines 486–7). He distinctly allies himself with the protection and renovation of tradition (just as he claims that he scrupulously obeys kings in earthly matters). But he also accepts and understands the future in a way that the other characters cannot. When the Chorus expresses its fear of the coming death, more fearful because it is unknown, John accepts it as his inevitable future to be revealed in the passage of time (*temporis longinquitas*, line 1012). He sees his progress towards death as part of the past and the future of the human race, his journey on 'the road established since the beginning of the world' ('namque institutam ab initio mundi viam in fata curro', lines 1052–3).[46]

With this vision, however, John is not a 'prophet' in a conventional or Greek sense, for in this play he tells us nothing of the momentous events to come, only briefly glimpsing the coming of one 'whose slippers I his servant would be unworthy to remove' ('cui detrahendis servus etiam socculis / indignus essem', lines 789–90).[47] Although John's actions have been represented as specifically political, his vision of salvation is personal rather than communal or historical. The play ends, not with an expectation of the future, but with the Chorus's despondent refusal of the Messenger's attempt at consolation: they still fear death and envision a life of misery (lines 1356–8). As Martin Mueller observes, 'no writer of scriptural tragedy went further than Buchanan in blocking any vision of transcendence that might mitigate the catastrophe by placing it in a wider context'.[48] Only the martyr has an enviable future in this play.

Baptistes thus shows the stress of Buchanan's imitation of classical tragic form in representing a political and spiritual subject. Responding to the formal constraints, Buchanan used a limited view of time to define political character. Even while he himself was constrained by time in composing the form, its politically corrupt or vicious characters are associated with the perception of a circumscribed time, in so far as they separate themselves from the past and cannot understand the future. This temporal construction is contrasted with the time of the martyr, who allies himself politically with the past, and who can know and accept his own future. It is even more significant, however, that Buchanan did not directly evoke the scheme of

---

events; the past or the future tense must be used in stating them; and yet the significance of every one of them was extrahistorical in that it denoted a change in the relations between men and that which was outside time altogether'.

[45] *Ibid.*, p. 44.   [46] Sharratt and Walsh, *Tragedies*, p. 157.   [47] *Ibid.*, p. 151.

[48] Martin Mueller, *Children of Oedipus and other essays on the imitation of Greek tragedy, 1550–1800* (Toronto, 1980), p. 171.

prophetic or eschatological time; in terms of the playwright's understanding of tragic form, the martyr is freed from the limits of secular time, but the community is not. The formal pressures here present a bleak picture of the kingdom's future. In this sense, Buchanan's neo-classical poetics betray his ambivalence about his own place, balanced between the past and the future.

At least in his contemplation of Scottish literary culture, the young James VI demonstrated considerably less anxiety about his ability to shape the present and future of his country. James's antipathy for his tutor's political views is well documented.[49] At the same time, he owed a great deal to Buchanan, and not just for his thorough acquaintance with Latin and Greek.[50] In addition to their drawing on the image of the ideal king of the *speculum principis*,[51] both similarly appealed to natural law: Buchanan, in identifying natural law with tradition; James, in a very different way, to legitimize kings without referring to tradition.[52]

This last difference in the two men's use of natural law is symptomatic of their divergent uses of Scottish political tradition. Both James and Buchanan were interested in the specific character of Scottish politics. Buchanan's important political writings are concerned almost exclusively with the contemporary turmoil in Scotland; James, in turn, in the *Basilikon doron*, advised his son how to rule Scotland, in particular, and professed ignorance of English customs.[53] However, although James carefully adjusted himself to the particular customs of Scottish politics and respected the example left by his immediate predecessors, he did not concern himself greatly with Scottish political history.[54] The *Basilikon doron* does briefly advise Prince Henry to read history:

I would have you to be well versed in authentick histories, and in the Chronicles of all nations, but specially in our owne histories (*Ne sis peregrinus domi*) the example whereof most neerely concernes you. I mean not of such infamous invectives, as *Buchanans* or *Knoxes* Chronicles ... But by reading of authenticke histories and Chronicles, yee shall learne experience by Theoricke, applying the bypast things to the present estate, *quia nihil novum sub sole*: such is the continuall volubilities of things earthlie, according to the roundnesse of the world and the revolution of the

---

49 See below, ch. 5.
50 See David Harris Willson, *King James VI and I* (London, 1956), p. 21.
51 See Mason, 'Rex stoicus', in Dwyer (ed.), *New perspectives*, on Buchanan's use of the *speculum* king; also see Rebecca W. Bushnell, *Tragedies of tyrants: political thought and theater in the English Renaissance* (Ithaca, N.Y., 1990), chs. 2 and 3.
52 See Williamson, *Scottish national consciousness*, p. 45, on the king's reliance 'upon the lessons and implications of the natural law'; also *ibid.*, p. 54, on what emerges from James's writings of the 1590s as 'the timelessness of insubstantial flux superimposed on an underlying eternal order'.
53 James VI, *Basilikon doron*, in McIlwain, *Works*, p. 11.
54 Cf. Wormald, *Court, kirk and community*, ch. 9, who claims that James in many ways was quite conservative.

heavenly circles: which is expressed by the wheeles in *Ezechiels* visions, and counterfeited by the Poets in *rota fortune*.[55]

Even here, however, James's notion of history appears different from that underlying Buchanan's 'infamous invective': instead of drawing on history to validate present practices, James posited the eternal, cyclical recurrence of events.[56]

James VI's theoretical arguments authorizing patriarchal monarchy rely most frequently not on history or tradition – except for the continuity of hereditary succession – but solely on natural law and the force of analogy. Buchanan and others turned to precedent, underwritten by natural law, to explain and legitimize their version of monarchy. However, when comparing the king to a father and to the body's head, James called on a nature imagined as an eternal and unchanging state of hierarchy. As Arthur Williamson observes, in the face of his own youthful political experience, James's 'paramount concern when visualizing politics within a purely Scottish context was to demonstrate the natural necessity of his status and authority as king', where 'only the timeless, changeless hierarchy of being ultimately withstood "the continuall volubilities of things earthlie"'.[57]

When he did use history to explain the Scottish kings' authority, James's strategy also differed from that of Buchanan. When in *The trew lawe of free monarchies* James rejected as irrelevant the claim that kings were originally chosen by the people, he defended his point by referring to the conquests of Fergus and William the Conqueror, after which, James wrote, kings have been 'the authors and makers of Lawes, and not the Lawes of the king'.[58] James thus here called up the past to construct a foundation myth which separates absolute rule from contingency and dependence on the consent of others. What Pocock says of other anti-traditional thinkers was also true of James: he is 'one who, having denied that the past authorises the present by vesting it with continuity, is obliged to create a new past and invest it with an authority which easily abolishes the necessity of referring to a past at all ... It tends to become unhistorical in the sense that it devises a mode of authority independent of social continuity'.[59] Characteristically, even when

---

[55] James VI, *Basilikon doron*, in McIlwain, *Works*, p. 40.

[56] See Achsah Guibbory, *The map of time: seventeenth-century English literature and ideas of pattern in history* (Urbana, 1986), p. 8: 'The classical view of history included two related concepts: nature is always the same, and history is a series of repetitive cycles'.

[57] Williamson, *Scottish national consciousness*, pp. 45–6.

[58] James VI, *Trew lawe of free monarchies*, in McIlwain, *Works*, pp. 62–3.

[59] Pocock, *Politics, language and time*, p. 260. In his self-image as the Roman emperor or god, James also reached into history to fashion an image which transcended time. As Jonathan Goldberg and others have described it, the iconography of James's reign represented him as reviving imperial Rome, with James himself the new Emperor Augustus. But this Stewart revival of Rome acted more to eclipse or suppress history, rather than to use history to

he claimed to write for a particular case at a particular time, James's understanding of his own authority veered away from history.

James's own early conception of the *poet's* responsibility to nature as opposed to tradition demonstrates the close link between this kind of political thinking and literary constructions of invention and imitation.[60] In his essay on the 'Reulis and cautelis to be observit and eschewit in Scottis poesie', written when James was nineteen, and published in 1585 in *The essayes of a prentise in the divine art of poesie*, the young king tried to do for Scotland what Du Bellay (cited in his preface) and the Pléiade had done for France.[61] At the same time, his poetics reflected a recent shift in concerns of literary neo-classicism. In the fifteenth century in Italy, and elsewhere in the sixteenth century, the neo-classical definition of imitation began to move from 'copying' to what Sidney calls 'a representing, counterfeiting, or figuring forth' of nature, a change which signalled a growing indifference to such historical problems.[62] With this gradual loss of interest in the imitation of ancient models and the increasing concern with decorum and verisimilitude, 'the historicism of Petrarch and Valla was largely repressed or exhausted',[63] and the poet's autonomy was magnified. Even while he held his poet to standards of verisimilitude, Sidney imagined a poet who is not 'subjected' to nature; rather, he goes 'hand in hand' with her, 'not enclosed within the narrow warrant of her gifts, but freely ranging only within the zodiac of his own wit'.[64] The dismissal of nature's 'warrant' rejects any 'licence' which implies a need for authorization. Sidney's *Defence* extends

---

ground or clarify the present. See Jonathan Goldberg, *James I and the politics of literature: Jonson, Shakespeare, Donne and their contemporaries* (Baltimore, 1983), pp. 51–2, on how Ben Jonson figured James's 'Roman' entrance into London as a moment outside history: in this spectacle, 'James's time is extraordinary, time fulfilled, a time out of time; a present state of unmoving'.

[60] See *ibid.*, pp. 22–3: 'A "free" monarch was how he styled himself in his first treatise on kingship, and it was the freedom of the mind that he addressed in his supposed first poem ... James's poems are exercises in freedom and subjection'.

[61] James may have learned about Du Bellay from Buchanan himself, who associated with members of the Pléiade when he was in Paris. McFarlane suggests that during his sojourn there Buchanan 'was in the forefront as a poet, rubbing shoulders with members of the Pléiade, and particularly with Joachim du Bellay'; see I. D. McFarlane, 'George Buchanan and French humanism', in A. H. T. Levi (ed.), *Humanism in France at the end of the middle ages and in the early Renaissance* (Manchester, 1970), pp. 295–319, at p. 299. In his commentary on James's treatise in *Elizabethan critical essays, vol. I* (Oxford, 1904), p. 404, G. Gregory Smith remarks that 'it has been surmised that the material of the volume of *Essayes of a Prentise in the Divine Art of Poesie*, in which this tract appears, was selected from the school exercises which James had done when he was Buchanan's pupil at Stirling. It may be that his effort towards an *Ars Poetica* was directly inspired by his master's *De Prosodia* and his annotations on Vives (*Opera*, Edin. 1715, vol. II).'

[62] Sidney, *Defence*, p. 25.   [63] Greene, *Light in Troy*, p. 180.

[64] Sidney, *Defence*, pp. 23–4.

this image of the poet as lawmaker to a rejection of the tyranny of history.[65] This notion of freedom was also to be imagined, as Sidney did, in the poet's ambivalent relationship to nature. In declaring that poets must be 'naturally' poets, even though natural talent alone cannot create immortal art, Du Bellay's *Deffence* anticipates Sidney's notion of the poet who is at once tied to, yet free from, nature. Analogously, even when he is restricted to imitating classical models, Du Bellay's poet is directed to develop his natural faculty of 'invention' by fashioning new images and ideas. Writers such as Du Bellay dreamed, as Sidney did, that the poet, indeed, could 'grow in effect another nature'.[66] The poet was thus both free 'by nature' and free from nature, although his inventions gained their power and authority from their resemblance to it.

Promoting the composition of Scottish vernacular poetry and instructing his 'docile' readers in the best practices of writing a new poetry, James was working out his sense of himself as a 'free' lawmaker and a Scot, in ways which would surface more clearly in his later political works. In the *Basilikon doron* James observed that it is a king's duty and privilege to develop the language of his country: for 'it best becommeth a King to purifie and make famous his owne tongue; wherein he may goe before all his subjects; as it setteth him well to doe in all honest and lawfull things'. Besides, he pointed out to his son, 'ynew of poore schollers would match you' in Latin and Greek.[67] For James, to write in his own language set him apart from mere 'poore schollers': it was the essence of his very kingliness as well as his 'Scottishness'.[68] So too, in his 'Reulis', he defended his writing of this

---

[65] For those earlier writers who concerned themselves primarily with the problem of the imitation of texts, in Struever's words, 'the essence of Humanistic method is a relationship between freedom and constraint which can be either an easy reciprocity or a difficult ambiguity' (Struever, *Language of history*, p. 153). Du Bellay's poetic self-image, which is alternately servile and defiant, was characteristic of the neo-classicists who were caught between tradition and innovation, inferiority and authority. See Margaret W. Ferguson, *Trials of desire: Renaissance defenses of poetry* (New Haven, 1983), p. 23, on how 'Du Bellay's treatise oscillates between presenting imitation as an act of reverent homage and as an act of aggressive theft'. See also Grahame Castor, *Pléiade poetics: a study in sixteenth-century thought and terminology* (Cambridge, 1964), p. 82, on how the Pléiade's poetics, in general, articulated a tension between 'the technical precepts and artifices of the "art" of poetry and the rapture of divine fury, between acquired rules and natural, spontaneous expression, between the first inspiration and the subsequent *labeur* of correction, between imitation of Nature and imitation of the ancients, and, most important of all, between imitation of other writers and the poet's own independent work'.

[66] Sidney, *Defence*, p. 23.   [67] James VI, *Basilikon doron*, in McIlwain, *Works*, p. 48.

[68] See Timothy J. Reiss, 'Poetry, power and resemblance of nature', in John D. Lyons and Stephen G. Nichols (eds.), *Mimesis: from mirror to method, Augustine to Descartes* (Hanover, N.H., 1982), pp. 215–47, who offers several examples of ways in which, in the late seventeenth century, it was imagined that 'the king, with his possession of, and power over, language, can guide all its other users in social action and in natural knowledge' (p. 230), in

treatise explicitly on the grounds that the Scottish language was unique, and implicitly on the grounds that he was the one to make the laws concerning its poetry. James indeed intended to be both the patron and lawmaker for his 'Castalian Band', who would produce a new, purely Scottish poetry.[69]

James distinguished his treatise from those written in other languages, either in the present or in the past, because of the difference of his time and culture. First, poetic treatises by those of other nations were irrelevant: 'That as for thame that hes written in it of late, there hes never ane of thame written in our language. For albeit sindrie hes written of it in English, quhilk is lykest to our language, zit we differ from thame in sindrie reulis of Poesie, as ze will find be experience.' Further, he discarded much of what had been written on poetry in the past (belying his later insistence in the *Basilikon doron* on history's repeatability), for 'as for them that wrait of auld, lyke as the tyme is changeit sensyne, sa is the ordour of Poesie changeit. For then they observit not *Flowing*, nor eschewit not *Ryming in termes*, besydes sindrie uther thingis, quhilk now we observe and eschew, and dois weil in sa doing'.[70] In the *Basilikon doron*, he demonstrated his impatience with the writing of the past more succinctly when he recommended composition in the vernacular, for 'ther is nothing left to be saide in Greeke and Latine alreadie'.[71] This mood of dismissing Latin and Greek distinguished James from Du Bellay: far from revering Greek and Latin languages and poetic models, at times the king seemed to have had little patience with them. Rather than the past representing the summit of perfection, for James poetry was then in its 'infancie and chyldhood': now it had come to 'mannis age and perfection'.[72]

Above all, what differentiates James's treatise from those of the Pléiade is this insistence that one improves Scottish poetry not by imitating classical models but rather by following the king's rules and developing one's own power of invention (however contradictory these two injunctions might be). The 'Reulis' is primarily a technical treatise on prosody, describing models for writing different kinds of lyric poetry, some borrowed from other national literatures and some native to Scottish poetry (in particular, the

---

so far as 'the king is both the principal poet of his country and the unique sovereign' (p. 229).

[69] See R. D. S. Jack, 'Poetry under King James VI', in Jack (ed.), *History of Scottish literature*, pp. 125–39, on the 'Scottish literary Renaissance' (p. 126).

[70] James VI, 'Ane schort treatise, conteining some reulis and cautelis to be observit and eschewit in Scottis poesie', in Edward Arber (ed.), *The essayes of a prentise, in the divine art of poesie* (Edinburgh, 1585; London, 1870), p. 54.

[71] This might echo his resentment, scribbled in a copy book, that 'they gar me speik Latin ar I could speik Scotis' (Willson, *James VI and I*, p. 23). See also Jack, 'Poetry under James VI', in Jack (ed.), *History of Scottish literature*, p. 125.

[72] James VI, *Basilikon doron*, in McIlwain, *Works*, p. 48.

genre of flyting). Equally important are the king's pronouncements on decorum, which reflect his vision of a fixed hierarchical social order: as Goldberg puts it, this poetic decorum is 'also a version of social decorum, all things in their place, unmovable, "ever framing zour reasonis, according to the qualitie of zour subiect"'.[73] Behind this minor form of 'lawmaking', however, one can detect in the 'Reulis' James's self-conception as a 'law-maker' and his desire to control the poetic practices of the self-described Castalian Band that he had gathered about him at court: as Jack interprets the situation, in seizing the role of 'leader/patron' so enthusiastically, James 'knew it allowed him to exert control over the more influential poets'.[74] The treatise is directed not to imperious schoolmasters but to the 'docile bairns of knowledge', supposedly willing to submit themselves to his paternal guidance.

Yet, even though James strictly set forth rules concerning prosody and decorum, in his estimate the main virtue of poetry was not to be found in its form. He wrote in the *Basilikon doron* that the 'chief commendation of a Poeme' is not 'to rime right, and flowe well with many pretie words', but that 'when the verse shall bee shaken sundrie in prose, it shall bee found so rich in quicke inventions and poeticke flowers, and in faire and pertinent comparisons; as it shall retaine the lustre of a Poeme, though in prose'.[75] That is, James saw as the main attribute of a poem the excellence of its 'inventions' or original ideas. This opinion was stated clearly in the 'Reulis', where he wrote: 'Bot sen Invention, is ane of the cheif vertewis in a Poete, it is best that ze invent your awin subject, zour self, and not to compose of sene subjectis. Especially, translating any thing out of uther language, quhilk doing, ze not onely essay not zour awin ingyne of Inventioun, bot be the same meanes, ze are bound, as to a staik, to follow that buikis phrasis, quhilk ze translate.'[76] (James violated his own rule, of course, in translating the *Urania* in the same volume.) The king was above all interested in the poet's ability to 'invent your awin subject, zour self', avoiding the practices of those who came before him.

In sixteenth-century poetic theory, such invention meant the discovery or fashioning of a new way of saying something, or a new idea. As Grahame

---

[73] Goldberg, *Politics of literature*, p. 19. James's treatise is also remarkable, as Jack has noted, precisely in extending the notion of decorum from a 'linguistic' to a 'social' phenomenon: that is, he recommends that not just style but the form of argument must fit the social position of the speaker. R. D. S. Jack, 'James VI and Renaissance poetic theory', *English*, 16 (1967), 208–11.

[74] Jack, 'Poetry under James VI', in Jack (ed.), *History of Scottish literature*, p. 125. In the *De jure regni*, Maitland is moved to make a comparison between the king's power to make the law and that of artists to set the rules for their own art, a claim which Buchanan vigorously denies (Buchanan, *De jure regni*, p. 31).

[75] James VI, *Basilikon doron*, in McIlwain, *Works*, p. 48.   [76] James VI, 'Reulis', p. 66.

Castor describes the way that invention was construed in early French poetics:

More usually, however, invention was set against imitation, taken in the sense of following literary models ... Both in translation and in imitation the poet is drawing upon other authors for his material. When he invents, on the other hand, he is relying entirely upon himself. He becomes the first to tread a particular poetic path, and all credit and honour are due to him for that primacy.[77]

Invention was distinguished from imagination, in so far as invention uses reason to construct images never thought before but pre-existing in nature (thus they are found or discovered rather than created).[78] Above all, invention was seen as anti-traditional, while linked to nature: so James wrote, 'Ze man also be warre with composing ony thing in the same maner, as hes bene ower oft usit of before'.[79] One of James's likely sources in this 'original' conception, George Gascoigne, construed this stance in more pejorative and class-tinged terms when he advised the writer to study some 'good and fine invention ... to avoyde the uncomely customes of common writers'.[80] It is not surprising, then, given James's emphasis on poetic invention, that he banned his poets from 'wryting any thing of materis of commoun weill, or uther sic grave sene subjectis (except Metaphorically, of manifest treuth opinly knawin, yit nochtwithstanding using it very seindil), because nocht onely ze essay nocht zour awin inventioun, as I spak before, bot lykewayis they are to grave materis, for a Poet to mell in'.[81] That is, the poet – other than the king – must *not* essay invention or original ideas about matters of state, apparently either because ordinary people should not have any original ideas about politics, or because such invention was the sole privilege of the king as author and poet.

Finally, in his 'Reulis', as in his political writings, James brought in nature to serve his invention, in so far as he claimed that one must be a poet 'naturally' and that invention must find its source in nature. In the preface, he wrote:

I will also wish zow (docile Reidar) that or ze cummer zow with reiding thir reulis, ze may find in zour self sic a beginning of Nature, as ze may put in practise in zour verse

---

[77] Castor, *Pléiade poetics*, p. 115.
[78] See *ibid.*, p. 128, where Castor notes how invention was primarily associated not with 'imagination' but with the power of reasoning; further, 'invention was thus the very antithesis of literary imitation, for it was the process of doing something which had not been done before, of treading *un sentier* hitherto *inconnu* ... [yet] To invent was simply to come into something which already existed and to make it manifest for the first time' (*ibid.*, pp. 189–90).
[79] James VI, 'Reulis', p. 65.
[80] See George Gascoigne, 'Certayne notes of instruction' (1575), in Smith (ed.), *Elizabethan critical essays*, vol. I, pp. 47–8.
[81] James VI, 'Reulis', p. 66.

many of thir foirsaidis preceptis, or ever ze sie them as they are heir set doun. For gif Nature be nocht the cheif worker in this airt, Reulis wilbe bot a band to Nature, and will mak zow within short space weary of the haill airt: Quhair as, gif Nature be chief, and bent to it, reulis will be ane help and staff to Nature.[82]

Like the Pléiade poets, James here attempted to negotiate the relationship between nature and art in the making of a poet and his poetry. As they did, he suggested that the poet must have a natural talent, which is shaped by art and learning: indeed, James implied that the true poet, by nature, will understand and articulate the 'laws' which he pronounces. In effect, the treatise represents James's own precepts as a kind of 'natural law' of poetry. Further, James's notion of invention is informed by nature: 'Bot because ze can not have the Inventioun, except it come of Nature, I remit it thairunto, as the cheif cause, not onely of Inventioun, bot also of all the uther pairtis of Poesie. For airt is onely bot ane help and a remembraunce to Nature, as I shewe zow in the Preface.'[83] This statement can be read two ways: first, a poet must be a poet naturally; but second, all inventions find their shape in nature. Thus James's poet's true freedom is freedom from artistic precedent. He is only subject to imitating the unchanging present which is 'nature'. As in the theory of divine right, it is not other men and their laws that define truth and authority; it is the timeless and never-changing 'rules' of nature, in which the king finds his own image.

For James and Buchanan, as Scottish humanists, literary neo-classicism offered two different ways of negotiating the issues of custom, authority and national consciousness. For Buchanan, the basic tenets of neo-classical poetics confirmed his sense of the continuity between Scottish and classical culture, so that imitation of the classical past could only serve to strengthen and redefine the present, just as the Scottish past was the basis of its present political life. Such a continuity between Scottish past and present, and classical past and present, was based in turn on the power of natural law, which bound them together. At the same time, however, Buchanan's works show a tension characteristic of early modern humanists, in representing his own isolation in the present moment, which is both a vulnerable and an elevated position: both his political and his poetic works demonstrate the conflict between his belief in the power of tradition and his rational distrust of it. James, in turn, adapted the neo-classicists' emphasis on the development of the vernacular but tied it to the power of poetic invention rather than the imitation of past models: the renovation of Scottish poetry would flow from the present, from court and king, rather than from submission to the example of the past. He betrayed little anxiety about confinement in the

[82] *Ibid.*, p. 55.   [83] *Ibid.*, p. 66.

present precisely because he imagined himself able to break free from precedent and custom. At the heart of the poetics of both is thus the Janus face of humanism, with one face turned toward the past and the other toward the future of modern Europe.

5   George Buchanan, James VI and the presbyterians

Roger A. Mason

I

It is now almost a century since J. N. Figgis first offered a coherent explanation of why James VI and I championed so enthusiastically the theory of royal absolutism commonly known as the divine right of kings. There were, he argued, two reasons for the king's insistence that, as his authority was divinely ordained, he was accountable for its exercise, not to his subjects, but to God and God alone. Firstly, according to Figgis, James was seeking to counter Catholic controversialists who as well as upholding the idea of papal supremacy over temporal rulers were also intent on undermining his claim to the English throne by advocating elective over hereditary monarchy and investing the people rather than the prince with sovereign power. Secondly, Figgis believed that, irrespective of his prospects in England, James faced in the Scottish presbyterians a still more dangerous challenge to his authority which was also best met by assertions of his divine right to rule. 'Presbyterianism in Scotland', he wrote, 'as expounded by Knox or Buchanan, and inwoven with politics by Murray [sic] and Morton, was a system of clericalism as much more irritating and meddlesome as it was stronger and more popular in its basis than that of the papal supremacy.' It was, therefore, 'no matter for surprise that at a time when the sons of Zeruiah were too strong for him and he felt his authority a mockery before the insolent representatives of ecclesiastical bigotry, James should promulgate with logical completeness and grasp with the tenacity of a narrow but clear-sighted intellect the theory of the Divine Right of kings'.[1]

The tone (and many of the details) of these remarks may be questionable, but Figgis was undoubtedly right to stress that what initially drove James to elaborate an absolutist theory of kingship was not so much his fear of Catholic controversialists in England and on the continent as his overwhelming need to ground his right to rule on principles other than those

---

[1] J. N. Figgis, *The theory of the divine right of kings* (Cambridge, 1896), pp. 135–6.

112

espoused by the presbyterian clergy in Scotland. He was certainly aware of the Catholic challenge and was later to engage in heated polemical exchanges with Catholic theorists over the oath of allegiance which he demanded of their co-religionists in England.[2] But it is perfectly clear from the text itself that, when James initially set out his ideas in *The trew lawe of free monarchies*, first published in Edinburgh in 1598, his principal target was his clerical opponents in Scotland.[3] It is all the more remarkable, therefore, that since Figgis wrote, although a good deal of attention has been paid to the place of the king's ideas in English political thought, few efforts have been made to explore the Scottish context in which they were first formulated.[4] What follows is an attempt to redress that imbalance by seeing the claim to rule by divine right as one side of an ideological debate which polarized Scottish political thinking in the immediate post-Reformation period. In many respects, what happened in Scotland paralleled developments elsewhere in Europe where the Reformation crisis precipitated debates over the nature and location of sovereignty which resolved themselves into more or less blatant clashes between the proponents of popular constitutionalism and the upholders of royal absolutism.[5] Two factors, however, lent the Scottish situation unique significance and provide the main focus for what follows.

[2] These debates are discussed at length in the introduction to McIlwain, *Works*. For a more recent analysis, see J. H. M. Salmon, 'Catholic resistance theory, Ultramontanism, and the royalist response, 1580–1620', in J. H. Burns and Mark Goldie (eds.), *The Cambridge history of political thought 1450–1700* (Cambridge, 1991), pp. 219–53, esp. pp. 247–53.

[3] As was pointed out some years ago in Jennifer M. Brown (now Wormald), 'Scottish politics 1567–1625', in A. G. R. Smith (ed.), *The reign of James VI and I* (London, 1973), pp. 22–39, at pp. 24–5; cf. Jenny Wormald, *Court, kirk and community: Scotland 1470–1625* (London, 1981), pp. 148–9. The same point is emphasized in Maurice Lee, Jr, *Great Britain's Solomon: James VI and I and his three kingdoms* (Urbana and Chicago, 1990), pp. 82–7.

[4] Two notable recent exceptions are Jenny Wormald, 'James VI and I, *Basilikon doron* and *The trew lawe of free monarchies*: the Scottish context and the English translation', in Linda Levy Peck (ed.), *The mental world of the Jacobean court* (Cambridge, 1991), pp. 36–54, and David Norbrook, '*Macbeth* and the politics of historiography', in Kevin Sharpe and Steven N. Zwicker (eds.), *Politics of discourse: the literature and history of seventeenth-century England* (Berkeley, 1987), pp. 78–116. On James's thought in relation to England, see for example W. H. Greenleaf, *Order, empiricism and politics* (London, 1964); Gordon J. Schochet, *Patriarchalism in political thought* (New York, 1975); Robert Eccleshall, *Order and reason in politics* (Oxford, 1978); and J. P. Sommerville, *Politics and ideology in England 1603–40* (London, 1986).

[5] The most obvious European parallel is France, for which see D. R. Kelley, *The beginnings of ideology: consciousness and society in the French Reformation* (Cambridge, 1981); R. Kingdon, *Myths about the St Bartholomew's Day Massacre* (Cambridge, Mass., 1988); and J. H. Franklin, *Constitutionalism and resistance: three treatises by Hotman, Beza and Mornay* (New York, 1969). Throughout this paper, I have occasionally fallen back on the anachronistic terms 'absolutism' and 'constitutionalism' as convenient shorthand. For a luminous discussion of contemporary terminology, see J. H. Burns, 'The idea of absolutism', in John Miller (ed.), *Absolutism in seventeenth-century France* (London, 1990), pp. 21–42.

Firstly, to an extent unmatched elsewhere in Europe, radical political ideas became 'inwoven' not just (as Figgis suggests) with Scottish politics, but with the very fabric of a nationally organized Protestant church which was legally recognized by the crown, but for long periods lay outside its control. In other words, the debate over the nature and location of sovereignty was a critical facet of the struggle waged between James VI and the Melvillian presbyterians for control of the Scottish kirk and over the caesaropapist implications of an English-style royal supremacy. Secondly, adding a fascinating personal dimension to the struggle was the fact that the principal political ideologue of Figgis's 'insolent representatives of ecclesiastical bigotry' was none other than that urbane and scholarly humanist, George Buchanan. Not only were Buchanan's ideas adopted wholesale by the presbyterians, but he was also the man charged with providing James VI with the education deemed suitable for a godly Protestant prince. The debate over the issue of sovereignty was thus both institutionalized in the conflict between the crown and the kirk and personalized in the relationship between the king and his tutor. In exploring the polarities of political debate in late sixteenth-century Scotland, therefore, we can do no better than to look in the first instance at the nature of the relationship between George Buchanan and James VI.

II

That their relationship was, to say the least, uneasy is perhaps best illustrated by an episode which occurred some forty years after Buchanan's death. In March 1622, the king's slumbers were disturbed by a dream in which his old tutor appeared to him and, speaking in verse, predicted that 'soon afterwards he would fall into ice, and then into fire, that he would endure frequent pain, and die after two years'.[6] By the time the Venetian ambassador in London picked up this tidbit of gossip and passed it on to his superiors in September 1622, James had apparently already had accidents with both fire and water, was painfully troubled by gout and was deeply apprehensive at the thought of his impending death. In fact, Buchanan's ghost was slightly out in his calculations: James was to live a further three years rather than two. Nevertheless, it was highly appropriate that the ageing king should receive such intimations of mortality from the spectral presence of his old tutor. For Buchanan had haunted the king's adult years just as he had tyrannized over his childhood.

It was hardly a happy childhood. Born in 1566, before James was a year

---

[6] *Calendar of state papers, Venetian, 1621–23*, ed. A. B. Hinds (London, 1911), pp. 444–5.

old his father had been murdered and his mother stripped of her crown and imprisoned. The following year, his mother escaped confinement in Scotland only to lose any chance of regaining her throne – or being reunited with her son – when she fled to England after the battle of Langside in 1568. James never saw her again. Instead, in 1570 he was placed under the supervision of Buchanan, who spent the next dozen years attempting to destroy the reputation of the exiled queen while moulding her son in a neo-classicist's image of a godly Protestant prince. Buchanan was a humanist poet and pedagogue of immense contemporary stature who had spent most of the middle years of his life on the continent before returning to Scotland in the early 1560s, very possibly in the entourage of Mary Queen of Scots herself.[7] Yet as well as having connections with the court of the Catholic Mary, he was also closely associated with the Protestant party, led by Mary's half-brother, the earl of Moray, which had engineered the Congregation's rebellion of 1559 against the queen's mother, Mary of Guise, and which was instrumental in ousting the queen herself from power in 1567 and placing the Scottish crown on the head of her infant son. It was as an appointee of this new anti-Marian regime that Buchanan, together with his junior colleague, Peter Young, took up his duties as preceptor to the four-year-old king.

By the time of his appointment Buchanan was already in his mid-sixties and was by all accounts a cantankerous old bachelor increasingly plagued by ill-health and with an evil temper to match. By the end of his long life in 1582, he had also (if a contemporary Spanish report is to be believed) 'given way to the vice of drunkenness' and was 'intoxicated every day'.[8] Whatever the truth of this, there is ample anecdotal evidence to suggest that, drunk or sober, his dour irascibility was guaranteed to make a life-long impression on the young king. On one occasion, Buchanan is alleged to have administered a severe whipping to James for persistently disturbing him in his reading. When the countess of Mar protested at his rough handling of the Lord's anointed, Buchanan's response was as crushing as it was crude: 'Madam, I have whipt his arse, you may kiss it if you please'.[9] However apocryphal, this both squares with what is known of Buchanan's choleric disposition and

[7] For these and other biographical details, see I. D. McFarlane, *Buchanan* (London, 1981); cf. the dated but still readable account of his life in P. Hume Brown, *George Buchanan: humanist and reformer* (Edinburgh, 1890).

[8] *Calendar of state papers, Spanish, 1580–86*, ed. M. A. S. Hume (London, 1896), p. 289.

[9] George Mackenzie, *The lives and characters of the most eminent writers of the Scots nation* (3 vols., Edinburgh, 1708–22), vol. III, pp. 179–80. Mackenzie based his story on 'some things I have heard from the Earl of Cromarty who had them from his Grandfather the Lord Invertyle who ... was Buchanan's scholar at the same time with King James'. The tale presumably lost nothing in the frequent retelling.

helps to explain why James remained so in awe of him that years later he is said to have trembled at the approach of a courtier because 'it minded him so of his pedagogue'.[10] Yet there was more to such fear and trembling than the king's vivid memories of Buchanan's overbearing treatment of him in the schoolroom at Stirling. There were other reasons why the ghost of his former tutor should have continued to haunt the adult king. For more than anyone else, with the possible exception of John Knox, Buchanan symbolized for James the forces of subversion, the agents of chaos and disorder, which throughout his reign in Scotland seemed to menace the throne on which he sat.[11]

During much of the 1570s, as James laboured under his instruction to master the complexities of Latin syntax, Buchanan was hard at work on the two books which, dedicated to the young king, served in James's eyes only to undermine his kingship. The first of them, the brief Latin dialogue *De jure regni apud Scotos*, was published in 1579, though it was composed a decade earlier, probably late in 1567, expressly to justify Mary's deposition.[12] In order to do so, Buchanan expounded a theory of popular sovereignty whose central premiss was that kings were appointed by the people to perform on their behalf a set of well-defined functions. It followed that if they failed to carry out their duties satisfactorily, thereby breaking the contract entered into by the terms of their coronation oath, the people had the right to depose them in favour of someone more able to fulfil the duties of the royal office. Monarchy, in short, was an elective form of government and kings were accountable to those who elected them. As a guide and safeguard, moreover, they were subject to the law as promulgated by the people in the image of an ideal prince and in the interests of the community as a whole. Far from being above the law, far from being the *fons et origo* of the law, the king was at all times subject to laws designed to ensure that his actions conformed to the dictates of reason, nature and the divine will. To flout the law was thus not simply to oppose the wishes and jeopardize the welfare of the people, it was also to declare oneself an enemy to reason, nature and God Himself. Such a tyrant, argued Buchanan, was no better than a brute beast and had

---

[10] Quoted in McFarlane, *Buchanan*, p. 449.

[11] The king's attitude to both Buchanan and Knox is discussed in Lee, *Great Britain's Solomon*, pp. 31–6. His general feeling is well conveyed in a report from Fontenay to Mary of January 1583 stating that James still loved and honoured his mother, while 'detesting ordinarily before the lords as traitors those who have caused to be said or written anything to your dishonour and prejudice, and above all Knox and Buchanan'. *CSP Scot., 1581–3*, pp. 279–80.

[12] There is no satisfactory modern edition or translation, but see *The art and science of government among the Scots*, ed. and trans D. H. McNeill (Glasgow, 1964), and *The powers of the crown in Scotland*, ed. and trans. C. F. Arrowood (Austin, Tex., 1949). On the date of its composition, see McFarlane, *Buchanan*, pp. 392–6.

no place in a society of rational human beings. Once denounced as a tyrant by a public assembly of the people, therefore, it was perfectly legitimate to depose such a monster and even for any individual to kill him. Indeed, argued Buchanan, the people should heap honour and reward on the citizen responsible for ridding the commonwealth of an irrational sub-human who *ipso facto* posed a grave threat to the welfare of the community over which he ruled.

Such a bald summary does less than justice either to the strengths or the weaknesses of Buchanan's political theory.[13] However, it is sufficient to indicate how his austere neo-Stoic rationalism issued in an essentially republican theory of government which severely restricted – and in the process completely demystified – the power and status of the monarch and led ultimately to an endorsement of the incendiary doctrine of single-handed tyrannicide. Not surprisingly, the publication of the *De jure regni*, long anticipated and encouraged by radical Protestants in England and elsewhere, caused a sensation well beyond the borders of Scotland.[14] Buchanan's theory, founded as he claimed on the immutable laws of nature and of God, struck at the roots of hereditary monarchy wherever it existed. Nevertheless, it was with Scotland that Buchanan was primarily concerned and, three years after the appearance of the *De jure regni*, in the year of his own death, his magisterial *Rerum Scoticarum historia* was finally published. Leaving aside the patriotic motives which originally prompted him to write a history of his native land, there are two aspects of the work which were clearly shaped by the revolutionary events of the 1560s and which are intimately related to the political ideas elaborated in the *De jure regni*.[15]

The first was that Buchanan deliberately manipulated existing accounts of the Scottish past in order to show how the laws of nature as set out in the *De jure regni* had been adopted by the Scots of remotest antiquity as the basis of their constitution and had operated successfully throughout much

---

[13] For a much fuller analysis, see Roger A. Mason, '*Rex stoicus*: George Buchanan, James VI and the Scottish polity', in John Dwyer *et al.* (eds.), *New perspectives on the politics and culture of early modern Scotland* (Edinburgh, 1982), pp. 9–33, and J. H. Burns, 'The political ideas of George Buchanan', *SHR*, 30 (1951), 60–8. Although dated, there is still much to be learned from W. S. McKechnie, '*De jure regni apud Scotos*', in George Nielson (ed.), *George Buchanan: Glasgow quatercentenary studies* (Glasgow, 1907), pp. 211–96.

[14] For some indication of Buchanan's contemporary reputation and the interest in his political writings, see J. E. Phillips, 'George Buchanan and the Sidney circle', *Huntington Library Quarterly*, 12 (1948–9), 23–55, esp. pp. 39–45. See also Buchanan's wide-ranging correspondence in *Georgii Buchanani . . . opera omnia*, ed. Thomas Ruddiman and Peter Burmann (2 vols., Leiden, 1725), vol. II, pp. 721ff.

[15] Though its analysis of Buchanan's ideas is highly suspect and best ignored, on the date of the *History's* composition, see H. R. Trevor-Roper, 'George Buchanan and the ancient Scottish constitution', *EHR*, supplement 3 (1966). The most accessible English version of

of the kingdom's history. In this he was greatly helped by the inventive approach to the past displayed by his predecessor, Hector Boece, whose *Scotorum historiae* of 1527 provided an extraordinarily detailed and largely fabricated account of the kingdom's earliest history in which kings were evidently accountable to the people and tyrants disposed of with monotonous regularity.[16] Buchanan jettisoned much of the detail which enlivened Boece's narrative, but this served only to bring into sharper relief the constitutional principles, based on the laws of nature, by which the ancient Scots had allegedly regulated the commonwealth. Thus, according to Buchanan, from the time of the kingdom's foundation by Fergus I in 330 BC, the monarchy was clearly elective and the monarch clearly subject to the law. It followed that those kings who broke the law were rightly dismissed from office and rightly – and often violently – disposed of by a virtuous nobility acting on behalf of the community as a whole. The reign of the debauched and lustful Durstus, for example, the eleventh king of Scots who, among other inhuman crimes, 'exposed his wife ... as a prostitute to his nobles', was legitimately cut short when the nobility rose against him and slew him in battle.[17] Here as elsewhere, the marked emphasis which Buchanan placed on sexual excess as a mark of tyranny was quite deliberate and points to the second way in which the political theory of the *De jure regni* impinged on the *History*.[18] For not only did it exemplify in typically humanist fashion the critical importance of subjecting man's baser instincts to the rule of reason, but it also provided a benchmark against which to measure the licentious conduct of Mary Queen of Scots. As described by Buchanan, Mary's rule was clearly patterned on the vicious tyrants who had in the past given free rein to their sensual appetites and jeopardized both the commonweal of the realm and their own right to rule over it. Mary's deposition, then, was not only a triumph for virtue and reason over brutish sensuality, it was also conducted in strict accordance with the dictates of reason and nature which underlay the constitutional practices of the ancient Scots.[19]

the chronicle is *The history of Scotland*, ed. and trans. James Aikman (4 vols., Glasgow, 1827).

[16] On Boece's chronicle, see my 'Scotching the Brut: politics, history and national myth in sixteenth-century Britain', in Roger A. Mason (ed.), *Scotland and England 1286–1815* (Edinburgh, 1987), pp. 60–84, at pp. 64–5.

[17] Buchanan, *History*, vol. I, pp. 166–7.

[18] A good deal of light is shed on the origins of this conception of tyranny, and its use by Buchanan and others in the sixteenth century, in R. W. Bushnell, *Tragedies of tyrants: political thought and theater in the English Renaissance* (Ithaca, N.Y. and London, 1990).

[19] Buchanan, *History*, vol. II, Books XVII and XVIII *passim*. Buchanan's anti-Marian writings, including these books of the *History*, are conveniently brought together in W. A. Gatherer (ed.), *The tyrannous reign of Mary Stewart: George Buchanan's account* (Edinburgh, 1958).

In the light of this, it is not hard to see why James found Buchanan's version of Scottish history so unsettling. It was not so much that it portrayed his mother as a lascivious whore who murdered her husband, James's father, Lord Darnley, in pursuit of an adulterous liaison with an unscrupulous thug, the earl of Bothwell. Much more serious were the political principles which Buchanan's account of the past was designed to exemplify. Peter Young recorded that when James as a boy was reading in Buchanan of the vicious life of Durstus, he exclaimed: 'How durst he be sa euil? Thai micht have callit him Curstus, because he was curst, and had acurst us.'[20] From a very early date James clearly recognized how serious a curse on his kingship the principles expounded by his tutor and graphically illustrated in the pages of the *History* might be. The long line of over 100 kings stretching back to the foundations of the kingdom in the fourth century BC was traditionally seen as the great glory of the Scottish monarchy, demonstrating its antiquity, its continuity and its stability. But the interpretation placed by Buchanan on many of their reigns opened up altogether different lines of speculation.[21] It is worth noting that when James made his triumphal entry into Edinburgh in 1579 the Salt Tron was decorated with a genealogy of all his royal forebears. Similarly, when his new wife Anne of Denmark entered the capital in 1590 'all the kings heertofore of Scotland' were once again placed on public display.[22] The sources give no indication of how this iconography was meant to be interpreted. But the king himself, so well-versed in Buchanan's *History*, can hardly have viewed them with equanimity.

Indeed, as James grew into manhood and out of the shadow of his tutor, he also grew into an awareness of just how weak the ideological underpinnings of Stewart rule in Scotland had suddenly become. Many of his predecessors had faced the problem of recovering from a period of regency government and reasserting the crown's authority in the face of truculent magnate interests. But none, with the exception of his mother, had been forced to confront so directly the awkward questions which the crises of the 1560s had thrown up and which some of his subjects persisted in pondering. Why should we obey you? What is the source, the nature, the extent of your authority? Where ultimately does sovereignty lie in the Scottish commonwealth? In fact, questions of this kind were not so much awkward as explosive: the product of a constitutional crisis such as Scotland had not experienced since the Wars of Independence.[23] Furthermore, the answers which Buchanan

---

[20] See G. F. Warner (ed.), 'The library of James VI 1573–83', in *SHS Miscellany I* (SHS, 1893), pp. xi–lxxv, at p. lxxiii.
[21] See Mason, 'Scotching the Brut', in Mason (ed.), *Scotland and England*, pp. 60–84.
[22] A. J. Mill, *Medieval plays in Scotland* (Edinburgh and London, 1927), pp. 194, 204.
[23] On this point, see my 'Kingship, tyranny and the right to resist in fifteenth-century Scotland', *SHR*, 66 (1987), 125–51.

supplied and which he tried to drum into the head of his royal pupil were quite devastating. They left the king no power save that which his subjects were prepared – conditionally – to grant him. It is not surprising that as soon as he escaped Buchanan's tutelage, James set about anathematizing the political doctrines associated with his name.

Cursing Buchanan, however, would do little to solve the problem of how the king could legitimize – or relegitimize – his kingship. The ideological foundations of his authority remained as questionable as ever. It is testimony, not so much to the excellence of his education at Buchanan's hands, as to the acute anxiety felt by James to re-establish the basis of his rule on unassailable grounds that he himself chose to counter his tutor's popular constitutionalism with a terse statement of royal absolutism. There are not many kings who have felt the need to go into print to explain to their subjects why it is that they ought to be obeyed. Yet such was the purpose of *The trew lawe of free monarchies*. It was in writing this tract that James came closest to laying to rest the ghost of his old tutor. But to understand the king's reaction, it is important to widen the focus and to look beyond the personal relationship between James and Buchanan to the institutional conflict between the crown and the kirk. For it was in this broader arena that Buchanan's political philosophy most fully realized its subversive potential.

III

In fact, irrespective of Buchanan, James was in no doubt of the grave threat that presbyterianism posed to his kingship. At roughly the same time as he was writing the *Trew lawe*, the king composed for his young son, Prince Henry, his celebrated treatise on kingship, *Basilikon doron*, first published in 1599 and subsequently revised and reissued, largely for the benefit of his new English subjects, in 1603.[24] In it James took the opportunity to warn his heir of the dangers of permitting such 'phanatick spirits' as the presbyterian clergy a foothold in the realm and advised him to exile the movement's leaders 'except you woulde keepe them for trying your patience, as Socrates did an euill wife'.[25] Amid the pithy saws and indignant abuse, however, James also ventured an account of the Reformation in Scotland which is as revealing as it is prejudiced:

---

[24] *The basilikon doron of King James VI*, ed. James Craigie (2 vols., STS, 1944–50) prints both versions as well as the original manuscript. Unless otherwise stated, quotations are from the 1603 version.

[25] *Ibid.*, vol. I, pp. 78–9.

But the reformation of religion in Scotland, being extraordinarily wrought by God, wherein many things were inordinatly done by a populare tumult & rebellion, of suche as blindly were doing the work of God, but clogged with their owne passions & particular respects, as well appeared by the destruction of our policie; and not proceeding from the Princes ordour, as it did in our neighbour country of England, as likewise in Denmark, and sundry parts of Germanie; some fierie spirited men in the ministerie, gote such a guyding of the people at that time of confusion, as finding the guste of gouernment sweete, they begouth to fantasie to themselves, a Democrat-ick forme of gouernment: and hauing (by the iniquity of time) bene ouer-well baited vpon the wracke, first of my Grandmother, and next of my owne mother, and after vsurping the liberty of the time in my long minority, setled themselues so faste vpon that imagined Democracie, as they fed themselues with the hope to become *Tribuni plebis*: and so in a populare gouernment by leading the people by the nose, to beare the sway of all the rule.[26]

Perhaps the most revealing aspect of this passage is that James felt the need to add to the 1603 version, presumably by way of apology to his English readers, that the Scottish Reformation was so 'extraordinarily wrought by God'.[27] Even had he so wished, the king was in no position to deny that Protestant reform had been necessary in Scotland, but he was plainly embarrassed by the manner in which it had been accomplished. Pervading the entire passage is a sense of regret, even anger, that God had moved so mysteriously His wonders to perform that He had allowed the Scottish Reformation to be achieved by 'popular tumult & rebellion' with all the mischievous consequences for the crown's authority which he then went on to lament. Why was it, he complained, that matters had not proceeded in Scotland as they had in England and elsewhere 'from the Prince's order'? Why, in other words, had not Scotland experienced a magisterial reforma-tion, led and closely controlled by the crown, and resulting in an Erastian system of ecclesiastical government capped by the royal supremacy? There was surely nothing James would have liked better than to have been recognized as supreme governor of a Scottish church administered, as appeared to be the case in England, by hand-picked bishops licensing hand-picked preachers to broadcast from their pulpits the divine origins of

---

[26] *Ibid.*, vol. I, p. 75.
[27] The briefer 1599 version reads: 'But the reformation of Religion in Scotland being made by a popular tumult & rebellion (as wel appeared by the destruction of our policie) & not proceeding from the Princes ordour (as it did in England) some of our fyerie ministers got such a guyding of the people at that time of confusion, as finding the gust of gouernement sweet, they begouth to fantasie to themselues a Democratick forme of gouernment; and hauing (by the iniquitie of time) bene ouer-well baited vpon the wrak, first of my Grand-mother, and syne of my own mother; & after vsurping the liberty of the time in my long minoritie, setled themselues so fast vpon that imagined Democracie, as they fed themselues with the hope to become Tribuni plebis: and so in a popular gouernement by leading the people by the nose, to beare the sway of all the rule.' *Ibid.*, vol. I, p. 74.

monarchy and the duty of unstinting obedience to their divinely appointed sovereign.

This is of course a caricature of the Elizabethan church, which had its own share of dissent and its own problems with presbyterians willing enough to challenge the royal supremacy.[28] Yet in England presbyterianism never gained a secure foothold within the structure of the established church and was driven underground by the concerted resources of the crown and a largely conformist ecclesiastical hierarchy. James had every reason to be envious of the way in which the royal supremacy operated under Elizabeth to bind together the English crown, the English church and the English people in a manner capable both of stifling dissent and of focusing national loyalties on the monarchy itself. Things were very different in Scotland. Precisely because Protestantism had been established there in defiance of the crown, it had developed an organization largely outside the crown's control and, within that independent ecclesiastical structure, presbyterianism had been allowed to spread relatively unchecked during the years of the king's minority. If the kirk's independence of the crown was in part a product of circumstance, however, it also stemmed from an ideological commitment on behalf of the first generation of reformers to a degree of ecclesiastical autonomy which was incompatible with the royal supremacy.[29] By design as well as by chance, conditions in Scotland proved eminently favourable to the reception of the systematized presbyterian polity which the young Andrew Melville, returning from Beza's Geneva in 1574, sought with ever-increasing determination to establish within the kirk.[30] By the late 1570s, Melville and his colleagues had not only secured a power-base within the kirk but had found a national forum in the yearly – often twice-yearly – meetings of the general assembly which, however ambiguous its constitutional position, could neither be ignored nor easily controlled by the crown. The stage was well set for the series of dramatic confrontations between the Melvillians and the monarchy which was to characterize church–state relations over the next three decades.

In essence, there were two aspects of Melville's presbyterian programme which James considered subversive of royal authority: the idea of minister-

---

[28] See in particular Patrick Collinson, *The Elizabethan puritan movement* (London and New York, 1967), and Peter Lake, *Moderate puritans and the Elizabethan church* (Cambridge, 1982). For a recent general survey, see Diarmaid MacCulloch, *The later Reformation in England 1547–1603* (London, 1990).

[29] On this point, see in particular James Kirk, *Patterns of reform: continuity and change in the Reformation kirk* (Edinburgh, 1989), ch. 6.

[30] The standard biography remains Thomas McCrie, *Life of Andrew Melville* (2nd edn, 2 vols., Edinburgh and London, 1824). His early career and involvement in educational reform in Scotland are well discussed in John Durkan and James Kirk, *The university of Glasgow 1451–1577* (Glasgow, 1977), chs. 14–15.

ial parity and the doctrine of the two kingdoms. In *Basilikon doron*, it was on ministerial parity that he chose to focus attention, denouncing it as 'the mother of confusion, and enemy to Vnitie whiche is the mother of ordour'.[31] The idea that no individual minister could hold authority over another spelled doom for the episcopate just as it did for any notion of ecclesiastical hierarchy other than that of a graded system of conciliar courts. But in James's eyes this kind of levelling would not only lead to anarchy in the church, it would lead 'the Politicke and ciuill estate' to the same 'greate confusion'.[32] Parity, he insisted, was simply incompatible with the hierarchical nature of things and could 'neither stand with the ordour of the Churche, nor the peace of a common-weale and well-ruled Monarchie'.[33] In other words, as he was to put it more succinctly at a later date: 'No bishop, no king'. But just as threatening to James, though oddly he made nothing of it in *Basilikon doron*, was the theory of the two kingdoms – the idea that church and state were separate powers with mutually exclusive jurisdictions. It was this belief which allowed Melville and his colleagues to defy the civil authority on the grounds that it had no power to act in ecclesiastical affairs.[34] Most memorably, it prompted Melville to declare to James in 1596 that the king was 'but God's sillie vassall'. Plucking his sovereign impatiently by the sleeve, he explained that there were 'two kings and two kingdomes in Scotland': as well as the temporal realm over which James Stewart presided, there was 'Christ Jesus, and his kingdome the kirk, whose subject King James the Sixt is, and of whose kingdome not a king, nor a head, nor a lord, but a member'.[35] There could be no royal supremacy in a presbyterian church: James was not head nor governor of the kirk, but merely a member of it and was subject, like any other member, to the clerical authorities who governed it on Christ's behalf. Unhappily for James, however, the converse did not necessarily apply. As regards civil affairs, the clergy did not hesitate to collapse the jurisdictional boundaries in order to instruct the magistrate in his duties and to ensure that in a godly commonwealth the godly prince acted in accordance with the will of God. James could surely be forgiven for thinking that the full implementation of the presbyterian programme would reduce him to the status of a puppet prince controlled by a clerical oligarchy.

Such, in James's view, were the terrible consequences of the Scottish Reformation being so 'extraordinarily wrought by God'. But there was one

---

[31] *Basilikon doron*, vol. I, p. 77.   [32] *Ibid.*, vol. I, p. 79.   [33] *Ibid.*, vol. I, p. 81.
[34] For one of many examples, see *The autobiography and diary of Mr. James Melville*, ed. Robert Pitcairn (Wodrow Society, 1842), p. 142, where Andrew Melville is said in 1583 to have 'declyned the judicator of the King and Counsall, being accusit upon na civill cryme or transgression, but upon his doctrine uttered from the pulpit'.
[35] Calderwood, vol. V, pp. 439–40.

further outcome of the process of reform which he evidently believed to be equally if not more threatening to royal authority. Just as the Reformation had involved rebellions against both his grandmother and his mother, so the presbyterian heirs of the revolution had a vested interest in perpetuating the radical political ideas – 'that imagined Democracie' – which the events of the 1560s had generated. This was true in a number of senses. Firstly, and most obviously, such ideas served to legitimize the process of reform itself and cleared those involved in the rebellions of any charge of treasonable or unconstitutional behaviour. Secondly, continued adherence to these radical political principles gave the presbyterian clergy enormous leverage over a potentially errant or ungodly prince and left the king in the exposed position to which he was clearly so sensitive himself. Thirdly, it is at least arguable that popular theories of government squared more readily with the presbyterian ecclesiastical polity. While one would hesitate to call sixteenth-century presbyterianism democratic in any real sense of the term, it was certainly more compatible with what – following Walter Ullmann – one might call an 'ascending thesis' of government than with the 'descending thesis' so obviously favoured by James VI.[36]

In any event, the latter point aside, Buchanan's writings played a critical role both in legitimizing the revolutionary events of the 1560s and in supplying the presbyterians with firm ideological foundations for their defiance of the crown.[37] While the *De jure regni* outlined a theoretical justification of popular sovereignty and the accountability of kings to their subjects, the *History* embodied those ideas in a sweeping survey of the Scottish past culminating in a whitewash of the rebels of the 1560s. To the presbyterians, it was an ideal 'official' history and was seen as such from the moment of its publication in 1582. James Melville, the great reformer's nephew, noted in his diary that it was 'a remarkable providence of God' that Buchanan's chronicle and *The second book of discipline* – the blueprint for a presbyterian Scotland – were published at the same time.[38] The relationship

---

[36] Walter Ullmann, *Medieval political thought* (Peregrine edn, Harmondsworth, 1975), pp. 12–13 and *passim*.

[37] This appears to have been so even before their publication. In 1577, a former colleague of Buchanan's at St Andrews, Archibald Hamilton, a recent convert to Catholicism, published in exile his *De confusione Calvinianiae sectae apud Scotos ... dialogus* (Paris, 1577), in which Buchanan and Knox were identified respectively as the Moses and Aaron of the Scottish Reformation and Buchanan's *De jure* was cited as giving expression to Calvinism's subversive political tenets. This attack on what were evidently perceived as the chief ideologues of reform in Scotland prompted Andrew Melville to commission the ex-Jesuit Thomas Smeaton to write in their defence *Smetonii ad virulentum Hamiltonii apostatae dialogum, orthodoxa responsio* (Edinburgh, 1579). For further details of this, see McKechnie, '*De jure regni*', in Nielson (ed.), *Buchanan: quatercentenary studies*, pp. 211–13, 270.

[38] Melville, *Autobiography and diary*, pp. 120–1; James Kirk (ed.), *The second book of discipline* (Edinburgh, 1981).

between Buchanan and Andrew Melville himself, although it remains largely unexplored, was very close and certainly extended well beyond their common devotion to neo-Latin verse.[39] Melville took a keen interest in the composition and publication of the *History* (himself contributing dedicatory verses to the first edition), and added extensive annotations to his own copy of the work.[40] It is likely that the charge later levelled against him that he made full use of Buchanan's ideas in lecturing at St Andrews on the civil magistrate is perfectly well founded.[41] In fact, such evidence as there is suggests that Buchanan's politics were rapidly internalized by Melville and his clerical colleagues and put to immediate use in their struggle with the king. David Calderwood recorded that in 1592 the king became incensed by ministers lavishing praise on Moray, Knox and Buchanan in their sermons. But when he 'found fault' with the *De jure regni* and 'with sindrie other things in these worthie men', Melville rounded on the king and told him bluntly that 'These men sett the crowne upon his head'. When James protested that the crown 'came by successioun, and not by anie man', Melville replied in terms laden with Buchananesque menace that 'They were the executioners and instruments'.[42] One could ask for no better illustration of either Buchanan's status among the presbyterian clergy or how haunting his ghost must have seemed to his former pupil.

There were good grounds, therefore, for the king in *Basilikon doron* railing against such 'infamous invectives' as the chronicles of Knox and Buchanan and advising his son to implement the legislation of 1584 by which he had sought to censor his old tutor's writings.[43] 'For in that point', he told Prince Henry, 'I would haue you a Pythagorist, to thinke that the very spirites of these archi-belloues of rebellion, haue made transition in them that hoardes their bookes, or maintaines their opinions; punishing them, euen as it were there authours risen againe'.[44] If here the ghosts of Knox and Buchanan are all but made flesh, it is worth noting that the act of 1584 by which James had sought to exorcize his tutor's rebellious spirit was part of a legislative package – the so-called Black Acts – which constituted

[39] McCrie, *Life of Melville*, vol. I, pp. 14–16; McFarlane, *Buchanan*, pp. 255–6, 470.
[40] Melville, *Autobiography and diary*, pp. 120–1. Andrew Melville's copy of the *History* is in St Andrews University Library – the annotations would undoubtedly repay closer study.
[41] McCrie, *Life of Melville*, vol. II, pp. 26–9. According to Durkan and Kirk, *University of Glasgow*, p. 321, Melville was accused at St Andrews 'of causing "the questione of the lawfulnes of deprivatione to be publictlie disputit" in which it was affirmed that "a successioun of kingis was lawfull but that all suld be electit". Such themes, it was felt, were not "questionis disputable in this cuntrey befoir the youth quha certanlie lernis nathing soever in that uneversetie or to tak ane evill opinione of his majestie, his hienes counsell and all their proceidingis quhilk may sumtym produce evill effectis"'.
[42] Calderwood, vol. V, p. 159.   [43] *Basilikon doron*, vol. I, p. 149.
[44] *Ibid.*, vol. I, pp. 149–51.

his first attempt to stem the presbyterian tide which was threatening to engulf him. Thus it was primarily concerned to re-establish the authority of bishops, to forbid unauthorized public meetings (such as those of the general assembly) and to place on the statute book what amounted to an act of royal supremacy.[45] It is testimony to their close association in the king's mind that in the middle of this patently anti-presbyterian series of measures is an act that singles out Buchanan's works – and Buchanan's alone – for censorship. On pain of a fine of £200, all persons possessing copies of either the *De jure regni* or the *History* were to hand them over to the privy council so that they could be 'purgit of the offensive and extraordinare materis'.[46] It would be fascinating to know what, if anything, would have remained once the censor had done his work. But the king's bark was worse than his bite: he lacked the teeth to enforce his legislation.[47] Indeed, the whole anti-presbyterian programme, while it checked the movement's immediate progress, proved premature. It was not until the mid-1590s that James was in a position once again to launch an offensive against his clerical opponents. Nevertheless, the Black Acts of 1584 are still significant in the present context. For they indicate that the king's search for more secure ideological foundations for his rule was intimately related to his attempt to establish in Scotland an equivalent of the English royal supremacy.

IV

When Henry VIII assumed the headship of the church in England, he did so by virtue of his claim to an imperial crown which vested him with complete jurisdictional authority over all matters spiritual as well as temporal within his realm. As John Guy has recently highlighted, however, decisive though the king's actions appear, the Henrician Reformation contained a 'dramatic internal contradiction'.[48] On the one hand, the king's supremacy over the church rested on scriptural, legal and historical arguments designed to prove that the English crown's authority was complete in and of itself. Yet on the other hand, the royal supremacy, like the English

---

[45] *APS*, vol. III, pp. 292ff.

[46] *Ibid.*, vol. III, p. 296. Knox's *History of the Reformation in Scotland* was not of course published until 1587. Had it been in print in 1584 it would presumably have been honoured in much the same way as Buchanan's work.

[47] For a discussion of the ineffectiveness of the king's attempts at censorship, see Julian Goodare, 'Parliament and society in Scotland, 1560–1603' (unpubl. Ph.D. thesis, University of Edinburgh, 1989), ch. 7.

[48] For this and what follows, see John Guy, *Tudor England* (Oxford and New York, 1988), pp. 369–78. Cf. the same author's 'Thomas Cromwell and the intellectual origins of the Henrician Revolution', in J. Guy and A. Fox, *Reassessing the Henrician age: humanism, politics and reform 1500–1550* (Oxford, 1986), pp. 151–78.

Reformation in general, was accomplished only through parliamentary enactment and rested ultimately on the authority of statute. Where then did sovereignty lie in the English commonwealth? With the crown or with the crown-in-parliament? For the most part, just as in practice crown and parliament were obliged to work together, so in theory the primacy of statute could hardly be ignored.[49] Nevertheless, the constitutional ambiguities of the Henrician Reformation ensured that lawyers and divines from Christopher St German in the 1530s to Richard Hooker in the 1590s remained deeply preoccupied with the caesaropapist implications of the royal supremacy.

Their concern was by no means misplaced. The ideology elaborated in defence of the supremacy relied heavily on an image of imperial omnicompetence which might well be used to underwrite the sovereignty of the crown alone.[50] The key figure of Constantine, for example, the first Christian emperor of Rome , but also (or so it was argued) a king of the Britons, was repeatedly invoked as a model of godly kingship to be emulated by his successors on the English throne. Most famously, successive English editions of John Foxe's *Actes and monumentes* lent massive prescriptive legitimacy to the idea of England as an empire and explicitly identified Elizabeth as Constantine *redivivus*. Such historical mythologizing proved powerfully effective as a means of justifying the royal supremacy and emphasizing the majesty – even sanctity – of Elizabeth's rule. But it did so by projecting an image of an English imperial monarch whose power – in the words of the Act in Restraint of Appeals (1533) – was 'plenary, whole and entire'.[51] Of course, apologists such as Foxe were concerned less with the powers of the crown in relation to its subjects than with its powers in relation to the papacy. In their eyes, the monarchy was 'absolute' primarily in the sense of recognizing no superior *external* jurisdiction.[52] Yet might not the idea of empire be interpreted also to validate the crown's perfect and complete authority *within* the realm? Was not the crown 'plenary, whole and entire' in relation to internal as well as external jurisdictions? Might it not be argued,

---

[49] See G. R. Elton, '*Lex terrae victrix*: the triumph of parliamentary law in the sixteenth century', in D. M. Dean and N. L. Jones (eds.), *The parliaments of Elizabethan England* (Oxford, 1990), pp. 15–36.

[50] For various perspectives on what follows, see Frances Yates, *Astraea: the imperial theme in the sixteenth century* (London, 1975), pp. 29–87; William Haller, *Foxe's 'Book of martyrs' and the elect nation* (London, 1963); Roy Strong, *The cult of Elizabeth* (London, 1977); and J. N. King, *Tudor royal iconography: literature and art in an age of religious crisis* (Princeton, 1989), esp. ch. 3.

[51] G. R. Elton (ed.), *The Tudor constitution: documents and commentary* (2nd edn, Cambridge, 1982), p. 353.

[52] Although focused on a later period, usage of the term 'absolute' is usefully analysed in James Daly, 'The idea of absolute monarchy in seventeenth-century England', *Historical Journal*, 21 (1978), 227–50; cf. Burns, 'The idea of absolutism', in Miller (ed.), *Absolutism in seventeenth-century France*, pp. 21–42.

then, that the English imperial monarchy was 'free' and 'absolute' in the further sense of possessing complete, perfect and, by definition, indivisible sovereignty? It was questions of this sort which later Elizabethan divines, among them Richard Bancroft and Hadrian Saravia, began to explore in the last decade of the sixteenth century. They did so, however, less in response to any threat posed by the papacy than in response to what they saw as a resurgence of support for presbyterianism within the English church and commonwealth.[53] In this context, Scotland's monarchy, the perceived victim of the overweening ambition of the Melvillian clergy, was to play a key polemical role in the development among English conformists of the first fully fledged theory of the divine right of kings.

But before exploring the place of the Melvillians in the demonology of Elizabethan Anglicans, it is important to review the impact of imperial thinking in Scotland itself. In fact, as is argued elsewhere in this volume, its influence was a good deal less pervasive than is sometimes assumed.[54] While it is true that earlier Stewart monarchs had been attracted to imperial symbolism, there is nothing to suggest that this was prompted by anything other than a desire to ensure that the Scottish monarchy was seen as the equal of its counterparts elsewhere. Moreover, in the decades following James V's death in 1542, two factors conspired to invest Scottish political thinking with a profoundly *anti*-imperial bias. Firstly, the unionist propaganda generated by the 'Edwardian Moment' made it all but impossible to dissociate the idea of empire from the English claim to suzerainty over Scotland. Just as unionists commonly legitimized their visions of Britain by recourse to England's historic claim to lordship over Scotland, so Somerset's military occupation of the Lowlands made brutally clear that the imperial crown bequeathed by Constantine to his successors was first and foremost a symbol of English hegemony. Secondly, when reformation was finally achieved in Scotland in 1560, it was spearheaded by Protestant ministers who, however strong their desire for amity with England, remained extremely suspicious of an English-style royal supremacy. Imperial language in general and Constantine in particular are notably absent from the literature of the Scottish Reformation. Conversely, the idea that church and state were separate powers with separate jurisdictions is plainly in evidence in the thought of the first generation of Scottish Protestants. The theory of the two kingdoms was not a novelty introduced to Scotland by Andrew Melville. On the contrary, the real innovator was the Regent Morton who, two years before Melville returned to Scotland in

---

[53] See Peter Lake, *Anglicans and puritans? Presbyterianism and English conformist thought from Whitgift to Hooker* (London, 1988), esp. pp. 53–66, 129–39.
[54] For what follows, see chapter 7 below.

1574, in pursuit of a policy of conformity with England, attempted to impose the royal supremacy on a Scottish kirk already stubbornly committed to maintaining its independence of the civil magistrate. When Buchanan in his *History* curtly dismissed Constantine – the 'meek Moses' of Foxe's *Actes and monumentes* – as the bastard son of a Roman general's concubine, he was articulating a widespread Scottish antipathy to the idea of empire which was at once both thoroughly patriotic and essentially presbyterian.[55]

In the light of this, it is perhaps appropriate that the publication of Buchanan's 'infamous invective' should have coincided with the Ruthven raid of August 1582. For this palace revolution, involving the seizure of the king by a group of disaffected aristocrats with presbyterian sympathies, appeared to herald the complete triumph of the Melvillians. Yet less than a year later, in June 1583, James escaped his captors and, aided by his then favourite, James Stewart, earl of Arran, initiated a conservative backlash which resulted in the flight of Melville and many of his associates to England. The Black Acts (so-called of course only by the presbyterians) were intended to give statutory backing to the new royal policy towards the church and their main thrust was summed up in a clause which confirmed 'the royall power and auctoritie over all statis alsweill spirituall as temporal within this realme in the persoun of the kingis maiestie our souerane lord his airis and successouris'.[56] There is no reason to doubt that James himself, now almost eighteen, fully supported this assertion of the crown's supremacy over the church as well as the state. But the man who sought to lend it intellectual substance and legitimacy was Patrick Adamson, an able if opportunistic cleric whom Morton had appointed archbishop of St Andrews in 1576 and who had been fighting an increasingly vicious battle with the presbyterians in the general assembly ever since his elevation to the primatial see.[57] In the autumn of 1583, Adamson had embarked on a mission to England with the intention of forging closer links with Archbishop Whitgift and seeking his co-operation in condemning the subversive views of the presbyterians.[58] Although he met with a cool reception from the English ecclesiastical establishment, his time in London was not entirely wasted. For when he returned to Scotland in the spring of 1584, shortly before the Black Acts passed through parliament, he came armed with an understanding of imperial kingship which was precisely what was required to underwrite the crown's assertion of supremacy over the kirk.

---

[55] Buchanan, *History*, vol. I, p. 199.   [56] *APS*, vol. III, pp. 292–3.

[57] The best account of Adamson's career is in D. G. Mullan, *Episcopacy in Scotland: the history of an idea 1560–1638* (Edinburgh, 1986), ch. 4.

[58] For details of Adamson's visit, see Gordon Donaldson, 'The attitude of Whitgift and Bancroft to the Scottish church', in his *Scottish church history* (Edinburgh, 1985), pp. 164–77.

Although not spelled out in as much detail as one would like, Adamson's views were made public in 1585 in a brief defence of the Black Acts entitled *A declaratioun of the kings maiesties intentioun and meaning toward the lait actis of parliament.* With specific reference to the Ruthven episode, he began by attacking the presbyterians in general and Andrew Melville in particular for preaching 'seditious & factious sermonis and steiring vp of the people to rebellion aganis their natiue King'. It was, he declared, 'the dewtie of ane faithfull Preachour of the Gospell . . . to exhort the people to the obedience of their natiue King . . . not be popular sermonis . . . to trouble and perturbe the countrey'.[59] The king no doubt was delighted to hear it. But more importantly Adamson then chose to confront head-on the Melvillian doctrines of the two kingdoms and ministerial parity and to launch in reply a spirited defence of both the royal supremacy and episcopacy. In respect of each of the latter, his case ultimately came to rest on the example of the primitive church under the Christian Roman emperors. Thus in defending the royal supremacy, he argued that it was 'a great errour to affirme . . . that Princes and Magistrats hes only power to take ordour in civile effaires', and went on to ground his belief not only on the authority of Scripture, but on 'the haill history of the primitiue kirk, in the quhilk, the Emperours iugeit ouer the Bishoppes of *Rome*, deposit them from their seates, [and] appointit Iudges to cognosce and decyde in causis Ecclesiasticall'.[60] Likewise, in defending the role of bishops within the church, he argued that episcopacy was established 'from the dayis of the Apostles' and that it became 'his Maiestie, as *Eusebius* wrytis of *Constantinus* the great, to be ane bishop of Bishops, and vniuersall Bishop within his Realme, in so far as his Maiestie should appoint every ane to discharge his dewtie'.[61] Such remarks make it a matter of regret that a further book in which Adamson intended that his case would be 'sufficiently prouen and verifeit' was never written.[62] Nevertheless, slight though it is, the *Declaratioun* leaves no doubt that Adamson was thinking along the Constantinian lines already so familiar in England.[63]

In 1585, however, James's imperial hour had not yet dawned. In Scotland

---

[59] Patrick Adamson, *A declaratioun of the kings maiesties intentioun and meaning toward the lait actis of parliament* (Edinburgh, 1585), sig. Aiii r–v.

[60] *Ibid.*, sig. Aiiii r.   [61] *Ibid.*, sig. Biiii v–Ci r.   [62] *Ibid.*, sig. Aiiii r–v.

[63] Certainly, that is how the presbyterian minister, James Melville, interpreted it. He lamented in his diary that once free of Buchanan's tutelage the young king – 'sa weill a brought up prince' – had been 'miserablie corrupted' by Arran and Adamson. While Arran was accused of putting 'the opinion of absolute powar in his Maiestie's head', Adamson was credited with inculcating the heinous view 'That a Christian king sould be the chief gouernour of the Kirk, and behovit to have Bischops under him, to hald all in order, conforme to antiquitie and maist flurissing esteat of the Christian Kirk under the best Emperor, Constantine. And the discipline of the Kirk of Scotland [i.e., presbyterianism] could nocht stand with a frie kingdome and monarchie, sic as was his Maiestie's in Scotland'. Melville, *Autobiography and diary*, pp. 119–20.

Adamson's proved a lone voice and one which was all but immediately drowned out, not so much by presbyterian rebuttals of the *Declaratioun*,[64] as by the collapse of Arran's administration shortly after its publication. The *Declaratioun*, indeed, might well have been forgotten altogether had it not been published in London under the more sensational title, *Treason pretendit against the king of Scots*.[65] It was the appearance of this edition which led to its inclusion in the 1587 version of Raphael Holinshed's chronicles where it was billed with some justification as an authoritative statement of the king's own views.[66] Given the fluidity of the Scottish political scene, however, it was unwise to take anything for granted. As a rule, James would have appreciated being told that the Ruthven raiders had erred mightily when they dared 'to lift up their sword or word against him, who being a God in earth, presenteth the Majesty of the God of Heaven'.[67] But such unctuous flattery belied to the point of risibility the reality of James's position in Scotland. For the Lord's anointed was even then in the process of patching up an alliance with the presbyterian clergy in order to mollify their aristocratic allies and provide a much-needed counterweight to the machinations of the Catholic earls.

It is unnecessary here to describe the complex political manoeuvrings which led the king to abandon the pretensions of the Black Acts and to pursue instead a policy of conciliation towards the presbyterians which was to last for the next decade.[68] More pertinent is the fact that it was against this background that in February 1589 an ambitious young English cleric, Richard Bancroft, preached his celebrated anti-presbyterian Paul's Cross sermon on the theme – taken from 1 John 4.1 – that 'many false prophets are gone out into the world'.[69] Prominent among those false prophets, their

---

[64] An 'Answere to the Declaratioun', possibly written by Andrew Melville, was followed by a 'Dialogue between Zelator, Temporizar and Palemon', probably written by James Melville. Both are in Calderwood, vol. IV, pp. 274–339. Cf. Mullan, *Episcopacy in Scotland*, p. 60.

[65] *Treason pretendit against the king of Scots, by certaine lordes and gentlemen, whose names hereafter followe* (London, 1585). As this suggests, the sensationalized title was justified by the inclusion of a brief (and extremely garbled) list of those involved in the Ruthven raid.

[66] See *The Scottish chronicle ... by Mr. Raphael Holinshed* (2 vols., Arbroath, 1805), vol. II, pp. 432–41. As 'Holinshed' or his editors put it in terms which seem ludicrously incongruous given the reality of James's position in Scotland: the king 'shewed himself of a rare and good disposition, in that he would humble himself beneath the majestie of his crown, politikelie to render a reason to his neighbour and to his subjects of his dealings towards such as were under his government, sith he was not bound thereunto ... ' (*ibid.*, vol. II, p. 432).

[67] *Ibid.*, vol. II, p. 441.

[68] A prime mover behind the policy was James's secretary John Maitland, who remained a patron of the presbyterians until his fall from power in 1596. See Maurice Lee, Jr, *John Maitland of Thirlestane and the foundations of Stewart despotism in Scotland* (Princeton, 1959).

[69] Richard Bancroft, *A sermon preached at Paule's Cross the 9 of Februarie ... Anno 1588* (London, 1589). For further details of the impact of the sermon on Scotland, see Mullan, *Episcopacy in Scotland*, pp. 67–70, and Donaldson, *Scottish church history*, pp. 170–7.

influence allegedly eroding the stability of the established church in England, were the presbyterian clergy of Scotland. Making extensive use of Adamson's *Declaratioun*, Bancroft painted a terrifying picture of the Melvillians as seditious traitors whose subversive politics – founded on 'the most strange and rebellious propositions stifly maintained, dilated and amplified' in the works of Beza, Mornay and Buchanan – posed as grave a threat to the English crown as they did to the beleaguered king of Scots.[70] In framing the Black Acts, argued Bancroft, the king had rightly perceived that the 'ecclesiasticall tyranny' of the presbyterians was 'the mother of all faction, confusion, sedition and rebellion: that it was an introduction to Anabaptisme and popularitie: that it tended to the overthrow of his state and Realme, and to the decaie of his crowne'.[71] Moreover, and here he struck an acutely sensitive Melvillian nerve, Bancroft even dared to suggest that the presbyterians were deluding themselves if they thought that the king had truly abandoned the view of the royal supremacy adumbrated in the Black Acts and defended in the *Declaratioun*. 'For the king, he is not altered ...', declared Bancroft knowingly: 'His crowne and their soveraigntie will not agree togither.'[72] He was almost certainly correct. Nevertheless, trying desperately not to offend his presbyterian allies, James found himself in the embarrassing position of having formally to repudiate Adamson's work while condoning instead the publication of a bitter attack on his future archbishop of Canterbury by the Melvillian minister John 'The Thunderer' Davidson.[73]

None of this was to deter Bancroft, who returned to the fray in 1593 with a further two works in which he again savaged the Scottish presbyterians and warned his countrymen of the grave dangers that 'Scottish Genevating' posed to the English church and commonwealth.[74] In particular, he laid great emphasis on the Melvillians' adherence to the Genevan political tenets of resistance and deposition associated with the names of Knox and Buchanan: 'such strange & seditious doctrine' as tended to 'the overthrow of the freest and most absolute Monarchies that are or can be in Christendome'.[75] As this suggests, by 1593 Bancroft's fear of the destabilizing influence of the presbyterians (whether real or merely rhetorical) was leading him towards assertions of divine-right absolutism. But Bancroft's polemical style was largely negative: having smeared the presbyterians as seditious traitors, he

---

[70] Bancroft, *A sermon*, p. 78.   [71] *Ibid.*, pp. 74–5.   [72] *Ibid.*, p. 75.

[73] *D. Bancrofts rashnes in rayling against the church of Scotland ...* (Edinburgh, 1590). Reprinted in the *Miscellany of the Wodrow Society I* (Wodrow Society, 1844), pp. 466–520, together with much of the material relating to Bancroft's sermon described above.

[74] *A survay of the pretended holy discipline ...* (London, 1593), and particularly Book I of his *Daungerous positions and proceedings, published and practised within this Iland of Brytain ...* (London, 1593) which is entirely devoted to the evils of the Scottish presbyterians.

[75] Bancroft, *Daungerous positions and proceedings*, p. 33.

offered little in the way of substantive argument for his own belief in the pre-eminent virtues of episcopacy, the royal supremacy and unstinting obedience to the crown.[76] There were, however, other Anglican divines who were better able to use the populist politics of the presbyterians as a springboard to a reasoned defence of the divine right of kings. Hadrian Saravia, Dutch by birth but long since settled in England, had as early as 1590 answered the *jure divino* claims of the presbyterians with arguments for the apostolic origins of episcopacy.[77] This he followed up, again in 1593, with a substantial volume *De imperandi authoritate et Christiana obedientia* in which, in the course of refuting the theories of popular sovereignty associated with both Protestant and Catholic radicals, he developed what Johann Sommerville has described as 'the best and most complete defence of divine right kingship to be produced in Elizabethan England'.[78] Indeed, Saravia spelled out in detail many of the arguments which James was to present as axiomatic in his *Trew lawe of free monarchies*. This is not to say that Saravia was the king's prime source for his divine-right theory. It is by no means certain that he had even read the Dutchman's work. Nevertheless, it is clear that by the early 1590s the king had valuable intellectual allies in England whose understanding of the nature and extent of imperial authority was unreservedly absolutist.[79]

Even if James was aware of the writings of Bancroft and Saravia, however, in 1593 he was in no position to take advantage of them. The previous year he had been obliged to lend the presbyterian polity in Scotland unprecedented statutory backing in the form of what became known (in contrast to the legislation of 1584) as the Golden Act. The Melvillians were understandably exultant and, for the next few years, revelled in their freedom to lecture the king with impunity. During this period, at the nadir of his fortunes in Scotland, James might well have concurred with Figgis's description of his authority as 'a mockery before the insolent representatives of ecclesiastical bigotry'. But between 1595 and 1597 circumstances changed very rapidly. Not only did these years see the king finally settle his differences with the Catholic earls, but they also saw the last of the maverick earl of Bothwell, an

---

[76] For similar comments on Bancroft's reticence, see Lake, *Anglicans and puritans?*, p. 131.
[77] For details of his career and thought, see Willem Nijenhuis, *Adrianus Saravia (c. 1532–1613): Dutch Calvinist, first reformed defender of the episcopal church on the basis of the ius divinum* (Leiden, 1980).
[78] J. P. Sommerville, 'Richard Hooker, Hadrian Saravia, and the advent of the divine right of kings', *History of Political Thought*, 4 (1983), 229–45, at p. 237.
[79] An exploration of the possible sources for James's ideas is well beyond the scope of this paper. However, in addition to English writers such as Bancroft and Saravia, he could readily draw on the writings of French theorists such as Jean Bodin as well as the Scottish 'anti-monarchomachs' discussed by J.H. Burns in the next chapter and Scottish legal thinking as discussed by Brian Levack in chapter 9 below.

acute source of political instability as well as a constant threat to the person of the king ever since his indictment for treason following the witchcraft trials of 1591. Moreover, with Bothwell in exile, the presbyterians lost their last and least reliable noble patron and, without aristocratic protection, the radicals in the kirk were a good deal more vulnerable than they appear to have realized.[80] The key moment when the tide turned for James is generally taken to be the mysterious Edinburgh riot of December 1596 which the king deftly turned to his advantage by summarily imprisoning the ministers whom he alleged had instigated it. But just as important was the general assembly held in Perth in February 1597 – an assembly which, contrary to all its kirk-controlled predecessors, was not only summoned by the king, but whose agenda was actually set by the king. James, in fact, took the unprecedented step of authorizing the publication of a slim pamphlet detailing *The questions to be resolvit at the convention of estaits and generall assemblie.* In an explanatory preface, his blatant interference in the affairs of Christ's kingdom was justified on the grounds that he was following 'the lovable Example of the Christian Emperours of the primitive Kirk'.[81] The echo of Adamson's *Declaratioun* and of the whole panoply of imperial thought and imagery is unmistakable. As one modern commentator has put it, the assembly of 1597 'was to see a new godly Constantine presiding at a Scottish Nicaea'.[82]

The most astonishing thing about these imperial pretensions is not that James advanced them, but that he was able to realize them. The Melvillians protested vehemently against the king's interference in the kirk's affairs, seeing his claim to have the right to call an assembly, to determine where and when it should be held and even to set its agenda as the thin end of the Erastian wedge. They were of course correct – that was exactly what it was – and to their utter dismay and future discomfiture James was able so to manipulate the terms of the Golden Act as to achieve his ends. As James Melville inveighed in his diary, hitherto the purpose of general assemblies had been to determine how 'Chryst's kingdome might stand in halines and friedome', but now their purpose would be to determine 'how Kirk and Relligioun may be framed to the polytic esteat of a frie Monarchie, and to advance and promot the grandeur of man, and supream absolut authoritie in all caussis, and over all persones, alsweill Ecclesiasticall as Civill'.[83] The king could hardly have put it better himself. Although John Davidson reminded him in 1598 that he attended the general assembly not as an

[80] See Keith Brown, 'In search of the godly magistrate in Reformation Scotland', *Journal of Ecclesiastical History*, 40 (1989), 553–81, esp. pp. 579–80.
[81] *The questions to be resolvit ...* (Edinburgh, 1597), p. 2.
[82] Mullan, *Episcopacy in Scotland*, p. 81.
[83] Melville, *Autobiography and diary*, p. 414.

emperor but as a Christian, James had good reason to think that he might after all be Constantine *redivivus*.[84]

V

The taming of the presbyterians and the re-establishment of diocesan episcopacy took more than another decade to complete. With hindsight, however, 1597 emerges as the crucial moment when the tide turned for James. The publication of the *Trew lawe of free monarchies* the following year was clearly no coincidence. It was a deliberate attempt by the king to lend intellectual substance to his sudden reassertion of authority over the kirk and, more broadly, a bid to provide himself at last with the ideological underpinnings which his kingship so desperately needed. A full analysis of the *Trew lawe* is well beyond the scope of this chapter.[85] The purpose here has been simply to recover the immediate context and longer-term pressures which led James to espouse a theory of the divine right of kings. Nevertheless, it is worth concluding with a brief glance at the arguments he rehearsed in the *Trew lawe*. For, despite his avowed intention of laying down 'the true groundes' of obedience 'without wasting time upon refuting the adversaries',[86] it is not difficult to discern who his principal opponents were. If his appeals to Scripture proved that he was as adept as any presbyterian at invoking biblical 'case law' to suit his needs, the two other sets of arguments on which he rested his case – the fundamental laws of the kingdom and the universal laws of nature – were patently directed at the ghost of his former tutor.[87]

In respect of the laws of nature, rather than following Buchanan in closely identifying natural law with reason and virtue, James fell back on the correspondences between patriarchal and political authority and on 'the similitude of the head & the body'. 'The King towardes his people is rightly compared to a father of children', he argued, 'and to a head of a bodie

[84] Calderwood, vol. V, p. 683.
[85] Such a study would also need to take into account the *Basilikon doron* and perhaps also the *Daemonologie* of 1597, for which see Stuart Clark, 'King James's *Daemonologie*: witchcraft and kingship', in Sydney Anglo (ed.), *The damned art: essays in the literature of witchcraft* (London, 1977), pp. 156–81.
[86] *The trew lawe of free monarchies*, in James Craigie and Alexander Law (eds.), *Minor prose works of King James VI and I* (STS, 1982), pp. 57–82, at p. 58.
[87] 'First then, I will set downe the true groundes, whereupon I am to builde, out of the Scriptures, since *Monarchie* is the true paterne of Diuinitie . . . : next, from the fundamentall Laws of our own kingdom, which nearest must concerne vs: thirdly, from the law of Nature, by diuers similitudes drawen out of the same . . . '. *Ibid.*, p. 60. For some fascinating insights into Buchanan's and James's understanding of natural and fundamental law, see above ch. 4.

composed of diuers members'. Just as it was 'monstrous and vnnaturall' for sons to rise up against their fathers, and just as the body could hardly cut off its head 'for the weale of it', so it followed that subjects could not resist, depose or kill their kings.[88] But important though such similitudes were to James, he struck his most telling blows against Buchanan when he turned his attention to the fundamental laws of the kingdom. For while he agreed with Buchanan that the first Scottish monarch had been Fergus I, he flatly denied that he was an elected king bound by laws made by the people. On the contrary, he insisted that Fergus had ruled by right of conquest; that it was he rather than his subjects who 'first established the estate and forme of gouernment'; and that it followed, 'of necessitie, that the Kinges were the authors & makers of the lawes, and not the lawes of the Kings'.[89] If there was an ancient Scottish constitution, therefore, it had been established, not by the people's consent, but by the king's right of conquest.[90] The king was, in effect, above the law and, though he might choose to rule according to it, 'yet is hee not bound thereto but of his good wil, and for good example-giving to his subjectes'.[91] To be sure, the king swore at his coronation to discharge his office 'honourably and truely', but it did not follow that, if he broke his promise, the people might pass judgement on him. No man, argued James, could be 'both partie and iudge in his owne cause'; if a contract existed between the king and his people, therefore, 'since God is the onely judge betwixt the two parties contractours, the cognition and reuenge must onely apperteine to him'.[92] Finally, according to James, the people as well as the king were bound by an oath of 'duty & allegeance'. In this case, however, it was not simply to an individual prince, but also to his 'lawfull heires & posteritie' that subjects swore obedience. Hereditary monarchy was established 'by the olde fundamentall lawes of the kingdome' and, as kings came to the throne 'by byrth, [and] not by any right of coronation', 'so to refuse him, or intrude an other' was 'to expell & put out their righteous King'.[93]

The *Trew lawe* is more a series of propositions than a fully reasoned defence of the divine right of kings. But it was perhaps no less effective for

---

[88] *Ibid.*, pp. 74–5. The king concluded: 'And whether these similitudes represent better the office of a King: or the offices of Maisters or Deacons of craftes, or Doctors in Phisike (which jolly comparisons are vsed by such writers, as mayntaine the contrarie proposition) I leaue it also to the readers discretion.' Perhaps needless to say, Buchanan had used these 'jolly comparisons' in his *De jure regni*.

[89] *Ibid.*, p. 70.

[90] The same argument was, of course, applicable in England and the king's reference to William I – who 'gaue the law & took none' – must have chilled the blood of common lawyers and parliamentarians. *Ibid.*, p. 71.

[91] *Ibid.*, pp. 72–3.   [92] *Ibid.*, pp. 78–9.   [93] *Ibid.*, p. 80.

that in demonstrating, at least to the king's satisfaction, 'the true groundes of the mutuall duetie and alleageance betwixt a free and absolute *Monarche*, and his people'.[94] In legitimizing his kingship in this way, James had effectively completed a process of ideological polarization which set the terms of political debate for the following century and more. If he had found an answer to Buchanan, however, his dream of 1622 suggests that he never completely escaped the shadow cast over his rule by his former tutor. In fact, Buchanan was still capable of rising from his grave to tease and torment James's son and successor. Charles I is unlikely ever to have had nightmares featuring his father's nemesis, but one Scottish royalist, Sir James Turner, wrote of the outbreak of the 1638 revolution that Buchanan's name was so universally invoked that 'I imagined his ghost was returned to earth to meander a little among the covenanters'.[95] There is no small irony in the fact that, ten years later, when Oliver Cromwell tried to persuade the Scots – unsuccessfully – to acquiesce in the execution of their king, he is said to have 'entered into a long discourse of the nature of regal power according to the principles of Mariana and Buchanan'.[96]

[94] *Ibid.*, p. 60.
[95] Quoted in Edward J. Cowan, *Montrose: for covenant and king* (London, 1977), p. 14.
[96] W. C. Abbott, *The writings and speeches of Oliver Cromwell* (4 vols., Cambridge, Mass., 1937–47), vol. I, p. 746.

6 George Buchanan and the anti-monarchomachs

J. H. Burns

The subject of this chapter is the Scottish response to the challenge offered by George Buchanan's radical political doctrine in *De jure regni apud Scotos*.[1] It is both true and important that the debate precipitated by Buchanan's dialogue was in the nature of the case European, not merely national – both the wider political significance of the deposition of Mary Queen of Scots, which Buchanan sought to justify, and the celebrity of the man who advanced that justification ensured this. It is also both true and significant that each of the three writers dealt with here was a Scot in exile, having had substantial experience of a wider intellectual and political world than was afforded them in their native land. Two of them, indeed – Adam Blackwood and William Barclay – spent so large a part of their lives outside Scotland as to be, arguably, more French than Scots in formation and outlook. Scots however they were and remained, and they were acutely aware of the specifically Scottish dimensions of the polemical controversy in which they chose to become engaged.

It is to be borne in mind that the precipitating cause of this particular flurry of controversial activity was the eventual publication of Buchanan's *De jure regni* in 1579. It is true that the dialogue had been written about a dozen years before that, and quite soon after the political events in Scotland which culminated in the deposition of Mary Stewart and her replacement by her infant son as James VI. The book did, to be sure, circulate quite extensively in manuscript in the late 1560s and the 1570s. We know this from Buchanan's correspondence and from other sources. It was, however, its appearance in print – in the same year, as it happened, as the *Vindiciae contra tyrannos* – that brought the controversy fully into the public domain. The three participants to be discussed here were, in the order in which their

---

[1] A modified and somewhat abridged version of this paper appears in Nicholas Phillipson and Quentin Skinner (eds.), *Political discourse in early-modern Britain* (Cambridge, 1993), pp. 3–22. For a much earlier examination of the subject, see J. H. Burns, 'Three Scots Catholic critics of George Buchanan', *IR*, 1 (1950), 92–109.

replies to Buchanan were published, Adam Blackwood (*Pro regibus apologia*, Poitiers, 1581); Ninian Winzet (*Velitatio in Georgium Buchananum*, Ingolstadt, 1582); and William Barclay – the coiner, it is worth observing, of the term 'monarchomach' (*De regno et regali potestate*, Paris, 1600). It should be noted in passing that Barclay's response to Buchanan is mainly (though not only) to be found in the first two of the six books of the *De regno*, which were apparently written, though not published, at much the same time as the Blackwood and Winzet texts.

There is an obvious case for following the order of publication in an analysis of the debate; and certainly Barclay must be left to the end, if only because, as we shall see, he drew extensively on Winzet's work. On the other hand, there are preponderant grounds for considering Winzet first. There is, to start with, the fact that, of his three Scottish adversaries, Winzet is the closest to Buchanan in time. Born in 1518 or 1519, he can be regarded – though such matters are always to some extent problematic – as belonging to the same generation as Buchanan, who was born in 1506. Blackwood (born in 1539) and Barclay (born about 1546) clearly belong to a later generation, with a decisively different perspective on events and ideas. The substance which underlies this point of formal chronology is, in particular, the fact that Winzet – like Buchanan himself, but unlike Blackwood and Barclay – had considerable adult experience of pre-Reformation Scotland and, more generally, of a Europe in which the transformations wrought by the religious conflict were still in their comparatively early stages. Again, the fact that Winzet had at least one personal encounter with Buchanan (at the time when they were both at Mary's Holyrood court), while coincidental in itself, is symbolic of a different kind of controversial confrontation. Winzet also had an immediate experience of polemical hand-to-hand fighting (as one might call it) quite unknown to his younger associates in the controversy with Buchanan. His personal debates with leading Protestants, including John Knox, at the critical moment in the Reformation struggle in Scotland (beginning when Winzet was still teaching in the burgh school of Linlithgow, strategically located as it was in relation to Edinburgh, Stirling and Glasgow) formed the prelude to the notable vernacular pamphleteering which eventually led to his seeking refuge abroad. Even after that, his involvement in affairs was to be of a different order from anything experienced by Blackwood or Barclay. Acting for a time as Mary's confessor during her captivity in England, he was closely associated with John Lesley, bishop of Ross, the indefatigable if less than resolute or reliable Marian schemer of the 1570s. It was thanks to Lesley that Winzet spent the latter part of his life as a Benedictine abbot, presiding over the first of the medieval *Schottenklöster* to be definitively if debatably taken over by Scottish monks in the last quarter of the sixteenth century.[2]

The man who, in his late fifties, became abbot of Ratisbon in 1577 was in many respects an unusual figure. He was by then a doctor in theology of the new university of Douai; but his formal study of the subject had lasted for no more than two years. Ten years before that, in 1565, he had studied in the arts faculty of Paris, where he subsequently taught. The university phase in his career, however, had begun only when he was already in his mid-forties. In his native Scotland, so far as can be ascertained, he had had no formal education after leaving school at (we may suppose) the age of fourteen or fifteen. He was ordained priest and acted as a notary; but the most interesting aspect of his life before the Reformation crisis, as schoolteacher and chaplain in Linlithgow, arises from fragmentary but significant indications of his having been one of a group of reform-minded Catholics actively interested in studying and exchanging ideas during the long years of the council of Trent. At the level of what we would call 'higher education', it was as a self-educated man that Winzet threw himself into the world of controversy; and it was as one whose interests and orientation were primarily theological that he re-entered that world some twenty years later.[3]

It must be emphasized that Winzet's decision to turn once more, and now with the technical scholarly equipment he had lacked in the early 1560s, to the polemical debate with the Protestants antedated his reading of Buchanan's *De jure regni*. In Lent 1581 (8 February–26 March) he had completed his *Flagellum sectariorum* when he encountered Buchanan's dialogue.[4] He appears to have set to work at once on his 'skirmish' against the *De jure regni*, and the *Flagellum* and *Velitatio* were published together, with continuous pagination, in the following year. In the most direct and immediate sense, then, Winzet deals with Buchanan's political ideas in the context of a general rejection of Protestant doctrine. We shall find a similar conjunction

---

[2] For this complex subject, see Mark Dilworth, *The Scots in Franconia: a century of monastic history* (Edinburgh, 1974), ch. 1 and the sources cited there.

[3] The account of Winzet's life by J. K. Hewison in his edition of *Certain tractates* (2 vols., STS, 1888–90) needs extensive correction and supplementation; but these are not yet systematically available in published work. See Dilworth, *Scots in Franconia*, as index, esp. pp. 22–31; and the same author's 'Ninian Winzet: some new material', *IR*, 24 (1973), 125–32. For Winzet's pre-Reformation contacts, see John Durkan, 'The cultural background in sixteenth-century Scotland', in David McRoberts (ed.), *Essays on the Scottish Reformation* (Glasgow, 1962), p. 315 at n. 247.

[4] *Flagellum sectariorum, qui religionis praetextu seditionem iam in Caesarem, aut in alios orthodoxos Principes excitare student ... Niniano Winzeto Renfroo ... Autore* (Ingolstadt, 1582); *Velitatio in Georgium Buchananum circa Dialogum quem scripsit de iure regni apud Scotos ... Niniano Winzeto ... Autore* (Ingolstadt, 1582). The dedication of the *Velitatio* is dated 15 May 1582. Winzet mentions (p. 153) that it was the second (1580) edition of Buchanan's dialogue that had reached him.

in Blackwood; and indeed the point is part of the common ground shared by all those who defended kingship against the 'monarchomach' attack. But where Blackwood and Barclay see a case to be argued primarily in juristic terms, Winzet sees above all an issue in political theology. The crux comes for him, whether he is concerned primarily with the church or with temporal government, in the question of authority. From the outset, in the situation which followed from the Reformation Parliament of 1560, Winzet came back repeatedly to that question, demanding to know by what authority the ministers of the newly (and precariously) established kirk preached and taught and administered those sacraments they still held to be valid.[5] The matter still preoccupied him when he wrote the *Flagellum sectariorum*. There, again, Winzet is still taking posthumous issue with Knox as the leader of the 'ministers of sedition'.[6] Not surprisingly he saw Buchanan's dialogue in essentially the same light.

For Winzet, then, authority in Christian society was a continuum extending across the entire structure, whether in its spiritual or in its temporal aspect. When this seamless garment was rent asunder by heresy and rebellion, it did not matter whether the first tear was made, so to speak, at the edge pertaining to kingship or at that which represented the traditional authority of the Catholic church. It was throughout a divinely constituted order that was being violated; and in this sense Winzet's political argument is a defence of the divine right of kingship against an onslaught which is as sacrilegious as it is seditious. To compare the *Velitatio* with the dialogue it attacked is to be struck especially by the contrasting ways in which biblical themes are handled. For Buchanan the argument from, or about, Scripture is subordinate and sometimes seems almost perfunctory; Winzet introduces that argument early and develops it elaborately. A very substantial part of the *Velitatio* is devoted to scriptural exegesis and to theological exposition based largely on patristic sources. Winzet's professional preoccupation with such matters takes him at times, indeed, some considerable distance from anything that was strictly relevant to Buchanan's case. A good deal of space is given over to such matters as the problematic character of *sola scriptura* theology in general and the nature of the Eucharist in particular.[7]

The political theme is not lost sight of, however. Much of the discussion

---

[5] See esp. *The buke of four scoir thre questionis*, in *Certain tractates*, ed. Hewison, vol. I.
[6] See esp. *Flagellum*, pp. 20–1, where Winzet, *inter alia*, gives a Latin translation of the propositions Knox intended to develop in the abortive *Second blast of the trumpet*. Winzet refers to these again in the dedicatory epistle of the *Velitatio* (sig. xx2v), where he has a marginal note 'Ioan. Nox alias Knox' (who becomes 'ille tenebricosus Nox' later, on p. 208).
[7] Winzet indicates his priorities in the dedication of the *Velitatio*: '. . . ego pro meo munere et loco, caeteris fere omnibus omissis, ea maxime quae ex Dei verbo, verisque illis veteribus Dei verbi interpretibus ab eo citatis, aut a iure nostri regni pro nouo hoc regno & imperio populi in Regem stabiliendo citat . . . agitare statui'.

is concerned with the evidence afforded by the Bible, and especially by the Old Testament, as to the nature of kingship. On that evidence, of course, God had expressly authorized and established royal rule over His chosen people. By so doing, according to a powerful tradition of Christian thinking to which Winzet firmly attaches himself, God had consecrated kings and kingship in such a way as to secure them against the kind of attack Buchanan had launched. That attack culminated in the justification and indeed the advocacy of tyrannicide. In Buchanan's argument, misgovernment, or even misconduct by a ruler in what might be regarded as matters of private, personal morality, constituted tyranny and made the delinquent king – or queen – a public enemy. For an individual citizen to kill such a self-declared criminal was legitimate and indeed praiseworthy. This is passionately rejected by Winzet. 'O tyrannical tyrannicide!' he exclaims: no one, amid all 'the pride, barbarity, and cruelty of the Calvinian spirit' had displayed its essential 'tyranny' more clearly than Buchanan.[8] In rebutting the attempt to justify the killing of a king even if his unjust rule does indeed amount to tyranny, Winzet relies in particular upon a scriptural instance to which he had already had recourse in his earlier vernacular writings. This was the treatment of Saul by David, his refusal to 'touch the Lord's anointed'.[9] The rite of anointing is crucial for Winzet as for other defenders of kingship in this period; and it confirms the impression that we are indeed dealing here with a 'divine-right' response to 'monarchomach' radicalism.

This being the case, and especially in view of the theological orientation of Winzet's thought, it is not surprising to find in the *Velitatio* an insistence on the parallelism between royal and priestly power. Kings, Winzet argues, are in political matters what priests are in matters divine – a kind of 'earthly gods' (*dii quidam terrestres*): they, like priests, are established by God as judges of His faithful people, and as such are answerable only to God.[10] That this sacred character should be combined with moral excellence is of course desirable; but such excellence – the essence of kingship as Buchanan portrays it – is neither a necessary nor a sufficient condition of royal power, which is, essentially, an effective power to *rule*. Winzet offers a list of the prerogatives this comprises. The detailed items need not detain us here. The most essential points are that the king alone disposes of the right to appoint magistrates, to enact laws (though this will require further consideration in a moment), to give judgment in doubtful cases, and to decide on issues of war and peace.[11] All this is summed up in the declara-

---

[8] *Velitatio*, p. 171.
[9] See *The buke of four scoir thre questionis*, q. 30 (in *Certain tractates*, ed. Hewison, vol. I, p. 95); and cf. *Velitatio*, p. 177 (one of several references).
[10] *Velitatio*, p. 181.   [11] *Ibid.*, pp. 265–6.

tion that 'all power in matters political flows from the king as from its source'.[12]

So far, it seems, we have a straightforward statement of the kind of 'absolutism' that had been characteristic of one strand in European thinking about monarchy since at least the early fifteenth century, to say nothing of its earlier origins. The metaphor in which political power in all its subordinate forms 'flows' from the king is strongly reminiscent of the neo-Platonic element in such thinking to which Antony Black among others has directed attention.[13] Yet the same metaphor occurs elsewhere in Winzet's text with what might well seem to be a diametrically opposite sense and effect; for he also envisages circumstances in which the king's power itself 'returns to the people, from whom it originally flowed'.[14] The contradiction here, if contradiction there be, takes us an important step further in understanding the position Winzet adopts. Certainly, for him, all power comes from God. Certainly God has endowed royal power with a special sanctity. Certainly hereditary monarchy as it prevails in Scotland is the best form of government.[15] Yet it is also the case that all this can and should be mediated through the community for whose benefit God has ordained it. Almost at the outset of the *Velitatio*, Winzet had acknowledged that 'in all well-ordered kingdoms the royal authority is in the first instance conferred by the people'.[16] It is true and important that, here and throughout, whether implicitly or explicitly, Winzet makes a sharp distinction between the *populus* and the mere *promiscua plebs*, having in mind always an organized body acting through some such mechanism as the three estates. The fact remains that the kingship he defends against what he calls Buchanan's *regnum populare* is a system in which king and people alike have an essential part to play. For example, fundamental changes in the law – changes in what Winzet calls the *leges politicae* – cannot be instituted by either party without the consent of the other.[17] And Winzet allows what Adam Blackwood had strenuously denied: namely, that there is a genuine sharing of power between king and community, each being (in a striking phrase) 'bound to the realm itself' (*ipsi regno . . . astrictus*).[18]

---

[12] *Ibid.*, p. 266: 'Quid pluribus insisto? cum tu nescire non potes in regno solum esse Regem, a quo tanquam a fonte omnis in politicis rebus potestas dimanat, omnesque dignitates & magistratus profluunt.'

[13] See A. J. Black, *Monarchy and community: political ideas in the later conciliar controversy 1430–1450* (Cambridge, 1970), pp. 57–67.

[14] *Velitatio*, p. 269: '. . . totum ius regni siue principatus . . . ad populum, unde profluxit, redire'.

[15] This is a point Winzet tends to take for granted without exploring the argument at any length; but the preference for hereditary monarchy pervades his whole discussion.

[16] *Velitatio*, p. 154.   [17] *Ibid.*, sig. xx3v; and cf. pp. 259–60.

[18] *Ibid.*, p. 283: '. . . ius regni, ad quod tuendum communi iurisiurandi vinculo atque foedere & populus regi & rex populo & uterque ipsi regno est astrictus'.

These mutual relationships constitute for Winzet the true *jus regni*. Plainly they imply limitations upon the king's power additional to those of divine and natural law which he shares of course with his subjects. Yet they leave intact, as Winzet understands the matter, that *liberum imperium* which the king must have if the realm is to be effectively ruled. The prerogatives of royal government are *not* shared with the community; nor does the community have any authority over its ruler corresponding (as Buchanan would have it) to his authority over each and all of his subjects. Though Winzet believes that what we would call constitutional restraints on royal power are effective, their effectiveness is not dependent upon any popular right to resist or depose a king guilty of misrule. Such a ruler – who becomes a tyrant only by stubborn persistence in misgovernment, not by isolated or occasional misdeeds – deprives himself by his tyranny of the authority which then reverts to the community. In such circumstances it would indeed be legitimate and even necessary for corporate action to be taken; but while it would be taken against one who was no longer, properly speaking, a king, the sanctity conferred by his anointing must still shield him from the violence Buchanan justifies and advocates.[19]

Such being Winzet's concept of kingship, we may now consider more briefly its application to the Scottish case he had immediately in view. This has two main aspects, which may be termed, on the one hand, the constitutional or institutional, and, on the other, the historical. Under the first heading Winzet makes a number of points to illustrate his understanding of Scottish kingship. He takes up, for one thing, Buchanan's reference to the coronation oath sworn by the king, accepting the point that this binds the king to rule according to the established laws and customs of the realm, but insisting that there is a reciprocal obligation on the part of the people, who undertake to obey the king in accordance with the same legal and customary rules.[20] The king, Winzet had argued earlier, is lord over both the land of Scotland and its people. So far as the latter are concerned, his traditional title is king *of Scots*; and every Scotsman is bound to follow the king in war whenever he is so commanded.[21] As for land, save when it is church property or otherwise exempted, payment from its revenues is due in every case to the royal treasury; and no one may enter into his father's estate without testimony to the effect that the previous holder died 'in loyalty and peace with the king'.[22]

The question of succession to the crown lies in a sense on the border between the institutional and the historical dimension of Winzet's argument. That the crown was now hereditary was for him beyond question; but

[19] *Ibid.*, pp. 273–5; and cf. p. 269.   [20] *Ibid.*, pp. 259–60.   [21] *Ibid.*, p. 184.
[22] *Ibid.*, p. 194.

he did not deny that there had in the past been an elective element in the matter. In one sense this posed no problem for his general concept of kingship, since he was committed to the view that authority in 'rightly ordered realms' was derived, under God, from the community. On the other hand, it was essential for him to rebut any suggestion that such elective origins could now have any relevance to a proper understanding of the present nature of royal power. This is why he is obliged to deal with what Buchanan had said about some supposed transactions in the reign of Kenneth III. The purpose of the law then enacted, Winzet declares, was not to establish, but simply to regulate, the hereditary succession to the crown in the family in whose possession it had by then been for centuries. Buchanan's suggestion that there was some yielding of royal authority as a *quid pro quo* is dismissed as 'a frivolous conjecture'.[23]

It is arguable – though this is not the place to develop the argument – that a kind of litmus test for polemical historiography in sixteenth-century Scotland is provided by what is conveniently designated in one contemporary source as 'the Baliols cause'.[24] Clearly the sequence of events between the death of Alexander III and the securing of the crown by Robert Bruce posed important questions about the basis of authority and the right of succession to the crown. Sixty years before Winzet wrote, John Mair had used those events to illustrate a theoretical position which gave decisive priority to the rights of the community. Winzet's interpretation is different. Following Hector Boece – or at least following one strand in the somewhat confused account Boece gives – he insists that the succession was strictly hereditary and that Balliol's leaving the throne was the result of a voluntary act of abdication. That act was indeed the sequel to Balliol's ignoble betrayal of his responsibilities as king; but there was, in Winzet's view, no question of an assertion of authority by the community.[25]

Undoubtedly, however, the most interesting historical episode analysed in the *Velitatio* is the reign of James III. That reign and its termination were critically important for Buchanan, since the events of the 1480s could be presented as a clear and recent case of the deposition of a Scottish king for tyranny. Much of the case has been shown by recent scholarship to turn upon what has become known as the 'legend' of James III – a legend developed for political purposes and elaborated by sixteenth-century historians.[26] Even Winzet's patron Bishop Lesley can be regarded as the

---

[23] *Ibid.*, pp. 245–6.
[24] The phrase comes from *Ane declaratioun of the lordis iust quarrell*, in James Cranstoun (ed.), *Satirical poems of the time of the Reformation* (2 vols., STS, 1891–3), vol. I, p. 62.
[25] *Velitatio*, pp. 254–6.
[26] See Norman Macdougall, *James III: a political study* (Edinburgh, 1982), ch. 12, esp. pp. 282 ff.

prisoner, in this connection, of an ideological myth ill-adjusted to his own polemical purposes.[27] What is striking in Winzet's case is that, despite his close association with Lesley and his inevitable reliance on essentially the same sources, he emphatically rejects the received interpretation of the story. In the first place, while he accepts the substance of the charges against James – and in particular his ill-judged reliance on the advice of counsellors other than the nobility, with their vested right to give such counsel – he denies that these charges amount to an indictment for tyranny. Secondly, however, and perhaps more importantly, Winzet insists that there was no vestige of 'due process', of any kind of judicial constitutional procedure, in James III's fate: he was, quite simply, killed by 'a few conspirators'.[28] The case will serve Buchanan's argument no better than the more remote instances of deposition and tyrannicide he claimed to find in the Scottish annals.[29]

What Ninian Winzet sought to vindicate against Buchanan's radicalism, then, was a view of kingship exemplified (he claimed) both in the Bible and in the concrete historical reality of the Scottish realm. It is not a view that can be fitted neatly into our conventional categories of 'absolute' and 'constitutional' or 'limited' monarchy. Yet the more closely it is examined against the background of political thinking in the later middle ages, the more deeply its roots will be seen to run into that cultural soil. In a sense what might be termed the 'amateurism' of Winzet's political thinking – and even as a theologian he cannot be regarded as a professional of high calibre – tends to enhance rather than to diminish its significance. His conservative response to the monarchomach challenge was grounded in the reflection of an intelligent observer upon the principles he believed to be embodied in the political system he had experienced. What we must now consider is whether and how the picture changes when we look at what the pro-fessionals – here, above all, the jurists – had to say in response to Buchanan's dialogue.

Adam Blackwood, the first of the two jurists to be considered here, was orphaned at an early age and was indebted for his educational opportunities, first of all, to his uncle, Robert Reid. Reid, who has been described as 'undoubtedly the most learned of the prelates' in Scotland on the eve of the Reformation,[30] died in 1558 as bishop of Orkney. He had been president of

---

[27] Cf. *ibid.*, p. 284: '... Bishop Lesley, the Queen's champion ... was trapped by the existing legend of James III'.

[28] *Velitatio*, pp. 238–41. Cf. also p. 254: 'Nec Iacobus tertius procerum sententia, sed quorun-dam coniuratorum inuidia e medio sublatus est.'

[29] *Ibid.*, pp. 242–3.

[30] James K. Cameron, 'Humanism and religious life', in John MacQueen (ed.), *Humanism in Renaissance Scotland* (Edinburgh, 1990), p. 166.

the college of justice and his active concern for the improvement of Scottish education included a particular interest in jurisprudence. One of the 'royal lectureships' that were to have been established in Edinburgh under the terms of his will would have dealt with civil and canon law; and it is reasonable to suppose that his nephew, in his late teens by the time Bishop Reid died, absorbed the nascent 'humanistic legal culture' of Scotland in that period.[31] He was, however, to imbibe humanism from less peripheral sources. Sent by his uncle to Paris, he had Adrien Turnèbe and Jean Dorat among his teachers; and though he returned to Scotland at the time of his uncle's death, he seems soon to have resumed his Parisian studies, now with the still more potent patronage of the queen of Scots herself. He pursued his studies further at Toulouse, having turned from the arts curriculum to civil law. In the later 1560s, however, he was again in Paris, where he was rector in 1567–8; and it is indeed worth emphasizing that Blackwood's strictly academic experience was largely in the humanities, with a particular interest in philosophy. His professional legal career did not begin until he was nearing his fortieth year. It was a career for which he was once more indebted to Mary Stewart; for it was she who, on the recommendation of Archbishop James Beaton of Glasgow, gave Blackwood the appointment as a counsellor of the *parlement* of Poitiers which he held for the rest of his life. Beaton for his part was expressing appreciation of Blackwood's first polemical work, the *De conjunctione religionis et imperii libri duo*, published at Paris in 1575. Subsequently Blackwood seems to have visited the captive queen of Scots several times, and in particular did so at or about the time when she was sentenced to death. His frequently reprinted *Histoire de la martyre de la royne d'Escosse* reflects this experience and his devotion to Mary's cause.[32]

Against this background, it is in no way surprising that Blackwood responded so vigorously and so promptly to the challenge of Buchanan's *De jure regni*. His *Apologia*, it may be noted, is the only one of the three works principally under discussion here to have been reprinted – once in the author's lifetime (Paris, 1588) and again, over thirty years after his death, in his *Opera omnia* (Paris, 1644). And a case can be made for maintaining that it merited such an accolade more than its rivals; for Blackwood's reply to Buchanan is, in terms of intellectual content, arguably the most rewarding. It is true that the *Apologia* struck A. J. Carlyle as 'somewhat crude'; but then Carlyle was always ill at ease when confronted with absolutist ideas, and a more recent assessment credits Blackwood with having 'provided an

---

[31] John W. Cairns *et al.*, 'Legal humanism and the history of Scots law: John Skene and Thomas Craig', in MacQueen (ed.), *Humanism*, p. 49.

[32] On Blackwood, see *DNB*, vol. V, pp. 149–50. Among the older sources, see esp. the *Elogium* by Gabriel Naudé prefixed to Blackwood's *Opera omnia* (Paris, 1644). The appearance of that edition at that date and Naudé's association with it are points of some interest.

original defence of absolute monarchy'.[33] Certainly the charge of 'crudity' is hard to sustain when set against the erudition and dialectical skill that are deployed in what is admittedly a vigorous piece of polemical writing.

It should be borne in mind when approaching Blackwood's riposte to the *De jure regni* that, as in the case of Winzet's *Velitatio*, we have an author building a specific case upon more general foundations laid earlier. The two books of the *De conjunctione religionis et imperii* – published before the rise of the Catholic League had begun to call into question the royalist alliance between religious orthodoxy and loyalty to the crown – were the product of the situation which followed the St Bartholomew's Day massacres. For Blackwood it was the Calvinist heresy that threatened to break the bond between *imperium* and *religio*. Again, when Buchanan's dialogue came to his notice, the politics and polemic of the League (which Blackwood was to attack in the third book added to the *De conjunctione* in 1612, after the assassination of Henri IV) had not entered the radical phase which began in the mid-1580s. It has indeed been argued that some elements in Blackwood's position – notably his deference to papal authority – were somewhat ill-adapted to the '*politique* royalism' which was directed against Leaguer monarchomach ideology.[34] It is however interesting to note that, despite this, the *Apologia* was reissued with no significant changes in the Paris edition of 1588, when the propaganda campaign against Henri III was developing in, for instance, the writings of Louis Dorléans, even if the extremism of Jean Boucher was still to come. Evidently Blackwood's royalism still retained its relevance.

The core of that royalism was, it seems fair to say, essentially juristic. The formidable marginalia of the *Apologia* are overwhelmingly drawn from the civil and canon laws and their interpreters. The range of Blackwood's sources is impressive, extending as it does from the leading civilians and canonists of the later medieval centuries down to the juristic scholars of his own century and generation. This juristic learning is exhibited in the framework of the wider humanistic culture to be expected in one who had sat at the feet of Turnèbe and Dorat. Blackwood also pays due attention to the fact that he is arguing in a specifically Scottish context. Yet, though there are points of interest to be noted later in connection with his com-

---

[33] *Adversus Georgii Buchanani dialogum, de iure regni apud Scotos pro regibus apologia* (Poitiers, 1581). The Paris edition is described as *aucta & emendata*; but there does not seem to be much additional material apart from the provision of an index. For Carlyle's comment, see A. J. and Sir R. W. Carlyle, *A history of mediaeval political theory in the West* (6 vols., Edinburgh, 1903–36), vol. VI, p. 437. The more recent view is that of J. H. M. Salmon, 'Catholic resistance theory, Ultramontanism, and the royalist response, 1580–1620', in J. H. Burns and Mark Goldie (eds.), *The Cambridge history of political thought 1450–1700* (Cambridge, 1991), p. 234.

[34] Salmon, 'Catholic resistance theory', p. 234.

ments on Scottish history, the most important point here is a general one, and it alerts us to the fact that what we are being invited to consider is indeed a general theory of kingship.

The point Blackwood makes at the very outset is that Buchanan's dialogue is misleadingly titled. It is *not* in any substantial sense a discussion of the *jus regni* 'among the Scots': it is a general – and utterly misconceived – account of the nature of royal government as such. In the first place, the system Buchanan describes is one in which supreme authority lies, not with the ruler, but with the people.[35] In addition, when he seeks to illustrate his argument by instances and institutions taken from, for example, Denmark or Venice, he is, on the one hand, digressing from his avowed concern with the situation in Scotland, and, on the other, drawing a false analogy, since those systems do not exemplify true kingship such as prevails among the Scots. The most important and striking case here is that of the Roman empire. This, after all, was the source of most of the language and conceptual equipment used by jurists in Blackwood's own civil-law tradition to describe and analyse political authority, and specifically to elucidate the power enjoyed by kings. For Blackwood, however, Roman imperial authority was essentially different from and inferior to truly royal power. One particularly remarkable passage is worth quoting:

The Senate and People of Rome had a certain authority over [the emperor]: the Senate and People of Scotland have no authority over [their kings]. The emperors had a limited power over the people: our kings have free and full power. The sovereignty (*imperium*) of the latter has always been pure and absolute (*merum . . . ac solutum*): that of the former depended on the will of others (*ex alieno nutu*). The first kind of lordship (*dominatio*) is called kingship (*regnum*), the second principate (*principatus*).[36]

The theme thus boldly enunciated pervades Blackwood's entire argument. Kingship – the ostensible subject of Buchanan's dialogue – is something quite different from the exemplary and dependent magistracy there envisaged. A king in the true sense of the term is a divinely constituted ruler, consecrated by the ceremony of anointing. That rite, Blackwood says, is *divinitatis symbolum ac veluti sacramentum*.[37] The point was one he had developed earlier, in the *De conjunctione*, where he had referred to 'the hidden and almost divine power' of the oil used in the Old Testament, by virtue of which 'those who were anointed with it became either kings or

---

[35] See, e.g., *Apologia*, 1581, p. 27: 'tu ademptam regi, populo maiestatem attribuis'.
[36] *Ibid.*, p. 51.
[37] The phrase comes from an opening chapter which seems to have been added to the *Apologia* between the 1588 edition and the inclusion of the work in Blackwood's *Opera omnia* (1644, p. 9). The theme, however, is a consistent one in his theory.

priests' and their persons thenceforward sacrosanct.[38] Kingship, however, unlike priesthood in the Christian dispensation, is strictly hereditary: the heir becomes king immediately upon the death of his predecessor.[39] With this we have evidently passed from political theology to public law, and here Blackwood the jurist naturally comes into his own. We know already from the comparison with the Roman principate that a king's power is *merum ac solutum*. This means that the king is bound by no human law or ordinance: his authority is unconditional.[40] The king has complete command (*summam ... imperii*); and in particular this means that he has full power over the laws.[41] Interestingly, Blackwood recognizes that a power of this kind is essential in any political society, and he does not suggest that all such societies are governed by kings. Yet he clearly associates 'sovereignty' (for that is what is at issue here) with kingship: the term he uses to denote it is *regia potestas*.[42]

To the statement that a king conceived in Blackwood's terms is subject to no human law there is in a sense one exception. His authority being by definition strictly hereditary, the rules governing succession to the throne are beyond his power to change. Kings, Blackwood claims, *non regum sed regni sunt haeredes*: they are heirs to the realm, not to the kings who have preceded them.[43] Now here, as in Winzet, we have a concept of the *regnum* as an entity in some sense independent of *rex* and *populus* alike. Whereas, however, Winzet saw that entity as one to which king and people might equally be regarded as bound, with the implication that there were consequential limits upon royal power, Blackwood's use of the idea is quite different. The conclusion he draws immediately is that since kings succeed to the realm and not to their predecessors they cannot be bound by any agreements entered into by those predecessors. To this he adds that the king can make no law which he may not subsequently abrogate or repeal.[44] With these points in mind (though much could be added), there is no difficulty in recognizing the vigour of Blackwood's absolutism; nor will it come as a surprise to find that his theory of government is grounded in a view of human society in which force is the essential basis of authority.[45]

When one turns from Blackwood's own position to the way in which, on that basis, he attacks Buchanan's, one finds, effectively, a dual strategy. On the one hand, there is an essentially theoretical argument directed to establishing the inconsistent and even contradictory character of the

[38] *Opera omnia*, pp. 232, 314.
[39] See generally *Apologia*, 1581, pp. 71–3, where there is an elaborate discussion of the hereditary principle, with references to, among others, Baldus and Johannes Andreae.
[40] *Ibid.*, p. 55.   [41] *Ibid.*, p. 59.   [42] *Ibid.*, pp. 197–8.   [43] *Ibid.*, p. 113.
[44] *Ibid.*, p. 114.
[45] *Ibid.*, pp. 61–3.

opposing view. This turns very largely upon a logical critique of Buchanan's concept of authority, intended to show that it implies an untenable division of the essentially unitary sovereignty that is crucial for ordered government. It is not possible here to pursue this part of Blackwood's case, beyond saying that it is here, above all, that we meet the Blackwood who had studied and taught philosophy in Paris as well as reading law in Toulouse.[46]

More germane to present purposes is Blackwood's handling of the Scottish dimension of the argument. Attention has already been drawn to his fundamental contention that Scotland exemplifies true kingship, with all that this (as we have now seen) implies. It was also necessary, however, to consider the more specific points Buchanan had taken for his polemical purposes from Scottish history and institutional practice. Here, inevitably, Blackwood drew primarily upon Hector Boece's *Scotorum historiae*, available since 1574 in the edition with Ferreri's continuation. He also consulted John Lesley's then recently published Latin version of his history; and there is, too, a reference to the *Recherche des singularitez plus remarquables concernant l'estat d'Escosse* by David Chambers, Lord Ormond.[47]

In Scotland, then, what Blackwood calls the *lex regia* rests, not on any kind of popular election, but simply and solely upon the oath of allegiance sworn by the Scots not simply to Fergus as their first king but to his posterity in perpetuity.[48] It follows that when we come to the situation following the lamentable reign of John Balliol, we shall find Blackwood taking essentially the same position as Winzet. After Balliol's abdication, that is to say, Robert Bruce became king not *populi suffragiis*, but by force of arms in vindication of his undoubted hereditary right.[49] And if the community has no say in the succession to the crown, then *a fortiori* it has no right to depose a king who has come to the throne by legitimate hereditary right. Buchanan's alleged instances to the contrary cut no ice with Blackwood; nor did he entertain the suggestion that the fate of James III provides an example of the punishment of a tyrant.[50]

It is not, in any case, in such particulars that the controversial force of Blackwood's argument lies. If he is dialectically at his best in dealing with general issues of principle, whether in the juristic or the philosophical mode, his rhetorical skill is at its height when he celebrates such themes as the antiquity and continuity of the Scottish polity. 'You will', he declares,

---

[46] See for this *Apologia*, ch. 33: 1581, pp. 293–307.

[47] *Ibid.*, p. 275. It may be noted that the copy of the 1581 edition of the *Apologia* now in the British Library belonged to Ormond. It was subsequently at one stage in the library of Thomas Gordon, professor at King's College, Aberdeen.

[48] *Apologia*, 1581, pp. 159–62.   [49] *Ibid.*, p. 188.

[50] *Ibid.*, pp. 188–9. Blackwood's assessment of James is more positively eulogistic than Winzet's, bordering indeed on the fulsome. Cf. p. 192 for an account of the king's death at Sauchieburn.

find many realms more powerful than ours in wealth and armed strength (for our forefathers, contented with little, had enough to do in protecting what they had without envying the possessions of others); but nowhere on earth will you be able to point to one that can compete with it in antiquity. What other royal house can be found in the world which, having begun nineteen hundred years ago in one nation, survives among them even today?[51]

And it was this ancient, hereditary, absolute kingship that Buchanan sought to overthrow. Such an undertaking, in Blackwood's eyes, was as futile as it was impious.

The sequence adopted in this paper takes us, in the historiography of political ideas, from the virtually unknown to the comparatively celebrated. If Blackwood occupies a position in the middle range of that scale, with Winzet somewhere near absolute zero, then William Barclay stands at its high point. This is in part because his writings ranged more widely than those of his two compatriots. Not only did his attack on the monarchomachs take account of opponents other than Buchanan, but he also produced work of some note in the more technical field of civil-law scholarship.[52] And (perhaps the most important point of all) his *De potestate Papae*, though published posthumously in 1609, took its place in the then vigorously raging controversy in which James VI and I and Cardinal Bellarmine were prominent participants, so that Barclay has his place not only in the sixteenth-century argument over resistance theory, but also in the conflict between Gallicanism and Ultramontanism in the seventeenth century and beyond. All this is reflected in the fact that Barclay's work has attracted a degree of scholarly attention which even Blackwood, let alone Winzet, cannot rival.[53]

William Barclay was born in 1546 or 1547 into the family of Barclay of Gartly in Aberdeenshire, though the genealogy of which he seems to have been inordinately proud remains somewhat problematic.[54] His father, it is perhaps worth noting, had been on terms of intimacy with John Mair.[55] After graduating at Aberdeen, Barclay seems to have frequented the court, at Holyrood and elsewhere, in the early 1560s.[56] By 1571, however, he was in France, pursuing the study of law first in Paris and then at Bourges. The teaching career on which he now embarked received its first important

---

[51] *Ibid.*, p. 306.   [52] *Commentarius in legem ... D. de iurisdictione* (Angers, 1604).
[53] See esp. C. Collot, *L'école doctrinale de droit public à Pont-à-Mousson* (Paris, 1965).
[54] The evidence consists essentially of the armorial bearings which surround the portrait of Barclay to be found in some rare copies of the *De regno*; but that evidence is not easy to interpret and verify.
[55] *De regno et regali potestate aduersus Buchananum, Brutum, Boucherium, & reliquos monarchomachos* (Paris, 1600), pp. 451–2.
[56] See for instance his description of the hunt organized for Mary Queen of Scots by the earl of Atholl in 1563: *De regno*, pp. 81–2.

advancement in 1578, when his Jesuit uncle Edmund Hay, rector of the recently established university at Pont-à-Mousson, by recommending his nephew to the duke of Lorraine, secured Barclay's appointment to the chair of law there. Barclay spent the next quarter of a century in the duchy, becoming counsellor of state and master of requests. Despite the Jesuit auspices under which, in a sense, he had begun his career at Pont-à-Mousson, Barclay's relations with the Society of Jesus, whose influence in the university he consistently opposed, rapidly deteriorated. The publication in 1600 of *De regno*, with its violent attack on Leaguer principles, reflected in part that animosity, which reached its height, of course, in the *De potestate Papae*. When Barclay left Lorraine in 1603, he went to Paris and then to London, where James VI and I offered him preferment if he would abandon his Catholicism. The staunch Gallican, however, would not become an opportunist Anglican. Barclay returned to France and in 1604 accepted the chair of civil law at Angers, where he died in 1609.[57]

Nearly thirty years before that, Edmund Hay had drawn Barclay's attention to the recently published *De jure regni apud Scotos*. Like Blackwood and Winzet, he set to work at once on a reply to Buchanan, which forms the substance of Books I and II of the *De regno et regali potestate* eventually published two decades later. The project of a specific and immediate entry into the controversy seems to have been dropped because Barclay felt he had been pre-empted by Blackwood and by Winzet. Interestingly, while he mentions the former's *Apologia* at the beginning of the book he eventually completed, Barclay seems never to cite Blackwood in support of his own arguments. With Winzet, as we shall see, matters are entirely different; and it is of course thanks to Locke's quotations from Barclay in the *Second treatise of government* that Winzet's name, otherwise quite forgotten in this context, was at once preserved and distorted.[58] Barclay was also aware, of course, of the Huguenot 'monarchomach' threat; and his second target in the *De regno* as it developed was the *Vindiciae contra tyrannos*. It is, at the same time, noteworthy that Buchanan is still very much in evidence in the polemics of Book III of the *De regno*. Indeed it is fair to say that the original challenge thrown down in the *De jure regni* is never far below the surface of Barclay's thought throughout the prolix length of his book. In Book IV, however, much of his attention is given to the *Vindiciae*, just as in

---

[57] On Barclay's career, see *DNB*, vol. III, pp. 173–4; D. B. Smith, 'William Barclay', *SHR*, 11 (1914), 136–63; and, for his professional work, Collot, *L'école doctrinale de droit public*.

[58] John Locke, *Two treatises of government*, ed. Peter Laslett, Cambridge Texts in the History of Political Thought (Cambridge, 1988), pp. 422–3. As Laslett observes (p. 422 n., 'Locke had obviously never heard of' Winzet: neither, it seems, had any of his editors until 1947, when T. I. Cook made the identification, though qualifying it as 'probably' correct and

Books V and VI his fire is concentrated upon what was to Barclay in some ways the worst case of all, coming as it did, not from a Protestant, but from a Catholic pen: the *De justa abdicatione Henrici tertii* of Jean Boucher.

One more preliminary point may be mentioned before turning directly to Barclay's engagement in controversy with Buchanan. Besides the works of Blackwood and, especially, Winzet, Barclay mentions rather frequently another work which he plainly regarded as an important Catholic counter-blast to the monarchomach ideology. This was the *De Christiani principis officio* published in 1580 by the bishop of Leeuwarden in Friesland.[59] The author, Cuner Peeters (1532–80), usually referred to as Cunerus, had been expelled from his see in 1571 by 'the Calvinists and Anabaptists'. Now in exile in Germany, he was writing in the hope of exerting some influence in what proved to be the abortive conference at Cologne in 1579, which tried to resolve the conflict between Spain and the Protestant provinces in the Netherlands. The book is not marked by any particular originality; but Barclay's use of it is a useful reminder of the fact that the late sixteenth-century debate on monarchical authority was no limited or parochial affair.

Barclay seems in fact, when writing his original reply to Buchanan, to have drawn extensively on Cunerus (as he was later to draw on Winzet) for the scriptural and theological elements in the debate. Books I and II of the *De regno* follow Buchanan in adopting the dialogue format; and it has to be said that, whatever the limitations of the *De jure regni* as an example of that genre, Barclay's are still more severe; nor is it surprising that, when he resumed work on the book in the later 1580s and the 1590s, he did not attempt to sustain it.[60] The strength of his book, such as it is, lies in its scholarly weight rather than in any great literary skill, and while there is in fact a good deal of scriptural exegesis and related theological discussion, the force of the argument tends to increase when Barclay is on home ground, buttressing his case with copious juristic citations. Even more than with Blackwood – as one might expect from an author who spent most of his career in academic activity – there is a striking and impressive range of learning here and a sharp awareness not only of the reserves of scholarship to be drawn from the past but of the current vigour of legal commentary and exposition.[61] It has been

---

without referring to the *Velitatio*; *Two treatises of government with a supplement Patriarcha by Sir Robert Filmer*, ed. T. I. Cook (New York, 1947), p. 243 n4.

[59] The first edition was published at Cologne, a second, in 1581, at Mons. Carlyle (*Mediaeval political theory*, vol. VI, p. 434), perhaps misled by finding references in Barclay, wrongly identified the author as 'a Scotsman ... who was bishop of Louvain'.

[60] Various references in the text indicate the dates at which different parts of the *De regno* were written; but the point calls for closer examination than can be undertaken here.

[61] There are, for instance, references to Bodin, Hotman, Cujas and Rebuffi. It is also worth noting, however, that Barclay cites with approval his later adversary Bellarmine, invoking his authority more than once against Jean Gerson.

argued that Barclay, in seeking to combine the older traditions of legal scholarship with the newer modes of juristic humanism, made particular use of 'the historical method'; and certainly there are distinct signs of such a method in his handling of Buchanan's ideas.[62]

It is to the fundamental positions adopted in the *De jure regni* that Barclay turns at the outset of his *De regno*. Buchanan, he says, had rejected the view that expediency or utility was the basis of social organization, looking instead to nature or the law of nature. This distinction has no force in Barclay's eyes: *utilitas* is for him clearly the foundation on which human society is built, while at the same time there will never be any conflict between the dictates of utility and those of nature.[63] More important, perhaps, is Barclay's criticism of the assumption that natural law provides a ready-made standard by which positive laws can be evaluated and judged. In fact, he points out – and it is here that 'historical method' manifests itself – positive laws vary widely in accordance with the different conditions in which human societies find themselves and the divergent traditions developed in those societies.[64] The essential consequence of this, in Barclay's argument, is the critical importance of legislative sovereignty vested in a king. Human affairs in all their diversity need firm government, and the most effective way of providing that government is royal power. That power is the source of positive law: it cannot therefore be subject to any law of that kind.[65] A wise king will of course always take counsel; but he cannot be obliged to follow it. Such bodies as assemblies of estates exist by the king's concession and leave; and similarly none of the magistracies requisite for the administration of the realm can claim any power beyond that which is conferred by royal appointment.[66]

This royal absolutism (to use a convenient term unknown, of course, to Barclay and his readers) is grounded, it need hardly be said, in the ordinance of God. Yet it is scarcely the case that Barclay's conception of 'divine-right' kingship is wholly unequivocal and straightforward. His book was, as we have seen, written over a period of two decades; and there is some reason to think that he hesitated or wavered during those years between different ways in which his basic doctrine might be expressed. Thus it was possible to hold that royal power was always and everywhere – as it had certainly been in some cases, notably among the people of Israel – the result of direct divine intervention. On the other hand, it was possible for Barclay to accept that the people had a part to play in the establishment of kings. The king thus established would still be endowed by God with the absolute power Barclay

---

[62] See Collot, *L'école doctrinale de droit public*, p. 105.   [63] *De regno*, p. 11.
[64] *Ibid.*, pp. 12–14.
[65] *Ibid.*, pp. 124–5, 207–8.   [66] *Ibid.*, pp. 40–2.

regarded as essential to the task of ruling. Yet, on this view, there could have been some kind of instrumental act by the community, albeit that such an act must necessarily involve a total and final grant of power to the ruler.[67] Both in *De regno* and in *De potestate Papae* Barclay can agree (with Bellarmine, for instance) that succession to the crown is a matter for human law and that popular consent may in some sense be a necessary preliminary to a king's accession. The fact remains that a king once enthroned is entitled to his subjects' submission and obedience with all due honour and reverence; and all this by nothing less than divine precept.[68]

To rebel against a king, then, was to rebel against God. There can, on such an argument as Barclay's, be no place (it seems) in any circumstances for the kind of action against a ruler Buchanan sought to justify in the *De jure regni*. Yet, once again, matters prove to be rather less clear-cut than this. John Locke, it will be recalled, was both to point out and to exploit what he took to be Barclay's ambiguities on the subject of resistance to rulers.[69] It is highly significant in the present context that the two chapters of *De regno* from which Locke quotes are among those in which Barclay had drawn heavily upon Ninian Winzet's *Velitatio*. At the same time, Barclay was evidently (and inevitably) influenced by a powerful element in his own professional civil-law tradition. According to that view of the matter, human beings had an ineradicable right, rooted in natural law, to self-defence. This right, Barclay accepts, must pertain to a people suffering intolerable oppression by a tyrannical ruler: such a ruler may therefore be resisted. Yet Barclay is not here conceding the points made by Buchanan. He still maintains the sanctity of the king's person and specifically denies that there can be any question here of *punishment*: the right of self-defence confers upon inferiors no right to punish their superiors. Even more important is the point that, if there is to be legitimate resistance, it must be by way of a collective or corporate act. There is no such right as that claimed by Buchanan for the individual subject to take upon himself the task of resisting the tyrant.[70]

When one looks at the crucial second passage from *De regno* cited by Locke, one finds, perhaps, a somewhat different perspective on the problem. Here Barclay will not allow that a king, as such, may be resisted – far less punished – even if the action is taken by the whole community and purports to be for their defence against oppression. Suppose, however, that the man who had been king were no longer so: suppose that he has, by certain extremities of misconduct, stripped himself of that royal dignity and

[67] *Ibid.*, pp. 110–14.

[68] See, e.g., *De potestate Papae an et quatenus in regna et principes seculares jus et imperium habeat* (Pont-à-Mousson, 1609), pp. 182–3.

[69] *Two treatises of government*, ed. Laslett, pp. 419–25.   [70] *De regno*, p. 159.

sanctity which subjects are bound to respect. Then indeed, Barclay says (closely following Winzet at this point), the ex-king may suffer all the sanctions against which the king he once was had been hedged. Then, it seems, the people may of their own power and authority proceed against their oppressor – by force of arms if need be.[71] There is indeed a difficulty in this for Barclay, and one that lies so near the heart of the whole problematic area in early modern political thought with which this chapter has been concerned that it may appropriately serve, in a moment, by way of conclusion. First, however, having regard to the specifically Scottish context of the discussion, it is necessary to take a brief look at Barclay's treatment of that context.

Barclay had left Scotland (never, so far as we know, to return) when he was in his mid-twenties. Yet his Scottish background and memories evidently remained vivid enough during the long years in Lorraine when, among other things, he wrote his *De regno*. This comes out in various ways – personal reminiscences, matters of which he must have heard talk in his youth (the assassination of Cardinal Beaton, for instance[72]), or remoter episodes in Scottish history such as the 'Black Dinner'.[73] So far as the historical record as such is concerned, Barclay's source is, inevitably, Boece; and he has harsh words, as one might expect, for Buchanan as an historian.[74] It is, however, the less formal points that are most striking – as when, in an aside, Barclay recalls James V's reputation as 'the carlis king'.[75] There is a special interest in his quoting a Scots law phrase – 'the lordis motives' – when dealing with that crucial element in absolutist theory which refers to the king's acting *de certa scientia*.[76] But it is, of course, the question of Barclay's general view of the Scottish past that has most bearing upon his political thought. And here perhaps – though the matter requires closer investigation than can be accommodated now – the most notable point is what may be termed the celebratory aspect of Barclay's view. He is concerned to recall the warlike valour of the Scots, their impatience of oppressive foreign rule, and at the same time their stubborn loyalty to the royal house which had ruled them for nearly two thousand years.[77] William Wallace was a second Gideon; John Balliol's submission to Edward I was a solitary, though ignominious,

---

[71] *Ibid.*, pp. 212–14. This follows a passage (pp. 207–12) in which Barclay opposes the view that a king can be brought before the ordinary courts of law.

[72] *Ibid.*, p. 433.   [73] *Ibid.*, p. 425.

[74] *Ibid.*, pp. 106–7. By the time he wrote this passage, at the beginning of Book III of *De regno*, Barclay had seen Buchanan's *Rerum Scoticarum historia* (published in 1582), and refers in ,particular to its last four books, covering the period from mid-1560 onwards.

[75] *De regno*, p. 229.

[76] *Ibid.*, p. 102; 'Plurima eos [*sc.* Principes] mouere possunt, aliis ignota ... in regno Scotiae eiusmodi causae vocantur simpliciter *the lordis motiues* ... '

[77] See, e.g., *ibid.*, p. 297.

exception to the consistent Scottish rejection of alien rule.[78] Barclay refers more than once to the issue between Balliol and Bruce, without (it seems) finding it necessary to refute at length those interpretations of the episode which might seem to undermine his theory of kingship and its application to his own country.[79] Yet, as has already been noted, the theory had its problems; and to that problematic area we must now, in conclusion, return.

The difficulty Barclay encounters may be elucidated by going back to Ninian Winzet's *Velitatio in Georgium Buchananum*. Whatever may be thought of the positions advanced in that text, it is at least clear that Winzet adheres to a tradition in which the community of the realm has institutional means of expressing its corporate will and, in certain circumstances, of acting in the execution of that will. To this extent indeed Barclay and Winzet are in agreement. An organized political society – specifically, the realm of Scotland – has, especially though not exclusively in the three estates, an articulate collective life and being. For most of the time, no doubt, Winzet would agree that this life is latent rather than overt: it is a potentiality to be actualized only if and when misgovernment or extreme emergency has produced a crisis with which the ordinary processes of royal government cannot deal. Now Barclay, in the phase of his argument which is so heavily indebted to precisely these elements in Winzet's thinking, plainly recognizes a similar need for institutional means of activating the corporate life of the community. The trouble is that his general theory has already denied and precluded the existence of such institutions except in so far as they are allowed by royal concession and brought into being by royal summons; and even when they are in being they are subject always to the king's overriding authority. That there was a genuine dilemma here for the theory of monarchy in the late sixteenth century is quite clear. What was to become even clearer, and especially so to James VI and I, was that the dilemma would travel southwards from Edinburgh to London; and its horns would lose none of their sharpness when a king reacting vehemently against the teaching of George Buchanan encountered a parliament with rather more vigorous life in it than the parliaments of Scotland.

---

[78] *Ibid.*, p. 213. Barclay points out in this connection that Bodin (*Six livres de la république*, 1576, I.ix) had misinterpreted the homage and fealty done by Scottish kings in respect of the lands they held in England.

[79] The disputed succession at the time of the 'Great Cause' and afterwards is dealt with in the passage just cited in n. 78; and cf. *ibid.*, p. 121 (where the reference to Wallace as 'a second Gideon' occurs).

Part III

Empire and identity

7   The Scottish Reformation and the origins of Anglo-British imperialism

Roger A. Mason

Although the unionist literature of the post-1603 period has recently attracted a good deal of scholarly analysis, much less attention has been paid to the
development of ideologies of British unionism in the century preceding
James VI's accession to the throne of England.[1] Historians are obviously
aware that the propagandists of the early seventeenth century did not
develop their ideas *ex nihilo*, but only Arthur Williamson has explored the
'prehistory' of British unionism in any detail. In particular, he has rightly
highlighted the significance of the 'Edwardian Moment' of the late 1540s as
a prime source of the triumphalist imperial rhetoric which came into its own
with the union of the Anglo-Scottish crowns in 1603. Likewise, though
rather less convincingly, he has argued that many of the reformers who
presided over the Protestant revolution in Scotland in the years after 1559
were imbued with a similar vision of Britain's imperial destiny.[2] Yet despite
Williamson's pioneering research, the significance of these episodes in the
history of the debate over Anglo-Scottish union remains largely unexplored.
The main aim of what follows, therefore, is to re-examine the relationship
between the Scottish Reformation and the development of British imperialism in the crucial decades of the 1540s and 1560s.[3] Before doing so,
however, it is important to review what meaning (or meanings) the idea of
Britain possessed for contemporary Scots and Englishmen; for the unionists
of the mid-sixteenth century, like those of 1603 and after, drew on a

---

[1] See Bruce Galloway, *The union of England and Scotland, 1603–1608* (Edinburgh, 1986), esp.
pp. 30–57; Brian P. Levack, *The formation of the British state: England, Scotland and the
union 1603–1707* (Oxford, 1987); and their SHS edition of some of the 1604 unionist
literature, *Jac. union*.
[2] Arthur H. Williamson, *Scottish national consciousness in the age of James VI* (Edinburgh,
1979), esp. pp. 1–47; and his 'Scotland, Antichrist and the invention of Great Britain', in
John Dwyer, *et al.* (eds.), *New perspectives on the politics and culture of early modern Scotland*
(Edinburgh, 1982), pp. 34–58. Though this paper takes issue with some of Williamson's
conclusions, it is enormously indebted to these writings.
[3] In some respects, this reworks and refines arguments first advanced in my 'Scotching the
Brut: politics, history and national myth in sixteenth-century Britain', in Roger A. Mason
(ed.), *Scotland and England 1286–1815* (Edinburgh, 1987), pp. 60–84. Parts of section 2 in
particular draw heavily on this earlier essay.

considerable heritage of ideas and assumptions about Britain's history and destiny whose roots lie deep in the middle ages.

I

Nowhere are these beliefs more clearly exposed than in the searching critique of the medieval view of Britain mounted by the Scottish scholastic theologian, John Mair, in his *Historia Maioris Britanniae tam Angliae quam Scotiae*, published in Paris in 1521.[4] Born near Haddington in East Lothian in 1467, Mair's talents as a logician and theologian ensured him a distinguished career at the university of Paris where in the first two decades of the sixteenth century he established a reputation as one of the leading lights of the Sorbonne. In 1518, however, he was persuaded to return to Scotland and it was there that, evidently appalled by what he perceived as the backward condition of his native country, he set out to explain it in historical terms and to provide some remedies for the future. The result is a bleak but penetrating analysis of Scottish political culture in general and the mores of the Scottish aristocracy in particular. For in Mair's view, Scotland was dominated by an over-mighty feudal baronage whose self-interested pursuit of power posed a constant threat to the authority of the crown and thus to the stability of the kingdom. The remedies which he proposed for this included both greater attention to the nobility's education in 'polite learning' and, more radically, changes in the system of land tenure aimed at lessening the ties of dependency which bound men to their lords and supplied the latter with their military retinues. However, just as Mair saw the inflated power of the aristocracy as a consequence of centuries of Anglo-Scottish warfare, so his solution too was ultimately to be found in a wider British arena. For in order both to curb the power of the nobility and to put an end to the debilitating rivalry between the Scottish and English crowns which had given rise to it, he came out strongly in favour of dynastic intermarriages – such as that of James IV to Margaret Tudor – which would in time unite the warring crowns and create a single British monarchy of unchallengeable authority.

Of course, by its very nature, dynastic intermarriage might take some time to produce a common heir to both kingdoms. In the interim, therefore, Mair sought through his *History* to provide the peoples of Scotland and England with an even-handed account of their respective pasts which would

---

[4] John Mair, *A history of Greater Britain as well England as Scotland*, ed. and trans. A. Constable (SHS, 1892). For the analysis that follows, see my 'Kingship, nobility and Anglo-Scottish union: John Mair's *History of Greater Britain* (1521)', *IR*, 41 (1990), 182–222.

help to overcome the deep-seated animosities which simmered between them. Crucial to this enterprise, at least as Mair saw it, was the demolition of a view of the British past which he repeatedly associated with the English printer and publisher, William Caxton. In the early 1480s, Caxton's commercial instincts had led him to publish two historical works which, already immensely popular in manuscript form, were to prove still more influential following their appearance in print. The first was a version of the common Brut history which had long gone under the alternative title *The chronicles of England*. The second was a vernacular translation of Ranulph Higden's fourteenth-century Latin *Polychronicon*, part of the first book of which Caxton also published separately as a *Description of Britain*.[5] The two works were very different in style and substance: while the *Polychronicon* was a learned universal history aimed originally at a clerical audience, the Brut was a popular history of England written primarily for the laity. But they do have one thing in common: that is, when they looked at the early history of the British peoples, they did so very largely through the eyes of the twelfth-century Norman–Welsh clerics, Geoffrey of Monmouth and Gerald of Wales.

While there are any number of studies of English historical writing in the middle ages, few make more than passing reference to the uses to which the past was put in explaining and sustaining the nature of a distinctively English identity.[6] There is little doubt, however, that it was the writings of Geoffrey of Monmouth and Gerald of Wales which, skilfully manipulated by later continuators and popularizers, contributed most to moulding English perceptions of themselves and their neighbours. How and why Geoffrey's *History of the kings of Britain* was appropriated so thoroughly by the Anglo-Norman elite of post-Conquest England, and how and why it continued to appeal to the more self-consciously English community of the later middle ages, are questions which remain to be fully answered and which can only be touched on here.[7] Yet at the very least, the so-called

---

[5] The *Chronicles of England* first appeared in 1480 and the *Polychronicon* in 1482. The *Description of Britain* was issued separately in 1480. All subsequently went through several editions, the latter – perhaps significantly – being retitled *The description of England*. The most accessible modern editions are F. W. D. Brie (ed.), *The Brut, or the chronicles of England* (2 vols., EETS, 1906–8); Ranulph Higden, *Polychronicon*, ed. C. Babington *et al.* (9 vols., Rolls Series, 1865–86); and *The description of Britain*, ed. Marie Collins (London, 1988).

[6] Useful though they are, standard works such as Antonia Gransden, *Historical writing in England* (2 vols., London, 1974–82); John Taylor, *English historical literature in the fourteenth century* (Oxford, 1987); and C. L. Kingsford, *English historical literature in the fifteenth century* (Oxford, 1913), show little interest in the uses to which the past was put in forging a collective English identity.

[7] For a recent attempt to answer the first question, see John Gillingham, 'The context and purpose of Geoffrey of Monmouth's *History of the kings of Britain*', *Anglo-Norman Studies*,

British History served to ensure that the English kingdom – though not, strictly speaking, the English people – could lay claim both to suitably classical beginnings in Brutus the Trojan and to the exploits of the greatest of all chivalric heroes in King Arthur. If neither Brutus nor Arthur were English by blood, they had nevertheless ruled over a kingdom of the Britons which was, as we shall see, quite literally England in all but name. Thus, long before the accession of the Tudors lent the ancient Britons renewed topicality, Brutus and Arthur had become as much a part of the history of England as Edward I or Henry V. Indeed, the very fact that early Tudor publicists deliberately exploited the new dynasty's British roots is telling evidence of the extent to which Geoffrey's account of the ancient Britons had become an integral part of what Englishmen considered their own national past.[8] It was presumably pure coincidence that the Galfridian lore embodied in the *Chronicles of England* and more deeply embedded in the wider frame of Higden's *Polychronicon* appeared in print on the eve of Henry VII's accession. But it was a coincidence which in the event served only to confirm the exalted place held by the Britons in the epic sweep of the English past.

Paradoxical though the English appropriation of the British History may seem, particularly in an era when myths of origin were concerned primarily with racial homogeneity, it did have the virtue of underlining the antiquity and continuity of what might best be termed a Brito-Anglian kingdom. At the same time, moreover, as this suggests, it did nothing to discourage the view that the terms 'England' and 'Britain' were in effect interchangeable. England was simply the new name given to his kingdom by the Saxon warlord Hengist following his conquest of the descendants of the eponymous Brutus. To all intents and purposes, therefore, England was Britain and Britain England. Gratifying though such an equation may have seemed to late medieval Englishmen, its implications for their neighbours were much less welcome. For according to Geoffrey of Monmouth, the kingdom of Britain over which Brutus and Arthur had ruled encompassed the entire British Isles.[9] Did it not follow, then, that those who fell heir to the British

13 (1991), 98–118; on the second, the best introduction remains T. D. Kendrick, *British antiquity* (London, 1950), though see also Walter Ullmann, 'On the influence of Geoffrey of Monmouth in English history', in his *The church and the law in the earlier middle ages: selected essays* (London, 1975), pp. 257–76.

[8] See R. A. Griffiths and R. S. Thomas, *The making of the Tudor dynasty* (Gloucester, 1985), ch. 13; Peter Roberts, 'The Welshness of the Tudors', *History Today*, 36 (January 1986), 7–13; and Sydney Anglo, *Spectacle, pageantry and early Tudor policy* (Oxford, 1969), ch. 1.

[9] On Geoffrey's use of 'Britannia' to denote the whole island, see J. S. P. Tatlock, *The legendary history of Britain* (Berkeley and Los Angeles, 1950), pp. 7–8. As he says, there is only one occasion where, 'perhaps inadvertently, Britannia is used merely for Leogria, England, as distinguished from Scotia'.

kingship – albeit under the name of England – fell heir to much more than the Roman province of Britannia?[10] Certainly, the later medieval chroniclers were in no doubt that this was the case. In their attitude to Scotland, for example, both the *Polychronicon* and the *Chronicles of England* are adamant in their insistence that Scottish kings were in the past and remained in the present vassals of the English crown. As the author of the *Chronicles* put it: 'And fro the tyme that Brut had conquerede Albyon, and nempnede the land after his owen name Brytayngn, that now is callede Engeland, after the name of Engist; and so was the reaume of Scotland holden of the reaume of Engelande, and of the croune, by feaute and homage'.[11]

The English claim to feudal superiority over Scotland has been discussed at length before and there is no need here to spell out the historical arguments first marshalled in its support by Edward I.[12] It is worth pointing out, however, that the legal case for superiority was lent additional weight in English eyes by the sense of cultural and moral superiority which they derived from the writings of Geoffrey of Monmouth's near contemporary, Gerald of Wales.[13] Gerald's extensive ethnographic studies betray a genuine interest in the manners and customs of the Welsh and Irish peoples whose cultures he observed. Himself a product of the Welsh Marches, as well as of the schools of the twelfth-century Renaissance, he was singularly well placed to analyse sympathetically the Celtic fringes of the Anglo-Norman world. Yet he left his readers in no doubt that the peoples of Wales

[10] The Roman legacy had already been exploited by Anglo-Saxon rulers who styled themselves *rex* or even *imperator totius Britanniae*. The geographical implications of this remained conveniently ambiguous. See Eric Johns, *Orbis Britanniae and other studies* (Leicester, 1966), pp. 1–63.

[11] Brie (ed.), *Chronicles of England*, vol. I, p. 256. As this passage suggests, and others confirm, the author of the *Chronicles* tends to identify Britain solely with England, while Scotland is seen as a separate but always dependent realm (cf. *ibid.*, vol. I, pp. 12–14, 69–81). Higden usually follows Geoffrey and Gerald in using Britannia to mean the whole island (e.g., *Polychronicon*, vol. I, pp. 6, 382–3; vol. II, pp. 31–3), though his medieval translators sometimes substituted England for Britain (e.g., *ibid.*, vol. II, p. 33). These various usages over time would doubtless repay closer study.

[12] For Edward I's letter to Pope Boniface VIII of 1301, see E. L. G. Stones (ed.), *Anglo-Scottish relations 1174–1328: some selected documents* (Oxford, 1965), no. 30. For commentary, see Stones, 'The appeal to history in Anglo-Scottish relations', *Archives*, 9 (1969), 11–21; and, from a Scottish perspective, William Matthews, 'The Egyptians in Scotland: the political history of a myth', *Viator*, 1 (1970), 289–306; and Marjorie Drexler, 'Fluid prejudice: Scottish origin myths in the later middle ages', in Joel Rosenthal and Colin Richmond (eds.), *People, politics and community in the later middle ages* (Gloucester and New York, 1987), pp. 60–76.

[13] For what follows, see Robert Bartlett, *Gerald of Wales 1146–1223* (Oxford, 1982), esp. chs. 6–7. For a wider perspective which stresses that Gerald was drawing on pre-existing feelings of 'English' superiority, see John Gillingham, 'The beginnings of English imperialism', *Journal of Historical Sociology*, 5 (1992), 392–409.

and Ireland were primitive barbarians who would only benefit from incorporation within the civilizing orbit of the English crown. Such an attitude was, needless to say, tailor-made to legitimize English territorial expansion, whether in Wales, Ireland or even, at a later date, the Americas.[14] Equally, it could be turned against the Scots. Gerald himself never fulfilled his ambition of adding Scotland to the list of countries he studied and one can only speculate on how he would have responded to its hybrid culture, part Celtic and part Anglo-Norman. Higden, however, was probably not far off the mark when in his *Description of Britain* he opined that 'The Scots are light of soul, barbarous enough and wild, but in part amended through mingling with the English'.[15]

Ironically perhaps, this was a view with which John Mair might well have agreed. His jaundiced view of the 'wild' Scots of the Highlands smacks of the same sense of cultural and racial superiority which Gerald of Wales bequeathed to his English readers and which Caxton's publications did nothing to dispel.[16] Crucially, however, despite his conviction that even Lowland Scots would benefit from closer association with their more civilized English neighbours, Mair did not share the belief in the English crown's claim to lordship over Britain. On the contrary, it was precisely this claim which led to his repeated attacks on Caxton and, by implication, on the whole panoply of the British History as elaborated in both the *Polychronicon* and *The chronicles of England*. Certainly, as a unionist, Mair was inclined to view Britain as a single geo-political entity and even to argue on the grounds of contemporary linguistic usage that 'all men born in Britain are Britons'.[17] But what he consistently refused to accept was the elision of the distinction between England and Britain which the British History had done so much to encourage and which the claim to superiority embodied in quasi-legal form.

The reasoning behind Mair's stance was both patriotic and pragmatic. Like almost all his fellow countrymen, he was intensely proud of what was then construed as the Scots' long and successful struggle to maintain their country's freedom in the face of English military aggression. If he could not accept the more fanciful aspects of the historical mythology which the Scots had developed in support of their claim to independence, Mair was adamant in his belief that no Scottish king had ever done homage to his English

---

[14] This theme is explored in John Gillingham, 'The origins of English imperialism', *History Today*, 37 (February 1987), 16–22.

[15] Higden, *Polychronicon*, vol. I, pp. 386–8; cf. Collins (ed.), *Description of Britain*, p. 145. It is noticeable that, without Gerald to help him, Higden's description of Scotland is much less full than that of Wales or Ireland.

[16] For Mair's views on the Highlanders, see *History*, pp. 48–50; cf. Mason, 'Kingship, nobility and Anglo-Scottish union', pp. 195–7.

[17] Mair, *History*, pp. 17–18.

counterpart for the realm of Scotland.[18] In addition, though more prag-
matically, he was clearly convinced that, if the Scots were to be persuaded of
the benefits of union, the case would have to be grounded on something
more appealing than the belief in Scotland's vassal status within a historically legitimized Anglo-British *imperium*. In other words, if union were to be
realized, and a new British kingdom were to be created, it would have to be
seen as a union of equals which explicitly recognized Scotland's historic
claim to autonomy. And this in turn would require the writing of a more
balanced and truly British history. But this was hardly likely so long as the
view of the British past propagated by William Caxton, and deriving
ultimately from Geoffrey of Monmouth, held sway in England. Hence
Mair's *ad hominem* attacks on the luckless Caxton and hence too his painstaking demolition of the 'silly fabrications' associated with the British
History.[19]

Mair's common-sense scepticism has won him widespread praise from
modern historians. Yet there is little to suggest that his immediate contemporaries were impressed by his arguments. In Scotland, although there
are echoes of his thinking in later unionist literature, his work was quickly
eclipsed by the publication in 1527 of Hector Boece's *Scotorum historiae*.[20]
Boece had been one of Mair's colleagues in Paris in the 1490s, but thereafter
he returned to Scotland where in 1505 he was appointed principal of Bishop
William Elphinstone's new university foundation at Aberdeen, a post which
he held until his death in 1536. A grammarian rather than a logician, Boece's
approach to the writing of history owed more to humanist rhetorical ideas
than to the scholastic skills practised so effectively by Mair. Nevertheless,
despite their wide differences in style and technique, they do share some
common ground. Like Mair, Boece was a passionate believer in the historic
and continuing autonomy of the Scottish kingdom and a vociferous critic of
the British History and all that it implied in terms of Scotland's feudal
dependence on England. It may even be the case that, like Mair, he saw the
advantages of Anglo-Scottish union, provided it was interpreted as a union
of equals.[21] If so, however, union figured low on his agenda. For what

---

[18] See *ibid.*, pp. 191–220, where Mair argues the point at great length in relation to John
Balliol's alleged submission to Edward I.
[19] For these attacks on Caxton, see for example *ibid.*, pp. 1–2, 143–4, 194, 226, 255, 287–8.
[20] Boece's work still awaits detailed scrutiny, but for a survey of the context in which it was
written, see my 'Chivalry and citizenship: aspects of national identity in Renaissance
Scotland', in Roger Mason and Norman Macdougall (eds.), *People and power in Scotland:
essays in honour of T. C. Smout* (Edinburgh, 1992), pp. 50–73.
[21] As pointed out in Williamson, *Scottish national consciousness*, p. 190, note 22. Yet Boece
clearly remained deeply suspicious of the Anglocentric connotations of British terminology
and followed earlier Scottish chroniclers in arguing that the correct name for the whole

distinguishes his work from that of Mair is not so much his uncritical reworking of the Scottish chronicle tradition as his apparent willingness to invent sources to plug the gaps which his medieval predecessors had left unfilled. The result is a continuous history of the Scots from their mythical origins in remote prehistory through the legendary foundation of the kingdom by Fergus MacFerchard in 330 BC to the subsequent reigns of each of his 104 successors on the Scottish throne. Much of this was, of course, fabrication. But it was a far more readable and flattering account of the Scottish past than that offered by Mair. Not surprisingly, therefore, it was Boece's racier and more satisfying version of events which was trans-lated into Scots by John Bellenden and published in Edinburgh in the 1530s. Mair's *History* was effectively swept into oblivion by the brash self-confidence which characterized Boece's chronicle just as it did the Scottish court of James V.

Nor did Mair's work fare any better in England. If Polydore Vergil welcomed a fellow sceptic in the north, there is little to suggest that anyone else did or that the kind of unionist arguments Mair advanced were taken at all seriously in 'South Britain'.[22] Certainly, they made no impression on Henry VIII who was willing enough when it suited him to lay claim to lordship over Scotland and who in 1542 issued his well-known *Declaration, conteynyng the iust causes and consyderations of this present warre with the Scottis, wherin alsoo appereth the trew & right title that the kinges most royall maiesty hath to the souerayntie of Scotlande.*[23] The latter half of the *Declaration* is little more than an updated version of the case for English suzerainty first compiled by Edward I. In a sense, this thoroughly medieval view of Scotland is precisely what one would expect of Henry VIII.[24] In one respect, however, the traditional feudal language of the *Declaration* is distinctly at odds with contemporary English thinking. For nowhere within it is there any reference to the imperial ideology which, eloquently crystal-lized in 1533 in the preamble to the Act in Restraint of Appeals to Rome, had served to underwrite Henry's repudiation of papal authority and his assumption of complete jurisdictional authority over both the English

---

island was Albion, while Britain referred only to its southern part. See Mason, 'Scotching the Brut', in Mason (ed.), *Scotland and England*, p. 66.

[22] Polydore was evidently aware of Mair's sceptical attitude to the Scottish origins' legend and remained distinctly dubious when Gavin Douglas tried to persuade him of the error of Mair's ways and supplied him with a version of the story of Gathelus and Scota. See J. Small (ed.), *The poetical works of Gavin Douglas* (2 vols., Edinburgh, 1874), vol. I, pp. clvii–clxi.

[23] Most accessibly printed as an appendix to J. A. H. Murray (ed.), *The complaynt of Scotlande* (EETS, 1872), pp. 191–206.

[24] On Henry's attitude to Scotland, see David M. Head, 'Henry VIII's Scottish policy: a reassessment', *SHR*, 61 (1982), 1–24.

church and the English state. Behind this claim to jurisdictional self-sufficiency lay in the first instance the Bartolist doctrine that 'the king is emperor in his own kingdom'.[25] But the rag-bag of 'proofs' – the *Collectanea satis copiosa* – which the king's officials assembled in its support also brought to the fore the English crown's historic right to lordship over Scotland, Wales and Ireland. In effect, the British History had been pressed into service to prove, in John Guy's words, 'that the authority of the English crown extended over other realms, and that the sum of the king's feudal rights amounted to a right of empire'.[26] The Henrician idea of empire was thus both inward looking and outward looking; nationalist and expansionist; quintessentially English but historically – and potentially – Anglo-British.

That the *Declaration* makes no reference to this imperial ideology is perhaps testimony to the traditional outlook which governed Henry's attitude to Scotland. Few historians would now subscribe to the old whig view of his foreign policy as dictated by a far-seeing desire to unify the British Isles in a grand imperial design. As J. J. Scarisbrick drily remarks, it is doubtful whether Henry was 'either guilty or capable of such high statesmanship'; he was motivated rather by the long-held desire of English kings to execute some 'notable enterprise' against France.[27] Even when, following the death of James V in 1542, Henry was presented with the opportunity of bringing about the kind of union envisaged by Mair, through the marriage of Mary Queen of Scots to his own son and heir, Prince Edward, his thinking continued to run along traditional lines. Neither then nor subsequently did Henry show any signs of recasting the claim to feudal superiority over Scotland in British imperial terms. Admittedly, the anonymous author of an account of the earl of Hertford's brutal invasion of 1544 does make passing reference to Henry's occupation of 'the imperial seat of the monarchy of all Britain'.[28] But the English king himself preferred to justify the use of military force in terms simply of his 'title and interest ... to this realm'.[29] In fact, the full flowering of a British imperial ideology only

---

[25] The background to the English use of the formula *rex in regno suo est imperator* is explored in Walter Ullmann, '"This realm of England is an empire"', *Journal of Ecclesiastical History*, 30 (1979), 173–203.

[26] J. A. Guy, 'Thomas Cromwell and the intellectual origins of the Henrician Revolution', in A. Fox and J. A. Guy, *Reassessing the Henrician age: humanism, politics and reform 1500–1550* (Oxford, 1986), pp. 151–78, at pp. 159–60; see also Graham Nicholson, 'The Act of Appeals and the English Reformation', in Claire Cross *et al.* (eds.), *Law and government under the Tudors* (Cambridge, 1988), pp. 19–30, esp. pp. 23–5.

[27] J. J. Scarisbrick *Henry VIII* (London, 1976), pp. 548–50. For an example of the older view, see A. F. Pollard, *Henry VIII* (London, 1905), ch. 14.

[28] *The late expedition in Scotland* (London, 1544), reprinted in A. F. Pollard (ed.), *Tudor tracts 1532–1588* (Westminster, 1903), pp. 37–51, at p. 46.

[29] J. Bain (ed.), *The Hamilton papers* (2 vols., Edinburgh, 1890–2), vol. I, no. 222.

occurred after Henry VIII's death in 1547 when the former earl of Hertford, now duke of Somerset and head of Edward VI's regency government, initiated a marked change in English military strategy and accompanied it with a propaganda campaign designed to persuade the Scots of the benefits of dynastic union with England.[30] The 'Edwardian Moment' had arrived and out of it was to emerge the enduring notion of a British monarchy which was both Protestant and imperial.

II

Undoubtedly the key word here is Protestant. For, as we shall see, it was an intense commitment to the reformed faith which energized the idea of empire and lent Somerset's propaganda its strong sense of urgency and expectancy. Of course, Protestantism had informed attitudes to Anglo-Scottish union throughout the latter part of Henry VIII's reign. Even before the death of James V opened the way to union through marriage, it was already possible to underwrite English expansionism with the sanction of 'godly' propriety. Early in December 1542, Lord Lisle advised Henry simply to annex Scotland south of the Forth as it would be a 'godly acte . . . to bring suche a soorte of people to the knowledge of godes lawes, the countrey soo necessarie to your domyneons'.[31] If Lisle's proposal was extreme, the Protestant dynamic which underlay it was becoming increasingly common. Nor was it necessarily confined to the English. In fact, it was Scottish Protestants who first exploited the British possibilities latent in the Henrician idea of empire. One such was John Elder who, shortly after James V's death, furnished Henry with a map of Scotland (now lost) which he accompanied with an obsequious letter expressing the wish that 'boithe the realmes of England and of Scotlande may be joyned in one; and so your noble Maiestie for to be superioure and kynge'.[32] A self-styled 'Redd-shanke' or Highlander, Elder did not share Lord Lisle's apparent contempt for Gaeldom. But he did share his Protestant zealotry, urging Henry to invade Scotland and drive out the 'traiterous priestis' who were thwarting

---

[30] On Somerset's regime and the change in military tactics, see M. L. Bush, *The government policy of Protector Somerset* (London, 1975), esp. ch. 2. The propaganda campaign is surveyed in very general terms in Marcus Merriman, 'War and propaganda during the Rough Wooing', *Scottish Tradition*, 9/10 (1979–80), 20–30; but see also the same author's 'The assured Scots: Scottish collaborators with England during the Rough Wooing', *SHR*, 47 (1968), 10–34.

[31] *Hamilton papers*, vol. I, no. 255.

[32] 'A proposal for uniting Scotland with England, addressed to King Henry VIII by John Elder, clerke, a Reddshanke', in *Bannatyne miscellany I* (Bannatyne Club, 1827), pp. 1–18, at p. 8.

his 'godly porpas and desire' for a union whereby, 'hypocrisy and supersti-
cioun abolissede, and the Frenche cleane pluckt out of our hartis, England
and Scotland, and the posteritie of boith, may live for ever in peax, love and
amitie'.[33] Here Elder struck a rhetorical chord which was to resound
throughout the unionist literature of the sixteenth century and beyond. But
it was not simply in terms of its rhetoric that Elder's letter anticipated what
was to come. For he also invoked the historical precedents embodied in the
British History to substantiate his belief that Scotland was 'a part of your
Highnes empyre of England'.[34]

Henry was sufficiently impressed with what Elder had to say to offer him
a pension.[35] But the vision of union which the Scotsman adumbrated was
never fleshed out during Henry's reign. It was only in 1547, in the context of
Somerset's more radically Protestant and self-consciously British regime,
that Elder's historical justification of English imperialism was seized upon
and developed. Then once again it was a Scotsman, James Henrisoun, who
took the lead. Henrisoun was a successful Edinburgh merchant who after
the first English invasion of Scotland in 1544 voluntarily accompanied
Hertford back to England. There, like Elder, he was pensioned by the
government, but he was given little opportunity to repay this largesse until
1547 when, on the eve of Somerset's Pinkie campaign, he wrote and
published his remarkable *Exhortacion to the Scottes to conforme themselves to
the honourable, expedient & godly union betweene the realmes of England &
Scotland*.[36] Here unionism reached new heights of Protestant-inspired
intensity; and here too, as we shall see, the idea of empire was legitimized by
recourse to England's historic claim to lordship over Scotland. In contrast
to Elder, however, Henrisoun was not content simply to refer to an *English*
empire. Like Mair before him, he believed it essential that 'those hatefull
termes of Scottes & Englishemen' should be 'abolisshed and blotted oute for
ever' and that the inhabitants of the British Isles should 'al agre in the onely
title and name of Britons ... and the selfe realme, beeyng eftsones reduced

---

[33] *Ibid.*, p. 16.
[34] *Ibid.*, p. 11. This is one of three occasions in the letter where Elder refers to 'the empire of
England' (cf. *ibid.*, pp. 8, 16). While one cannot be certain from the context that he intended
the phrase in the sense pioneered in the Act in Restraint of Appeals, it is strongly suggested
by his blatant anti-papalism and all but confirmed by his reference to Henry as 'Defender of
the Christen Faith, and in erth next vnto God, of the Churche of England and Irland
Supreme hed' (*ibid.*, p. 7).
[35] Merriman, 'Assured Scots', pp. 21–22.
[36] Reprinted in Murray (ed.), *Complaynt of Scotlande*, pp. 207–36. For a full account of his
career, see Marcus Merriman, 'James Henrisoun and "Great Britain": British union and
the Scottish commonweal', in Mason (ed.), *Scotland and England*, pp. 85–112. It is very
probable that Henrisoun had some contact with Elder when both were settled in London
after 1544.

into the fourme of one sole Monarchie, shalbee called Britayn'.[37] Henrisoun's British enthusiasm even led him to develop a novel racial argument in favour of union. For although, as he admitted, the British Isles had often been invaded by other peoples, he insisted that the original Britons and the original British blood had never been extinguished. 'I doubte not to saie', he wrote, 'and am able to prove, that the great parte of bothe realmes, is come of ye old Britayns. And thoughe we have been mixed with foreyn nacions, whereby the Britayne tongue is chaunged & out of use, yet doth the bloud and generacion remain'.[38] In Henrisoun's view, the idea of a unitary Britain was based, not as Mair had implied on an accident of geography, but on a common racial identity.

Perhaps even Henrisoun himself remained unconvinced by this argument, however, for having advanced it briefly, he at once reverted to more conventional reasons for considering Britain as a single geo-political entity. Rejecting out of hand the historical mythology developed by his countrymen in support of Scottish autonomy, he chose instead to follow Elder in endorsing and developing the case for English lordship 'so exactelie set furthe' in Henry VIII's *Declaration*.[39] And with the full panoply of the British History behind him, he confidently concluded that the proposed marriage of Mary and Edward would bring about, not just an Anglo-Scottish union, but the final re-creation of the British monarchy 'as it was first, & yet still ought to be'.[40] But it was not in fact on Brutus, the eponymous founder of the British kingdom, that the weight of Henrisoun's historical analysis rested. That honour fell to the heroic figure of Constantine the Great, the first Christian emperor of Rome, but also, according to Geoffrey of Monmouth and his disciples, a king of the Britons.[41] There were two reasons for the extreme importance which Henrisoun attached to Constantine in the *Exhortacion*. Firstly, it allowed him to argue that, as in Constantine were united both Roman emperorship and British kingship, so his successors in Britain fell heir not just to his kingdom but also to his imperial status. This was an argument which had appealed fleetingly to Henry VIII in his attempts to justify the royal supremacy in the early 1530s and to which Polydore Vergil had given some currency in the version of his *Anglica historia* published in 1534.[42] Henrisoun was merely following the

---

[37] Henrisoun, *Exhortacion*, p. 230.   [38] *Ibid.*, p. 216.   [39] *Ibid.*, pp. 219–25.
[40] *Ibid.*, p. 234.
[41] See Geoffrey of Monmouth, *The history of the kings of Britain*, ed. and trans. Lewis Thorpe (Harmondsworth, 1966), pp. 131–3. The belief that Constantine was the son of the Roman general Constantius through his marriage to Helen, daughter of Coel, king of the Britons, is also to be found in Brie (ed.), *Chronicles of England*, vol. I, pp. 39–40, and Higden, *Polychronicon*, vol. V, pp. 114–17.
[42] For a useful, though probably exaggerated, account of Henry's use of Constantine, see Richard Koebner, '"The imperial crown of this realm": Henry VIII, Constantine the Great and Polydore Vergil', *BIHR*, 26 (1953), 29–52.

Italian's example in arguing that Constantine's successors in Britain – the kings of England – had always worn 'a close crowne Emperiall, in token that the lande is an empire free in it self, & subject to no superior but GOD'.[43] In contrast to Polydore, however, Henrisoun's agenda was self-consciously British and the second reason for his attachment to Constantine was his belief, repeatedly affirmed, that he 'had al Britayn in possession'.[44] The empire of Constantine's successors, of Henry VIII and Edward VI, was not merely English, therefore, but encompassed the entire British Isles. Scotland too was incorporated within the orbit of the closed imperial crown given statutory recognition in the Act in Restraint of Appeals, and Scotsmen too could participate in the imperial and Protestant future which the break with Rome inaugurated.

In the light of this, it is not surprising that Henrisoun viewed the marriage of Mary and Edward as an event charged with momentous historical import. Through it the English king would at last and without bloodshed gain 'his righteous possession of the whole monarchie of Britayn'.[45] It represented the final consummation of God's providential – and emphatically Protestant – design for Britain. In concluding the *Exhortacion*, Henrisoun has a personified 'Britain' – Britannia in all but name – ask rhetorically of her warring children:

Hath not the almighty providence severed me from the reste of the worlde, with a large sea, to make me one Islande? hath not natures ordinaunce furnished me with asmany thinges necessary, as any ground bringeth furth? hath not mans pollicie at the beginning subdued me to one governoure? And hath not the grace of Christ illumined me over all, with one faith; and finally the workes of all these foure, tended to make me one? Why then wil you divide me in two?[46]

To do so, 'Britain' continues, is unnatural folly: neither birds nor beasts indulge in such parricide; neither then should reasonable men. Civil war leads only to destruction, as the examples of the Greeks, the Romans and so many other realms proclaim. Britain's problems have stemmed from the same internal discord. Consequently, 'Britain' exhorts the Scots to seize the opportunity of 'this most honorable, most godly and profitable attonement

---

43 Henrisoun, *Exhortacion*, p. 218. Cf. Henry Ellis (ed.), *Polydore Vergil's English history* (Camden Society, 1846), pp. 98–9: 'Albeit the imperie remained not long after in the stock of Constantine (so sodaine is the fall of humaine treasures), neverthelesse the maiestie of the imperie could not perish, sithe that even at this presente the kinges of England, according to the usage of their aunciters, doe weare the imperiall diadem as a gift exhibited of Constantinus to his successors'.

44 Henrisoun, *Exhortacion*, p. 218: 'wherunto whether he came by Helene his mother, or by Constancius his father, forceth not much: for it sufficeth for our purpose, to prove yt al Britayn was under one Emperor, and beeyng under one Emperor then was Scotlande and Englande but one Empire'.

45 *Ibid.*, p. 225.   46 *Ibid.*, p. 232.

with Englande', and to share in the latter's 'concorde and unitie, her tranquilitie & quiet, her wealth & luckey fortune, her conquestes & triumphes: & finally of all her incomparable ioyes & felicities'.[47] Above all, however, Henrisoun has 'Britain' remind her Scottish brood:

> how that by this calling of us into this unitie, proceding plainly from god him selfe, he would also unite and ioyne us in one religion. For how godly were it, yt [that] as these two Realmes should grow into one, so should thei also agre in the concorde & unite of one religion, & the same ye pure, syncere & incorrupt religion of Christ, setting a part all fond supersticions, sophistications, & other thousandes of devilries brought in by the bishop of Rome & his creatures, wherby to geve glosse to their thinges & darknes to Gods true worde.[48]

The new Protestant and imperial British realm would usher in an era of peace, prosperity and godly concord: 'For beeyng then . . . bothe under one kyng, the more large and ample the Empire wer: the more honorable and glorious: the kyng of greater dominion, governance, power and fame: and the subjectes more renoumed, more happy and more quiet'.[49]

It is worth quoting at length from Henrisoun's work as it plainly illustrates that the rhetoric characteristic of the unionist literature of 1603 and after was already well developed in the late 1540s. In fact, the *Exhortacion* itself does not appear to have exerted any direct long-term influence. But another product of the 'Edwardian Moment', published in 1548 as an *Epistle or exhortacion to unitie and peace*, is frequently mentioned by later unionist writers.[50] Ostensibly written by Somerset himself, and usually referred to as Somerset's *Epistle*, it was clearly cut from the same rhetorical cloth as Henrisoun's tract and may well have been penned by the Scotsman himself.[51] While the *Epistle* spares us the detailed historical survey which underpins Henrisoun's imperial vision, it leaves the reader in no doubt of the providential nature of the opportunity being offered the Scots to create a united British monarchy. It is argued, for example, that the death of James V in 1542, leaving the infant Mary as his sole legitimate heir, far from being a 'miracle' or the work of 'blynd fortune', was rather the work of God's

---

47 *Ibid.*, pp. 232–3. Henrisoun's 'text' for the *Exhortacion* as a whole was 'Omne regnum in se divisum desolabitur: that is to saie: every kingdom divided in it self, shalbe brought to desolacion' (*ibid.*, p. 211).

48 *Ibid.*, p. 234.   49 *Ibid.*, p. 229.

50 For the text of the *Epistle*, see Murray (ed.), *Complaynt of Scotlande*, pp. 237–46. Unlike the *Exhortacion*, the *Epistle* was translated into Latin and, incorporated in Sleidan's *Commentaries* of 1557, received wide circulation. See Williamson, *Scottish national consciousness*, p. 152. For references to it in later unionist literature, see *Jac. union*, pp. 29–31, 63, 102–3, 119–20, 167–8.

51 As Williamson rightly suggests, if Somerset was the author, he had 'an émigré Scot at his elbow'. See 'Scotland, Antichrist and the invention of Britain', in Dwyer (ed.), *New perspectives*, p. 37.

'infinite mercie and most inscrutable providence'.[52] Such an opportunity for uniting the realms had not occurred for 800 years, and the Scots are therefore urged to accept the manifest will of God, 'to take the indifferent old name of Britaynes again', and 'to make of one Isle one realme, in love, amitie, concorde, peace, and charitie'.[53] After all, not only had God 'in maner called us both unto it', but union, as Henrisoun had similarly emphasized, would have distinct advantages:

we two beyng made one by amitie, be most hable to defende us against all nacions: and havyng the sea for wall, the mutuall love for garrison, and God for defence, should make so noble and wel agreyng Monarchie, that neither in peace wee maie bee ashamed, nor in warre affraied, of any worldely or forrein power.[54]

To reap the benefits which perpetual peace under a British monarchy would inevitably bring, the Scots had only to break their useless alliance with France, repudiate the usurped authority of Rome, and reaffirm their commitment to the marriage of Mary and Edward. Meanwhile, the author of the *Epistle* could only marvel that two peoples 'annexed and ioyned in one Island ... so like in maner, forme, language, and all condicions as we are' were nevertheless locked in 'mortall warre'.[55]

While there is no doubting the power of such unionist rhetoric, many Scots remained, not surprisingly, less than convinced. After all, despite the beguiling prospect of peace and prosperity conjured up by the propagandists, the creation of a British monarchy was being pursued on the ground by a policy of brutal military conquest and occupation. As Henrisoun himself warned in the *Exhortacion*, Somerset approached 'with a puissant & invincible army', intent on befriending those who sought his 'mercy, grace & favour', but on punishing those who persisted 'in their stubborn & wilful disobedience'.[56] The *Epistle* put the matter still more succinctly, informing the recalcitrant Scots that 'you wil not have peace, you will not have aliaunce, you will not have concorde: and conquest commeth upon you whether you wil or no'.[57] Could Somerset's fair words be trusted any more than Henry VIII's? Just as the claim to superiority was never far from Henry's mind, so Somerset's *Epistle* insisted that, whatever the Scots did, they could never 'extynguish the title which we have to the Croune of Scotland'.[58] Despite protestations to the contrary, therefore, was it not clear that Somerset's ultimate objective was the subjugation of Scotland to the crown of England, albeit under the pretence of a 'renewed' British monarchy? Such a conclusion was amply borne out by the publi-

---

[52] Somerset, *Epistle*, pp. 239–40.   [53] *Ibid.*, p. 241.   [54] *Ibid.*, p. 245.
[55] *Ibid.*, p. 239.
[56] Henrisoun, *Exhortacion*, p. 235.   [57] Somerset, *Epistle*, p. 244.
[58] *Ibid.*, pp. 242–3.

cation in 1548 of a further propaganda piece entitled *An epitome of the title that the kynges maiestie of Englande hath to the sovereigntie of Scotlande*.[59] For here the author appealed to the Scots to stop fighting 'against the mother of their awne nacion: I mean this realme now called Englande, the onely supreme seat of thempire of Great Briteigne', and then went on to 'prove', in still more detail than the *Declaration*, that Scotland had acknowledged English superiority from the days of Brutus and his sons.[60]

The continuous use of this kind of historical evidence in support of the unionist cause made complete nonsense of the *Epistle's* appeal to the Scots 'to take the indifferent [i.e. impartial or neutral] old name of Britaynes again'.[61] In fact, the terms 'Briton' and 'Britain' were loaded with connotations of English hegemony which the propaganda of the 'Edwardian Moment' served only to entrench. Understandably, the only published response to Somerset's onslaught, the *Complaynt of Scotland*, continued the Scottish tradition of insisting that the term 'Britain' was applicable only to England and, by implication, had never encompassed Scotland.[62] But this kind of argument was unlikely to convince those who, whether Scots or English, were mesmerized by the vision of an Anglo-British monarchy which was both Protestant and imperial. Nowhere perhaps is the urgency and insensitivity with which this vision was pursued more evident than in William Patten's pamphlet *The expedicion into Scotland*.[63] Patten was a Londoner who had joined Somerset's Scottish campaign of 1547 as an official of the Marshalsea court and had witnessed the battle of Pinkie and the subsequent military occupation of the Scottish Lowlands. Back in London in 1548, flushed with Somerset's success, he published his *Expedicion* in the form of a diary of the events of the campaign. To this, however, he added a preface – to serve 'in stede of argument for the matter of the storie ensuing'[64] – which is well worth looking at as a final example of the Protestant triumphalism which characterizes the Anglo-British imperialism of the 'Edwardian Moment'.

Not unexpectedly, the preface begins by praising Somerset's 'valiaunce

---

[59] Printed in greatly abridged form in Murray (ed.), *Complaynt of Scotlande*, pp. 247–53. Its alleged author was one Nicholas Bodrugan, alias Adams.

[60] *Ibid.*, p. 250.   [61] Somerset, *Epistle*, p. 241.

[62] A. M. Stewart (ed.), *The complaynt of Scotland* (STS, 1979), pp. 67–8. The author, possibly Robert Wedderburn, argued that English kings came of the 'false blude' of the Saxon invaders 'sergestes and engestes' who usurped the throne of 'the kyng of grit bertanze quhilk is nou callit England' and 'trasonablie banest the rytheus kyng and his posteritie fra the realme'. Since that time, he went on, England had been ruled by a series of 'tirran kyngis' who, having no 'rytht to the crone of ingland, ergo thai hef na titil to the crone of Scotland'.

[63] Most accessibly printed in a modern English version in Pollard (ed.), *Tudor tracts*, pp. 53–157. The version used here, however, is in John Dalyell (ed.), *Fragments of Scottish history* (Edinburgh, 1798).

[64] Patten, *Expedicion*, p. v.

and wisdome' in all his dealings with the Scots and by describing him as sent by God to 'woorke his divine wyll'.[65] Perhaps as a consequence of this, Patten did not think it necessary to justify English aggression in any detail – he alluded only to 'the iust title of our Kynge unto Scotland, [and] the Scottes often deceites, untrueths of promyse, and periurie'[66] – preferring instead to dilate in now familiar terms on the providential nature of the union which the Scots had thus far scorned:

whearby, like countreymen and countreymen, like frend & frend, like broother and broother, we might in one perpetual and brotherly life, ioyn, love, & lyve together, according as thearunto, bothe by the appointment of God at the firste, and by the continuaunce of nature since, we seme to have bene made and ordeyned: seperate by seas from all oother nacions, in customes and condicions littell differinge, in shape and langage nothing at all.[67]

The Scots, Patten continued in the same conventional vein, could not live 'lawles and hedles without a Prince', and who better for their queen to marry than Edward VI, 'a right Briton bred and borne' and virtuous to boot. Such a marriage, he assured the Scots, would mean, 'not the mastership of you, but the felowship', for England wished not to conquer Scotland – though doubtless she could – but rather to free her from 'the fained frendship of Fraunce'. Not just from France, however, for England also, and more importantly, wanted to free Scotland 'from that most servile thraldome and bondage under that hydeous monster, that venemous *Aspis* and very Antichrist the Bisshop of Rome'.[68] It was Rome rather than France which Patten saw as the principal enemy; and it was his perception of Britain as the 'beleaguered isle' – an insular Protestant fortress surrounded by the massed forces of continental Catholicism – which lent his desire for union apocalyptic urgency.

For Patten was undoubtedly possessed of that peculiarly Protestant exultation generated by the conviction that he was participating in the final battle with the forces of the papal Antichrist in the latter days of the world.[69] How prudent and providential, then, that England, 'not so much led by themsamples of others ... as mooved by the mere mercie and grace of Almighty God', had cast off the pope's usurped authority and 'most happely exterminate & banisht hym our bounds'. England, in short, had reasserted her imperial status:

Whearby, as we have now ye grace to knowe and serve but one God, so are we subiect but to one Kynge; he naturally knoweth his owne people, & we obediently knowe hym our onely Soveraigne; hys Highnes estate brought and reduced from

---

[65] *Ibid.*, p. ix.   [66] *Ibid.*, pp. x–xi.   [67] *Ibid.*, p. xiii.   [68] *Ibid.*, pp. xv–xvii.

[69] Henrisoun too believed he was living in the 'latter days' (*Exhortacion*, p. 212), but while this certainly imparted urgency to his plea for union, it did not lead him, as it did Patten, to identify the pope as 'ye only antichrist' (*Expedicion*, pp. xvii–xviii).

perdicion, & in maner subieccion, unto the old princely, entyer, and absolute power again, and ours redemed from the doubt, to whome we should obey.[70]

The Scots too could enjoy these godly blessings: they too could free themselves from popish ceremonies, popish taxes and popish jurisdiction. Indeed, if they did not, they would feel the full force of the wrath of God. More specifically, as the Bible aptly put it, so Patten warned the Scots that God would 'set out his vyneyard to oother good husbandes that wil yeld him frute in due times' and that 'the kingdome of God shalbe taken from you, & be geven to the nacion yt will do profit'.[71] If Patten did not quite go so far as to say that England would receive Scotland as a reward for her righteousness, the idea was clearly not far from his thoughts. Meanwhile, he saw Somerset's army as a meet instrument for inflicting God's plagues upon the Scots for their disobedience to His manifest will. For only thus – paradoxically enough – would they come to realize:

whoo be your frendes, & whyther we will you well: wyth whoome, by soo many meanes sith God of good will hath so nie ioyned you, seme not you of frowardnes to seaver a sunder, agaynst the thyng that should be a generall wealth and common concorde, the provision of nature, and ordinaunce of God; and against his holy woord, which not at all unaptly, perchaunce, here may be cited: *Quos Deus coniunxit, homo ne separet.*[72]

In defying Somerset, the Scots were defying the will and the instrument of God. Under the influence of Protestantism, the union of Scotland and England in a new (or renewed) British imperial monarchy had become an apotheosis to be pursued with apocalyptic urgency. Quite clearly, however, for Patten, as for the other propagandists of the 'Edwardian Moment', Britain was simply England writ large.

III

John Mair, whose death in 1550 at the ripe old age of eighty-two spared him none of the horrors of the Rough Wooing, was no doubt more appalled by the death and destruction wrought by the military campaigning than by the Anglocentric terms in which the unionist cause was promoted.[73] Nevertheless, the Anglo-British empire envisaged by Somerset's publicists was a far cry from his own ideal of a union of equals. Far from recognizing the Scots' historic autonomy and identity, the unionists of the 'Edwardian Moment'

---

[70] Patten, *Expedicion*, pp. xviii–xix.   [71] *Ibid.*, pp. xix–xx.   [72] *Ibid.*, p. xxi.

[73] It seems likely that one motive behind Mair's unionism was the concern he shared with other Parisian theologians that the unity of Christendom was threatened by warfare among its constituent states. On this generally, see W. F. Bense, 'Paris theologians on war and peace 1521–29', *Church History*, 41 (1972), 168–85.

had deliberately sought to deny the former and emasculate the latter. It may have pained Mair, but it surely did not surprise him, that in 1548 his countrymen shipped Mary off to France and to an eventual French marriage. Perhaps his only comfort, orthodox Catholic as he remained, was that the close association of Protestantism with English imperialist aggression had done little to advance the cause of reform in Scotland and led to the collapse of Somerset's regime in England. The 'Edwardian Moment' was over and, with its passing, the dream of a united and Protestant British monarchy appeared to evaporate. Within less than a decade, however, Anglo-Scottish union was back on the agenda. Changed political circumstances – the accession of Elizabeth Tudor in England in 1558 and the rebellion of the Protestant Congregation in Scotland in 1559 – breathed new life into the unionist rhetoric of the late 1540s and once again the prospect of a Protestant British monarchy appeared tantalizingly on the horizon.

Among the most prominent and influential of the new generation of unionists was John Knox. Although a Scot by birth, Knox had emerged as a leading Protestant activist in the England of Edward VI. Subsequently, when forced into continental exile by the Catholic reaction of Mary Tudor's reign, he developed quite distinct programmes of action for his persecuted brethren in England and Scotland. There were, as Jane Dawson has argued, two John Knoxes, one English and one Scottish.[74] It is worth suggesting, however, that the reformer also possessed a third, British, persona which lamented the lost opportunity of the 1540s and looked in the future to the creation of a united British monarchy. Although he never wrote at length on the subject of union, in 1558, in the course of his notorious *First blast of the trumpet against the monstrous regiment of women*, Knox construed the persecution then afflicting his brethren in Britain as a result of 'the proude rebellion and horrible ingratitude of the realmes of England and Scotland', and went on to explain that when God had offered 'the meanes by the whiche they might have been joyned together for ever in godly concorde, then was the one proud and cruel, and the other inconstant and fickle of promise'.[75] Later that year, when his *Appellation to the Scottish nobility and estates* was published, it appeared bound together with another pamphlet

---

[74] Jane Dawson, 'The two John Knoxes: England, Scotland and the 1558 tracts', *Journal of Ecclesiastical History*, 42 (1991), 555–76. In Knox's view, by publicly embracing Protestantism in Edward VI's reign, the English had entered into a covenant with God which bound them on pain of damnation to fulfil the divine ordinance that idolaters – including royal idolaters – must 'die the death'. Protestant Scots, on the other hand, had never publicly covenanted with God in the same way as their English brethren and, while obliged to defend and promote the 'true religion', were cautioned against the wholesale destruction of the Catholic powers who ruled over them. The development of this distinction is traced in the introduction to my *John Knox: on rebellion* (Cambridge, 1994).

[75] David Laing (ed.), *The works of John Knox* (Wodrow Society, 1846–64), vol. IV, p. 394.

entitled *An admonition to England and Scotland to call them to repentance*. Written by the English Marian exile, Anthony Gilby, but surely reflecting Knox's own views, the *Admonition* castigated the people of 'Britanie' for not effecting the 'godlie conjunction' which the marriage of Mary and Edward had promised. Satan, lamented Gilby, 'and Antichrist his sonne, could not abyde that Christ should grow so strong by joyning that Ile togither in perfect religion, whom God hath so many waies coupled and strengthened by his worke in nature'.[76]

Knox himself was later to express sentiments very similar to these in his *History of the Reformation in Scotland* where he talked of the marriage as a 'wonderfull providence of God' and went on to characterize the Rough Wooing in terms of God's 'anger', 'judgement' and 'revenge' in the face of Scottish recalcitrance.[77] More pertinently, however, when he returned to Scotland in May 1559 to lend his weight to the Congregation's rebellion, he did so with the prospect of union firmly in mind. As he wrote to William Cecil in June of that year, 'my eie hath long looked to a perpetual concord betuix these two Realmes, the occasion whareof is now present'.[78] By no means every member of the Congregation shared these unionist sympathies, but by mid-July the rebels as a whole (presumably under Knox's influence) were writing to Cecil of a 'confederacie, amity, and leigue' between the two realms which, being done 'for God's cause', would be quite unlike 'the pactions maid by warldlie men for warldlie proffeit'.[79] Thereafter, throughout the course of the rebellion, hardly a letter crossed the border without some reference to the 'perpetuale freyndschip betwene the tuo Realmes which presently is easy to be done'.[80] Of course, friendship with

[76] Gilby's *Admonition* is reprinted in *ibid.*, vol. IV, pp. 553–71. Quotations from pp. 554, 558, 560.

[77] *Ibid.*, vol. I, pp. 101–2, 119, 122, 214. Also indicative of his thinking is his comment that: 'After the death of this most verteous Prince [Edward VI], of whom the godles people of England, (for the most parte,) was nott worthy, Sathan intended nothing less than the light of Jesus Christ utterly to have bein extinguissed, within the hole Ile of Britannye' (*ibid.*, vol. I, pp. 242–4).

[78] *Ibid.*, vol. VI, pp. 31–2. See also *ibid.*, vol. VI, p. 46, where in a further letter to Cecil Knox wrote suggestively that he 'understood the materis in which I have labored ever sence the deathe of King Edward, now to be opened unto you'.

[79] Knox, *Works*, vol. II, p. 25. In the same letter, the Congregation wrote: 'As tuicheing the assurance of a perpetual amity to stand betuix these twa Realmes; as no earthlie [thing] of us is more desyred, so crave we of God to mak us instrumentis by whiche this unnatural debaite, whiche long hath continued betuix us, may anis be composed, to the prais of Goddis name, and to the confort of the faithfull in boyth realmes' (*ibid.*, vol. II, p. 24). Similar sentiments are expressed (somewhat less fulsomely) in a letter sent to Elizabeth at the same time (*ibid.*, vol. VI, pp. 43–4).

[80] William Kirkcaldy of Grange to Sir Henry Percy, in *ibid.*, vol. VI, p. 33. For many other such references, see Book 3 of Knox's *History* (*ibid.*, vol. II, pp. 1–92), and the Congregation's correspondence with England as collected by Knox's editor (*ibid.*, vol. VI, pp. 11–148).

England was a practical necessity for the Congregation, but there is no reason to doubt that many of the rebel leaders were genuinely committed to dynastic union and the creation of a Protestant British monarchy.[81] What is much less clear, however, is the extent to which Knox and his colleagues conceived of union in the same imperial terms which animated the propaganda of the 'Edwardian Moment'.

Given the unionist sentiments expressed in their correspondence, it is certainly tempting to see the architects of the Scottish Reformation as the direct heirs of the imperial ideology of the late 1540s.[82] Yet closer inspection suggests that, while they undoubtedly shared their predecessors' unionist sympathies, they deliberately shunned the close association between union and empire which characterized the propaganda of the Rough Wooing. On reflection, this is hardly surprising. In England, neither Elizabeth nor her privy council showed any interest in pursuing the British policies which had brought financial and political ruin on Somerset's regime.[83] As a result, Elizabeth's reluctant intervention in Scotland in 1560, while of critical importance in ensuring the Congregation's success, was undertaken in a spirit of pragmatism far removed from the heady apocalypticism of the 'Edwardian Moment'. That it occurred at all was due largely to the persuasive powers of William Cecil who, perhaps alone among Elizabeth's counsellors, possessed a British strategy based on the recognition that England's security would always be at risk so long as Scotland (and Ireland) lay outside her control. Cecil's policy was probably shaped by his personal experience of the Rough Wooing when he served with William Patten on the Marshalsea court during Somerset's Pinkie campaign of 1547. If so, he had clearly learned the ideological as well as the military lessons of Somerset's abject failure. For although familiar enough with the English claim to feudal superiority over Scotland, Cecil wisely saw that to use it as grounds for intervention on the Congregation's behalf would do nothing to further the English cause in Scotland.[84] Not only would it associate Elizabeth with the high-handed military aggression of the Rough Wooing, but it

---

[81] The idea of a marriage between Elizabeth and James Hamilton, earl of Arran, son of the heir presumptive to the Scottish throne, was mooted at least as early as June 1559 (see *CSP Scot.*, vol. I, no. 465) and negotiations to that end were to continue for some considerable time. Cecil, and probably also some members of the Congregation, considered simply setting aside Mary Stewart's claim and hastening complete dynastic union through the Arran match (see *ibid.*, vol. I, no. 537).

[82] A temptation to which I succumbed in my 'Scotching the Brut', in Mason (ed.), *Scotland and England*, pp. 71–2. The linkage is central to the thesis developed in Williamson, *Scottish national consciousness*, ch. 1.

[83] What follows in this paragraph is greatly indebted to Jane Dawson, 'William Cecil and the British dimension of early Elizabethan foreign policy', *History*, 74 (1989), 196–216.

[84] *Ibid.*, p. 206; cf. Conyers Read, *Mr Secretary Cecil and Queen Elizabeth* (New York, 1955), pp. 150–1.

would make nonsense of the Congregation's own attempt to seize the patriotic initiative and portray themselves as selfless defenders of Scotland's ancient laws and liberties.[85]

Such considerations go a long way towards explaining why the language of empire is conspicuously absent from the literature of the Scottish Reformation. Quite simply, in propaganda terms, there was nothing to be gained in either Scotland or England from invoking the Anglo-British imperialism of the 'Edwardian Moment'. In a purely Scottish context, however, there is an additional and less cynical explanation for the reformers' unwillingness to employ imperial rhetoric. For the evidence suggests that Scottish Protestants were deeply suspicious of the Erastian-type church which the idea of empire served to underwrite. Knox's own attitude to the royal supremacy, although not wholly unambiguous, seems increasingly antagonistic.[86] While he consistently assigned the civil power a key role in establishing and defending the 'true religion', and appeared in 1558 to be vesting the secular authorities with supreme authority over the spiritual estate, by the following year he was arguing that the church's jurisdictional rights derived directly from God Himself and that the prince, like any other member of the church, must submit himself to the yoke of ecclesiastical discipline.[87] It was the latter views which were espoused by the Congregation in a letter addressed to Mary of Guise in May 1559 and usually attributed to John Erskine of Dun. Here it was argued that the government of the church belonged only to Christ – 'ffor he is the heid thairoff, all wther ar her memberis vnder him' – and the regent was warned to 'tak na authoritie wpone you abwe the kirk of Christ, for than seik ye to be equall with him quha can hef na merrowis'.[88] That Knox by this stage fully

---

[85] For a detailed analysis of the Congregation's propaganda and the implications of their patriotic stance, see my 'Covenant and commonweal: the language of politics in Reformation Scotland', in Norman Macdougall (ed.), *Church, politics and society: Scotland 1408–1929* (Edinburgh, 1983), pp. 97–126.

[86] Curiously, very little has been written on this aspect of Knox's thought. Richard Kyle, 'The church–state patterns in the thought of John Knox', *Journal of Church and State*, 30 (1988), 71–87, contrives not to mention the royal supremacy at all. The most useful discussion is in James Kirk, *Patterns of reform: continuity and change in the Reformation kirk* (Edinburgh, 1989), ch. 6.

[87] In his *Appellation*, Knox's efforts to persuade the nobility that they were bound not only to defend the faithful but also to punish the persecuting Catholic clergy led him to compare the relationship between the civil and ecclesiastical powers to the subjection of Aaron to the authority of Moses (e.g. *Works*, vol. IV, pp. 486–7). But in 1559, he advised the brethren in England that 'yf the King himself wolde usurpe any other autoritie in God's religion then becometh a membre of Christ's body', he must first be admonished 'according to God's Worde' and, if necessary, 'be subject to the yoke of discipline' (*ibid.*, vol. V, pp. 519–20).

[88] For the full text of the letter, see *Spalding Club miscellany IV* (Spalding Club, 1849), pp. 88–92 (quotations from p. 89). On its broader significance, see Kirk, *Patterns of reform*,

supported the church's claim to jurisdictional independence is strongly suggested by the *First book of discipline* of 1560 where he and his colleagues declared that the kirk was empowered 'to draw the sword which of God she hath received' and to discipline its members 'as well the Rulers, as they that are ruled'.[89] Such views were clearly incompatible with the imperial ideology which underpinned the English royal supremacy. They suggest, in fact, that Scottish Protestant thinking was from the outset profoundly – and consistently – *anti*-imperial.

Suspicion of an English-style royal supremacy, then, combined with hostility to English claims to feudal superiority over Scotland, had the effect in 1559–60 of decoupling the idea of empire from the idea of union. If there was much excited talk of the imminent creation of a Protestant British monarchy, there was no revival of the Anglo-British imperialism of the 'Edwardian Moment'. Nor, at least in Scotland, was there any move to revive imperial rhetoric in the immediate aftermath of 1560. The return of the Catholic Mary in 1561 served the dual function of focusing Scottish patriotism on the figure of a free Scottish monarch and entrenching still further the belief in the kirk's independence of the civil magistrate. Subsequently, Mary's deposition in 1567, followed by the prolonged uncertainties of James VI's minority, while going a long way towards realizing Cecil's policy of reducing Scotland to a satellite of the English crown, witnessed also the emergence of the full-blown theory of the 'two kingdoms' associated with the Melvillian presbyterians. Even when, in the 1570s, the Regent Morton sought to establish what amounted to a Scottish royal supremacy, there was no attempt to cast this in imperial terms. Earlier Stewart monarchs – James III, James IV and James V – had all in different ways deployed the insignia of empire to proclaim the Scottish monarchy's parity of status with its European counterparts.[90] But neither before nor after 1560 was there any attempt to Protestantize this tradition and fashion out of it a specifically Scottish imperial past. Moreover, when in the 1570s the cult of Elizabeth generated in England renewed enthusiasm for the imperial glories of the British past, typified by the publication in 1572 of Humphrey Lhuyd's thoroughly Galfridian *Breviary of Britayne*, it elicited in Scotland a venomous rebuttal from no less a figure than George Buchanan.[91]

pp. 235–40; and F. Bardgett, 'John Erskine of Dun: a theological reassessment', *Scottish Journal of Theology*, 43 (1990), 59–85, esp. 67–71.

[89] James K. Cameron (ed.), *The first book of discipline* (Edinburgh, 1972), pp. 167, 173.

[90] See Mason, 'Chivalry and citizenship', in Mason and Macdougall (eds.), *People and power*, pp. 60, 64. The evidence cited there is by no means exhaustive and the subject still requires detailed investigation.

[91] See H. R. Trevor-Roper, 'George Buchanan and the ancient Scottish constitution', *EHR*, supplement 3 (1966), for Buchanan's response to Lhuyd's work. But for some strictures on

Historians have yet to come to terms with the full significance of the publication in 1582 of Buchanan's *Rerum Scoticarum historia*. Quite clearly, however, just as it played a key role in fashioning a distinctively Protestant Scottish identity, so its republican politics and presbyterian sympathies rendered it wholly inimical to any form of imperial thinking.[92]

In fact, as is argued elsewhere in this volume, it was largely in reaction to Buchanan's views as interpreted by the Melvillian clergy that James VI developed his own self-image as Constantine *redivivus*.[93] Yet Constantinian imperialism found few echoes among the king's Scottish subjects. Admittedly, in the years after 1603, a number of Scots, most notably John Gordon, James Maxwell, and Sir William Alexander, devoted immense intellectual energy to exploring the implications for James of having donned his illustrious predecessor's imperial mantle.[94] But the Anglo-British perspective of these exiled Scots, all of them based at the English court, was hardly typical of opinion in Scotland itself. There, not unexpectedly, union and empire continued to prove uneasy bedfellows. Much more representative were those whose enthusiasm for union was tempered by the fear that Scotland would become, in John Russell's memorable words, 'ane pendicle' of the realm of England.[95] In effect, such sentiments bring us back full circle to John Mair's plea for a union of equals in which Scotland's historic claim to autonomy would be explicitly recognized in England.[96] Certainly, it was precisely this concern which preoccupied the Scottish lawyer and unionist, Sir Thomas Craig of Riccarton, who in 1602 was moved to write a massive defence of Scotland's freedom from English lordship in answer to the 'Fooleries and Scurrilities' contained in the chronicles of Raphael Holinshed.[97] In fact, the real object of Craig's fury was not so much Holinshed

---

Trevor-Roper's interpretation, see my 'Scotching the Brut', in Mason (ed.), *Scotland and England*, pp. 73–4.

[92] By far the fullest and most revealing analysis of Buchanan's context and significance is in Williamson, *Scottish national consciousness*, pp. 117–39.

[93] See above, ch. 5.

[94] On the thinking of these British enthusiasts, see Williamson, 'Scotland, Antichrist and the invention of Britain', in Dwyer (ed.), *New perspectives*, pp. 44–52.

[95] John Russell, 'A treatise of the happie and blissed unioun', in *Jac. union*, pp. 75–141, at p. 97.

[96] For example, Russell claimed in one of the many patriotic outbursts that enliven his tract that 'Scotland is ane verray ancienne kingdome – mair ancienne nor Ingland, nevir conquest as yit be any forraine force, hes gevin repulss to Ingland and overthrauin utheris thair enemies, Pechtis, Danis, Northuegians' (*ibid.*, p. 89). He was also one of the few contemporary Scots to talk explicitly in terms of a union 'betuixt the two imperiall crounes of Scotland and England'. Curiously, however, despite his obvious concern to defend Scottish integrity within the union, he could still refer to James as 'the vive image of Lucius and Constantine' (*ibid.*, p. 80). For fuller analysis of his thought, see ch. 9 below.

[97] Originally written in Latin, it remained unpublished until translated by George Ridpath as *Scotland's soveraignty asserted* (London, 1695).

as William Harrison, the author of the 'Description of Britain' which prefaced both the 1577 and 1587 editions of the chronicles. For Harrison not only devoted an entire chapter to rehearsing England's historic claim to sovereignty over Scotland, but added insult to injury by claiming *inter alia* that the ancient Scots were uncivilized barbarians 'who used to feed on the buttocks of boies and womens paps, as delicate dishes'.[98] It would seem that neither the experience of reform nor the common bond of Protestantism had done much to alter the age-old assumption of English cultural as well as political superiority over Scotland.

Such deep-rooted prejudices hardly augured well for the union of 'hearts and minds' proposed by James VI and I and advocated with enthusiasm by Craig himself. In the wake of his chastening experience as one of the Scottish union commissioners in 1604, Craig wrote another lengthy tract in which he repeatedly stressed the need for the English to treat the Scots as equal – and equally civilized – partners in union.[99] More significantly, however, he went on to echo John Mair's plea that the new British kingdom be underwritten by a new British history. 'As far as possible', he wrote, 'the public annals of the two countries should be revised. Errors and irritating expressions must be expunged (though in this matter our own histories are not so provocative as those of our neighbours), and a new history of Britain should be written with the utmost regard to accuracy'.[100] It is perhaps some indication of what Craig was up against that, as Jenny Wormald has noted, when Francis Bacon similarly proposed the writing of a new history of Britain, it was transmuted in the mind of Lord Chancellor Ellesmere into 'the Story of England'.[101] By now, however, it should come as no surprise to find that Englishmen found it impossible – and unnecessary – to conceive of a history of Britain as something distinct from the history of England. On the title page of his *Book of martyrs*, John Foxe could refer quite unselfconsciously – and with singular lack of discrimination – to 'this realm of England and Scotland'.[102] It may well be that this curious phraseology was

---

[98] Raphael Holinshed, *Chronicles of England, Scotland and Ireland* (6 vols., London, 1807–8), vol. I, pp. 1–220. Harrison's account of the English claim to 'the souereigntie of this Ile' was actually based on the 1548 tract by Nicholas Bodrugan or Adams and on a work of John Leland presented to Henry VIII (*ibid.*, vol. I, p. 196). For the comment on Scottish cannibalism, founded on the authority of St Jerome, see *ibid.*, vol. I, p. 10.

[99] See Sir Thomas Craig, *De unione regnorum Britanniae tractatus*, ed. and trans. C. S. Terry (SHS, 1909), esp. ch. 8, where Craig set out to refute the English belief that the Scots were 'uncivilised, wild, and barbarous, strangers to the humanities and the study of them', and went on to address Harrison's calumnies about primitive Scottish cannibalism.

[100] *Ibid.*, p. 468.

[101] Jenny Wormald, 'The creation of Britain: multiple kingdoms or core and colonies?', *TRHS*, 6th series 2 (1992), 175–94, at pp. 179–80.

[102] That it was not a slip of the pen is confirmed by a further textual reference to 'this my country of England and Scotland', *The acts and monuments of John Foxe* (8 vols., London,

prompted by a charitable desire to accommodate the Scots within the epic sweep of England's Protestant and imperial past. In effect, however, Foxe was merely perpetuating the assumption that the history of England *was* the history of Britain and that there was no need for even the smallest semantic concession to signal the difference between them.[103]

One might well conclude from this that 'Scots *or* Britons' would be a more appropriate title for this volume than 'Scots *and* Britons'. For so long as the history of Britain remained undifferentiated from that of England, the Scots were bound to have the utmost difficulty in reconciling the dual identities and allegiances which union demanded. As things stood in 1603, to conceive of themselves as Scots with loyalties to a greater British whole was tantamount to admitting their incorporation within English ecclesiastical, legal and political structures. Clearly, some Scots, the successors of the Anglo-British imperialists of the 'Edwardian Moment', were prepared to do just that. Historically, Scotland was for them a part of a greater English *imperium*. Many others, however, were unable to accept the denial of Scotland's historic autonomy and identity which this entailed. For them, the new Britain dictated the writing of a new kind of British history. Their problem was that their partners in union could not or would not participate in the invention of a past capable of accommodating Scottish as well as English aspirations. Nor did they need to. Inevitably, as Henry VII is alleged to have foreseen, the greater drew the lesser; and the increasing dominance of English political institutions within Britain gave the Scottish past less and less purchase on the realities of the British present. After 1603, Geoffrey of Monmouth and the old British History rapidly lost credibility and British terminology was consequently freed of its Brut-ish connotations. But the parallel rise of Anglo-Saxonism and the search for an ancient Gothic constitution merely reinforced the irrelevance of the Scottish past and the Englishness of Britain.[104]

1843–9), vol. I, p. 5. The full title of the 1563 edition reads *Actes and monumentes of these latter and perilous dayes, touching matters of the church, wherein ar comprehended and described the great persecutions & horrible troubles, that have bene wrought and practised by the Romishe prelates, speciallie in this realme of England and Scotland* ...

[103] I have found nothing in Foxe to suggest that he drew on the Anglo-British imperialism of the 'Edwardian Moment'. While he certainly endorsed the English claim to superiority over Scotland, he betrays no interest in union or the prospect of a Protestant British monarchy. However, it would be well worth exploring further whether his belief in Scotland's dependent status was integral to his view of England as an empire.

[104] The processes alluded to here are discussed more fully, though from very different perspectives, in Colin Kidd, *Subverting Scotland's past: Scottish whig historiography and the creation of an Anglo-British identity* (Cambridge, 1993), and Linda Colley, *Britons: Forging the nation 1707–1837* (New Haven, Conn. and London, 1992). See also John Pocock's essay, below ch. 12.

8 Number and national consciousness: the Edinburgh mathematicians and Scottish political culture at the union of the crowns

Arthur H. Williamson

Ars sine scientia nihil est.   Anonymous

I

In the summer of 1617 the town of Perth greeted James VI with a proclamation which averred that 'the ancient nation of the Scots' had descended
from 'victorious Greeks and learned Egyptians'.[1] In one sense of course the
people of Perth were uttering a very old commonplace indeed. From the
high middle ages, if not earlier, Scots claimed to have found their origins in
ancient Egypt. From Egypt their primordial ancestors had journeyed to the
mouth of the Mediterranean Sea, settling in Iberia, and from thence they
journeyed still further to Ireland, ultimately to establish themselves in what
became the Scottish kingdom. The Egyptian migration had been led by the
painfully eponymous 'Gathelus' along with a number of his associates – all
Greek military heroes and mercenaries who had married into good Egyptian
families (Gathelus himself marrying no less than the Pharaoh's daughter,
the equally eponymous 'Scota'). These traditions had long served Scotland
well, counteracting the analogous English mythologies which asserted the
suzerainty of the southern crown.[2]

But if the story itself (and the 'victorious Greeks') had been around for a
very long time, Egyptian learning was considerably more recent. During the
Renaissance Scotsmen looked beyond this medieval assertion of dynastic
dignity and historico-legal autonomy to search out the cultural meanings of
the experience. The outstanding figure in this undertaking was the Aberdeen University principal, Hector Boece, whose enormously influential

---

[1] *Τὰ τῶν μουσῶν ἔξοδια, The muses welcome*, ed. John Adamson (Edinburgh, 1618), p. 137.
[2] William Matthews, 'The Egyptians in Scotland: the political history of a myth', *Viator*, 1
(1970), 289–306; Marjorie Drexler, 'Fluid prejudice: Scottish origin myths in the later
middle ages', in Joel Rosenthal and Colin Richmond (eds.), *People, politics, and community in
the later middle ages* (Gloucester and New York, 1987), pp. 60–77; Arthur H. Williamson,
Scottish national consciousness in the age of James VI (Edinburgh, 1979), chs. 1 and 5; Roger
A. Mason, 'Scotching the Brut: politics, history and national myth in sixteenth-century
Britain', in Roger A. Mason (ed.), *Scotland and England 1286–1815* (Edinburgh, 1987),
pp. 60–84.

Scotorum historiae (Paris, 1527) can only be described as one of the major cultural events within sixteenth-century Scotland. Scotland, Boece declared, had once possessed the ancient Egyptian wisdom, the wisdom of the hieroglyphs. As the *Historia* indicated in John Bellenden's contemporaneous translation:

Thay usit the ritis and maneris of the Egyptians, fra quhome thay tuk thair first beginning. In all thair secret besines, thay usit not to write with commoun letteris usit amang othir pepil, bot erar with sifars and figuris of beistis maid in manner of letteris; sic as thair epithafis, and superscriptioun abone thair sepulturis, schawis: nochtheles, this crafty maner of writing, be quhat sleuth I can not say, is perist; and yit thay have certane letteris propir amang thaimself, quhilis was sum time vulgare and commoun.

Even if the ancient wisdom had been lost, the original Scottish language, the archaic Gaelic of the bards, seemed yet to possess something of the sound of its Mediterranean source: 'thay that spekis with the auld toung ... hes thair asperatioun, thair diptongis, and thair pronunciatioun, better than ony other pepill'. Other ancient wisdom, Graeco-Roman rather than Egyptian, could also be found in the earlier Scotland. Among 'mony craftis and science' which they translated into Gaelic, they were particularly skilled in classical medicine. Moreover, Gaelic Scotland had preserved the record of the ancient past (the even now mysterious chronicle of 'Veremund'), while its political history offered politico-moral exempla which spoke to far more than just the Scottish realm.[3]

Scotland's experience thus embraced a range of wisdom, some primal and Egyptian, other parts more mediated and classical. The Renaissance typically regarded such ancient wisdom – and especially Egyptian wisdom – as embodying pristine, original and uncorrupted knowledge. Very often it possessed close associations with neo-Platonism and other magical religious traditions. If no less a figure than Desiderius Erasmus had legitimized the hieroglyphs as a subject of humanist study – and Boece had been his patron at Montaigu College in Paris and became, effectively, his spokesman in

---

[3] Hector Boece, *Heir beginnis the hystory and croniclis of Scotland*, trans. John Bellenden (Edinburgh, 1540?), sig. D2 r; cf. Hector Boece, *Scotorum historiae a prima gentis origine, cum aliarum & rerum & gentium illustratione non vulgari ...* (Paris, 1527), fol. xixb.49–62, also Lib. I, fol. xb.58–66, Lib. II, fol. xxb.60–8. Whoever 'Veremund' may or may not have been, it is important to recognize that Boece was truly linked via clan Campbell to the bardic traditions (John Bannerman, 'Literacy in the Highlands', in I. B. Cowan and Duncan Shaw (eds.), *The Renaissance and Reformation in Scotland* (Edinburgh, 1983), pp. 229–30). Gaelic medicine derived from classical texts which had been translated into the local language. Although the tradition was intensely conservative, it made Gaelic one of the languages in which classical medicine could be studied, in addition to Latin, Greek and Arabic (John Bannerman, *The Beatons: a medical kindred in the classical Gaelic tradition* (Edinburgh, 1986), esp. pp. 82, 89–90, 96).

Scotland – the symbols themselves were often regarded as a divinely inspired system which articulated the true nature of the objects they named. Unlike other languages whose terms acquired their meaning simply through convention, Egyptian truly linked words and things, and its grammar, presumably, paralleled the underlying logos of nature.[4]

Boece never speculated about the Egyptian learning. Nor did he indicate that it could ever be recovered. But the Egyptian connection – with its crucial linkages to culture and civilization – was a matter of the utmost importance in the sixteenth century to an extraordinary range of Scottish intellectuals as well as to the Stewart court – and perhaps never more so than at the moment when Boece published the *Historia*. The volume at once became a virtually official statement of court ideology: James V had it translated into Scots and it would eventually see publication under royal privilege, a major event in the thin annals of sixteenth-century Scottish printing. Moreover, it is surely no accident that the Gypsy community within Scotland, consistently well received by the court, should receive the king's favour at just that moment (1530) and eventually became his protégés – in marked contrast to their experience elsewhere in contemporary Europe.[5] If by the 1570s there began a steady stream of enactments against 'certane ydill and countirfute people of diverse nationis falslie namyt Egiptians', Scotland's Egypt lost none of its cogency as a result. Quite the reverse – from the 1590s onwards into the eighteenth century Boece's history would be summarized and popularized in brief abridgements and, eventually, in pocket almanacs. The ancient stories, prophecies and statements were real

---

[4] John Durkan, 'The beginnings of humanism in Scotland', *IR*, 4 (1953), 5–24, at p. 6; *Hectoris Boetii Murthlacensium et Aberdonensium episcoporum vitae*, ed. and trans. J. Moir (New Spalding Club, 1894), p. 88; For Boece, Erasmus was 'the glory and ornament of our age'. 'There is no spot in Europe so inaccessible that his praises are not found there'. Erik Iversen, *The myth of Egypt and its hieroglyphics in European tradition* (Copenhagen, 1961), pp. 64, 75–6; Don Cameron Allen, *Mysteriously meant: the rediscovery of pagan symbolism and allegorical interpretation in the Renaissance* (Baltimore, 1970), ch. 5, and esp. pp. x, 108, 118–19; cf. Allison Coudert, 'Some theories of natural language from the Renaissance to the seventeenth century', in Albert Heinekamp and Dieter Nettler (eds.), *Magia Naturalis und die Entstehung der Modernen Naturwissenschaften*, Studia Leibnitziana, sonderheft 7 (Wiesbaden, 1978), pp. 56–113.

[5] David MacRitchie, *Scottish Gypsies under the Stewarts* (Edinburgh, 1894), ch. 4, esp. pp. 36–7; Walter Simson, *A history of the Gypsies* (New York and London, 1866), p. 109; Brian Vesey-Fitzgerald, *Gypsies of Britain: an introduction to their history* (London, 1944, 1946), p. 28; Angus M. Fraser and François de Vaux de Foletier, 'The Gypsy healer and the king of Scots', *Journal of the Gypsy Lore Society*, Third Series 51 (1971), 7. Both James IV and James V received the Gypsies favourably, but the latter felt particularly strongly – despite bad experiences and growing hostility towards them at Aberdeen and apparently from members of the court – and the traditional accounts have portrayed his reign as the Gypsies' best moment in early modern Britain. Just before his death James banished them, but the legislation was immediately rescinded during the regency.

enough to fire the popular imagination and on occasion even informed practical policy.[6] What had begun in the earlier sixteenth century as a court phenomenon had become the common currency of the realm.

To be sure, Scotland's was not the only humanist and then Protestant culture to identify itself with peoples at the outset of time and subsequently to find in this identification significant intellectual, political, and even soteriological meaning. Scandinavian intellectuals such as Olaus and Johannes Magnus, Johannes Buraeus and, eventually, Olof Rudbeck undertook a strikingly similar enterprise. All of these scholars sought to create a coherent vision of their societies and to imagine them (despite their cold climate, obscure location and unfortunate reputation) as at once civilized and relevant to Europe.[7] For the Scots these preoccupations proved culturally important and surprisingly creative. If few Scottish writers had the linguistic tools to pursue the putative Egyptian wisdom through its Gaelic sources – and the one individual who did, George Buchanan, perhaps wisely declined to do so – Scottish society would prove remarkably receptive to and tolerant of magical religious ideas. Although it is certainly true that occult traditions also in part became prominent in Scottish discourse from some late sixteenth-century Scottish intellectuals who looked to a magico-apocalyptic future rather than seeking such meaning in the past, the Egyptian mythology retained its persuasiveness for most people. The first abridgements of the *Historia* simply restricted themselves to brief summaries of the careers of the kings within Scotland, but soon thereafter subsequent editions were expanded to include the earlier material. That, it seems, is what people such as the citizens of Perth wanted to read.[8] Boece had established the 'Egyptian learning' as a feature of Scottish identity, and it would certainly have a long history.

---

[6] Even to matters as basic as mining: Stephen Atkinson, *The discovery and historie of the gold mynes in Scotland* (Bannatyne Club, 1825), esp. pp. 24–6, 28–9, 39, 57, 59; see Arthur H. Williamson, 'Scotland, Antichrist and the invention of Great Britain', in John Dwyer *et al.* (eds.), *New perspectives on the politics and culture of early modern Scotland* (Edinburgh, 1982), pp. 34–58.

[7] Iversen, *Myth of Egypt*, pp. 88–9; Kurt Johannesson, *The Renaissance of the Goths in sixteenth-century Sweden: Johannes and Olaus Magnus as politicians and historians*, trans. James Larson (Berkeley, 1991); Susanna Åkerman, *Queen Christina of Sweden and her circle: the transformation of a seventeenth-century philosophical libertine* (Leiden, 1991), esp. pp. 108–21; Arthur H. Williamson, 'The Jewish dimension of the Scottish apocalypse: climate, covenant, and world renewal', in Y. Kaplan *et al.* (eds.), *Menasseh Ben Israel and his world* (Leiden, 1989), pp. 7–30, esp. pp. 7–12.

[8] [John Monipenny], *Certayn matters concerning the realme of Scotland, composed together* (Edinburgh, 1594?, 1597; London, 1603); John Monipenny, *The abridgement or summarie of the Scots chronicles* (London, 1612, and numerous editions after that into the eighteenth century).

II

The decades on either side of 1600 experienced an unprecedented surge of interest in natural magic throughout Europe. In most instances it was associated with a concomitantly deepening interest in prophecy and in the great events thought to be reserved for the latter days of the world. Unprecedented assertions of power and promise occurred in what was a moment of extraordinary hope. A vast flowering of speculation about a Protestant *imperium* took place in Germany, Scandinavia and elsewhere on the continent during these years, speculation founded upon an integration of apocalypticism and magic. These decades marked the historical high point of Protestant academic astrology – altogether ignoring Calvin's objections and Luther's unease – and witnessed as well enormous interest in Paracelsianism, number mysticisms, neo-Platonism and even cabbala. Such expectations issued in Rosicrucianism and the magico-scientific utopias of Andreae, Campanella and Bacon. It is no accident that the first Faust book appears in the late sixteenth century (1587) – to be translated into English, Dutch and French during the next decade. Robin Bruce Barnes is surely right when he remarks that 'the broadly-based Lutheran [apocalyptic] expectancy contributed strongly to the magical and occult strivings so characteristic of German thought in the decades around 1600', but his observation holds true for far more than the Lutheran world.[9] These years saw an altogether new fascination with Jewish mystical traditions and the beginnings of apocalyptic philo-Semitism. In the early 1590s, it seems, Abraham Cohen de Herrera began his immersion in the Lurianic cabbala which would eventually find fruition in the *Puerta del Cielo*. During the 1590s the Swede Johannes Buraeus launched his enormously learned fusion of 'Gothic' historiography, neo-Pythagoreanism, Runic studies and apocalypticism – a project which eventually envisioned a final *dominium maris Baltici*. In fact, these years witnessed increasingly confident prophetic projections almost everywhere and the beginnings of modern millenarian speculation. European intellectuals have found themselves more attracted to magic in some periods than in others – indeed a number had felt its attraction a century earlier[10] – but magic had never before been nearly as

9 R. B. Barnes, *Prophecy and Gnosis: apocalypticism in the wake of the Lutheran Reformation* (Stanford, 1988), p. 184, also pp. 119, 135, 139, 177, 181, 187, 201, 216, and esp. chs. 4 and 5; Martin Brecht, 'Chiliasmus in Würtemberg im 17. Jahrhundert', in Martin Brecht *et al.* (eds.), *Chiliasmus in Deutschland und England im 17. Jahrhundert, Pietismus und Neuzeit* Band 14 (Göttingen, 1988), pp. 25–49; E. M. Butler, *The fortunes of Faust* (Cambridge, 1952; repr. 1979), p. xiii; Frances Yates, *The Rosicrucian Enlightenment* (London, 1972); Frances Yates, *Giordano Bruno and the Hermetic tradition* (London, 1964).
10 Frank Borchardt, 'The *Magus* as Renaissance man', *Sixteenth Century Journal*, 21 (1990), esp. pp. 66, 72–5. M. Vereté, 'The restoration of the Jews in English Protestant thought,

widespread nor associated, as it now so often was, with social reform and eschatology. Wired into the historical redemption, magic became for the first time in its long history more public than private, more political than contemplative.

Scotland participated fully in most of these intellectual developments. The phenomenon later called freemasonry emerged there at this time. A remarkable number of Scottish figures appear to have had an interest in various occult traditions. Most important, a highly significant group of Edinburgh intellectuals – all of them intensely Protestant, all of them interested in mathematics, in biblical exegesis and, in most cases, in prophecy and in the occult as well – appear to have legitimized the pursuit of such esoteric knowledge. Indeed they enabled such styles of thought to penetrate the very tissues of Scottish culture. None of these individuals, every one of them from social elites, are at all likely to have joined a masonic lodge, yet they seem to have made freemasonry socially possible. Several were clearly regarded by later masons as spiritual kindred. Moreover, their analyses of the apocalypse increasingly concretized the prophetic future and opened the way to millenarian speculation. The contrast with other Protestant cultures can be striking. When the contemporaneous Tübingen jurist and Paracelsian physician Tobias Hess speculated about a future millennium, he found himself in some theological difficulty for proposing 'ein Newe Opinion von einem tertio seculo'. James Melville, by contrast, strongly recommended Thomas Brightman's philo-Semitic millennium to his clerical colleagues – many of whose doctrines were adopted by no less an establishment figure than Patrick Forbes of Corse, the future bishop of Aberdeen. The notion of a British *imperium* in the last age, one fully rivalling any continental counterpart, was clearly proposed by a still more establishment figure, Sir William Alexander, and completely accepted by the young Prince Henry.[11] In the years straddling 1600, speculation about the occult and about the millennium could be legitimate as rarely before, and legitimate for a surpris-

1790–1840', *Middle Eastern Studies*, 8 (1972), pp. 15, 45; David Katz, *Philo-Semitism and the readmission of the Jews to England, 1603–1655* (Oxford, 1982), p. 91; Arthur H. Williamson, 'The Jewish dimension,' in Kaplan *et al.* (eds.), *Menasseh Ben Israel*; Kenneth Krabbenhoft, 'The structure and meaning of Herrera's *Puerta del Cielo*', *Studia Rosenthaliana*, 16 (1982), p. 1; Åkerman, *Queen Christina*, pp. 92–3; Åkerman, 'The Gothic cabbala: Johannes Buraeus' runic theology and northern European apocalypticism', paper presented to University of California, Davis, conference on 'The expulsion of the Jews: 1492 and after', 4 April 1992.

[11] David Stevenson, *The origins of freemasonry: Scotland's century, 1590–1710* (New York, 1988), esp. pp. 50–1, 127; Brecht, 'Chiliasmus in Würtemberg', pp. 25–6; Williamson, 'Jewish dimension,' in Kaplan *et al.* (eds.), *Menasseh Ben Israel*; E. J. Cowan, 'The darker vision of the Scottish Renaissance: the devil and Francis Stewart', in Cowan and Shaw (eds.), *Renaissance and Reformation*, pp. 125–140; J. W. Williamson, *The myth of the conqueror: Prince Henry Stuart, a study in seventeenth-century personification* (New York, 1978).

ing range of people. Early modern Calvinist Scotland certainly did not seek to become a tolerant society, yet within limits – and, to be sure, these were severe – it was just that.

By far the most socially significant of the mathematicians was the Reverend Robert Pont. A founding father of the Scottish Reformation and junior colleague to John Knox, he was one of the most eminent of Scottish clergy. For four decades a leader in the general assembly and frequently its moderator, he (with John Winram) had conveyed Knox's last wishes to it. But Pont was also a lawyer and long served in the secular courts, indeed as nothing less than a senator of the college of justice. A militant Calvinist but no doctrinaire presbyterian, Pont at once enjoyed the confidence of the government while participating in the most important and strategic deliberations of the church. If he defended church property rights, he nevertheless strongly endorsed the king's British vision. If he had prosecuted Bishop Bothwell, he would nevertheless appear on government lists of prospective episcopal appointments – an appointment ultimately blocked by his clerical colleagues. An author on Scots law at the church's request, sometime missionary to Morayshire, translator of both Pindar's odes and David's psalms as well as of the Helvetic Confession, lexicographer, poet and preacher, by the decade before his death in 1606 he had become a venerable figure – 'an aged pastour' in the Scottish kirk as the frontispiece to his books repeatedly described him. The young King James VI referred to him respectfully as 'an old theologue' – even when they deeply disagreed – and may actually have hedged his comments on astrology in the *Daemonologie* in deference to him. Pont could even get away with that most dangerous of prophecies, the death of monarchs. Respected on all sides, he had acquired in these years a stature virtually unique within Scottish society. The Reverend Robert Pont spoke with great learning, vast experience and enormous authority, and, when he did so, all Scotland listened.[12]

Of his many intellectual undertakings one clearly stood out. Pont wanted to chart the cycles which he believed to be inherent within the structure of nature and within human experience. The project appears to have taken

---

[12] *DNB*; Robert Pont, *Against sacrilege, three sermons* (Edinburgh, 1599); Robert Pont, *A newe treatise of the right reckoning of yeares and ages of the world and mens lives and the estate of the last decaying age thereof, the 1600 yeare of Christ (erroniouslie called a yeare of Iubilee) which is from the creation, the 5548 yeare* (Edinburgh, 1599); Calderwood, vol. V, p. 131; Robert Wodrow, *Analecta* (4 vols., Maitland Club, 1842–3), vol. II, pp. 341–2. For the king's attitude to Pont, see discussion in the fourth section of this essay. More generally on Pont, see Williamson, *Scottish national consciousness*, pp. 30–1; K. Firth, *The apocalyptic tradition in Reformation Britain, 1530–1645* (Cambridge, 1979), pp. 191–6. Pont's views on astrology appear to be similar to those of Tycho Brahe: Åkerman, 'Queen Christina of Sweden and Messianic thought,' in J. I. Israel and D. S. Katz (eds.), *Sceptics, Millenarians, and Jews* (Leiden, 1989), pp. 144–5; Åkerman, *Queen Christina*, p. 161.

shape during the 1590s and it involved a massive integration of the apocalypse, number mysticism, chronology and astrology. Its intention was to
endow both political history and natural phenomena with a deeper sense of
cause and thus meaning. Pont's synthesis would not only vindicate the
Protestant vision of the past and expectations for the future but would
simultaneously establish a secure framework for understanding nature and
her purposes.

   Like virtually all sixteenth-century Protestants, Pont believed that he was
living in the 'latter days' of the world. Time's final millennium had begun
long ago, the papacy would shortly 'come to utter ruin', and 'the prophecies
and signs' declared that 'the world was near an end'. The apocalypse of
course provided time's underlying programmatic. The chronology of events
it described could be best understood through the periodic sequences of
sacred time. Numbers comprised the key both to nature and to God's design
in history. Although Pont eschewed 'Pythagorical superstition', he strongly
subscribed to the 'manifold mysteries of the number seaven'. Scripture
taught men to reckon time within sabbatical weeks of years which yielded
the central recurring scriptural period of 490 years with important subsets
of half that time. Pont's younger colleague, friend and parishioner, John
Napier of Merchiston, had worked it out in compelling detail for the New
Testament shortly before in his acclaimed *A plaine discovery of the whole
Revelation* (Edinburgh, 1593). It remained to determine how this powerful
insight would fit into the full scheme of things. It needed to be integrated
into the Augustinian millennial week of world history and the recurring
periodicities within that week – most recently described, for Pont, by
Scheltco à Geveren's *Of the end of the worlde and seconde commying of Christe*
(London, 1578) and derived from the metallic imagery in Daniel. It
required at least cognizance of non-scriptural prophecies such as that of the
Rabbi Elias ('not that great prophet Elias but a certaine Rabbin of the Jews
so named'). The seculum's termini also required calculation. By measuring
backwards in sabbatical periods from the advent of Christ, Pont reached the
same creation date, 3947 BC, that Joseph Scaliger had derived by a quite
different method in his *De emendatione temporum* (1583). The future was
more problematic: although Napier's calculation located the Last Judgement in the eighteenth century, Pont like so many of his generation
expected time to be foreshortened in the years immediately after 1600. In
addition, the sacred time sequences needed to be linked with or related to a
sure chronology of world history and alternative chronologies – the Greek
Olympiads described by Pindar and the Egyptian perceptions – demanded
the full range of Pont's erudition.

   In broad terms, time followed a pattern at once linear and yet informed by a
range of cyclicities. The first millennium following the creation was a golden

one, an age of peace, quietness, innocence dominated by Saturn, the planet of quietness and peace 'if we give credit to the Astrologues' (as Pont clearly did). But the age declined into an evening ending with the flood and Noah. That in turn initiated the second great age (under the benevolent planet Jupiter) with a world renewed but inferior to its predecessor. But that age too had an 'evening' when the posterity of Noah declined to idolatry and Nimrod founded the first tyranny. Thereafter Abraham was separated out from the idolaters inaugurating the age of brass which yet again declined to end with the period of the four great monarchies (the iron age). In the fifth age, the world was restored with Christ (in an age of peace under Augustus Caesar) only to deteriorate once again with the rise of the papal Antichrist, a process completed by Pont's reckoning in the year 1056 with Pope Sylvester II. Then followed the age of the antichristian night whose end rapidly drew near before the prospect of the third and final golden age which would end time itself. Men therefore lived in a great Noahidic reprise and, in anticipation of the end, should be purging their societies and separating themselves from the idolaters within it. Within this overarching framework the rhythms of the human experience worked themselves out in the sabbatical and sub-sabbatical periods which Pont calculated with great detail and formidable exactitude.

All of this had to be connected with the processes of nature, and, for Pont, that meant astrology. If the apocalyptic programmatic, firm chronology, and the influencing patterns of nature could be effectively integrated, then the rise and fall of societies, the fatal periods of monarchies, the periodicities of creation would at last be certain and fully understood.[13] In the end Pont's project would give rise to a vast astral sociology. As the sun, planets and stars possessed periodic natures

so ... also in the common-wealthes and policies established by men for holding up mutuall societies amongst themselves, there be certain periods of time, which make them to change and alter: which may be found out by experience and ensample of Histories of all ages, as well ecclesiasticall as profane. The cause thereof cannot be ascribed to chance and Fortune as unskillfull men doe: for then all these changes would be most uncertaine; neither is it altogether to be ascribed to the corrupt manners of men that cannot long remain in one estate but ever more seek novationes and changes: ... although that maie be as a concurrente cause, but it must needs proceede from an high grounde.

If 'the divine science of Astrology' had 'certaine limites and bounds' and its predictive powers were as yet problematic, its history (and thereby its

---

[13] *Newe treatise*, pp. 35–6, 24, 93, 62, 84, 86, 17, 76, 77, and 'Propositions' 6 and 7. For Pont's chronologies, see *Newe treatise*, pp. 36–42, 71–4 and the *Sabbaticorum* (discussed further below).

correlations) were obviously unarguable.[14] Intelligibility for Pont therefore arose through an extraordinary naturalizing of the sacred and drawing together of those two fundamental realms of being. The results were powerful. In the latter days of the world the Christian faith, the Protestant scenario, would find itself anchored ultimately on naturalistic bases. The forces of Antichrist would be confuted, and the self-deceived Jews shown – quite literally – the miscalculation which had given rise to their expectations about the coming of the Messiah.

The new certitude in the world, which Pont sought to delineate, of course turned on the persuasiveness of astrology, and it was no small part of his project to vindicate 'this science' against 'mockage and contempt'. Astrology had acquired a bad name because 'vulgare prognosticators' who understood neither the heavens nor their influences had made predictions which all but inevitably failed:

there are superstitious observations used by many in the artificial setting up of the figure of the heaven and applying the same without any sufficient natural cause or reason to every purpose, which I for my parte altogether improove [i.e. reprove] and condemn. And yet it followeth not hereof that this divine science should be all utterly rejected and condemned as many that be ignorant of it do.

Popular astrology failed for many reasons, but primarily it did so because the shifting of the heavens since antiquity meant that 'the old rules' of the Chaldeans and Arabians would 'serve not our dayes and time'. In the days of Ptolemy the vernal equinox had intersected the sign of Aries not far from its first star, but by the sixteenth century the equinox had shifted some 27 degrees 15 minutes backwards *vis-à-vis* that sign. Altered positions had led naturally enough to altered influences:

the signes taking their nature and properties from the fixed starres and having now changed their place render other influences to the aire and earth then they did of before. So that they which sometime were hoat are now become cold and they that were dry humide ...

Pont, who saw himself in the tradition of the great academic astrologers such as Johann Stoeffler, Caspar Peucer and Erasmus Rheinholt, wanted to save the phenomenon by providing it with a rigorous scientific basis.[15] So anchored, prophecy became fortified rather than supplanted: had not

---

[14] *Ibid.*, pp. 45, 66 [printed 65].

[15] *Ibid.*, esp. pp. 44–50, 62, 21–2. Don C. Allen, *The star-crossed Renaissance* (Durham, 1964), esp. pp. 53–69; Barnes, *Prophecy and Gnosis*, pp. 99, 107–8, 148, 175, 159. Characteristic of the age, Pont's thought was an eclectic amalgam of neo-Platonic, Stoic and Aristotelian traditions. Number mysticism was of course Platonic, but his heavily naturalistic concern to reform astrology suggests Hellenistic Aristotelianism and sounds somewhat like the early preoccupations of the Elizabethan magus John Dee (see Nicholas H. Clulee, *John Dee's natural philosophy: between science and religion* (London, 1988), esp. pp. 40–1, 70–3).

Matthew warned of the stars departing their accustomed places in the latter days?

Pont's project looked to a reconstituted astrology, founded upon more accurate astronomical measurements and mapping – not altogether unlike that of Tycho Brahe, who was in contact with several of Pont's mathematical colleagues. If in the end the project must strike moderns as utterly barren, it visibly demanded an enormous erudition, it attempted to naturalize the most basic processes in the universe, and it sought the advancement of human learning. But in context it possessed still greater significance. Its initial statement appeared in the vernacular as *A newe treatise of the right reckoning of yeares and ages of the world and mens lives and the estate of the last decaying age thereof* ... (Edinburgh, 1599), and was quite specifically and almost apologetically intended for a popular audience – while Pont's major work on chronology *De sabbaticorum annorum periodis chronologica a mundi exordio ad nostra usque secula et secula et porro digestio* (London[?], 1619; 1623) only appeared much later and posthumously. Thus the project was the highly public undertaking of probably the most renowned member of the Scottish intellectual establishment, and it inherently legitimized lines of inquiry and modes of cognition that had long been suspect (and often more than suspect) to any orthodoxy. If Pont continually warned about the misuse of astrology and about its present limitations, he was emphatic that the heavens provided light, enabled men to measure time, and made possible the prediction of the future. If Pont also insisted upon the efficacy of human will against the influences of the stars, his vision of the universe and its processes seems at moments remarkably Stoical. In Pont, Daniel the prophet and Daniel the magician became one.

For upwards of thirty years Pont's neighbour, colleague, friend, and the leading layman in St Cuthbert parish was John Napier of Merchiston. Pont referred to him as 'honoratum et apprimê eruditum amicum nostrum fidelem Christi servum Joanem Naperum' whose *Plaine discovery* was 'profound and learned' – and much used. More radical and much more militantly presbyterian than Pont, Napier took pains to discredit Constantine and the godly Roman emperors as models for Christian kingship and thereby undermined much of the ideological basis of King James's British designs. Napier's preface to the first edition of his commentary in 1593 urged the presbyterian programme upon the young James in remarkably sharp terms. That same year he led a delegation from the general assembly to confront the king about the crisis of the plotted Spanish invasion and specifically for his trafficking with the popish earls. His commentary on the apocalypse and his work in mathematics had endowed him with enormous authority to contemporaries from the early 1590s, and he clearly came to be regarded as one of the ornaments of the realm. Even for those such as Bishop Cowper, who strongly disagreed with both his religious politics and its apocalyptic, the laird of Merchiston was

> our countrey-man worthily renowned as peerless indeed for many other learned works and especially his great pains taken upon this Booke [i.e. Revelation], out of rare learning and singular ingyne, which are not commonly found in men of great ranke.

If Napier's commentary on the Revelation and his invention of logarithms, his working out of decimal notation, his work in developing and systematizing spherical trigonometry had established his international reputation, his domestic reputation turned on still other achievements. He developed a number of elementary calculating devices, known to contemporaries as 'Napier's bones', invented a hydraulic screw and revolving axle to keep the water level down in coal pits, apparently experimented with manures and discovered the value of common salt for this purpose, and designed a number of extraordinary military devices to protect the realm in its time of crisis. The presbyterian party would recurringly turn to Napier for his erudition about antiquity and the early church. Sir John Skene would look to Napier – 'a gentleman of singular judgement and learning especially in mathematic sciences' – for his erudition about the various methods to be used in land measurement.[16]

Napier had another kind of erudition and, it seems, another kind of reputation which went with it. Like Pont, Napier practised astrology. At St Andrews University he not only encountered Christopher Goodman's analysis of the Revelation but also encountered Mark Kerr of Newbattle who had very powerful interests in magic and a long association with the Napier family. Although Napier's apparently voluminous papers were lost to fire in the eighteenth century, his alchemical interests are well established, and an alchemical manuscript of his son and literary executor, Robert, has survived ('Mysterii aurei velleris Revelatio; seu analysis philosophica qua nucleus verae intentionis hermeticae posteris Deum timentibus manifestatur' ('Revelation of the mystery of the Golden Fleece or philosophical analysis whereby the marrow of the true Hermetic intention is made manifest to God-fearing posterity')). Napier was familiar with various Jewish mystical traditions – perhaps not surprisingly given his fascination with the Old Testament – which he could 'neither affirm nor condemn'. In

---

[16] Mark Napier, *Memoirs of John Napier of Merchiston* (Edinburgh, 1834), pp. 102, 62–3; *Newe treatise*, pp. 62–3; William Cowper, *Works* (London, 1623), p. 822; see Williamson, *Scottish national consciousness*, pp. 21–30, 34; and Williamson, 'Scotland, Antichrist, and the invention of Britain', in Dwyer (ed.), *New Perspectives*. Pont's description of Napier may be rendered as: 'that faithful servant of Christ, my honoured and surpassing learned friend, John Napier'.

1594 he contracted with Robert Logan of Restalrig, the outlawed ally of
Francis Stewart, earl of Bothwell, to find 'be al craft and ingyne' hidden
treasure thought to be located somewhere in Fastcastle. Although the contract does not disclose the divining techniques Napier would employ, they
were certainly occult. Given his interests and his (albeit brief) association
with the most notorious occultist in Scottish history, it is probably not surprising that, even before his death, his name had become linked with Galfridian prophecies, that he was reported to have compacted with the devil,
that he was believed to have a familiar in the form of a black cock (a family
emblem), and that oral traditions about his magic persisted even into the
early nineteenth century. Margaret Baron is probably right to suspect that
only his quintessentially establishment position saved him from prosecu-
tion as a warlock. But, in a way, that is precisely the point: the establishment, or at least a good part of it, clearly and publicly accepted the
occult traditions.[17]

Aside from astrology, we will probably never know in detail the kinds of
magic that interested Napier. Nor will we probably uncover how they
informed his many projects. Even the arcane symbols on his portrait
remain undeciphered. But it seems likely that, for him, numbers and
mathematical manipulations possessed a mystical or even magical character. He seems to have regarded his investigation of imaginary roots as a
great algebraic secret – perhaps not unlike the way hermetic mysteries were
regarded (and protected). He saw a 'marvellous harmony' between the
trinity and the dimensions inherent within God's 'holy Jerusalem', a
concern at least broadly analogous to preoccupations of Johannes Kepler.
In fact Napier was put in contact with Tycho Brahe by Dr John Craig, a
mathematician who was also James VI's physician, when the royal party
visited Brahe's observatory at Hven in 1590. A letter of Kepler's written in
1624 seems to indicate that he had received information on Napier's work

---

[17] Napier, *Memoirs*, pp. 92, 147, 148, 218–23, 236–7, 260, 301, 320–1; Cowan, 'The darker
vision', in Cowan and Shaw (eds.), *Renaissance and Reformation*, p. 139; G. Murray, M. R.
Apted and I. Hodkinson, 'Prestongrange and its painted ceiling', *Transactions of the East
Lothian Antiquarian and Field Naturalist Society*, 10 (1966), 92–132; M. R. Apted and
W. N. Robertson, 'Four "Drollities" from the painted ceiling formerly at Prestongrange,
East Lothian', *Proceedings of the Society of Antiquaries of Scotland*, 106 (1974–5), 158–60;
long ago John Read described Napier's encounter with the German alchemical adept Daniel
Müller in 1607 and 1608 which indicated in some detail Napier's alchemical interests and
that he had been 'for some time a serious student of alchemy' ('Scottish alchemy in the
seventeenth century', *Chymia*, 1 (1948), 139–51); *A plaine discovery* (1593), pp. 8–9, 118; cf.
the 1611 edition at p. 336. The letter of Napier's half brother Archibald to Mark Kerr
discussing astrology is an extraordinary document, not least in its concerns paralleling those
of Robert Pont. (Napier, *Memoirs*, p. 321n); *DSB*. Napier's biblicism and his preoccupation
with the ancient Jewish commonwealth and with Jewish systems of time reckoning would
lead him naturally enough into Jewish wisdom and Jewish studies generally.

as early as 1594.[18] Napier and Pont both therefore need to be seen as participants in the magico-scientific world of the northern Renaissance. That world was prominently established in Scotland.

Napier was well aware of younger men in the field and urged James to become 'the patron and accepter of their godly exercises':

For let not your majestie doubt but that there are within your Realme (as wel as in other countries) godly and good ingynes, versed and exercised in al maner of honest science and godly discipline, who by your Majesties instigation might yeelde foorth workes and fruites worthie of memory, which otherwise (lacking some mightie Maecenas to incourage them) may perchance be buried with aeternall silence.[19]

Pont too spoke of 'the rare Mecenases of this land' and specifically noted the work of another scholar which correlated the sub-sabbatical periods with the natures of the seven planets. 'The authors name I will suppress till he himself publish it ... for I will not ascribe unto me the prayse of other mens labours'.[20] One of the men whom Pont and Napier surely had in mind – he is likely to have been the author of the table to which Pont referred – was the young James Maxwell. Maxwell had initially intended to pursue his 'mathematicall studies' in Denmark with 'the famous and noble philosopher and astrologician' Tycho Brahe, possibly encouraged to do so by Craig or Napier. But in the end he was dissuaded by Robert Rollock and instead finished his Master of Arts at Edinburgh University in 1601.[21] His interest in mathematics, like that of Pont and Napier – and Brahe for that matter – clearly extended to the astrological and prophetic. Indeed Maxwell had an altogether consuming passion for the apocalypse and all forms of prophecy. At the age of nineteen he began what must have been a massive study in Latin of both Protestant and Catholic commentary on Daniel and Revelation which focused on the 'being continuance and ending of those great tribulations'. Dedicated to the church and college of Edinburgh, it apparently formed the basis for a lifetime of apocalyptic study, whose range of contemporary and medieval sources has struck Marjorie Reeves as 'remarkable'. In Scotland he was, as he later said, 'a professed Puritane' and surely shared the outlook of Pont and Napier. But at the union of the crowns he experienced a dramatic conversion and followed the king south

---

[18] *DNB*; *DSB*; Napier, *Memoirs*, pp. 206, 354–5; Read, 'Scottish alchemy'; Thomas Riis, *Should auld acquaintance be forgot ... Scottish Danish relations, c.1450–1707* (2 vols., Odense, 1988), vol. I, p. 121.

[19] *A plaine discovery*, 'The Epistle Dedicatorie'.   [20] *Newe treatise*, pp. 3, 68.

[21] James Maxwell, *A new eight-fold probation of the church of Englands diuine constitution ...* (London, 1617), sig. B1 r; see Williamson, *Scottish national consciousness*, pp. 103–6; 'Scotland, Antichrist, and the invention of Britain', in Dwyer (ed.), *New Perspectives*; and 'Jewish dimension', in Kaplan (ed.), *Menasseh Ben Israel*, for an introduction to Maxwell and his intellectual context.

to become one of the most relentless apologists for the Jacobean British order and its imperial implications. The conjunction of Saturn and Jupiter in Aries in 1603 (occurring only once in 800 years) apparently suggested to Brahe that 'the eternal sabbath of all creation is at hand', and the date of this expectation doubtless encouraged Maxwell's decision. Like so many Scots in this period and later, Maxwell found the prospect of a British empire to be irresistible.[22]

Like Pont and Napier, Maxwell had an abiding interest in chronology. But in his *Dies Domini*, a work never printed and apparently now lost, he went well beyond anything contemplated by either of them and 'shewed in what season of the year and on what day of the week, by all likelihood, the world is to end'.[23] Not surprisingly he also saw great significance in popular Galfridian prophecy and in the sayings of Merlin – something neither Pont nor Napier would ever touch. Maxwell learnedly distinguished between the two Merlinic traditions, suggesting naturally enough that the Caledonian Merlin seemed more persuasive than the Welsh one. He then dissented from both the Scottish scholastic John Mair and the Spanish Jesuit demonologist Martin Del Rio about Merlin's legitimacy:

I doe thinke that he was not a diabolicall but onely a natural magician, well seen in the admirable secrets of nature and especiallie in astrologie, and that his horoscope or constellation did incline him to ayme at fore-knowledge and fore-telling of things to come; the like whereof hath befallen to many others more.[24]

Maxwell's perceptions constitute an advanced form of the excited thinking associated with the prospect of a new British age. The government itself willingly printed the ancient sayings attributed to Merlin, Bede, Thomas the Rhymer, Gildas and a great many others which seemed to indicate that James I's new monarchy was fulfilling the hoariest of expectations. A 'leaf' out of Robert Bruce's left side to the ninth degree had long been prophesied one day to reconstitute ancient Britain, and these expectations now appeared to be in the process of fulfilment. Robert Birrell noted in his diary that 'at this time the haill commons that had red or understanding, were

---

[22] *Eight-fold probation*, sigs. B1 r, B1 v, p. 53; James Maxwell, *Admirable and notable prophecies* (London, 1615), sigs. A2 v, A3 v; see note 17; Åkerman, 'Queen Christina', in Israel and Katz (eds.), *Sceptics, Millenarians and Jews*, p. 145; Åkerman, *Queen Christina*, p. 161. Maxwell's great manuscript 'book' was apparently lent by the university to the Reverend John Welsh for what was to be a few days, and he subsequently took it with him into exile in France; Marjorie Reeves, *The influence of prophecy in the later middle ages* (Oxford, 1969), pp. 499–500.
[23] *Admirable and notable prophecies*, sig. A3 r; Maxwell, *A demonstrative defence, or ten-fold probation of the doctrine of the church of England* ... (London, 1617), p. 15.
[24] *Admirable and notable prophecies*, p. 14.

daylie speiking of Thomas Rymer hes prophesie and of uther prophesies quhilk wer prophesied in auld times'.[25] Even Archbishop Spottiswoode marvelled at the obvious fulfilment of the ancient sayings in the person of King James. Maxwell characteristically went further than most: not only the new Britain, but even the king's Irish policies had been anticipated by Merlin. All of these attitudes – for which Maxwell sought to provide intellectual basis – represent an enormous reversal of earlier reformed thought. William Perkins, whose writings and federal theology proved extremely influential in Scotland, took as little account of 'Merlins drunken prophecies' as he did of the tales of Robin Hood. Marian exiles and founder reformers such as John Knox and John Foxe had wanted no part of Merlin. Knox emphatically insisted that 'My asurances are not the Mervallis of Marlin nor yitt the dark sentences of prophane prophecies'. For Foxe such profane prophecies were simply demonic:

By these experiments [= experiences] and mischievous ends of such prophecies and by the nature of them, it is soon to be seen from what fountain or author they proceed; that is, no doubt, from Satan, the ancient enemy of mankind ... In the same number are to be put all the blind oracles of the idolatrous gentiles, which although they proceed of a lying spirit, yet sometimes hit the truth to mischevous purpose. The like judgement is to be given of Merlin's prophecies. ... For as once in the old time of Gentility, he gave his oracles by idols and priests of that time; so the same devil, although he worketh not now by idols, yet he craftily can give now answer by astrologers and conjurers in these our days.

Not only had Galfridian prophecy been rejected by reformers and counter-reformers, by clerics such as Mair, by humanist scholars such as George Buchanan, and by royal authority such as Henry VIII's, there had even existed a popular scepticism articulated in verses such as 'Mum and the Sothsegger': '... there nys [= is not] wight in this world that wote bifore eve/ How the wind and the weder wol wirch [= work, make] on the morrowe'. Perhaps the lawyer Thomas Craig, one of the finest minds in sixteenth-century Scotland, best captured this extraordinary moment. On the one hand he dismissed the prophecies of Merlin as so 'full of ambiguities, turnings, and windings, that the oracles of Delphos are not to be compared to them'. Yet, in the same volume, he agreed that if the prophecy of Cadwallader applied to anyone, it was surely King James. The new

---

[25] *A collection of ancient Scottish prophecies* (Bannatyne Club, 1833); *The romance and prophecies of Thomas of Erceldoune*, ed. J. A. H. Murray (EETS, 1875); G. B. Harrison (ed.), *A Jacobean journal ... 1603–1606* (London, 1941), pp. 50–1; John Spottiswoode, *History of the church of Scotland*, ed. M. Russell and M. Napier (3 vols., Spottiswoode Society, 1847–51), vol. I, pp. 93–4; Williamson, *Scottish national consciousness*, p. 94.

century promised to open the way to radically new possibilities, and James Maxwell sought to be its theorist.[26]

The wisdom of the ancient world had always appealed strongly to Maxwell, and he wanted to believe that 'vertuous Gentiles' such as Hermes Trismegistus, Zoroaster, Socrates, Plato, Aristotle, Pythagoras, Homer, Lycurgus and others – a list which visibly included pre-Christian equivalents to Merlin – had escaped damnation. Of the ancient traditions, the more mystical clearly held particular attraction,

especially of the diuine Plato unto whom I was alwayes more deuote [than to Aristotle] and of the renowned Ægyptian philosopher Hermes Trismegistus; following therein the example of those four famous Italian philosophers Franciscus and Joannes Picus Mirandula, Marsilius Ficinus, and Franciscus Patricius.

Among Maxwell's now lost writings is what he describes as a 'Pythagoreticall play at cards, representing the excellencie and utilitie of Union, with the ignobilitie and incommodities of Division'. Prophecy, magic and mathematics would underwrite the reunion of mankind under the new British aegis. Here lay his fundamental concern. Confronting an increasingly fragmented and discordant world, Maxwell sought the mystical keys to a new coherence, and in this preoccupation he probably was the closest thing Scotland ever produced to Italy's Tommaso Campanella or to France's Guillaume Postel – or for that matter to Sweden's Johannes Buraeus. It led to his rejection of 'Geneuisme' – Napier's presbyterian apocalyptic, Pont's Calvinist theology – and fired his consuming commitment to a new, imperial British era.[27]

---

[26] For Maxwell, Merlin's prophecies joined sacred prophecy, astrology, number symbolism and genealogy in explaining and legitimizing James's British vision – all of which looked forward to a prophetic British age ('yea, the same Merlin hath likewise foretold long ago the plantation and conformation of Ireland by his Maiesties meanes'). Merlin's confirmation of the new imperial Britain and James's Irish policies seemed only natural, for, according to Maxwell, James's person had united all the ancient dynasties – Irish, English, Welsh, Scottish (*The treasure of tranquility, or a manuall of moral discourses, tending to the tranquility of the minde* (London, 1611), 'The Epistle Dedicatory', sigs. A11 v–A12 v). For Maxwell's expectations for the British age, see Williamson, 'Scotland, Antichrist, and the invention of Britain,' in Dwyer *et al.* (eds.), *New Perspectives*; Walter B. Stone, 'Shakespeare and the sad augers', *Journal of English and Germanic Philology*, 52 (1953), 457–79; John Knox, *Works*, ed. D. Laing (6 vols., Wodrow Society, 1846–64), vol. III, p. 168; John Foxe, *The Acts and monuments . . .*, ed. S. R. Cattley (8 vols., London, 1837–41), vol. III, pp. 756–61; *Mum and the Sothsegger*, ed. M. Day and R. Steele (EETS, 1936), p. 77; Thomas Craig, *Scotland's sovereignty asserted*, trans. George Ridpath (Edinburgh, 1695), pp. 116, 125. Merlin's most vigorous non-religious critic was probably the great humanist and political theorist George Buchanan: 'Merlin ... must be considered an egregious imposter and cunning pretender rather than a prophet' (*History of Scotland*, trans. James Aikman (4 vols., Glasgow, 1827), vol. I, pp. 233, 236–44). See generally for this topic, Williamson, *Scottish national consciousness*, pp. 101–2, 178–9.

[27] *A demonstrative defence*, p. 9; *A new eight-fold probation*, sig. B1 r; *Carolanna* (London[?], 1619), p. (3); the play was named in honour of the king and queen, 'Iamesanna, alias Hearts-Union'; Williamson, 'Jewish dimension', in Kaplan *et al.* (eds.), *Menasseh Ben Israel*,

Not all of the Edinburgh mathematicians seem to have shared this obsession with apocalypticism and magic. James Hume of Godscroft studied Scripture closely enough to write a Hebrew grammar (*Ραδιομαθεια linguae haebraeae, hoc est Grammatica haebraea copiosissima et compendiosissima . . .* (Hamburg, 1624)), but appears never to have written about the latter days. He was very interested in the measurement of time, but his interest took the form of a *Méthode universalle et très facile pour faire et déscrire toutes sortes de quadrans & d'horologues, équinoctiaux, horizontaux, méridionaux, verticaux, & polaires* (Paris, 1640). Hume's Calvinist credentials could hardly be bettered. He was the son and heir of David Hume of Godscroft, one of the key theoreticians of the presbyterian party, a man who had been widely regarded as the intellectual successor of George Buchanan and who had served as tutor and secretary to Archibald, eighth earl of Angus, probably the most significant and militant of the presbyterian lords. A self-conscious borderer from the Merse, the elder Hume espoused a 'country Calvinism' and – while he never dissented from his colleagues' apocalyptic expectations – also never used that imagery other than as metaphor.[28] James Hume's Calvinism appears to have assumed a similar shape, and it led to a more modest approach to mathematics. He would focus upon devising a simplified notation for François Viète's algebra, developing spherical trigonometry, and battling the egregious counter-Reformation toady, Jean-Baptiste Morin, on matters ranging from the Copernican system to plagiarism:

The author [Hume] . . . set forther a treatise on trigonometry in 1635 which demonstrated certain propositions of Napier of Merchiston never before proven. And Morin criticized them in his book on trigonometry wherein he showed one of these to be of no use in proofs. In the following year 1636 Morin added an appendix to his book on trigonometry, in which he transcribed out of Hume's book these propositions and theorems, and in order to conceal the theft, he mixed them up, one with another in an astounding way. And with the greatest of impudence he tried to pass this off as his own, as if in the city of Paris frequented by so many men of the greatest learning and in the presence of the author himself, such manifest plagiarism could not be perceived. As Morin is held the most unlearned of all mathematicians, so he can justly be also called either the most impudent of all mortals or else the most imprudent.[29]

---

p. 18. Maxwell also appears to resemble the contemporaneous Italian Giordano Bruno in his search for primal (magical) knowledge which would go beyond confessional conflict. Unlike Campanella or Buraeus, Maxwell never found his Urban VIII or his Gustavus Adolphus. He never even obtained the position he sought at the Chelsea College, which was to be the new Britain's intellectual centre. Moreover, by the time he reached London, Maxwell's mathematical studies had been abandoned for theology and prophecy.

[28] See Arthur H. Williamson, 'A patriot nobility? Calvinism, kin-ties, and civic humanism', *SHR*, 72 (1993), 1–21.

[29] David Hume, *Poemata omnia* (Paris, 1639), third section, pp. 43/44–45/46. James Hume's work is appended to this reissuing of his father's poetry and selected prose. For J. B. Morin

When James Hume spoke of prophecy it came out as ironic Rabelaisian romance. When he wrote about architecture it was a distinctly unmasonic analysis of the French and Dutch styles of military fortification. His enemy Morin mightily promoted astrology – 'la plus haute et plus diuine des sciences naturelles' – but Hume only joked about it. Morin had early developed an interest in the cabbala and was much exercised by the imminent appearance of Antichrist, subjects about which Hume had nothing to say.[30] Hume's Calvinism undoubtedly ran deep, but his outlook, classical rather than biblical, might best be described as post-apocalyptic. Numbers no longer held the mystery that they had for his eminent elders.

Magic, mathematics and prophecy visibly flourished in Edinburgh in the late sixteenth and early seventeenth centuries. Often they interacted with one another and could even form part of an integrated world view. All three were enormously creative, if in different ways, and they all attest to the great vitality of intellectual life in Jacobean Scotland. The migration of the court at the union of the crowns proved disruptive. Craig and Maxwell pursued the new British order south, while Hume eventually settled in France. Most telling of all, Napier ended his days without successors and with his closest

---

(1583–1656), see *DSB*. Hume's verse comments on Morin's 'eruditio', 'ingenium', 'verecundia', and 'fama' might well be imagined. James Hume, *Traité de la trigonométrie, pour résoundre tous triangles rectilignes et sphériques, avec les démonstrations des deux célèbres propositions du baron de Merchiston non encore demonstrées* (Paris, 1636), 'Au Lecteur', pp. 141, 145–6, 184–202; *Sphères de Copernic et Ptolémée, avec l'usage et constructions des tables sphériques de Regiomontanus* ... (Paris, 1637), esp. 'Au Lecteur', pp. 17–36, 65–6, 81–4, 90, 96, 485; *Algèbra de Viète, d'une méthode nouvelle, claire et facile. Par laquelle tout l'obscurité de l'inventeur est ostée, & ses termes pour la pluspart inutiles, changez ès termes ordinaires des artists* (Paris, 1636); *Méthode universelle* (Paris, 1640); *La Théorie des planettes, contenant l'usage et construction de toutes sortes de tables astronomiques* ... *avec response aux premières invectives du sieur Morin* ... (Paris, 1637).

30 *Pantaleonis vaticina, satyra* ... (Rothomagi [= Rouen], 1633), a send-up of John Barclay's enormously popular *Argenis*; *les fortifications françoises, d'une méthode si facile qu'on les pourra apprendre sans maistre* (Paris, 1634); I have not been able to locate his *De arte muniendi more Hollandico* (Paris[?], 1634[?]) which he says was based upon Samuel Marolois (1572?–1627), *Opera mathematica ou oeuvres mathematiques, traictés de géometrie, perspective, et fortification* ... (Hagae-Comitis, 1614–[17], and many subsequent editions); J. B. Morin, *Remarques Astrologiques* ... (Paris, 1654), p. 3; *Astrologia Gallica* ... (The Hague, 1661); According to Pierre Bayle, Queen Christina wanted to see Morin on her first trip to Paris because of his reputation as an astrologer. His battles with Gassendi on the subject are well known. See Pierre Bayle, *Dictionary historical and critical* (5 vols., London, 1734–8), vol. IV, pp. 258, 261; M. [Joseph] Delambre, *Histoire de l'astronomie moderne* (2 vols., Paris, 1821), vol. I, p. xliii, vol. II, p. 344; James Hume, *Algèbra de Viète*, p. 424; Åkerman, *Queen Christina*, pp. 170, 171. Regarding cabbala and Antichrist, see Bayle, *Dictionary*, vol. IV, pp. 265–6 and J. B. Morin, *Astronomicarum domorum cabala detecta* (Paris, 1623). Ironically, Morin first studied astrology with a Scot, the physician William Davidson. (Bayle, *Dictionary*; *DSB*; John Read, 'William Davidson of Aberdeen: The first British professor of chemistry', *Ambix*, 9 (1961), 70–101). Characteristically, Morin made a point of taxing Hume for his Calvinist faith (*Défense de la verité contre la faussete & l'imposture* (Paris, 1636), pp. 10, 12, 21, 30).

intellectual links to English mathematicians. And yet for all that, their impact on Scottish society can only be described as extraordinary. The 'Mecenas' for Pont's *Newe treatise*, so rhetorically and intellectually anti-papal as it was quite literally from its first line, turns out to be the Catholic Alexander Seton, earl of Dunfermline. Less than four years earlier Seton's career nearly ended summarily in a radical Protestant riot in Edinburgh. Yet such was the earl's well-known interest in mathematics and such was the eminence of Pont that he could sponsor a work utterly inimical to his faith. Later he would also patronize the presbyterian Napier's work on calculating mechanisms, the *Rabdologia, seu numentionis per vingulas libri duo* (Edinburgh, 1617).[31] Every one of the Edinburgh mathematicians had a Protestant political agenda, but their undertakings seemed so momentous and so promising that they transcended political and even religious dissent. There could hardly exist more eloquent testimony to their status, power and influence.

III

> Thou has ordered all things in measure and number and weight.
> The Wisdom of Solomon

In the late 1590s Scottish stonemasons organized themselves into semi-secret 'lodges' which were independent of their incorporated municipal guilds. Undertaken at the behest of William Schaw, the king's master of works, the masonic lodges were a national phenomenon even though no centralized authority emerged. The masons saw themselves as the successors to the ancient Egyptians among whom architecture and its mystical

---

[31] *DNB*; Maurice Lee, Jr, *Government by pen: Scotland under James VI and I* (Urbana, 1980), esp. pp. 9, 19, 47–8, 122–3; Lee provides a detailed and persuasive analysis of Seton's deeply politique career in 'King James's popish chancellor', in Cowan and Shaw (eds.), *Renaissance and Reformation*, pp. 170–82. Although Lee notes that Seton was a 'fastidious intellectual', he sees this as significant only in that it would attract him to King James's 'intellectualism' (p. 181). Napier commented in his dedicatory epistle to the *Rabdologia* that but for Seton's encouragement (and warning that others would very likely publish his discoveries as their own) the work would not have appeared. [sig. P3 r–3 v]. Perhaps inevitably in these circumstances Seton became rather a second parent than a patron ('ad quem non modo ut patronum, sed potius ut alternum parentem') – even if the work was also unworthy of so great a Maecenas ('tanto Maecenate indigni'). It is entirely in keeping with Seton's career that he should sponsor a *New grammar* written by the Melvillian Alexander Hume and then rally to its defence against the hostility of the episcopal establishment. He numbers among the very few Catholics indeed to be remembered at all fondly in Calderwood's *History*. (J. Durkan, 'Education: laying fresh foundations', in J. MacQueen (ed.), *Humanism in Renaissance Scotland* (Edinburgh, 1990), pp. 140–1; Lee, 'Popish chancellor', in Cowan and Shaw (eds.), *Renaissance and Reformation*, p. 182; Calderwood, vol. VII, p. 549).

mathematical meanings were first perceived and developed (Euclid, it seems, was an Egyptian). The Israelites subsequently took this wisdom with them and gave it physical form as Solomon's temple – all of which became especially real and relevant for any Scot because of the centuries-old national mythologies now newly recast by Boece. Underlying the masons' vision of themselves was a series of assumptions which had entered Latin Christian culture long before through works such as Augustine's *De musica*, Boethius's *De arithmetica*, and the commentaries of Macrobius. According to this tradition, certain numbers and especially certain numerical proportions possessed a metaphysical dignity in that these relationships constituted the fundamental ordering of the cosmos – and, like the heavens, the basic structure of the heavenly city at the end of days. To think of these proportions – which could be articulated acoustically through music or spatially through geometry and architecture – was to have one's mind raised 'anagogically' to the highest forms of truth and to an intimation of the experience of redemption. The building of Solomon's temple (and presumably the building of the pyramids and other Egyptian structures) duplicated on a smaller scale what God Himself had performed in Genesis. In this tradition Solomon 'taught' architecture, and God appeared, dividers in hand, as the master builder of the cosmic temple. Thus, in claiming these ancient (and yet curiously Scottish) traditions as their own, the Scottish masons asserted that they were no mere craftsmen practising a mechanical art, but theoreticians of a *scientia* that rivalled any other form of learning.[32]

The emergence of freemasonry should probably be seen therefore as part of a growing fascination with mathematics both as symbol system and as mystery which took place within much of Scottish culture during the 1590s. Freemasonry is quite typical of the period in other ways as well. Natalie Davis's description of the confraternity of journeymen printers in sixteenth-century Lyons – the Company of the Giffarins – whose secular rituals and mythology concerned Minerva, 'the Mother of Printing and the Goddess of Knowledge', suggests striking parallels with that of the masons. The Giffarin preoccupation with upstart 'forfants' also rather closely resembles masonic preoccupation with upstart 'cowans'. To be sure, France was a much larger and more complicated society – in the sixteenth century Lyons was easily six times the size of Edinburgh – and nothing like comparable tensions between masters and journeymen would occur in freemasonry until the late seventeenth century. Although the Giffarins

---

[32] Stevenson, *Origins of freemasonry*; David Stevenson, *The first freemasons: Scotland's early lodges and their members* (Aberdeen, 1989), ch. 1; Otto von Simson, *The Gothic cathedral*

maintained fraternal relations with comparable organizations elsewhere (especially Paris), their focus remained municipal. But by the earlier seventeenth century, semi-secret journeymen's associations had emerged in France on a national scale – the phenomenon of 'compagnonnage' – whose rites (according to several variants of its mythology) similarly derived from the builders of Solomon's temple. At some point, it has been suggested, compagnonnage began incorporating masonic materials, and, given the similar features of these organizations, this is hardly surprising.[33]

Freemasonry was therefore in its origins neither intellectually nor organizationally peculiar. What *was* peculiar was Scottish reaction to it. In the words of freemasonry's most recent historian: 'One of the most startling aspects of the sudden appearance of the masonic lodges and their rituals in seventeenth-century Scotland is that no attempt was made to suppress them.'[34] French Calvinism categorically opposed confraternities, even overwhelmingly Protestant ones like the Giffarins (who had proved instrumental in the 1562 Calvinist seizure of Lyons). Once alerted to its existence, counter-reformed France consistently sought the destruction of compagnonnage as at once sacrilegious and subversive. It seems clear that more was at issue than simple class tension: the Catholic church absolutely rejected its rituals as 'abominable impieties', while secular authority saw not only economic subversion but also the illegal usurpation of authority in the compagnons' constituting themselves as a corporate body.[35]

Scottish authorities too took an exceedingly dim view of secret fraternities which often enough truly constituted a species of organized crime. In 1606 the privy council called loudly for the suppression of the 'deboscheit and laules lymmaris' who had associated themselves into 'The Society and Companie of Boyis'. 'They haif most unlauchfullie and seditiouslie bound thamselffis in ane fellowschipp with aithis, vowis, and protestationis of mutuall defence and persute, and that every one of thair quarrellis salbe commoun to all.'[36] Even the private bonds of manrent and of friendship – so

(New York, 1956; repr. Princeton, 1988), ch. 2; M. C. Jacob, *Living the Enlightenment: freemasonry and politics in eighteenth-century Europe* (New York, 1991), pp. 35–6.

[33] Natalie Z. Davis, 'Strikes and salvation at Lyons', in *Society and culture in early modern France: eight essays by Natalie Zemon Davis* (Stanford, 1975; originally published in 1965), pp. 1–16; Cynthia Truant, 'Solidarity and symbolism among journeyman artisans', *Comparative Studies in Society and History*, 21 (1979), 214–26; William H. Sewell, Jr, *Work and Revolution in France: the language of labor from the old regime to 1848* (New York, 1980), esp. ch. 3; Douglas Koop and G. P. Jones, *The genesis of freemasonry* (Manchester, 1947), pp. 59–60.

[34] Stevenson, *First freemasons*, p. 9; also Stevenson, *Origins*, pp. 50–1, 128–9.

[35] Emmanuel Le Roy Ladurie, *Carnival in Romans* (New York, 1979), p. 294; Truant, 'Solidarity and symbolism', pp. 217–18.

[36] *RPC*, vol. VII, p. 418.

long a staple of Scottish political life – fell into disrepute after 1603, and their incidence rapidly declined.[37]

The answer to the riddle of freemasonry must surely lie in Scottish cultural and social self-consciousness. Scottish culture not only broadly experienced in the 1590s what we might loosely call a neo-Platonizing moment, but the phenomenon was in some ways seen as a collective undertaking. A spectrum of occult and mystical traditions was promoted and legitimized by the Scottish intellectual elite to a popular – that is, vernacular – audience. Neither Napier, nor Pont, nor Maxwell had ever intended other than to write in Latin and to address other than a learned and international readership, as each of them quite specifically indicates.[38] But circumstances constrained these highly academic, but also highly political individuals to do otherwise. Certainly the masons wanted to see themselves participating in the learned traditions – that was after all the point of their mythologies and rituals. Pre-modern Europe associated physical labour and the mechanical arts with servility and with the pain of damnation, associations escaped through the *scientia* of the masonic mysteries. Moreover, these mysteries held real plausibility within the Scottish context. In the mid-seventeenth century masons recalled that 'in the purest tymes of this kirke maisons haveing that word have been ministers'. Within the mental world of the Edinburgh mathematicians, this is far from impossible, and there does exist some evidence to suggest that a laird became a mason as early as 1600. When, again at mid-century, masons thought of their intellectual purposes, they found themselves thinking of Napier, 'the Generalissimo of all wise men'.[39]

It is simply inconceivable that Pierre Viret or any of the Lyonnais consistory would join the Giffarins. It is hard to imagine what could induce a parish priest however radical to become a campagnon. But it is altogether plausible that a minister with Pont's preoccupations – if not the aged reverend himself – might become a mason. Such was the remarkable intellectual and social plasticity of early modern Scotland.

---

[37] Jenny Wormald, *Lords and men in Scotland: bonds of manrent, 1442–1603* (Edinburgh, 1985); cf. Keith M. Brown, *Bloodfeud in Scotland 1573–1625* (Edinburgh, 1986).

[38] See the dedication in *The newe treatise* and the 'Epistle Dedicatorie' to *The plaine discovery*; both wrote in the vernacular, somewhat apologetically, in response to urgent politico-religious needs (the armada crisis; the concern to debunk the false jubilee scheduled to be celebrated by the papacy in the year 1600). Maxwell's original manuscript book was in Latin, but all of his publications appeared in English and most often as quaint verse summaries of learned arguments. Only Napier's mathematical treatises were published in Latin; Pont's formal Latin treatise of chronology, *De sabbaticorum*, only appeared much later and posthumously.

[39] Stevenson, *Origins*, pp. 127–8; Stevenson, *First freemasons*, pp. 8, 32; Anthony Low, *The Georgic revolution* (Princeton, 1985); Anthony Low, 'New Science and the Georgic revolution in seventeenth-century English literature', *English Literary Renaissance*, 14 (1984), 231–59.

IV

> Men shall run to and fro in the latter days and knowledge shall increase.
>
> Daniel 12.4

Freemasonry arose in a context of intellectual excitement and of relative toleration. But not everyone in Jacobean Scotland shared these enthusiasms. The young King James, intellectually conservative – and both politically and emotionally terrorized by the earl of Bothwell – utterly condemned 'magie' and the Egyptian wisdom. Although he could accept the apocalypticism of the age, he stood firmly opposed to 'the Divels schoole' of judicial astrology. Astronomy was certainly 'most necessarie and commendable'. But astrology – not a true branch of mathematics – possessed no such legitimacy. At most, James grudgingly admitted, it might lawfully be used 'moderatelie' in medicine and in predicting the weather. But even so it should not be regarded as 'so necessarie and commendable' as astronomy. James's overriding concern, understandably, was to prevent political prophecy. What astrology could not – must not – do was to

> fore-tell what common-wealthes shall florish or decay: what persones shall be fortunate or vnfortunate: what side shall winne in anie battell: what man shall obteine victorie at singular combate: what way and of what age shall men die ... and diuerse such like incredible things, wherein *Cardanus, Cornelius Aggrippa*, and diuerse others haue more curiouslie then profitably written at large. Of this roote last spoken of, spring [the] innumerable branches [of the occult sciences].

Moses may indeed have learned 'all the sciences of the Ægyptians', as Scripture expressly stated, but that did not include the occult. Or, if in fact it did, Moses certainly did not practise such nastiness. Or, if actually he did, he stopped doing this sort of thing when he led the Israelites out of bondage. Egyptian wisdom was either legitimate (and, we might add, Aristotelian) or it was irrelevant.[40]

'But', conceded the king, almost certainly thinking of the vastly respected Robert Pont, 'manie of the learned are of the contrarie opinion.' James then declined to develop his opposing argument (it would take too long) and simply cited Jeremiah's prohibition before hurrying on to another topic.[41] Yet even if James ducked a direct confrontation the issue remained: the *Daemonologie* had reduced 'the divine science of astrology' to a trifle (at best) and altogether precluded Pont's project. The publication of the *Newe*

---

[40] James VI, *Daemonologie* (Edinburgh, 1597; Bodley Head repr., London, 1924), pp. 10, 12–14, 24–5. The lines in Scripture (Acts 7.22) are hard to escape.

[41] *Ibid.*, p. 14; James met Tycho Brahe in Denmark and may have had him in mind as well; see note 18 above.

treatise within two years of the king's great retro-active proof of the reality of witches and of the obligation to prosecute them is an extraordinary event. The treatise's confrontation with the king undoubtedly accounts for its careful admission that men had not 'yet so farre' mastered the science so as to predict the political future and 'the general chaunges and alterations of kingdomes and common-wealthes' – though most likely 'they have found out many particulars concerning particular persons'. Still, even if large-scale political prophecy currently involved 'great obscurities and imperfite', if there were 'boundes and limites', if the influence of the stars could never overturn free will, if the Chaldeans were now irrelevant, if 'vulgar prognosticators' gave everyone a bad name, there remained a fundamental truth – and man's grasp of it was improving.[42] The two books dance around each other, stake their territory, and – ever so politely – define the fundamental argument. As is so often the case with the pre-modern period, the radical merges with the traditional, the discredited with the genuinely innovative. James's debunking of astrology, dissociating it from astronomy and mathematics, formed a part of his assertion of the manifest danger of witchcraft and the urgent validity of the witch-hunt. Pont's defence of the occult urged a more confident view of human capacity, while it sought and in part achieved a more open society. Both Pont and Napier were well aware of the role of the 'necromantick' popes in the rise of Antichristian power and they wanted people to be well aware of it, but they were no less concerned to expand the range of legitimate inquiry and the sum of human knowledge. To do so was, after all, nothing less than to fulfil the promise of the latter days and thereby work the historical redemption. During the lifetime of the king, the *Daemonologie* never received a more direct rebuttal.

More than books confronted one another. On the day of Elizabeth's death, Pont reportedly managed to gain access to the king 'at a very unseasonable time' and greeted him as 'king of Great Britain France and Ireland'. James's reaction, quite restrained from one perspective, ran: 'I still [= always] told ʒou ʒou would go distracted in ʒour learning and nou I see ʒou are so!' It is not reported whether Pont's prophecy resulted from astrology or some sort of natural insight (the minister denied being a seer). More telling is the mixture of both exasperation and deference in James's response. The *Daemonologie* had bitterly criticized 'diuers Christian Princes and Magistrates' who prosecuted witches and then ignored or even celebrated magicians. In the case of Robert Pont, leading theologian and, not

---

[42] *A newe treatise*, p. 67 and *passim*. Pont's treatise is studded with political astrology virtually throughout, but see especially p. 82.

incidentally, a powerful backer of James's corporate Britain, the king simply had no choice.[43]

With the Renaissance, magic had become a part of Scotland's historical identity. The wisdom of Gathelus and Scota, the eponymous founders of the Scots, was of a piece with that of Moses. The hieroglyphs, yet extant, both contained and concealed this natural revelation. It was therefore perhaps only appropriate that Scotsmen should participate in what was in fact the wisdom of Solomon. In itself this offered no striking political implications – beyond validating the mason's trade and, possibly, asserting Scotland's dignity and autonomy within popular culture. But semi-secret organizations practising arcane mysteries were typically regarded by early modern authorities as subversive and frightening. Number mysticism and magic only became intellectually legitimate and socially possible because of highly important individuals, some of whom – like Pont and Napier – showed little or no interest in Scotland's Egyptian past. But whatever their attitude towards Scottish antiquity, the Edinburgh mathematicians looked to a magico-apocalyptic future and in the process provided a language for both imagining an imperial Britain and for criticizing it. Yet their writings achieved more than intended and legitimized species of cognition which had become part of popular culture. Against a ferocious intellectual reaction in which the king played a leading role, the mathematicians, both imperial and anti-imperial, expanded the realm of the intellectually acceptable. This action became particularly important in a context where, unexpectedly, the elite spoke to broader audiences. The imagination of intellectuals and that of working people interacted to produce a social phenomenon which would prove enduringly significant to western political history. Modern liberal values would have been utterly alien to Pont, Napier, Maxwell, Craig and Hume, but each helped create the cultural environment whereby such might become conceivable.

---

[43] Robert Wodrow, *Analecta* (4 vols., Maitland Club, 1842–3), vol. II, pp. 341–2; *Daemonologie*, p. 24; for Pont's commitment to Britain, see Williamson, 'A patriot nobility?'. Pont, *Newe treatise*, p. 39; Pont believed that, as some animals could foretell the weather, so too could people: 'For if it be granted (as we know it is) to certyaine foules of the aire and beastes of the earth, to fore-know and feel the aire and tempestes to come, how should we altogether denie fore-knowledge to be graunted to men, to conjecture of these accidents, having reason, judgement, and experience to lead the thereto?' (*Newe treatise*, p. 46). It is not clear whether some natural men's abilities might extend to matters beyond the weather.

9   Law, sovereignty and the union

Brian P. Levack

The purpose of this chapter is to explore the influence of lawyers and the law on the development of Scottish political thought at the time of the union of the crowns. This subject has not received a great deal of attention from historians. One reason for this is that very few lawyers appear to have engaged in political discourse at this time, a situation which in turn may be attributed to the relatively small size of the Scottish legal profession. A second reason, closely related to the first, is that very little Scottish political thought, regardless of its authorship, appears to bear much of a juristic character. This situation stands in contrast to continental European political thought, which was profoundly influenced by the study of Roman law long before the turn of the seventeenth century.[1] It also stands in contrast to English political thought, which reflected the growing dominance of the common-law frame of mind during the Tudor and early Stuart periods.[2] John Pocock has suggested that in the late seventeenth and eighteenth centuries the study of civil jurisprudence may have been a major influence on the political thought of Scotsmen.[3] But the study of legal influences on political thinking in the early seventeenth century has only barely begun.[4]

Despite the apparent poverty of the sources, there is enough material available upon which such an investigation can proceed. The basis of it is a substantial number of treatises that were written by Scots during the first two years following the personal union. Two of these treatises were written by Scottish lawyers: Sir Thomas Craig's *De unione regnorum Britanniae*,

---

[1] Myron Gilmore, *Argument from Roman law in political thought, 1200–1600* (Cambridge, Mass., 1941); William F. Church, *Constitutional thought in sixteenth-century France* (New Haven, Conn., 1941); Ernst H. Kantorowicz, *The king's two bodies: a study in medieval political theology* (Princeton, 1957), pp. 87–143.

[2] J. G. A. Pocock, *The ancient constitution and the feudal law* (2nd edn, Cambridge, 1987); G. R. Elton, 'The rule of law in sixteenth-century England', in A. J. Slavin (ed.), *Tudor men and institutions* (Baton Rouge, La., 1972), pp. 265–94.

[3] J. G. A. Pocock, 'Cambridge paradigms and Scotch philosophers', in I. Hont and M. Ignatieff (eds.), *Wealth and virtue* (Cambridge, 1983), pp. 235–52.

[4] See especially Arthur H. Williamson, *Scottish national consciousness in the age of James VI* (Edinburgh, 1979), ch. 3.

which was completed in 1605 and published by the Scottish History Society in 1909, and John Russell's *The happie and blissed unioun,* which was written in 1604 and more recently published by the Scottish History Society.[5] These two works shall form the basis of this study, but it will also draw on three other works by these two men: first, Craig's famous *Jus feudale,* a study of European feudal law with particular attention to its application in Scotland, which was written during the first decade of the seventeenth century and first published in 1655; second, Craig's *De hominio,* or *Scotland's soveraignty asserted,* which was written in 1604 and first published in 1695; and third, Russell's manuscript tract, 'Ane wther treatise contieninge the deuty and office of ane christiane prince ... in the administratioun of his imperiall crounes', which was appended to his union treatise in 1604.[6] A final group of materials consists of other Scottish union tracts of 1604, which were not written by lawyers but which sometimes reveal the influence of the law upon their thinking, and the works of Sir John Skene, who was one of the other lawyers active in public life at the time of the union.

The writings of Craig and Russell address two political issues that were thrown into sharp relief by the union of the crowns. The first was the nature of 'Britain' and the relationship between England and Scotland under the personal union. This became the main political question in Scotland during the reign of James VI and I, and in a certain sense it retained that urgency throughout the seventeenth and early eighteenth centuries. One important aspect of this question was the nature of Scots law and its relationship to English law. The second issue was the power and authority of the king and his relationship to the law. That was a central question for political theorists both in Britain and on the continent, and it became the subject of considerable debate in 1604 as a result of the union. Before exploring these issues, however, it is important that we look briefly at both Craig and Russell and the profession to which they belonged.

I

Of the two lawyers, Sir Thomas Craig of Riccarton (1538–1608) is by far the more famous. Indeed, he is still today recognized by Scottish lawyers as the earliest of the institutional writers, which means that his works have authority equivalent to that of judicial decisions. He is also recognized by historians as a major figure in the development of modern historical

---

[5] *Jac. union,* pp. 75–102.
[6] NLS, Advocates' MS 31.4.7, fols. 21 r–27 v; BL, Royal MS 18 A LXXVI, fols. 23–7.

thought.[7] Craig's legal education, like that of many of his colleagues, took place overseas. After beginning his studies in the arts at St Andrews, he travelled to Paris, where he read civil and canon law under Petrus Rebuffus and Franciscus Balduinus. He also may have studied under the great humanist legal scholar Jacques Cujas at another French university. In any event, he acquired from his studies in France an appreciation of the humanist approach to legal texts as well as the neo-Bartolist appreciation of customary law that characterized the work of François Hotman. His application of this approach to the feudal law, his knowledge of Greek, his elegant Latin style, his familiarity with ancient classical texts, and his finely honed philological skills all mark him out as one of the leading exponents of legal humanism in Renaissance Scotland.[8]

Craig was admitted as an advocate in the court of session in 1563, and from that time until his death he maintained an extremely busy legal practice, with which he combined his scholarly undertakings. He held very few public offices, although he did act as a commissioner to revise the laws and print the statutes in 1587, and he also served in the general assembly in 1589. His main involvement in public life did not come about until 1604, when he and the other great lawyer of the early seventeenth century, Sir John Skene, were appointed to the commission to negotiate a treaty of union with England. His union treatise, written in late 1604 and early 1605, was in many ways a defence of the ill-fated treaty he had helped to negotiate.

Concerning John Russell much less is known. We can be fairly certain that the John Russell who wrote *The happie and blissed unioun* was the John Russell who practised as an advocate in the central courts from the early 1590s until his death in 1613 and whose son John followed in his footsteps.[9] We have no information regarding Russell's formal education, although internal evidence from his works suggests a comfortable familiarity with the civil law, so it is likely that he, like Craig, was educated overseas. Russell also demonstrates a fairly wide knowledge of classical history and philosophy, and he even uses Greek quotations, although his works bear fewer of the signs of humanistic education than are evident in those of Craig. His style of argument follows the traditional model of academic disputation, and his work displays more signs of the Aristotelian terminology that characterized earlier political writing in Scotland. We might conclude from all this that Russell, while by no means a scholar in Craig's mould, displayed

---

[7] Pocock, *Ancient constitution*, pp. 79–90. On the limitations of Craig's historical scholarship, see J. J. Robertson, 'The illusory breve testatum', in G. W. S. Barrow (ed.), *The Scottish tradition* (Edinburgh, 1974), pp. 84–90.

[8] John W. Cairns, T. David Fergus and Hector L. MacQueen, 'Legal humanism in Renaissance Scotland', *Journal of Legal History*, 11 (1990), 48–52.

[9] *Jac. union*, pp. liv–lv.

much broader learning than one might expect of an average Edinburgh advocate. He does not appear to have held any public office, but he was sufficiently well connected at court to arrange for a copy of his union treatise to be presented to King James at Westminster.[10]

The profession to which both Craig and Russell belonged was, at least by contemporary English standards, both small and vaguely defined. Records of advocates pleading in Edinburgh date from the fifteenth century, but it was not until the establishment of the faculty of advocates as part of the college of justice in 1532 that they achieved some kind of institutional identity. Originally numbering only eight men, many of whom were churchmen trained in the canon law, the faculty grew in size during the sixteenth century, reaching a total membership of 54 in 1587, a few years before Russell was admitted. By that time the faculty had been completely laicized.[11] The faculty of advocates did not constitute the entire Scottish legal profession during these years; there were clerks who did essentially the job of soliciting and were organized in the writers to his majesty's signet as well as advocates practising in some of the other Scottish towns. But the faculty represented the elite of the Scottish legal profession.

One might expect that the members of the faculty of advocates in the time of Craig and Russell had developed a distinctive professional ethos and corporate mentality. The model in this regard were the English common lawyers, who by the end of the sixteenth century exhibited a deep sense of pride in, and reverence for, the law they practised, a recognition of its antiquity and superiority over all other legal systems, and a frequently intense rivalry with the practitioners in the ecclesiastical and conciliar jurisdictions, many of whom were men trained in the civil law. There is little evidence that such a strong sense of professional identity had emerged in Scotland by the turn of the seventeenth century. Certainly there was nothing in Scotland to compare with the 'common-law frame of mind' that had developed in England. The main reason for the absence of such an outlook was the amorphous and uncertain nature of Scots law at this time.

Scots law in the early seventeenth century was an amalgam of many different elements, consisting mainly of English law that had been imported and Scotticized during the late middle ages, Roman and canon law that had been 'received' in the fifteenth and sixteenth centuries, and a large sub-

---

[10] On the differences between the Edinburgh and London versions of Russell's manuscript, see *Jac. union*, pp. lv–lvii.

[11] Nan Wilson, 'The Scottish bar: the evolution of the faculty of advocates in its historical social setting', *Louisiana Law Review*, 28 (1968), 235; Gordon Donaldson, 'The legal profession in Scottish society in the sixteenth and seventeenth centuries', *Juridical Review*, new series 21 (1976), 9; Alexander Murdoch, 'The advocates, the law and the nation in early

stratum of custom, much of which was feudal in origin. This law, moreover, had been preserved and transmitted in a number of different forms, including various bodies of written law, such as the *Regiam majestatem* of the fourteenth century, the acts of the Scottish parliament, the decisions of the court of session, and the commentaries of learned civilians. The multiplicity of these sources and the absence of a clearly defined 'common custom of the realm', which formed the nucleus of the English common law, lent credence to the contemporary characterization of Scots law as an 'undigested mass'.[12] To make matters worse, there were legitimate doubts regarding the authenticity of many of the texts that were currently in use, including all the statutes passed before 1424.

In the late sixteenth century there were a number of attempts to remedy this deplorable situation by achieving some kind of codification, an enterprise that attracted widespread support in both legal and religious circles.[13] Royal commissions were appointed in 1566, 1574 and 1592 with the express purpose of establishing 'ane certaine writtin law ... to judge and decide be'.[14] These commissions never produced a digest of Scots law, but the work of codification did result in the publication of a number of legal texts which became available for use by Scottish lawyers. In 1597 Sir John Skene, who served on all three commissions and whose scholarship also reflected the influence of humanism, published the *Lawes and actes of parliament*, which was a new edition of all of the statutes passed since 1424, and in 1609 he followed this with *Regiam majestatem; the auld lawes and constitutions of Scotland*.

Even more important than the publication of these texts was the attention that men such as Skene and Craig gave to the relative value of the various sources of Scots law. This resulted in two decisions of broad significance. The first was a relegation of Roman law to an inferior place to that of native Scottish sources. This point needs emphasizing, since there is a long tradition in the study of Scots law that stresses the importance, if not the dominance, of Roman law. To be sure, Scots law, unlike English law, has long been a 'mixed' legal system, and retains that character to the present day. Roman law has always had a place in the formulation of Scots law, and that was as true for Craig and Viscount Stair as it was for the civil and canon lawyers of the fifteenth century. It is also true that Scots lawyers continued to receive their education in Roman law well into the modern period, and

modern Scotland', in Wilfrid Prest (ed.), *Lawyers in early modern Europe and America* (London, 1981), pp. 147–63.

12 John Cowell, *Institutiones juris Anglicani* (Cambridge, 1605), preface. George Ridpath compares Scots law before the time of Sir Thomas Craig to an 'undigested Chaos' in his preface to Sir Thomas Craig, *Scotland's soveraignty asserted* (London, 1695), p. xxx.

13 Williamson, *Scottish national consciousness*, ch. 3.   14 *APS*, vol. III, p. 89.

that this education had a powerful influence on some of their political ideas. But the Romanist element in Scots law must be kept in perspective. Just as legal historians are now discovering the strength of native Scottish influences and the relative weakness of Roman influences on the development of both substantive and procedural Scots law,[15] so the lawyers of Craig and Russell's day witnessed the relegation of Roman law to the status of 'the custom of foreign people' (which is the way Skene referred to it) or a rough equivalent of 'natural law', which was to be resorted to only when the superior, native sources of law were found to be deficient (which was roughly the position taken by Craig).[16] As we shall see, it is possible that this clear de-emphasis of non-Scottish influences, which reflects the Bartolist insistence on all learned law being considered as suppletive, had an impact on the close association of native Scots law with Scottish sovereignty during the union debates of the seventeenth century.

The second decision that was apparent in the work of both Craig and Skene was the elevation of parliamentary acts to a place of primary importance as a source of Scots law. The reason for this elevation of statute had nothing to do with the legal power of Scottish statutes. The passage of Scottish acts had never affected the course of Scots law in the decisive way that English statutes had.[17] The reason was quite simply that the Scottish acts were the most authoritative source of law that Scots had. As Craig wrote in *Jus feudale*, 'We have no other body of positive written law of comparable authority ... The Scots Acts are practically the only written source of law we have'.[18] The reason that Craig reached this conclusion was that after applying his skills as a philologist to the ancient laws and constitutions of the country, he found reason to call their authenticity into question. Indeed, it appears to have been Craig, perhaps aided by others, who recognized that the celebrated *Regiam majestatem* was copied from the twelfth-century English text that we customarily refer to as Glanvill. Consequently Craig would not accept its authority except to the extent that it embodied native custom.[19] There were also limitations to the authority of judicial decisions, such as those collected by Sir James Balfour in his *Practicks*, since many of them contained serious errors. Even the early acts – those passed before 1424 – could not be accepted as authoritative, since the original records of them had vanished.

---

15 See for example Hector L. MacQueen, 'Pleadable brieves, pleading and the development of Scots law', *Law and History Review*, 4 (1986), 403–22.

16 Sir Thomas Craig, *Jus feudale* (Edinburgh, 1732), 1. 8. 16–17; Cairns *et al.*, 'Legal humanism', p. 53.

17 Brian P. Levack, *The formation of the British state: England, Scotland and the union, 1603–1707* (Oxford, 1987), p. 92.

18 Craig, *Jus feudale*, 1. 8. 9–12.   19 Cairns *et al.*, 'Legal humanism', pp. 57–8.

The reverence paid to statute continued throughout the seventeenth century. Until the appearance of Viscount Stair's *Institutions* in 1681, the acts were considered the 'chief pillar of our law'.[20] This elevation of, and reverence for, statute was evident in a number of contexts, including the debates over Anglo-Scottish union. Not only did it influence the position taken by both Craig and Russell on Anglo-Scottish union in their treatises of 1604, it also characterized Scottish protestations against the religious policies of Charles I in 1638, which appealed to a Scottish act passed in James VI's reign.[21] It was the Scottish acts, rather than Scottish custom or common law, which formed the basis of the Scottish conception of their law.

II

Let us turn now to the specific political issues which occupied the minds of these two broadly educated, legally trained advocates in the first decade of the seventeenth century. The main issue that engaged both of them was the nature of Britain after the regal union of 1603, which was the subject of their union treatises. On first examination the tracts appear to be so dissimilar, and their approaches to the question of union so different, that one may wonder why they should even be compared, much less searched for evidence of a common political and legal outlook. Craig's treatise was a defence of the Anglo-Scottish union commission of 1604, of which he had been a member. It bears many characteristics of a piece of special pleading. After a long historical introduction, in which Craig proves that the separation of the two crowns had been the cause of 'all the calamities that had befallen Britain' and that the greatest English kings had attempted the task of union, he discusses the work of the English and Scottish commissioners at Westminster. In the course of this discussion he recounts all the objections that had been raised against the articles of union which the commissioners had agreed upon. Then, setting the tone for the rest of the treatise, he declares his intention to 'meet these criticisms'.[22] This he more than succeeds in doing, although in the process he digresses on a number of topics, including an extended commentary on the similarity of the laws of the two countries and a reply to the contention of Robert Parsons that the union will promote political unrest. After enumerating the advantages of the proposed union,

---

[20] J. Irvine Smith, 'The transition to the modern law, 1532–1660', in G. C. H. Paton (ed.), *An introduction to Scottish legal history* (Stair Society, 1958), p. 29.
[21] Williamson, *Scottish national consciousness*, p. 141.
[22] Sir Thomas Craig, *De unione regnorum Britanniae tractatus*, ed. and trans. C. S. Terry (SHS, 1909), p. 275.

Craig concludes with a set of measures 'whereby this union may stand firm and solid for all time'. Many of these recommendations are in effect restatements of the plan for union embodied in the treaty of 1604.[23]

On the surface John Russell's union treatise appears to be a very different specimen from Craig's apologetic piece. Intended to advise James on the issue of the union, it was written some time between May and October 1604, before the king had either assumed the style of king of Great Britain or convened his commissioners to negotiate a treaty.[24] A second, revised copy of the treatise, now included among the Royal manuscripts, was almost certainly presented to him. The treatise takes the form of an academic disputation, in which arguments both for and against the union are presented and then resolved, ostensibly in favour of union. It is a highly rhetorical piece in which the union is frequently depicted in religious, sometimes providential or apocalyptic terms, a tendency that characterized many of the other Scottish treatises but which is virtually absent from Craig's work.[25] It is also a more philosophical work, concentrating in the manner of many other union treatises on the metaphysical nature of union. The only stylistic similarity to *De unione*, aside from the virtually universal tendency to seek guidance from a study of the unions of other kingdoms, is a concluding section in which Russell offers a set of fifteen recommendations regarding the future relationship between England and Scotland in the union, much in the fashion of Craig's final chapter.[26]

Even when we begin to explore the substantive arguments regarding the union, the two treatises appear to be different. It is possible to read Craig's work not simply as an apology for the treaty of 1604 but as a plea for an incorporating union between the two kingdoms, by which is meant a union of the two kingdoms into one state. The possibility of such a union was certainly considered shortly after the personal union, when King James referred to a 'perfect union' as his goal and when the possibility of parliamentary and legal – as well as ecclesiastical – union was raised. The subject of an incorporating union also came before parliament in 1607 when Sir Edwin Sandys, perhaps simply as a tactical move to defeat the proposed treaty of union, suggested that Scotland surrender its sovereignty and become completely incorporated within the English state.[27] In many places Craig uses the language of perfect or incorporating union. He speaks of the 'fusion of the two sovereign states into a single realm' and of the 'infusion or

---

[23] Craig, *De unione*, pp. 460–72.   [24] *Jac. union*, p. lvi.

[25] This is most clearly evident in John Gordon. Craig does occasionally adopt a providential approach to the union, but it is relatively restrained in its expression. See Craig, *De unione*, p. 264.

[26] *Jac. union*, pp. 135–7.

[27] Levack, *Formation of the British state*, pp. 29, 44; Wallace Notestein, *The house of commons, 1604–1610* (New Haven, Conn., 1971), pp. 233–4, 249.

engrafting of the two kingdoms', while in one famous passage he speaks of promoting the union of the two countries in 'one body politic'.[28]

There was very little possibility of gaining such an impression from Russell's work. From very early on it was clear that Russell was discussing the pros and cons of what he called a personal union. Now it is true that this personal union was much more than the merely dynastic union that had been achieved in 1603. Not only would it permanently fuse the two monarchies into one (which was actually not accomplished until 1707), it would also involve a union of the English and Scottish peoples. 'Ane personall unioun', wrote Russell, 'is the conjunctioun of persounes: the prince and the people mutuallie, the husband and the uyfe in mariage, uith utheris of the lyik nature, Christiane people unitit in thair head and saviour Jesus Chryst'. It was this type of personal union, 'the concord and harmonie of hairtis and myndis', that was the 'principall unioun of all'.[29] All of this was by no means inconsequential, but it still was a far cry from the type of perfect union that was under discussion in England. In no place does Russell suggest that he is in favour of an incorporating or perfect union which would involve the laws and parliaments of the two kingdoms.

The difference of opinion between Russell and Craig on this crucial issue was more apparent than real. Both men in fact shared virtually the same position with respect to union, and what is more, they based their position on a similar legal foundation. To understand Craig's position, we must appreciate the nature of the union treaty that he was defending. Although this treaty provoked a torrent of anti-unionist sentiment in the English parliamentary session of 1606–7, its proposals for strengthening the ties between the two countries were fairly modest in scope. It called for the repeal of the hostile laws passed by the two kingdoms against each other, an improvement of justice along the border, a commercial union between the two nations, and the mutual naturalization of Scots and Englishmen. It specifically did not propose an incorporating union, both because the Scottish parliament had forbidden its commissioners to consider such issues, and because King James's unionist supporters, such as Sir Francis Bacon, had developed misgivings about proceeding quickly with either legal or parliamentary union. The union that Craig defended, and which he even occasionally referred to as perfect or incorporating, was this union. It would be essentially a union of the English and Scottish peoples under one king, a union similar to that described by Russell, and in fact not all that different from the religiously inspired union that covenanters were to propose in the early 1640s. What it was emphatically not to be was a union of laws or parliaments, as Craig made clear in his final recommendations:

[28] Craig, *De unione*, pp. 282, 283, 328.   [29] *Jac. union*, p. 85.

The third essential to a permanent union is, that each nation be governed in accordance with its own laws and customs; that no change be made in them, or in the established methods of judicial procedure, without the express sanction and approbation of either kingdom; that legal causes be determined in accordance with ancient practice and without appeal from the courts of one kingdom to those of the other, a procedure intolerable to both and expressly forbidden in all the examples of union which I have mentioned above ... The parliaments of the two nations must also retain their own status and authority ... The resolutions of one parliament must not be liable to rejection or amendment, as it is called, by the other. No new laws or ordinances must be promulgated, no existing law must be repealed, without the authority of the Parliament concerned.[30]

That Craig was taking such a strong position on the legal and political autonomy of Scotland should not surprise us. An ardent Scottish patriot, Craig devoted a considerable amount of scholarly energy to the task of defending the historic sovereignty of his country against the claims made by the English chronicler Raphael Holinshed. The argument of Holinshed and his associates was that since some Scottish kings had paid homage to the king of England in the distant past, the country was still held of England as a fief. In refuting these claims Craig, utilizing his skill as both a legal scholar and a historian, established the jurisdictional independence of his country. It was the same autonomy that he found himself defending in his union treatise.[31]

If Craig was indeed defending the sovereignty of Scotland in *De unione*, we still must deal with the long chapter in that work in which he argues for the legal union of England and Scotland. There is no question that Craig was fascinated with the possibility of a union of English and Scots law. His legal studies in the feudal law had convinced him that the land laws of the two countries had derived from the same European source, and in both *De unione* and *Jus feudale* he explores the possibilities of legal union.[32] He laboured at great length to prove the fundamental similarity between the two legal systems, although his critics have been quick to point out how much he had to ignore in order to make his point,[33] and even Craig remained uncertain upon what foundation a common code of law would be based.[34] He con-

[30] Craig, *De unione*, pp. 465–6.
[31] George Ridpath, who was an opponent of incorporating union in the early eighteenth century, argues in his preface to Craig, *Scotland's soveraignty asserted*, p. xxxi, that Craig's writings revealed him to be a 'faithful Patriot throughout the whole Course of his Life'.
[32] On this generally, see Brian P. Levack, 'English law, Scots law and the union, 1603–1707', in A. Harding (ed.), *Law-making and law-makers in British history* (London, 1980), pp. 105–19.
[33] David M. Walker, *Scottish jurists* (Edinburgh, 1985), pp. 54–64; W. David Sellar, 'The common law of Scotland and the common law of England', in R. R. Davies (ed.), *The British Isles, 1100–1500* (Edinburgh, 1988), pp. 82–99.
[34] The possibilities he suggested were the Norman codes, the original feudal law or, failing that, the civil law. See Levack, *Formation of the British state*, pp. 78–81.

cluded his investigation with the observation that there was 'no reason to despair of the possibility of so harmonising the legal systems of the two peoples as to fashion one body of law applicable equally to both'.[35]

Craig's enthusiasm for legal union was by no means incompatible with his staunch defence of Scotland's legal and political sovereignty. He was never opposed to making changes in Scots law, in the way that some English lawyers were reluctant to make alterations in their common law. In this respect the openness of Scots law to outside influences, its lack of a large body of ancient custom, and the primacy of acts of parliament over all other forms of law may have made the prospect of change more palatable than it was to English common lawyers. Craig's only concern was that 'no change be made in them [the laws], or in the established methods of judicial procedure, without the express sanction and approbation of either king-dome'.[36] As long as that proviso was respected, as long as legal change was not imposed on Scotland, Scottish sovereignty would not be violated. For the time being, however, change could not be recommended or even seriously contemplated.

The foundation of Scottish sovereignty on the laws of the country and the determination that those laws be preserved within the union are even more evident in Russell's treatise than in Craig's. In *The happie and blissed unioun* we find a resistance to legal change that was every bit as impassioned as the protests of anti-unionist English common lawyers.[37] Russell quotes the dire predictions from Plato and Aristotle that legal alteration will bring about the subversion and extermination of the commonwealth, and then he warns (quoting Paulus Aemilius) that the process could begin with the 'resisting to the auld lauis; for seeing the lauis ar the suir fundatioun of every civill societie, giff that fail it most niedis fall furth that the haill politicall building man come to ruine'.[38] These statements regarding the dangers of legal change stand as early expressions of a developing Scottish concept of fundamental law, which was to play such an important part in later Scottish arguments against an incorporating union. In Russell's treatise they are combined with prophecies of Scottish dependence upon England, which anti-unionist Scots claimed would accompany this destruction of its laws and estates. 'Sall ane frie kingdome possesing sua ancienne liberteis become ane slave . . .?' asks Russell in one passage, while raising the prospect of Scotland's becoming 'ane pendicle of thair kingdome' in another.[39] In this way Russell anchors Scottish sovereignty in its fundamental and ancient laws.

[35] Craig, *De unione*, p. 328.   [36] *Ibid.*, p. 465.
[37] See for example BL, Harleian MS 1314, fol. 16 v.
[38] *Jac. union*, p. 92.   [39] *Ibid.*, pp. 89, 98.

The reason for Russell's presentation of these arguments against legal change was not to make a case against union as such; quite to the contrary, his treatise strongly favours union. He was, after all, calling for the establishment of a 'soverane and heich monarchie forevir, to be callit the Kingdome of Great Britanie'.[40] The reason for presenting all the 'negative' arguments in the second part of the treatise was to make an important qualification of that unionism:

> Bot housoevir I inclyne to the affirmative, it is with this speciall limitatioun that it sall not import ony alteratioun of the kingdomes in haill or in pairt, in religioun, policie, lauis, liberteis and ancienne priviledgis, bot to tend to the gude of baith, prejudice of nane.[41]

With this statement, and with the final set of recommendations favouring commercial and social union – 'the unioun of the inhabitantis and thair successoris amangis thameselffis' – Russell brings us back to the position of Craig. Russell is adamantly opposed to any possible violation of his country's legal and constitutional integrity, but he is not opposed to change itself. If that change were not to be prejudicial to Scotland, and if it were to work to the benefit of *both* countries, then the objection would not apply. This was not only the position of Craig, as mentioned above, but also of David Hume of Godscroft, whose second tract on the union (1605) envisioned a number of legal changes, provided they worked to Scotland's advantage.[42]

Russell's strong concept of Scottish sovereignty is reflected in one additional way in his treatise: in his use of the terms 'empire' and 'imperiall'. Throughout *The happie and blissed unioun* and 'The deuty and office of ane christian prince', Russell makes frequent reference to separate 'imperiall crounes' of England and Scotland and the status of both realms as 'impyires'. In one place he refers to Scotland as King James's 'first and auldest impyir'.[43] Now there is nothing exceptional in Russell's designation of either England or Scotland as an empire, or in his claim that James possessed two imperial crowns. References to England as an empire date back to the 1530s, when the preamble to the Act in Restraint of Appeals declared that England was, and had long been, an empire. The king of England, so it was claimed, had possessed the imperial crown since the reign of Constantine, who had bestowed it on his successors.[44] References to the imperial status of Scotland appear even earlier than those regarding

---

[40] *Ibid.*, pp. 126, 134.   [41] *Ibid.*, p. 125.

[42] David Hume, 'Tractatus secundus', NLS, Advocates' MS 31. 6. 12, fol. 52 v.

[43] *Jac. union*, p. 121.

[44] Richard Koebner, '"The imperial crown of this realm": Henry VIII, Constantine the Great and Polydore Vergil', *BIHR*, 26 (1952), 29–52.

England, the first occurring in 1469 during the reign of James III.[45] Indeed, James III, who was known for his high concept of kingship, appeared on a Scottish coin wearing the closed crown of the emperor three years before a corresponding image of Henry VII appeared on the English sovereign of 1489.[46] James VI, whose theories of kingship were even more exalted than those of James III, also had himself depicted as a Roman emperor, wearing a laurel wreath, on the medals struck in 1590 to commemorate his marriage to Anne of Denmark.[47]

What makes Russell's use of these terms so surprising is that most unionists in the early seventeenth century abandoned such traditional designations and began describing James's imperial monarchy and empire in unified, British terms. The most enthusiastic unionist of them all, King James VI and I, set the tone for this, referring to 'our imperiall monarchie of thease two greit kingdomes' and proclaiming the union of the two countries under 'one Imperiall Crowne'.[48] The authors of most union treatises followed suit. John Thornborough, the bishop of Bristol, celebrated the birth of a new imperial monarchy, while William Cornwallis observed the beginning of the 'happiest empire that ever was'.[49] Two Scottish writers, John Gordon and James Maxwell, lauded James as the successor to the 'British' emperor of Rome, Constantine,[50] while the English dramatists Ben Jonson and Thomas Dekker celebrated the creation of a British empire upon the official entry of King James into the city of London in 1604.[51]

In this chorus of British imperial adulation the voice of Russell was

[45] *APS*, vol. II, p. 95. This recognizes the king's claim to 'ful Jurisdictioune and fre Impire within his Realme'. This use of the term 'empire' in this document does not possess the same territorial connotation of the later English usage.

[46] Leslie J. Macfarlane, *William Elphinstone and the kingdom of Scotland* (Aberdeen, 1985), pp. 188–9; P. Grierson, 'The origins of the English sovereign and the symbolism of the closed crown', *British Numismatic Journal*, 33 (1964), 118–34. It is uncertain whether Henry VII intended to symbolize the imperial status of his monarchy or simply to distinguish the English crown from that of France.

[47] Jonathan Goldberg, *James I and the politics of literature* (Stanford, Calif., 1983), p. 45. For similar depictions of James at the time of his accession to the English throne, see H. A. Grueber (ed.), *Medallic illustrations of the history of Great Britain and Ireland* (3 vols., Oxford, 1907–11), vol. I, plate XIV, nos. 1, 11.

[48] *RPC*, vol. VII, p. 17; J. F. Larkin and L. P. Hughes (eds.), *Stuart royal proclamations I: royal proclamations of King James I, 1603–1625* (Oxford, 1973), p. 95. James also referred to his succession to the 'Imperiall Crowne of England' and to the imperial crown of England, Ireland and France. *Ibid.*, pp. 1, 18.

[49] John Thornborough, *The joiefull and blessed reuniting the two mighty and famous kingdomes* (Oxford, n.d.), p. 7; William Cornwallis, *The miraculous and happie union of England and Scotland* (London, 1604), sig. D2 v.

[50] Arthur H. Williamson, 'Scotland, Antichrist and the invention of Great Britain', in John Dwyer *et al.* (eds.), *New perspectives on the politics and culture of early modern Scotland* (Edinburgh, 1982), pp. 34–58.

[51] Graham Parry, *The golden age restor'd: the culture of the Stuart court 1603–42* (New York and Manchester, 1981), pp. 4, 16.

strangely hushed. The reason for this had nothing to do with a lack of enthusiasm for union. Russell was calling for the creation of a kingdom of Great Britain, a permanent union of the monarchies and peoples of the two kingdoms. We know that he shared the sentiments of Scottish episcopalian writers such as Gordon and Maxwell, who anticipated union with England as the first step of a European Reformation presided over by a new Constantine, a British emperor. In one passage in *The happie and blissed unioun* Russell explicitly asserts that God 'hes raysit his Majestie in this age to be the vive image of Lucius and Constantine'.[52] The only reason that Russell, in the midst of such apocalyptic enthusiasm, continued to emphasize the imperial status of both England and Scotland is that he wished to preserve the sovereignty of Scotland within the union.

Certainly the repeated designation of Scotland as an empire by itself could have this effect. The concept of 'empire' has a long and complicated history, and the term bears many different connotations. One of those meanings, which certainly inspired much of the imperial rhetoric of the early seventeenth century, was the concept of empire as the sum of many kingdoms, an idea which derived ultimately from Roman imperial rule over large territories.[53] The first and most important connotation of the term, however, was that of sovereign rule, and that is clearly the way in which Russell was using it. As a student of Roman law, he would have had a special awareness of this meaning of empire. The original word *imperium*, which can be found throughout the texts of Roman law, connoted the legal power of command, and in the late middle ages the term was frequently used to describe the sovereign power of European monarchs. A king was *imperator in regno suo*, which meant that he had no temporal superior within his realm.[54] By extension the realm over which he ruled could be described as an empire, and it is in this sense that Russell referred to both England and Scotland.[55]

[52] See *Jac. union*, p. 80. This is one of the few places in the text where the word 'impyir' appears to refer to a united Britain, the others being where he discusses the 'increase of empire' in the appended treatise regarding the duty of the king (see below). For the Scottish apocalyptic tradition of 'empire', see Williamson, 'Scotland, Antichrist and the invention of Britain', in Dwyer (ed.), *New perspectives*, pp. 34–58.

[53] Robert Folz, *The concept of empire from the fifth to the fourteenth century* (London, 1969), pp. 6–7; Richard Koebner, *Empire* (Cambridge, 1961), pp. 4–11. For early seventeenth-century examples of this usage, see Thornborough, *Joiefull and blessed reuniting*, p. 7; John Speed, *The theatre of the empire of Great Britaine* (London, 1611), title page; Thomas Dekker, *The magnificent entertainment given to King James*, in Fredson Bowers (ed.), *The dramatic works of Thomas Dekker* (2 vols., Cambridge, 1964), vol. II, p. 298.

[54] Folz, *Concept of empire*, pp. 156–7; G. L. Harriss, 'Medieval government and statecraft', *Past and Present*, 25 (1963), 9–12.

[55] Russell also referred to Ireland as an 'ancienne impyir': *Jac. union*, p. 123. Ireland continued to claim its own imperial crown on the basis of Henry VIII's statute of 1542: *The statutes at large, passed in the parliaments held in Ireland* (London, 1765), vol. I, p. 176.

Russell's idea that both Scotland and England had imperial crowns of their own, an idea shared by Craig, became an important aspect of Scottish political thought in the later seventeenth and early eighteenth centuries. In particular, it underlay the determined efforts of Scots such as James Anderson to refute the claims that Scotland had always been under the jurisdiction of the English imperial crown because of Scotland's feudal subjection to England.[56] But the influence of Russell and Craig was not limited to the narrow question of Scotland's imperial crown. More generally, by insisting upon Scottish sovereignty within the union, by appealing to Scottish law as the basis of national identity, and by contributing to the development of a Scottish notion of fundamental law, they developed a vocabulary for the articulation of the case for 'federal' union both in the mid-seventeenth and the early eighteenth centuries.

III

The second political issue which Craig and Russell addressed in the context of the union debate was the power of the king and his relationship to the law. This was a more theoretical issue than the nature of the British polity, and one which occupies a central place in the overall history of early modern political thought. The contribution that these two men made to the development of that thought may not have been particularly original, especially in Russell's case, but it still warrants investigation to see if it can illuminate the influence of the law on Scottish political discourse.

The two issues of union and regal power were not unrelated. The prospect of union at the beginning of the seventeenth century stimulated extensive and intense debate regarding the extent of the king's power. At every stage of the union proceedings the question was raised whether the union should be achieved by royal or parliamentary power. The fear that changing the name of England and Scotland to Great Britain would be undertaken without parliamentary approval raised the spectre of a conquered kingdom, in which the king would make and unmake law at his pleasure.[57] What is more, the prospect of legal and political union forced men to consider in detailed fashion the nature of the prerogative in both kingdoms, while the union treaty itself included a highly controversial saving clause allowing the king to make appointments and denizations of

---

[56] William Ferguson, 'Imperial crowns: a neglected facet of the background to the Treaty of Union of 1707', *SHR*, 53 (1974), 22–44.

[57] Brian P. Levack, 'Toward a more perfect union: England, Scotland and the constitution', in Barbara Malament (ed.), *After the Reformation* (Philadelphia, 1980), p. 59. Pocock, *Ancient constitution*, pp. 284–5.

ante-nati Scots by virtue of the royal prerogative.[58] More generally, the prospect of an absent king not only raised Scottish fears of increased royal power but also led to demands that he exercise his powers with greater care.

In general terms, the political views of both Craig and Russell can be characterized as royalist. Both men placed sovereignty with the king, and both rejected certain aspects of the constitutionalist tradition of Scottish political thought that finds its most radical expression in the work of George Buchanan. Whether the position Craig and Russell took was representative of most men of their profession, or of most Scotsmen who studied the civil law in continental universities, is impossible to determine. Suffice it to say that there is a strong royalist tradition among Scottish lawyers, one which reaches well into the eighteenth century and which identifies Sir George Mackenzie of Rosehaugh as its quintessential spokesman. In this connection it may be worthy of note that in *Jus regium* (1684) Mackenzie attacks Buchanan and other radical authors for having 'adventured upon a debate in law not being themselves lawyers and should have written books on that subject without citing one law, civil or municipal'.[59]

Although the positions taken by Craig and Russell were similar, they appear to have derived from different aspects of their work as lawyers and legal scholars. Craig's royalism, like that of his fellow humanist Skene, appears to have emerged primarily from his efforts to determine the authenticity of the sources of Scots law. As we have seen, both Craig and Skene insisted upon the pre-eminence of written law as a source, and in Scotland written law meant acts of parliament. The question for Craig was how such written laws acquired their authority. In his studies of European feudal law Craig had developed theories regarding the evolution of society that in many respects were not all that different from those of Buchanan. But as Cairns, Fergus and MacQueen have demonstrated, Craig believed that when kings were appointed only they, as men with no superiors, had the right to make law.[60] In making this argument Craig was strongly influenced by Jean Bodin, whose *Les six livres de la république* had done so much to popularize the idea of the sovereign law-giver, not just in Europe but in Britain as well.[61]

It might be questioned whether this conception of a sovereign Scottish law-giving king squared with the more apparently constitutionalist aspects

[58] Levack, *Formation of the British state*, p. 37.
[59] Sir George Mackenzie, *Jus regium, or the just and solid foundations of monarchy* (Edinburgh, 1684), sig. B3 v.
[60] Cairns *et al.*, 'Legal humanism', 53–5.
[61] Jean Bodin, *Les six livres de la république* (Paris, 1576); G. Mosse, 'The influence of Jean Bodin's *République* on English political thought', *Medievalia et Humanistica*, 5 (1948), 73–83.

of Craig's thought. Craig did, after all, write extensively about the partnership between king and people. He also described the acts of the Scottish
parliament as 'the constitutions and statutes of the three estates of the
kingdom with the consent of the prince'.[62] Could it be that the sovereign
law-making authority of the king, essential in primitive society, was now, in
Craig's view, shared? The answer, which separated Craig from Buchanan,
was no, for in his conception of the contemporary legislative process, Craig
still placed the main emphasis on the role of the king. It was the king who
summoned parliament, and it was the king who embodied the sovereignty of
the country.[63] In this respect Craig's political ideas did not differ greatly
from those of James VI and I, even though they found expression in
different ways.[64]

It is possible then to locate Craig within a tradition of emerging absolutist
Scottish thought, one which served as a counterweight to the constitutionalist tradition of George Buchanan and his associates. In so doing, however,
we must recognize that Craig, like many royal absolutists throughout
Europe in the late sixteenth and early seventeenth centuries, did not argue
that the king's power was unrestricted.[65] Quite to the contrary, Craig placed
some serious limitations on the power of the king. One of the most important of these was the inability of the king to alienate his kingdom. In his
treatise on Scottish sovereignty, Craig addresses the question 'Whether
Soveraign Princes can render themselves, and their Subjects Vassals to
another Prince'. As one might expect of a Scottish patriot and feudal lawyer,
Craig answers in the negative, claiming that a prince 'who governs a free
people cannot render them Slaves'.[66] The reasoning behind Craig's conclusion can be placed within a solid royalist tradition which insists that the
sacra sacrorum, the rights of majesty, cannot be separated from the crown.
Hence those rights cannot be renounced, taken from the prince, or suffer
prescription. From this it follows that 'those who are entrusted with the
chief care of the Common-wealth cannot so much as diminish one foot of the
Public Patrimony, much less give away the Property of it'.[67] Once again
citing Bodin ('a most famous Lawyer'), Craig explains that sovereign
princes do not have dominion or property of the public estate but are only

---

[62] Craig, *Jus feudale*, 1. 8. 9.
[63] Craig, *Scotland's soveraignty asserted*, p. 422, claims that 'Laws cannot be made by any one
who has a Superior, nor can any Man call a Parliament who hath not the Right of
Sovereignty and Majesty'.
[64] In this respect Craig parted company with many legal humanists. See Quentin Skinner, *The
foundations of modern political thought* (2 vols., Cambridge, 1978), vol. II, p. 131.
[65] The limitations on royal power recognized by French absolutists are discussed in Church,
Constitutional thought, pp. 63–4, 231–2; Skinner, *Foundations of modern political thought*,
vol. II, pp. 293–301.
[66] Craig, *Scotland's soveraignty asserted*, pp. 369–79.   [67] *Ibid.*, pp. 369–70.

proctors or administrators who are entrusted with the use of it. Hence it follows that if a king 'who is subject to none' were to serve and obey another, either of his own accord or against his will, he would lose the 'Title and Rights of Majesty'.[68]

In making this final statement, Craig draws explicitly upon the work of François Hotman, the radical French political thinker who is often considered to be in the same constitutionalist tradition as George Buchanan. Craig also reveals a close affinity to John Mair, who advanced a similar argument in his discussion of the homage controversy in *The history of Greater Britain* in 1521. Mair, in turn, drew upon the work of the conciliarist Jean Gerson, who contended that the king was merely a trustee exercising authority delegated to him by his subjects.[69] Thus Craig, in claiming that the king could not alienate his kingdom, establishes a connection with the constitutionalist as well as the absolutist tradition in both French and Scottish political thought.

The difference between Craig and the constitutionalists, however, is that Craig does not, like Mair, advance a theory of popular sovereignty or a justification of resistance. He does not claim that a kingdom could not be alienated without the consent of the people. Nor does he establish the right of subjects to deprive the king of his title when he fails to fulfil his duties. Had he done so, he would have contradicted most of the other royalist principles of his political thought. Craig's argument is simply that a king who acted, or was forced to act, in this way would forfeit his title, just as he would if his kingdom were to be conquered. In Craig's view the inalienability of the kingdom has the status of a fundamental law, one which is necessary for the preservation of the kingdom itself.[70]

The influence of the law on the political thought of John Russell was no less pronounced than with Craig, but it took an entirely different form. In this case the formative influence appears to have been Russell's education in the civil law. Concerning the impact of Roman jurisprudence on the development of European political thought much has been written, but there is little consensus regarding what its precise effects have been. This is understandable, since the civil law contains many texts of potential political significance, and those texts can sustain radically different interpretations. The traditional argument has been that the famous texts of the *Digest* and

---

[68] *Ibid.*, p. 370.

[69] Roger A. Mason, 'Kingship, nobility and Anglo-Scottish union: John Mair's *History of Greater Britain* (1521)', *IR*, 41 (1990), 207–8.

[70] Early sixteenth-century French Roman lawyers, most of whom were absolutists, insisted upon two fundamental laws: the Salic law and the inalienability of the royal domain. Church, *Constitutional thought*, p. 49. Thomas Hobbes, *Leviathan*, ed. C. B. Macpherson

the *Institutes* – most notably 'Whatsoever has pleased the prince has the force of law', 'The prince is free of the laws', and 'The king is a living law' – encouraged the growth of royal absolutism. Against this argument it has been shown not only that the absolutist texts themselves are subject to a constitutionalist interpretation, but that other texts in the civil law, such as the *digna vox* of the *Code*, which stressed the subordination of the prince to the law, did more to shape the outlook of princes and lawyers than the texts which appeared to give *merum imperium*, or full power, to the prince.[71]

There is little question that the Justinianic texts could have a real impact on the political thought of their students. In his study of William Elphinstone, Leslie Macfarlane has illustrated the influence of the civil law on both French and Scottish conceptions of royal power in the fifteenth century.[72] Walter Ullmann has argued that the first title of the *Digest*, which defined the extent of the public law, influenced Henry VIII's ideas regarding the royal supremacy and the imperial status of his crown.[73] The education that seventeenth-century English civil lawyers received in Roman law often helped to shape their political views, regardless of whether they were royalist or parliamentarian.[74] It has also been suggested, although never fully demonstrated, that James VI drew some of his ideas from the civil law, for which he seems to have had a strong penchant.[75]

John Russell is another case in point. His 'Treatise contiening the deuty and office of ane christiane prince', which was appended to both copies of his manuscript treatise on the union, reflects a solid influence of an education in the civil law. It is instructive, however, to see how he uses these texts and what conclusions he draws from them. 'The deuty and office' has two ostensible purposes: first, to set down the two chief principles annexed to the duty of a good and Christian king; and second, to present a short description of his office, with the special qualities thereof. The latter objective consumes the bulk of the treatise, and it need not concern us here. It is one of many examples of the 'ideal prince' literature that proliferated in

---

(Harmondsworth, 1968), p. 334, defines a fundamental law as that, 'which being taken away, the Common-wealth faileth, and is utterly destroyed'.

[71] See Brian P. Levack, 'Law and ideology: the civil law and theories of absolutism in Elizabethan and Jacobean England', in Heather Dubrow and Joseph Strier (eds.), *The historical Renaissance* (Chicago, 1988), pp. 225–6; Kantorowicz, *The king's two bodies*, pp. 103–7; Skinner, *Foundations of modern political thought*, vol. II, pp. 123–34.

[72] Macfarlane, *Elphinstone*, pp. 39–47, 188.

[73] Ullmann, '"This realm of England is an empire"', *Journal of Ecclesiastical History*, 30 (1979), 179–83.

[74] Brian P. Levack, *The civil lawyers in England, 1603–1641* (Oxford, 1973), ch. 3. See also Levack, 'Law and ideology', in Dubrow and Strier (eds.), *Historical Renaissance*, *passim*.

[75] McIlwain, *Works*, pp. xl–xli; Francis Oakley, *Omnipotence, covenant and order* (Ithaca, N.Y., 1984), p. 117.

the sixteenth century.[76] The first objective, however, reveals a great deal regarding Russell's thought and the sources he was drawing on. Discussing his first principle, he writes:

Non quod libet mihi licet, sed legibus me subjectum profiteor: et secundum leges vivere, et imperare debere, and thairfoir they ar nott to be suffered in ane commonueill, far les to be in companie uith ane godlie prince, qha will persuade him to violat or break the law. For that detestable speach utterit by Julia, the stepmother of Caracallus (qhairof Spartiane makis mentioun) is uorthie to be abhorrit be all gude christianes, *Regis voluntas et libido, est pro lege.* Ulpian the Jurisconsult is easielie reconcilit with the posterior princes, for albeit he hes affirmit *Princeps legibus est solutus, et quod principi placuit legis habet vigorem*, zit the last Imperoris maist uyselie geuand thair confessioun, hes professit *quod digna vox est majestate principis regnantis, legibus se alligatum profiteri.* This apparent contradictioun salbe taine away with this solu- tioun: The prince alsuiell as ane private persoun is oblist to the lauis of God, nature, Justice and publict honestie, the transgressioun qhairof importis to him ane great dishonor, seing according to Aristotle and Xenophon, the prince is callit *lex loquens et animata, plus peccans exemplo quam peccato.* On the uther pairt, as for civill constitutiones, they ar aluyis in his pouer, according to the necessesitie of tyme and place, bot yit fundamentall lawis of every monarchie sould aluyis be preservit, and neuir to ressave concussioun … It is evident that the Soverane prince, qha is baith author and minister of the law, sould lykuyis be subiect thairto.[77]

Now it should be clear from this passage that Russell's political ideas were profoundly influenced by his knowledge of the civil law. Although he also draws upon classical literature and theology in his treatise, in the manner of most political writers of his day, in the crucial statement regarding the king's powers and duties he relies mainly upon the texts of Roman law. Indeed, the quoted passage contains all of the most famous Justinianic texts that touch on that question: *quod principi placuit*; *legibus solutus est*; *lex animata*; and the *digna vox*.[78]

Russell treats these texts in such a way as to resolve some of the apparent contradictions between them. As we have seen, some of these texts empha- size the king's superiority to the law, whereas others stress his subordi- nation. Russell's solution is to make a distinction that was commonplace in both medieval and early modern political thought between the king's public and his private capacities, one which is closely related to the theory of the king's two bodies.[79] When the king was acting as a private individual, he was subject to the natural and divine law in the same way his subjects were. The

---

[76] Russell's treatise can be compared in different ways with the fifteenth- and sixteenth- century political literature discussed in Roger A. Mason, 'Kingship, tyranny and the right to resist in fifteenth-century Scotland', *SHR*, 66 (1987), 125–51.

[77] NLS, Advocates' MS 31.4.7, fols. 21 r–21 v.

[78] The *digna vox* also appears in *The happie and blissed unioun*, p. 93.

[79] Kantorowicz, *The king's two bodies*, pp. 95–6.

London version of Russell's manuscript, which was the one presented to James, makes this even clearer than the Edinburgh version cited above: 'The Prince is asweill subiect to the lawis of pietie, religioun, nature, justice and publict honestie as the meanest subject.'[80] But when the king was dealing with the laws of Scotland, or his 'civill constitutiounes', he was not subject to the law. Once again, the London manuscript is clearest: 'Bot as to the solemnitie of his ouin lawe, he is not subiect, but maie dispense thereuith, and qhen the transgressioun of the law importis na preiudiuce to pietie, justice or publict honestie, hie is not subiect'.[81]

Now it can be argued that there is nothing in Russell's treatment of this problem to which a hard-nosed absolutist could object. Most absolutists, including Bodin, argued that the prince was subject in one way or another to natural or divine law. The crucial point was that he could not be subject to the public law of his kingdom. Not only could he dispense with such laws according to time and place, but he could never be held accountable for his actions. He might be considered to be subject to the directive force of the law, but not the coactive or coercive force. In the final analysis, his subjection to the civil law of his kingdom was moral and voluntary.

Russell does not deny any of these absolutist tenets. Like Craig, he never violates the royalist principles that lie at the source of his political thought. Nevertheless, Russell places such heavy emphasis on the king's subjection to the law that his treatise often reads as if it were part of a constitutionalist rather than an absolutist tradition. Indeed, the king's subjection to the law was the theme of the entire treatise. The very first rule that Russell lays down for princes in the administration of their 'impyir' is that 'the prince is subject to the law and should leive conforme thairto, according to the confessioun of the romane Imperor, *legibus me subiectum fateor, et secundum leges vivere, et imperare debere*'.[82]

One illustration of Russell's theme is his discussion of the famous maxim of Roman law, *rex est lex animata*, the prince is the living law. Now there is no question that this statement could be and quite frequently was interpreted in an absolutist light: the prince is the living law or the speaking law, *lex loquens*, because he is the sole source of that law. That was certainly an interpretation that could have been acceptable to either Russell or Craig in the light of the emphasis they placed on the king as the source of the authority of Scots law. But this was clearly *not* the interpretation that Russell gave to the phrase. Tapping a subordinate but never absent tradition of medieval thought, and referring back to Aristotle and Xenophon, he gives the phrase a distinctly constitutionalist flavour, one in fact that George

---

[80] BL, Royal MS 18 A. LXXVI, fol. 23 v.   [81] *Ibid.*   [82] *Ibid.*

Buchanan gave to it in *De jure regni apud Scotos*.[83] The king is the living law because he should embody that law or live that law. Since he is a public figure, moreover, it is even more important for him to adhere to the law than for his subjects to do so. If he did not obey the law, then how could he expect his subjects to do the same?

A further illustration of Russell's theme comes in his treatment of the king's power to dispense with his own law, or the public law of the kingdom. Here three points are worth making. First, all the examples Russell gives of the king's exercise of this power are for the benefit of his subjects. Indeed, the sole reason for the king's possession of this power is to serve the good of the people. This illustrates the Aristotelian axiom that Russell quotes at the very beginning of his treatise, *Princeps pro populo, non populus pro principe constitutus*.[84] Second, the king does not have the power to dispense with the law when such action would violate the laws of justice and piety to which he is subject as an individual. This idea, also common among contemporary theorists, resembles the argument that the pope, while possessing absolute power, did so only with respect to his own laws, not the laws of nature and God.[85] Finally, and most important, the king is not given the power to dispense with the fundamental laws of the monarchy.

What exactly did Russell mean by the fundamental laws of the monarchy? We can be fairly certain that he did not give to this term the meaning English MPs and common lawyers gave to it in the 1620s at the time of the discussion of the Petition of Right. In that context the phrase meant certain basic rights that the king could not violate under any circumstances.[86] There is nothing in Russell's work that would sustain such an interpretation. What Russell probably meant by the fundamental laws was what James VI meant by it in *The trew lawe of free monarchies*: the laws the king made in framing his government, or the basic constitution of the monarchy itself. What Russell is saying is that James had no power to destroy the properly established Scottish monarchy.

This of course brings us back to Craig's statement regarding the inability of the king to alienate his kingdom. Russell does not go as far as Craig. He does not state that if the king were to do so, he would forfeit the just title of king. But the implication is certainly there, and it would be difficult not to make such a deduction, given the definition of fundamental law that Russell adhered to. Just like the king described by Craig, Russell's monarch was

[83] Roger A. Mason, 'Rex stoicus: George Buchanan, James VI and the Scottish polity', in Dwyer *et al.* (eds.) *New perspectives*, p. 18.
[84] NLS, Advocates' MS 31.4.7, fol. 21.
[85] Oakley, *Omnipotence, covenant and order*, p. 113.
[86] See generally, J. W. Gough, *Fundamental law in English history* (Oxford, 1955).

considered incapable of destroying the very principles upon which his rule was based.

Russell's reference to fundamental law brings us back not just to Craig, but also to the union of England and Scotland, for it was in the context of that issue that both men wrote. Just as Craig was saying that James should not and *could not* surrender the country's sovereignty (which of course was *his* sovereignty), so Russell was referring to the fundamental laws that figure so prominently in his union treatise. And as Russell makes clear in his treatise, the violation of those fundamental laws would result in the destruction of Scotland's freedom as a nation. 'Sall ane frie kingdome possessing sua ancienne liberteis, become ane slave, furth of libertie in bondage and servitude ...?'[87]

The second principle that Russell discusses in his treatise on the duty of the prince, that 'an increase in kingdoms produces an increase in care', also brings us back to the question of union. Indeed, it is this statement that explains why Russell appended this particular work to *The happie and blissed unioun*. The king always had a duty to serve his people, but he had to be especially careful to do this when his 'empire' increased. The principle is phrased almost as a warning; it is a statement of the dangers inherent in imperial expansion:

The gude emperor affirmit that the sea and the impyre war the tua pleasant thingis to luik upon bot perilous to taist ... And thairfoir ane uyse prince should not think himselff the happier becaus he succeides to ane greater impyre nor he had of befoir, bot rather to remember that he has the greter cair and paine imposit wpon his schulderis, in the gude ruling thairof.[88]

These words, which are echoed in Craig's *De unione*,[89] were well chosen, and much could be written about the failure of both James VI and Charles I to take heed of them. For our purposes, however, it is sufficient to point out that the principle to which Russell is referring comes from Roman law. Just as the historical examples that he gives to illustrate this point (such as the Emperor Trajan) were taken from Roman history, the actual text is a quote from the Justinianic texts. And Russell is not quoting from this text simply to strengthen a conclusion he had already reached on other grounds. Quite to the contrary, the Justinianic text appears to have inspired and given shape to this entire section of his treatise. Once again Russell's familiarity with the texts of Roman law had a major influence on both the style and the content of his political writings.

The similarity between Russell and James VI on the nature of fundamental law has already been noted. Another speech of James tended to

---

[87] *Jac. union*, p. 89.   [88] BL, Royal MS 18 A LXXVI, fols. 23 v–24 r.
[89] Craig, *De unione*, p. 461.

underline this similarity between the political views of the two men. Addressing the English parliament in 1610, James spoke thus:

> So in the first originall of kings, whereof some had their beginning by Conquest, and some by election of the people, their wills at that time serued for law; Yet how soone Kingdomes began to be setled in ciuilitie and policie, then did Kings set downe their minds by Lawes, which are properly made by the King onely; but at the rogation of the people, the King's grant being obteined thereunto. And so the King became *Lex loquens*, after a sort, binding himselfe by a double oath to the obseruation of the fundamentall Lawes of his kingdome ... And therefore a King gouerning in a setled Kingdome, leaues to be a King, and degenerates into a Tyrant, assoone as he leaues off to rule according to his Lawes. In which case the Kings conscience may speake unto him, as the poore widow said to Philip of Macedon; Either gouerne according to your Law, *Aut ne Rex sis*. And though no Christian man ought to allow any rebellion of people against their Prince, yet doeth God neuer leaue kings unpunished when they transgresse these limits ... Therefore all Kings that are not tyrants, or periured, wil be glad to bound themselves within the limits of their Lawes; and they that perswade them to the contrary, are vipers, and pests, both against them and the Commonwealth.[90]

Now it should be clear from the foregoing discussion that there is nothing in James's speech with which Russell, or for that matter Craig, would have disagreed. The idea of the king as the sole proper source of law; the meaning of the phrase *lex animata*; the king's obligation to observe the fundamental laws of his kingdom; the difference between a tyrant and a king; and the theory of non-resistance all find a place in the thought of these two lawyers. Even James's account of the origin of royal power, while absent from Russell's treatise, is in perfect accordance with the position taken by Craig.[91]

To mention these similarities is not to argue for the influence of either man on the king, even though both Craig and Russell were in a position to have had such an effect and might very well have helped to shape his views. It is extremely difficult to establish the personal, let alone the literary, sources of James's thought. He derived his ideas from many different intellectual traditions, and those ideas were conveyed to him through a succession of different teachers and counsellors, including George Buchanan.[92] The reason for making these comparisons is merely to reveal how difficult it is to label all three men's political thought. The passage quoted from King James's speech was vintage James, and it is usually cited as the epitome of absolutist thought in England at the beginning of the seventeenth century. There is no question that within an English context, these

---

[90] McIlwain, *Works*, pp. 309–10.
[91] Sir Thomas Craig, *The right of succession to the kingdom of England* (London, 1703), p. 17.
[92] On Buchanan, see above, ch. 5.

ideas bear an absolutist interpretation. But it is also clear that within both a European and a Scottish context, James's absolutism is hedged with a series of serious limitations, and that on certain questions, such as the concept of the king as *lex loquens*, there is little that separates him from Buchanan.[93] Those very same moderating influences, most of which centre on the king's obligation to adhere to the law, are the most salient features of the thought of Russell and Craig, and this fact should make us hesitant to categorize early seventeenth-century Scottish legal thought as uniformly 'absolutist'. Scottish lawyers at the beginning of the seventeenth century certainly recognized the sovereignty of the law-giving king, but they also emphasized his obligation to adhere to those laws and to preserve them within a united Britain.

[93] For a sympathetic interpretation of James's political thought, and in particular his speech of 1610, see Oakley, *Omnipotence, covenant and order*, ch. 4.

Part IV

The covenanters

10 The political ideas of a covenanting leader: Archibald Campbell, marquis of Argyll 1607–1661

Edward J. Cowan

'Questionless the greatest subject the King had; sometime much known and beloved in all the three dominions: it was not thought safe he should live'.[1] So wrote a distinguished contemporary of Archibald Campbell, eighth earl, first (and only) marquis of Argyll, as epitaph on one of the most significant and tempestuous careers of the British civil wars. Having embraced his earldom and the National Covenant in 1638 he remained for a decade the principal leader of the covenanting movement. He received his marquisate from Charles I, collaborated with the Cromwellians and was executed on the order of Charles II in 1661. Once characterized as 'the dangerousest man in the state',[2] he was undoubtedly the major Scottish figure of an illustrious generation. He was also *MacCailein Mor*, chief of the Campbells, the most powerful clan in all of the *Gaidhealtachd*.

There has hitherto been virtually no effort to discover what political ideas, if any, influenced Argyll, probably for the good reason that, in the words of his only biographer, 'he was one of those who rather *did* things worthy of being related than *wrote* things worthy of being read'.[3] It is true that Argyll preferred the *vita activa* to the more languorous pursuits of the study, but as a committed politician he confessed a pragmatic inconsistency not generally associated (at least by scholars) with political theory or thought – 'wise men walk not always in the same way, nor keep always the same pace, they advise according to the occurrence of affairs, and vary according to the alterations of time and interests'.[4]

Some suggestions have already been made about the sources of inspiration surrounding the drawing up of the National Covenant in 1638, includ-

---

[1] *The letters and journals of Robert Baillie*, ed. David Laing (3 vols., Bannatyne Club, 1841–2), vol. III, p. 465.

[2] Philip Yorke, second earl of Hardwicke, *Miscellaneous state papers 1501–1726* (2 vols., London, 1778), vol. II, pp. 113–15.

[3] John Willcock, *The great marquess. Life and times of Archibald, eighth earl and first (and only) marquess of Argyll* (Edinburgh, 1903), p. 304. On Argyll, see also Edward J. Cowan, 'Fishers in drumlie waters: clanship and Campbell expansion in the time of Gilleasbuig Gruamach', *Transactions of the Gaelic Society of Inverness*, 54 (1987), 269–312.

[4] Archibald Campbell, marquis of Argyll, *Instructions to a son* (Glasgow, 1743), p. 123.

ing the influence of the German political philosopher Johannes Althusius.[5] This chapter will attempt to trace the influence of some Scottish and European traditions in political thinking upon Argyll and will examine one particular episode – in 1640 – to suggest that Argyll at least anticipated some practical application of his ideas. Another potentially significant contribution to Argyll's thought will be noted in that conferred upon him by his Celtic or Gaelic heritage. As virtually all of his contemporaries, from Vane to Cromwell, from Montrose to Charles II, testified, the man truly bestrode Scotland like a colossus; but if the heel of one foot was firmly planted in the Lowlands with a toe pointed towards England, the other rested securely in the Highlands.

One of the main difficulties in assessing the career of Archibald Campbell is rooted in his carefully nurtured reluctance to commit his ideas to paper. Although some hundreds of his letters survive they seldom reveal much of the man. His correspondence tends to convey minimal information. He studiously avoided reflection or the expression of opinion, favouring an almost Tacitean reticence. On occasion his epistles were designed deliberately to mislead. A remarkable and fascinating exception was a series of letters which he exchanged with Thomas Wentworth, earl of Strafford, beginning in the summer of 1638. Robert Baillie, the assiduous chronicler of the covenant, noted that 'in some two or three well penned letters [Argyll] justified our cause against that man's acute and subtill challenges'.[6] The letters were copied and circulated in both England and Scotland as evidence of the attitudes of the covenanting leaders, one copy reaching Laud.[7] This correspondence provides an invaluable insight into Argyll's mind, the justification of his course of action and the philosophy which sustained him (despite temporary lapses) throughout his troubled career.

The sequence began in July when Argyll warned Strafford of potential trouble from the clans on both sides of the Irish Sea. The deputy in his reply took the opportunity to lecture Argyll on the duty of obedience:

In a time so uncertain and declining towards disobedience it becomes us all, especially persons of your lordship's blood and abilities, actively and avowedly to serve the crown ... To be lazy lookers on, to lean to the king behind the curtain or to whisper forth only our allegiance will not serve our turn; much rather ought we to

---

[5] Edward J. Cowan, 'The making of the National Covenant', in John Morrill (ed.), *The Scottish National Covenant in its British context 1638–51* (Edinburgh, 1990), pp, 68–89. See also my 'The Solemn League and Covenant', in Roger A. Mason (ed.), *Scotland and England 1286–1815* (Edinburgh, 1987), pp. 182–202.

[6] Baillie, *Letters and journals*, vol. I, pp. 192–3.

[7] The following discussion is derived from W. Knowler (ed.), *The earl of Strafford's letters and dispatches* (2 vols., Dublin, 1740), vol. II, pp. 11, 192, 210, 220, 246–8, 290–1, 299–300. Copies of the letters are noted in *HMC*, 12th report, appendix, part 2: *Cowper MSS*, vol. II, pp. 213–4; and *HMC*, 12th report, appendix, part 8: *Athole MSS*, p. 24.

break our shins in emulation who should go soonest and furthest in assurance and in courage to uphold the prerogatives and full dominion of the crown, ever remembering that nobility is such a grudged and envied piece of monarchy, that all tumultuary force offered to kings doth ever in the second place fall upon the peers, being such motes in the eyes of a giddy multitude, as they never believe themselves clear sighted into their liberty indeed, till these be at least levelled to a parity as the other altogether removed, to give better prospect to their anarchy.

Strafford went on to lament that religion should be used to 'patronise the disobedience of subjects towards their king', deploring that such sentiments could be preached in a Protestant church against so good a king as Charles Stewart.

Could Bellarmine, Mariana, with all the rest of that rebellious college do more? ... Certainly no. For they never absolved subjects of their allegiance but where the king in their opinions was heretic in fundamentals. But to shake off that straight bond for discipline, for ceremonies, for things purely and simply indifferent is more in truth, I think, than the church of Rome itself can justly be convinced or accused of.

Argyll riposted on 9 October with one of the few recorded facetious remarks of his career, acknowledging Strafford's 'undeserved favour, that has been pleased to take so much pains to inform me of my duty rather like a father and friend than a stranger'. He continued with a statement of the greatest significance:

the best being but subjects, and by our places everyone in his degree his majesty's shadow, therefore our care should ever be so to carry ourselves to his people, as we desire his majesty should appear to them, and so make up to him a treasure of their love. For whensoever we fail in this, the greatness of our places aggravate so much the more our offences.

In expressing these sentiments at a time, it must be stressed, when he had not yet declared for the covenant, Argyll was invoking the historical role of the Scottish nobility throughout the centuries. He both appealed to the past and formulated the justification for present or future action. He evidently subscribed to the view that 'foresight regards future affairs by considering the outcome of past events'.[8] It was quite clear that Argyll could no more agree with Strafford than could any of his Campbell forebears that the interests of the nobility and the monarchy were identical. So deeply ingrained was the idea that the nobility, in a sense, existed independently of the monarchy, and so widely recognized in Scotland through custom and usage, that it was the single greatest ideological force behind the covenanting revolution, a revolution initially both aristocratic and conservative.

---

[8] Peter Gregory, *De republica libri XXVI* (Pont-à-Mousson, 1596), lib. X, p. 4, quoted in *The politics of Johannes Althusius*, trans. Frederick S. Carney (London, 1964), p. 131 (hereafter Carney, *Politics*).

The Scottish nobility had claimed the right to control their kings since time immemorial. The principle is enunciated in the Declaration of Arbroath (1320) and in subsequent treatises and parliamentary legislation. Perhaps one of the most remarkable tracts to enshrine the ideas with which Argyll tried to counter Strafford's arguments was *The Porteous of nobleness* copied into the Asloan manuscript from a volume published by Walter Chepman and Andrew Myllar in 1508. It belongs to the *speculum* or mirror genre so popular throughout the middle ages and it is concerned to discuss the twelve virtues necessary for the nobleman who wishes to 'understand how nobillis ar maid perfyte'. The anonymous author adheres to the traditional view of the Great Chain of Being, 'for to hald and stable this warld in concord and unitie [God] has ordanit everything in his proper office, sum till haf lordschipe and otheris to lif in subiectioun'.

Those appointed to lordship are obliged to possess honour, devotion and justice; they must eschew vice and villainy. 'Thai ar nocht sa hie set nor ordanit for to reif or tak be force in ony way but thai ar haldin in werray richt and resoun for to serf thair king and defend thair subiectis'. The latter memorable phrase is repeated three times in a single paragraph. 'Thai suld do na wrang nother to gret nor less than thamself, for thai suld without varians or dreid of ony man serve thair king and defend thar subiectis.'[9] If the nobility failed in this duty complete disruption of the social order would follow. From the assertion that the role of the nobles was 'to serve the king and defend the people' it was but a short step to Argyll's position – 'our care should ever be so to carry ourselves to his people, as we desire his majesty should appear to them and so make up to him a treasure of their love'. Given the decentralized nature of medieval and early modern Scottish government, Argyll's observation was based upon an empirical situation. The nobility represented their kin, vassals, tenants and retainers at the king's court; but in localized Scottish society monarchy was revealed to the people through those same nobles, a point which probably explains the failure, for example, of James I's attempts at parliamentary representation from the shires in the early fifteenth century.[10] If James aimed to erode the monopolizing powers of the great lords he met with signal failure. James VI later advised his son that the nobles should be encouraged to attend court 'sen they must be your armes and executors of your lawes', but he recognized that heritable jurisdictions 'wracke the whole country' and advised their

---

[9] W. A. Craigie (ed.), *The Asloan manuscript* (STS, 1923), pp. 173–4. The fact that the *Porteous* is a translation from the French of Alain Chartier does not negate its relevance. It was presumably translated by the Aberdeen burgess and notary Andrew Cadiou because it so aptly reflected the Scottish situation.

[10] *APS*, vol. II, p. 9 c. 8; p. 15 c. 2. Ranald Nicholson, *Scotland: the later middle ages* (Edinburgh, 1974), p. 303.

destruction,[11] so forging, as time would reveal, another nail for the coffin of Charles I who legislated their abolition in the shadow of the Act of Revocation (1625). As chief of the most powerful clan in the Highlands, Archibald Campbell was as defensive of custom and tradition as he was suspicious of Charles Stewart's innovatory legislation.

The *Porteous* developed the theme that a nobleman must be noble in his actions. Birth alone did not confer true nobility, a point which was to be elaborated by the great schoolman, John Mair – 'there is no true nobility but virtue and its acts. Vulgar nobility is nothing but a windy mode of talk'. Although Mair was decidedly hostile towards the nobility, believing that they had betrayed William Wallace, the hero of Scottish independence, they were central to his view of the Scottish constitution. 'It is from the people, and most of all from the chief men and the nobility who act for the common people that kings have their institution; it belongs therefore to princes, prelates and nobles to decide as to any ambiguity that may emerge in regard to a king.'[12] Such ambiguity might be decided, in extreme cases, through deposition.

Consistently aristocratic in tone was the superb *Complaynt of Scotland* (1549) in which Dame Scotia urges her sons, the three estates, to co-operate with one another in order to eradicate the friction between them which is destroying the kingdom. The dame, a veritable harridan, thinks that none of the common people should enjoy liberty 'but rather ye suld be daily dauntit and halden in subjectioun because that your hartis is full of malice, ignorance, variance and inconstance ... There is nocht ane mair ignorant and ane mair blind thing in this warld as is till adhere to the judgement of the commont people, quhilk hes nother consideratioun nor raison'.[13] The nobility, in her view, are poor champions of her honour but on them she has no option but to depend.

John Knox wrote an important series of letters from Dieppe in 1557 in which he chafed at the apparent inactivity of the Protestant lords. Since Scotland lay in religious bondage it rested with the nobles to deliver her:

For only for that cause are ye called princes of the people, and ye receive of your brethren honour, tribute and homage at God's commandment; not by reason of your birth and progeny ... but by reason of your office and duty which is to vindicate and deliver your subjects and brethren from all violence and oppression to the utmost of your power ... The reformation of religion and of public enormities doth appertain to more than to the clergy or chief rulers called kings.[14]

---

[11] McIlwain, *Works*, p. 87.
[12] John Mair, *A history of Greater Britain*, ed. and trans. A. Constable (SHS, 1892), p. 215.
[13] J. A. H. Murray (ed.), *The complaynt of Scotland* (EETS, 1872), pp. 139–40.
[14] W. C. Dickinson (ed.), *John Knox's history of the Reformation in Scotland* (2 vols., Edinburgh, 1949), vol. I, p. 135.

Knox, who was always refining his theories to meet contingencies of the moment, went rather further the following year with his *Appellation ... addressed to the nobility and estates of Scotland*, the same year in which the dying fourth earl of Argyll, the first of his house to commit to Protestantism, ordered his son to set forward the public and true preaching of the Gospel and to suppress all superstition and idolatry to the uttermost of his power:[15]

Be not deceaved my Lordes, ye are placed in auctoritie for an other purpose then to flatter your king in his folie and blind rage; to witt, that as with your bodies, strength, riches and wisdome ye are bound to assist and defend him in all things, which by your advice he shall take in hand, for God's glorie, and for the preservation of his communewealth and subjects; so by your gravities, counsel and admonition, yee are bound to correct and represse whatsoever ye know him to attempt expressedly repugning to Goddes word, honour and glorie, or what ye shall espie him to do, be it by ignorance, or be it by malice, against his subjects great or small. Of which last part of your obedience, if ye defraud your king ye commit against him no lesse treason, than if ye did extract from him your due and promised support, what time by his enemies injustly he wer pursued.[16]

That Knox struck a chord is suggested by the letter of the lords of the Congregation to Mary of Guise in May 1559 in which they declared a preference for exposing their bodies to a thousand deaths rather than risking the perpetual damnation of their souls by denying Christ.[17] In the event the nobility failed Knox as they failed the Reformation. His next appeal was to the commonalty who responded with a reformation which was, as Gilbert Burnet succinctly observed, 'popular and parliamentary'.[18] The Scottish aristocracy, however, adhered to its own rhetoric during the crisis promoted by Mary Queen of Scots.

Serious investigation of Mary's deposition has been notoriously ignored by her biographers although it was probably the single most important episode in her crowded career, far outstripping her love affairs and intrigues. Such theorists as Mariana, Suárez, Mola and Hotman have been cited to justify Mary's involvement in the Babington plot by historians who are apparently oblivious of the fact that Mary herself was the tyrant who had to be removed in 1567.[19] Two years earlier those nobles who, through their objections to the queen's marriage with Henry Stewart, Lord Darnley, became embroiled in the Chaseabout raid mounted what became something of a dress rehearsal for 1567. The declaration which the disaffected issued at Dumfries contains obvious echoes of Knox and suggests that the revolt was

[15] *Ibid.*, vol. I, p. 138.
[16] David Laing (ed.), *The works of John Knox* (6 vols., Wodrow Society, 1846–64), vol. IV, p. 495.
[17] Calderwood, vol. I, p. 444.
[18] Gilbert Burnet, *Bishop Burnet's history of his own time* (3 vols., Edinburgh, 1753), vol. I, p. 2.
[19] E.g., Antonia Fraser, *Mary Queen of Scots* (London, 1969), p. 491.

something more than 'a jealous disaffection springing from feudally inspired hatred of the Lennoxes with religious overtones introduced for the sake of English subsidies rather than a genuine revolt of conscience'.[20] They claimed that they had done nothing except fulfil their obligations to their prince, native country and commonwealth in the defence of the reformed religion:

Concerning the policie and commoun wealth, we that are of the cheefe of the nobilitie and counsellors of this realme, to whom of duetie it apperteaneth to have a speciall care of the publict effaires of the same, and of the preservation of the estate therof as weill by reasoun of our birth and blood as also be defence of the countrie, having advisedlie considered the great misorder and danger ensuing to the estat forsaid by diverse enormities and misorders, can doe no lesse than by all meanes possible sue the same to be repaired and redressed.

The queen had abandoned 'the wholsome advice and counsell of her Majesties ancient nobilitie and barons' in order to follow 'the advice and counsell of such men, strangers, as have nather judgement nor experience of the ancient lawes and governance of this realme, nor naturall love toward her Majestie nor subjects thereof'.[21] Although the rebellion was abortive the Dumfries declaration neatly states the arguments behind Mary's deposition in 1567 and indeed it could stand to explain the opposition to her grandson in the 1630s. Strafford had many precedents for asserting that Argyll and others were using the 'cloak of religion'.

One of Mary's most fervent apologists, the worthy John Lesley, bishop of Ross, subscribed to the same theory as the confederate lords – 'na republik or commounweil evir yit flurished that contemned the nobilitie'. The most important governmental affairs depended upon their support or, as Lesley's translator, Father Dalrymple, rendered the Latin, 'Scotland sa honoured thame, that it thocht the cheifest parte of the republic to consist of thame, and a sueit succour to the commoune weil.' The alienation of the nobility and the people, he conceded, sometimes led in the past to 'the king's slauchtir'.[22] Even though Lesley deplored the deposition of Mary, he could conceive of no other Scottish constitution.

Another worthy who unrepentantly ransacked the annals of Scottish history to document his own bias was Robert Lindsay of Pitscottie. He related how the nobles in the reign of James III formed a convention to debate how they might best persuade the king to rule justly, defend his honour and promote the well-being of the commonwealth. They 'put sic

---

[20] *Ibid.*, p. 233.   [21] Calderwood, vol. II, pp. 569–76.
[22] *The historie of Scotland wrytten first in Latin of the most revered and worthy Jhone Leslie bishop of Rosse and translated in Scottish by Father James Dalrymple*, ed. E. G. Cody (2 vols., STS, 1888), vol. I, pp. 111–12.

nobill men about him to serve him quhairby vertew might be mantenit and wyce punischit quhairby he might win the favouris of his lordis and barrouns and to bring his realme to sic peace and rest as his father left it to him'. They begged the king to shed his suspicions of the nobility and take their advice in all matters. If he refused 'they tuik God to witnes that they sould be guiltles of the misgoverance of the realme'.[23] As a consequence of his failure to heed the nobility, James III 'happinit to be slane' in 1488. If corroboration be required for the assertions of the garrulous and tendentious Pitscottie, whose horizons seldom extended beyond Fife, it is to be found in the parliamentary record which preserves that memorably laconic obit.[24]

Although Lesley and George Buchanan found themselves on opposite sides in the Marian controversy their views on the role of the nobility in Scottish society were practically identical. Buchanan's ideas on tyrannicide have received a good deal of attention from scholars though his more extensive discussion of the nobility has been somewhat ignored. He wrote a version of his *De jure regni apud Scotos* before December 1567 and it was quite widely circulated prior to its publication in 1579.[25] Although the *De jure regni* is the best known repository of Buchanan's theories they are also to be discerned spasmodically in his poetry and other works, while they are central to his *Rerum Scoticarum historia* published in 1582. It has also been argued that Buchanan's hand was behind a document presented at Westminster by the earl of Morton in 1571. Morton's paper, like Buchanan's *History*, was explicit on the function of the Scottish nobility. 'Wicked and unprofitabel' princes had been deposed or replaced 'be commoun and ancient conswetude, unreprovit, agaynsaid or abrogat, quhilk inducis lawe'. It stated quite categorically that 'the nobilitie of Scotland hes power to correct thair kingis ... a part may als wele do it as the haill'.[26]

The *De jure regni* is primarily a discussion of the difference between *rex* and *tyrannus* and of suitable means for preventing the former becoming the latter. Buchanan believes that kings were originally chosen by the people and that laws were created as a check on royal prerogative. What clearly emerges as his argument develops is the idea of the contractual theory of monarchy. The people should have the power to prescribe the limits to royal

---

[23] Robert Lindsay of Pitscottie, *The historie and chronicles of Scotland*, ed. A. J. G. Mackay (2 vols., STS, 1899), vol. I, pp. 170–1.

[24] *APS*, vol. II, p. 210.

[25] On the *De jure regni*, see I. D. McFarlane, *Buchanan* (London, 1981), index; W. S. McKechnie, '*De jure regni apud Scotos*', in George Nielson (ed.), *George Buchanan: Glasgow quatercentenary studies* (Glasgow, 1907), pp. 211–96. Evidence of dating is provided by H. R. Trevor-Roper, 'George Buchanan and the ancient Scottish constitution', *EHR*, supplement 3 (1966), 16n.

[26] Trevor-Roper, 'Buchanan', pp. 40–50.

authority – 'what affects the joint safety of all should have the backing of an open general council acting with the king'. To the charge that the people is 'a monster with many heads', Buchanan replies that he would never entrust such matters to the people at large but 'roughly in accordance with our standing practice, selected people of all classes should assemble to advise the king'. These guarantors for the mutual fulfilment of the contract so assembled would inevitably in the sixteenth century be dominated by the nobility, politically the most powerful of the estates.[27] To this point we shall return.

Religion figured prominently in Argyll's discussions with Strafford who, he said, had been misinformed in assuming that the present debate in Scotland involved the 'substance of religion', while he also believed the deputy mistaken to dismiss the importance of discipline and ceremony. The Scots had rejected Rome through their laws; they believed that whoever loved popery more than the reformed religion loved the pope 'better nor the king'. All adherents of the true religion distinguished dangers in the recent innovations and consequently they were concerned to indicate the error to a religious king. The justice of their case seemed to be confirmed by the king's willingness to 'grant their humble supplications', that is, his permission to summon a free general assembly.[28]

Strafford hotly denied that he had misread the situation in Scotland citing the recently published 'Montrose's Protestation' to support his arguments. The document, of September 1638, was compiled by Wariston but it earned Montrose a reputation for total intransigence because his name appeared for the noble Table. The protestation dealt with the question of why those who had signed the National Covenant could not now subscribe to the King's Confession of 1581 as Charles insisted they should. The protesters argued that to sign the confession would imply rejection of the covenant thus perjuring the covenanters, and would also implicitly condone acceptance of all religious innovations since 1581, innovations which the second and third parts of the covenant totally abjured.

The protestation is full of references to the Scriptures and to acts of parliament. 'The tears that began to be poured forth at the solemnizing of the Covenant are not yet dryed up and wiped away, and the joyful noise which then began to sound hath not yet ceased.'[29] Charles dismissed the closely worded arguments of the protesters as 'lacking in reason' and 'crack-brained'. Strafford followed his royal master, lifting quotations out of context and manifesting a complete miscomprehension of the points

---

[27] Buchanan, De jure regni (1843 edn), caps. xxvi, lvi, trans. by D. McNeill, The art and science of government among the Scots (Glasgow, 1954), pp. 41, 68.
[28] Strafford, Letters, vol. II, pp. 246–7.
[29] Walter Balcanquhal, A large declaration concerning the late tumults in Scotland (London, 1639), pp. 163–7; Strafford, Letters, vol. II, p. 247.

made. One example of his faulty dialectic must suffice. He asserts that the protesters state 'there be indeed no substantial difference between that which we have subscribed and the confession of 1581', so implying that they totally destroy their own case. The document actually states, 'no substantial difference between that which we have subscribed and the confession subscribed [in] 1581 more than there is between that which is hid and that which is revealed ... betwixt the hand closed and open, betwixt a sword sheathed and drawn ... or (if we may with reverence ascend yet higher) between the Old Testament and the New'. Strafford considered the bishops to be constituted by the lawful and superior magistrate (namely the king). He regretted that the English liturgy composed by 'learned and Christian bishops who sealed their confession and departure from the Church of Rome with their blood and their lives should be termed Popish books'. Charles had granted their supplications as the father, out of compassion to his son, bears with that which he disapproves hoping to 'undeceive him'; so the king deals with the Scots, his 'political children'. It was pernicious to use religious arguments to resist the king. Citing passages from the protestation he demonstrated that the covenanters assumed a 'papal plenipotency'. Finally he denied that the idea of a covenant 'sealed from Heaven' had any precedent.[30]

Argyll countered that the bishops were under attack because they transgressed the laws and laudable customs of the kirk and kingdom. The English did not move far enough from Rome while the Scottish church was constituted by her laudable assemblies. The Scots did not oppose Charles himself but only 'voluntair and constrained actions in religious duties'. Their inspiration was the Scriptures and not such artefacts as books of martyrs. They wished to be like Moses who would not allow one house to remain in Egypt 'lest it should give occasion to return, or like Lot that durst not look back on Sodom or like Paul when he was converted advising no more with flesh and blood'. He concluded by deploring the meddling of Strafford and others like him to upset the peace of the Scottish church.[31]

The Strafford correspondence contains the most explicit statements that Argyll ever made on his religious and political views with the exception of what he had to say in the *Instructions*, which were addressed to his children as he awaited trial. He believed that religion was of the greatest importance for illustrious personages – other glories had lifted them beyond the pitch and reach of men, but 'this is a ray of divinity which advanceth them near to the Deity'. He enjoined his son to make obedience to his sovereign one of the chief points of his religion. He denied that the Scots kirk preached sedition but he believed that obedience to the sovereign must be consistent

[30] Strafford, *Letters*, vol. II, pp. 246–7.   [31] *Ibid.*, vol. II, p. 291.

with obedience to God. To his dying day he adhered to the perfection of the established doctrine of the Scottish church discovering none better in all the religions throughout the world.[32] Is there, then, any indication that Argyll envisioned any practical application of his theories? The evidence is somewhat ambiguous but nonetheless suggestive.

In the summer of 1640 word leaked out that Argyll was planning nothing less than 'ane Dictatory and incantoning of the kingdome, by which the countrye was to be enslaved and reduced to all thralldome'. His rival, Montrose, was asked to subscribe a band or bands 'importing the schaiking off of Authoritie and establisching the wholl power and rule of Scotland' in the hands of three men – General Alexander Leslie, James, marquis of Hamilton and Argyll himself who was to be responsible for Scotland 'benorth the Forth'. An alarmed Montrose immediately drew up and, with a group of moderates, subscribed the Cumbernauld Band to foil 'the particular and indirect practicking of a few'.[33] It remained secret for several months but its existence was revealed by one of the signatories, Lord Boyd, on his deathbed in mid-November. Argyll immediately questioned another signatory, James Livingstone, Lord Almond, a son of the earl of Linlithgow and a professional soldier of such distinction that he had been rewarded with a peerage and a commission as Leslie's second-in-command.[34] It took two days for Archibald to winkle the required information out of him. When he was informed of the names of the signatories he was reluctant to publicize the division within covenanting ranks since some of the subscribers commanded regiments in the army and any such revelations could only damage the negotiations with the king. He contented himself with having the Band burned by the common hangman. Clarendon observed that Montrose and Argyll were like Caesar and Pompey since the one could not endure a superior nor the other an equal.[35] At this point, however, it was essential to present a common front to the king and to paper over the cracks in the covenant. Argyll, although he already suspected Montrose's motives and instincts, was content for the moment to let the matter rest.[36]

Montrose was of a different mind. Earlier in the year he had offered to prove that some of the 'pryme leaders' of the covenant 'had entered in motiones for deposing the king'. His informant was Mr John Stewart of

[32] Argyll, *Instructions*, pp. 25–9.
[33] Mark Napier (ed.), *Memorials of Montrose and his times* (2 vols., Edinburgh, 1858), vol. I, pp. 254–6. The Band is also printed in Baillie, *Letters and journals*, vol. II, pp. 467–8. Laing noted a copy in the Balcarres MSS and he possessed another in a contemporary hand.
[34] On Almond, see J. B. Paul, *The Scots peerage* (9 vols., Edinburgh, 1904–14), vol. II, p. 361.
[35] W. D. Macray (ed.), *Clarendon's history of the rebellion* (6 vols., Oxford, 1888), vol. I, p. 392.
[36] For a fuller discussion of the Cumbernauld Band, see Edward J. Cowan, *Montrose: for covenant and king* (London, 1977), pp. 96–9.

Ladywell, commissary of Dunkeld, who reported certain discussions in which Argyll had allegedly participated while he held the earl of Atholl captive at Balloch Castle. At Perth and Scone in February 1641 Montrose reiterated his accusations which soon reached the ever-attentive ears of the committee of estates. On being questioned by that body, Montrose confidently affirmed that he had named Argyll as the man 'who was to have rule benorth the Forth and as the man who discoursed of deposing the king'.[37] When Stewart was interrogated four days later he boldly reminded Argyll of his remarks at Balloch whereupon the earl 'broke into a passion and with great oaths denied the whole or part thereof'. 'Many wondered there-at', commented Guthry, as wonder they might at the colourful oaths of *Mac-Cailein Mor*.

According to Bishop Guthry, who preserves the most detailed information on Argyll's allegedly treasonable discussions at Balloch, Argyll argued that in the opinion of certain lawyers and divines deposition was legitimate in the case of desertion, invasion or vendition, 'and that once they thought to have done it at the last sitting of parliament and would do it at the next sitting thereof'.[38] Some corroboration may be provided by Johnston of Wariston who reported that, in the debates which prefaced the parliament of June 1640, 'Montrose did dispute against Argyll, Rothes, Balmerino and myself because some urged that as long as we had a king we could not sit without him; and it was answered that to do the less was more lawful than to do the greater'.[39] The sense is obscure but the intended suggestion was probably that to indict parliament without the king was more lawful than to depose him altogether. The other possible piece of corroboration derives from the potentially suspect testimony of Stewart of Ladywell; he asserted that Argyll had darkly claimed to be 'the aucht [eighth] man from Robert Bruce' and that Argyll's followers boasted that they 'were King Campbell's men, no more King Stewart's'. Certain lines in Gaelic were in circulation which he translated as 'I gave Argyll the praise because all men sees it is treuth; for he will tak geir from the lawland men; and he will tak the croun per force; and he will cry King at Whitsonday.'[40]

The question of whether there was any substance in these allegations is

---

[37] Mark Napier, *Memoirs of the marquis of Montrose* (2 vols., Edinburgh, 1856), vol. I, p. 263; see also *ibid.*, vol. I, chs. 14–17 *passim*, and Napier, *Memorials*, vol. I, pp. 296–301.

[38] *The memoirs of Henry Guthry, late bishop of Dunkeld* (Glasgow, 1749), p. 93. Guthry attended the subsequent beheading of Stewart of Ladywell and he clearly believed that Stewart's original testimony had been the true one. Stewart was brutally tortured to the point that when he retestified before the committee he could neither stand nor walk. Ironically he was condemned for leasing-making, technically, slandering a king to his subjects; in this case the charge was applied *vis-à-vis* a king-like subject slandered to his king.

[39] Napier, *Memoirs*, vol. I, p. 236.   [40] Napier, *Memorials*, vol. II, p. 477.

obviously crucial to any understanding of Argyll's career. It is clear that some limitation of the royal prerogative was implicit in Argyll's condemnation of the bishops, explicit in the covenanters' abolition of episcopacy. His attitudes had been well known since at least 1635 while his recorded statements during the 1639 and 1640 parliaments indicated a desire to alter the constitutional position of the king. The proposal to partition the country between Leslie, Hamilton and Argyll recalls the days of the Roman triumvirate but such a measure need not have implied deposition. A dictatory or dictatorship on Roman lines would have been regarded as a purely temporary expedient, though many would have been uncomfortably aware that it required the dagger of Brutus to remove Caesar from office. Argyll's powers beyond the Forth were already extensive; he was without doubt the most powerful subject in the kingdom. Although he was perfectly familiar with the classics he could have equally well appealed to Scottish history. As we have seen, he told Strafford that the function of the Scottish nobility was to 'carry ourselves to his people as we desire his majesty should appear to them and so make up to him a treasure of their love ... Whensoever we fail in this the greatness of our places aggravate so much the more our offences.'[41] He could have argued that, as so often in the Scottish past, he was simply acting for the king who was temporarily incapacitated, as in the many examples of royal minorities in the fifteenth and sixteenth centuries. Argyll's fault, however well intentioned or otherwise, was that he apparently drew up bonds without consulting the committee of estates or the covenanting leadership. Montrose objected that his name had been attached to one such bond without his consent. That bond, however, was concerned to provide a noble committee comprising the earls of Mar, Cassillis and Montrose to advise Argyll as general-commander.[42] Of the three, only John Kennedy, sixth earl of Cassillis, could truly be described as a consistent covenanter – Burnet thought him so sincere that 'he would suffer no man to take his words in any other sense than he meant them'.[43] John Erskine, nineteenth earl of Mar, had spent much time at court, was known to be a pro-royalist and would sign the Cumbernauld Band.[44] Montrose had been under suspicion since his meeting with Charles in 1639, which experience, many thought, had turned his head. If Argyll had truly sought an absolute dictatorship he would hardly have selected two such potentially lukewarm supporters for his committee.

Argyll's opinions on the role of the prince, as they appear in his *Instructions*, are inconveniently coloured by hindsight, but they do shed some light

41 Strafford, *Letters*, vol. II, p. 220.   42 Napier, *Memoirs*, vol. I, pp. 255–6.
43 Paul, *Scots peerage*, vol. II, p. 481.
44 Napier, *Memorials*, vol. I, p. 255.

on his general attitudes. He believed that 'princes begin to lose their estates when they begin to break the ancient laws, manners and customs under which their subjects have long lived; for princes must have as much regard for the safety of their subjects (which consists in the protection of the laws) as of their lives'. He was convinced that 'the greatness of that prince is sure and stable which his subjects know to be as much for them as above them'. On the other hand he took pains to warn against the dangers of tyranny. 'Nothing can please a good king so much as concord among his subjects, whereas that makes a tyrant to fear them.' Tyranny was to be avoided at all costs for 'nothing is impossible or unfeasible for an enslaved people to do against tyrants and usurpers'.[45]

Given such sentiments and considering the situation in which Argyll found himself in 1640 it is not difficult to believe that he did indeed discuss, in general terms, the possibility of deposition when the king was charged with the desertion, invasion and vendition of his kingdom. When Stewart of Ladywell was invited, under torture, to reconsider his testimony, he recalled that Argyll's speech was 'general, of all kings'.[46] It could be objected that anyone generalizing on the subject of deposition in the troubled Scotland of 1640 was more than somewhat lacking in political sagacity since the particular predicament of Charles Stewart was in the forefront of all Scottish minds. Yet these discussions were heard by the earl of Atholl, his brother-in-law Sir Patrick Ogilvie of Inchmartin, Sir Thomas Stewart younger of Grandtully and Archibald, brother of Campbell of Lawers, as well as Stewart of Ladywell.

The Scots had complained since 1603 that the Stewarts had 'deserted' their kingdom. Argyll stated that 'kings must sometimes visit the remotest parts of the country, that their subjects may see that by their care of them that they are truly pastors of the people'.[47] Charles may have been deemed guilty of desertion by failing to appear in his native country in 1639 and 1640. Alexander Henderson, whose views were broadly shared by Argyll, distinguished in his *Instructions for defensive arms* between 'the king resident in the kingdom ... rightly informed and the king far from us, in another kingdom misinformed by our adversaries'. Henderson was much concerned with the second criterion for deposition, namely invasion. He wished that all might know 'how unjustly we are invaded'. There was all the difference in the world between the king, 'as king, proceeding royally according to the laws of the kingdom against rebels and the king as a man coming down from his throne ... Princes principally are for the people and their defence and not the people principally for them. The safety of the

---

[45] Argyll, *Instructions*, pp. 95, 100, 103, 106, 126.   [46] Napier, *Memorials*, vol. I, p. 298.
[47] Argyll, *Instructions*, p. 97.

people is the supreme law.'[48] The matter of vendition is more problematical, though the meaning of the word extends beyond its commercial sense to embrace such concepts as alienation or disposal. John Spalding used the more appropriate term – prodition (betrayal or treachery) – which he defined as seeking the damage and loss of the kingdom by destroying its laws and liberties.[49] Argyll adhered to the time-honoured and sacrosanct principle of the inalienability of sovereignty when he observed that 'a king is obliged as diligently and carefully to keep the goods of his crown, as a tutor those of his pupil'.[50] On this count also Charles could be deemed to have failed.

Argyll clearly envisaged a sovereignty shared by king and parliament. All his instincts and his own position as 'prince'[51] of his family and clan would lead him to stop short of deposition.[52] But he may have aired his views because he feared that if the centre did not hold others would undoubtedly take advantage as things fell apart. Few had forgotten the bizarre episode in the 1630s when Hamilton had allegedly schemed to seize the crown for himself, utilizing his own royal pedigree and 6,000 troops levied for the armies of Gustavus Adolphus.[53] Throughout 1639 and 1640 rumours that the marquis sought to supplant Charles resurfaced.[54] If Charles were overthrown, Archibald Campbell, earl of Argyll, was doubtless prepared to put himself selflessly forward in his country's hour of need in order to block someone like Hamilton.

The allusion to 'eighth man from Robert Bruce' was a garbled reference to a prophecy of Thomas the Rhymer whose enduring fame owed more to the obscurity than to the veracity of his vaticination:

> A French wife shall beare the son
> Shall rule all Bretaine to the sey
> that of the Bruce's blood shall come
> as neere as the ninth degree.[55]

---

[48] Printed in Andrew Stevenson, *The history of the church and state in Scotland from the accession of King Charles I to the restoration of King Charles II* (2 vols., Edinburgh, 1754), vol. II, pp. 686–95. The earliest version of this 1639 pamphlet that I have seen is dated 1642.

[49] John Spalding, *Memorialls of the troubles in Scotland and England AD 1624–AD 1645* (2 vols., Spalding Club, 1850), vol. II, p. 47.

[50] Argyll, *Instructions*, pp. 98–9.   [51] *Ibid.*, p. 16.

[52] 'In all negotiations between the Presbyterians and the king it had been stipulated that the king's person must be protected and his honour remain undiminished. Argyll was reported to have remarked that this would be amply fulfilled if Charles were kept permanently in prison, provided he was guarded against assassins and that his attendants served him on their knees.' Willcock, *Great marquess*, p. 217.

[53] Ian Grimble, *Chief of Mackay* (London, 1965), pp. 1–9.

[54] *CSP Dom. 1639*, p. 451; *CSP Dom. 1640–1*, p. 10.

[55] *The whole prophecies of Scotland* (Edinburgh, 1718), p. 22.

Since this version was printed by Waldegrave in 1603 (and reprinted in 1615), it enjoyed, like most prophecy, the immeasurable boon of hindsight since it referred to none other than James VI, son of that French wife, Mary Queen of Scots. Prophecy was extremely popular in this period. James VI, who consulted several prophets, believed that in 1603 he had fulfilled the prophecies of Merlin as did the covenanting army invading England in 1640. Millennial prophecies attributed to John Knox and John Napier bolstered the covenanting revolution. Prophecies were applied to almost every significant figure in that revolt, including Argyll. The latter's relationship with Robert Bruce was considerably beyond the ninth degree, although he was a descendant of Bruce's sister, Lady Mary. The point of the allegation was simply to suggest once again that Archibald had designs upon the throne.

Although the Gaelic original does not appear to have survived, the sentiments of the praise poem which Stewart translated certainly match those of surviving poetry by the MacEwens, hereditary bards to Clan Campbell. Indeed the claims of the translated piece may be considered mild in contrast to the extravagant eulogistic language of a poem such as *Triath na Gaoidheal* which traces Gill-easbuig's pedigree from none other than Arthur himself:

No wonder that all men's obedience is rendered to equal-minded Arthur's blood; a balance to weigh his nobility will not be found in Britain; at this time to withstand his will is hard.

MacCailein is the rightful ruler of the Hebrides, 'the headship of the Gael is his of due'. He commands the largest number of warriors but equally · important 'Gill-easbuig the Generous surpasses Europe's warriors in maintaining poet bands'. The MacEwen bards were willing and able to reinforce any passing dreams that Archibald may have allowed himself of elevation to the kingship.

The kin of Arthur, the great son of Ambrose, many a king has been crowned therefrom; its counterpart is not in Scotland, a blood with greater share of noble blood. Since thou art noblest of British blood, history has exalted thee beyond the due men pay to earls; to match another with thee is unmeet: no man has a right to do it.

From the bounds of Lewis to the coast of Banbha there is no region that pays not tribute due to thee; in the whole kingdom no kingship matches thine; thou art of the noblest of every land and lord.[56]

One such poem could spawn a dozen English translations claiming that Argyll would 'tak the crown per force; and he would cry King at Whitsonday'.

---

[56] W. J. Watson, 'Unpublished Gaelic poetry', *Scottish Gaelic Studies*, 3 (1931), 143–51.

Certainly, contemporary chroniclers found kingship an appropriate metaphor with which to clothe Argyll. Gordon of Rothiemay accused Argyll of 'playing *rex* in the Highlands',[57] while Menteith of Salmonet remarked that he commanded 'like a little sovereign'.[58] Burnet noted that the earl was 'much set upon raising his own family to be sort of king in the Highlands',[59] and Gordon of Ruthven noted his 'ambitious desire of supreme and absolute rule'.[60] He was, indeed, King Campbell.

The question arises of whether, since Argyll's ideas about kingship were clearly fostered by the bards, it is possible that his notions about deposition were also reinforced through his Gaelic heritage? The answer is very probably in the affirmative. In his discussion of the problem George Buchanan provides a fascinating – and suggestive – analogy:

Apart from the fact that bad kings have always been brought to book when they set up a tyranny over the citizens, our ancient families still retain some traces of that old custom. Those of us Scots who retain our time-honoured practices to this day elect the chief of our clan and associate with him a council of wise men – and the chief is liable to lose his office if he does not obey this council. Is it likely that those who are so careful in sections of the community would ignore what affects the welfare of the whole nation?[61]

He cites the specific example of John Balliol 'deposed by our leading men on account of his having subjected himself and his kingdom to Edward the Englishman'. Through their coronation oath the kings swear obedience to the laws. Later in his argument he claims that 'whatever power is given to anyone by the people can be revoked on just grounds'. Various examples are cited, including that of James III adjudged by the estates 'to have been lawfully slain on account of his appalling cruelty and wicked turpitude'. Parliament on that occasion wished to establish a precedent – 'there is little difference, on the whole, between the judgement on a deed that is done and an ordinance providing for a future event'. Hence Buchanan concludes that 'there is a mutual contract between king and people'.[62]

That Buchanan should have invoked the Gaelic past to justify the Scottish present in the matter of contractual theory was highly significant. Ninian Winzet referred to Buchanan's Gaelic-speaking mother. Gaelic was still spoken in the vicinity of his native parish of Killearn a hundred years

---

[57] J. Gordon of Rothiemay, *History of Scots affairs from MDCXXXVII to MDCXLI*, ed. J. Robertson and G. Grub (3 vols., Spalding Club, 1841), vol. III, p. 200.
[58] Robert Mentet [Menteith] of Salmonet, *The history of the troubles of Great Britain*, trans. James Ogilvie (London, 1735), p. 179.
[59] Burnet, *History*, vol. I, p. 35.
[60] Patrick Gordon of Ruthven, *A short abridgement of Britane's distemper* (Spalding Club, 1844), p. 56.
[61] Buchanan, *De jure regni*, cap. lvi.   [62] *Ibid.*, cap. lxxxvi.

after his death.[63] John Lesley remarked on the antiquity of Gaeldom, an area where language, manners, institutions, clothing and way of life had not changed in two thousand years.[64] Although Buchanan wrote most perceptively on the subject of the Gaelic language, as a talented classicist he anticipated without regret a time when the 'rusticity and barbarism' of Gaelic would give way 'to the softer and more harmonious tones of the Latin'.[65] In the document of 1571, there is an allusion, as there is in the *De jure regni*, to the nobility and people of Scotland choosing their king and 'adjoining to him ane counsall of the wisest quhilk ancient custom the men of the Ilis and utheris in choosing of thair chiftainis yit still observes'.[66] In compiling his *History* he included a section on the Hebrides drawn from Donald Monro's description of the Isles which discusses the composition of the council of the lords of the Isles.[67]

Buchanan's appeal to the Gaelic past must have made a profound impression upon *MacCailein Mor* who provided in his own person a devastating combination of the political tenets of presbyterianism and a shrewd knowledge and understanding of the Gaelic experience. During the previous century and a half John, lord of the Isles, Iain MacDonald, chief of Keppoch, and Dougal MacRanald, chief of Clan Ranald, had all been deposed by their clansmen.[68] The Campbell conspiracy of 1592 could be similarly interpreted, while the departure of Gill-easbuig Gruamach in 1617 could be seen as a sophisticated alternative to the often bloody expedient of deposition.[69] A chief as potentially vulnerable as Argyll could draw comfort and a measure of protection from Calvin's *Institutes*. Calvin was uncomfortably aware that the promise of liberty in the Gospel was bound to encourage those who refused to tolerate any secular power. 'They will think that nothing will be safe until the whole world is changed into a new form, when there will be neither courts, nor laws, nor magistrates, nor anything of the kind to interfere, as they suppose, with their liberty!' What then might offer a check to revolution? In reviewing different types of government Calvin found monarchy prone to tyranny, democracy to sedition. 'The form that

---

[63] Arthur H. Williamson, *Scottish national consciousness in the age of James VI* (Edinburgh, 1979), p. 190n. J. Guthrie Smith, *Strathendrick and its inhabitants from early times* (Glasgow, 1896), p. 105. Buchanan's discussion of Gaelic is in Book I of his *History*.

[64] Lesley, *Historie*, trans. Dalrymple, vol. I, p. 95.

[65] George Buchanan, *History of Scotland*, trans. James Aikman (4 vols., Glasgow, 1827), vol. I, p. 9.

[66] Trevor-Roper, 'Buchanan', p. 42.

[67] Buchanan, *History*, vol. I, pp. 39–55; R. W. Munro (ed.), *Monro's Western Isles of Scotland and genealogies of the clans 1549* (Edinburgh, 1961).

[68] Audrey Cunningham, *The loyal clans* (Cambridge, 1932), pp. 55, 95–6.

[69] Edward J. Cowan, 'Clanship, kinship and the Campbell acquisition of Islay', *SHR*, 58 (1979), 132–57; see also Cowan, 'Fishers in drumlie waters', *passim*.

greatly surpasses the others is aristocracy either pure or modified by popular government ... Owing to the vices or defects of men, it is safer and more tolerable when several bear rule that they may thus mutually assist, instruct and admonish each other and should any one be disposed to go too far, the others are censors and masters to curb his excess.'[70]

The coincidence of Calvin's appeal to pre-Davidic Israel and the predominantly aristocratic concept of the Scottish constitution was truly historic. These two strands were nowhere more tightly spliced than in the mind of Archibald Campbell. It was essential in his view that the excesses of the first Scottish Reformation in 1560 were not repeated. He believed that 'popular furies would never have end if not awed by their superiors ... the people will learn their own strength, that great power is rooted in the wishes of men and from thence infer that the popular power excels that of the noblesse'.[71] Popular power was no problem in Gaeldom where the initiative was taken by the aristocratic council which acted to 'curb the excess' of the chief. Calvinism, indeed, could only reinforce and reinvigorate the patriarchal powers of the chief of Clan Campbell.

All of this must appear rather tenuous to colleagues accustomed to working on great books which are the products of great minds. Argyll's did not belong to the latter category. Rather, as he confessed at the end of his life, 'whatever hath been said by me and others in this matter, you must report and accept them as from a distracted man, of a distracted subject, in a distracted time wherein I lived'.[72] This chapter has attempted to investigate the 'native' or 'Scottish' tradition in Argyll's intellectual heritage. His debt, in common with his colleagues Wariston, Henderson, the earl of Rothes and Samuel Rutherford, to Johannes Althusius has been discussed elsewhere.[73] Although it is not possible to demonstrate conclusively that Argyll was totally familiar with the entire contents of the *Politica methodice digesta* there are hints in his correspondence and in his *Instructions to a son* that he was not altogether unacquainted with it. He must have acquired some knowledge of the work in discussion with his covenanting associates and if he did own a copy of the *Politica* it was presumably not to hand as he penned his *Instructions* during five months' imprisonment in the Tower of London in 1660.[74] What can be stated with confidence is that there is little in Althusius with which Argyll would have taken issue.

The position of the Campbell chief was perfectly described in Althusius's observation that 'he is called *princeps* of the family, or of any tribe of people

---

[70] John Calvin, *The institutes of the Christian religion*, trans. Henry Beveridge (2 vols., London, 1962), vol. II, pp. 651, 654, 656–7.
[71] Argyll, *Instructions*, p. 6.   [72] *Ibid.*, p. 5.
[73] Cowan, 'Making of the Covenant', in Morrill (ed.), *Scottish National Covenant*, pp. 78–82.
[74] Willcock, *Great marquess*, pp. 304–5.

... who has the right to coerce the persons of his family individually or collectively'. Both writers touch upon clan or family insignia which, Argyll notes, his famous ancestors 'have borne with commendation and honour'.[75] Althusius's discussion of the administration of the (presbyterian) province whose heads or administrators 'have rights of sovereignty in their territory and stand in place of the supreme prince' contains a possible echo of Argyll's sentiments in the Strafford correspondence cited above. *Mac-Cailein* clearly administered the most impressive presbyterian province in the country conscientiously, exercising 'diligent watch and care over sacred and provincial affairs'.[76] He was an intensely devout individual, an elder in the kirk at Inveraray who, reputedly, often supplied the sermon[77] and who, as the *Minutes of the synod of Argyll* demonstrate, strenuously fulfilled another of Althusius's requirements in removing 'corruptions, idolatries, superstitions' etc. as well as promoting the establishment of kirks and schools.[78] Indeed, there can be little doubt that Argyll agreed with everything that Althusius had to say on safeguarding the church.

Possibly Campbell would have drawn his greatest inspiration from the *Politica*'s lengthy section on 'ephors' (governors and administrations below the rank of king) and their duties, the most important of which was to 'overcome the wicked actions or tyranny of the supreme magistrate'. The actions of the ephors were understood to embody those of the entire people – 'what they do through [the ephors] is regarded as if it had been done by them all and to pertain to them all'.[79] Ephoral duties included the constitution or appointment of the supreme magistrate and containing him within the limits of his office as well as acting as trustees during interregnum or incapacitation. Ephors had power to remove the tyrant and a duty to defend the magistrate and his office against conspiracies, plots and factions.[80]

There are some topics on which the two men coincide exactly and upon which the terminology is almost identical, the problem being that their opinions could legitimately be dismissed as commonplace and heavily derivative of Scripture and the classics. Thus the magistrate should be 'attentive to everything' (Althusius), 'universally knowing' (Argyll), but should 'keep many things secret' (Althusius) or 'be more reserved than he

[75] Carney, *Politics*, pp. 24–5; Argyll, *Instructions*, pp. 3, 7, 11, 16. For the Latin text, see Johannes Althusius, *Politica methodice digesta*, ed. Carl J. Friedrich (Cambridge, Mass., 1932).

[76] Carney, *Politics*, pp. 57–8.

[77] Robert Wodrow, *Analecta, or materials for a history of remarkable providences*, ed. M. Leishman (4 vols., Maitland Club, 1842–3), vol. I, p. 22.

[78] Carney, *Politics*, p. 50; D. C. MacTavish, *Minutes of the synod of Argyll 1639–1661* (2 vols., SHS, 1943–4).

[79] Carney, *Politics*, p. 96.   [80] *Ibid.*, pp. 98–103.

to whom all is permitted' (Argyll).[81] Both recommend the reading of histories but promote conversation as the best teacher while advocating the Ciceronian caution against the acquisition of superfluous knowledge.[82] Both deplore novelty or innovation at the start of a new reign or administration; both disapprove of wars with neighbouring countries; both commend honourable public diversions such as games or amusements 'without debauchery or excess'.[83] Both recommend the educational and political value of limited residence in a foreign country.[84] Althusius opined that 'there is nothing that makes the magistrate more beloved and pleasing to others than clemency', to be closely followed by Argyll, doubtless still nurturing some hope of pardon in 1660: 'there is nothing in the world which ... makes a prince more revered and desired than clemency'.[85]

Throughout his discussion Argyll is much more solicitous of the well-being of monarchy than is Althusius, but again, in common with the covenanting leadership, he could have drawn inspiration from the latter's remarks on tyranny. Did *MacCailein* have Althusius in mind during the machinations of 1640? A single ephor could not act alone but it was permitted for those in one part of the realm to withdraw from tyranny in order to defend themselves. Remedies other than deposition were to be first attempted and resistance by words and deeds was to be defensive, as opposed to offensive, by action within the territory of the resisting ephor. It was permissible to resist by enlisting an army 'so long as tyranny endures ... or acts contrary to the declared covenant'.[86]

Given the sketchy nature of the evidence the case for Argyll's indebtedness to Althusius must remain possible, perhaps even probable, but ultimately not proven, at least in the present state of our knowledge. It may be that in the final analysis Argyll did not need Althusius – he had deeper roots on which to draw. If it is accepted that Argyll's ideas on deposition were indeed, in part, conditioned by his Gaelic background, then nothing could better indicate the conservative nature of the covenanting revolution over which he presided. Perhaps the last word can most appropriately be left to George Buchanan:

So old the tale; but whether merely old I leave to each man's judgement. Some may smell mustiness in anything raked out from ancient records; others may call that fresh which matches what is green in memory.[87]

---

81 Carney, *Politics*, p. 132; Argyll, *Instructions*, p. 97.
82 Carney, *Politics*, p. 133; Argyll, *Instructions*, pp. 73–4.
83 Carney, *Politics*, pp. 147–8, 151.
84 Carney, *Politics*, pp. 144–5; Argyll, *Instructions*, pp. 52–8.
85 Carney, *Politics*, p. 148; Argyll, *Instructions*, p. 93.   86 Carney, *Politics*, p. 189.
87 Quoted in T. D. Robb, 'Sixteenth-century humanism as illustrated in the works of George Buchanan', in Nielson (ed.), *Buchanan quatercentenary studies*, p. 178.

11 Lex, rex iusto posita: Samuel Rutherford on the origins of government

John D. Ford

> Our Scene is again in *Scotland*, who hath accepted his Son, whom for distinction sake, we will be content to call *Charls* the Second. Certainly these People were strangely blind as to Gods judgement perpetually poured out upon a Familie, or else to their own interest, to admit the spray of such a stock; one that hath so little to commend him, and so great improbabilitie for their designs and happiness.
>
> J. H., *The grounds and reasons of monarchy considered out of Scottish history*
> (Edinburgh, 1651)

I

When Charles II was crowned king of Scotland, England, France and Ireland at Scone in 1651 he was subjected to a well-known lesson on kingship by Robert Douglas, moderator of the general assembly. Douglas took the conventional line, reminding Charles of his duty to maintain true religion and the liberties of his people, exhorting him to cultivate the virtues of piety, fortitude, justice and prudence, and urging him to abide by the laws of the land as well as by God's law, and to accept the counsel of his traditional advisers.[1] Like an earlier Scottish tutor in kingship,[2] Douglas managed to inject a radical message into an otherwise conservative doctrine by teaching that 'When a king is Crowned, and received by the people, there is a Covenant or mutuall Contract, between him and them, containing

---

Thanks are due to all those who participated in the Folger seminar at which this paper was first presented, and to John Coffey who made helpful comments on a later draft.
[1] Robert Douglas, *The forme and order of the coronation of Charles the Second, king of Scotland, England, France, and Ireland* (Aberdeen, 1651), pp. 6–7. On the conventional doctrine, see R. J. Lyall, 'Politics and poetry in fifteenth- and sixteenth-century Scotland', *Scottish Literary Journal*, 3 (1976), 5–29; and Roger A. Mason, 'Kingship and commonweal: political thought and ideology in Reformation Scotland' (Ph.D thesis, University of Edinburgh, 1983), and 'Kingship, tyranny and the right to resist in fifteenth-century Scotland', *SHR*, 66 (1987), 125–51.

[2] Roger A. Mason, '*Rex stoicus*: George Buchanan, James VI and the Scottish polity', in John Dwyer *et al.* (eds.), *New perspectives on the politics and culture of early modern Scotland* (Edinburgh, 1982), pp. 9–33, and 'Kingship and commonweal', pp. 358–415.

conditions, mutually to be observed', and by warning Charles that 'A King abusing his power, to the overthrow of Religion, Laws and Liberties, which are the very Fundamentals of this Contract and Covenant, may be controled and opposed'.[3] As has often been remarked, Douglas's insistence that 'a Kings power is a limited power, by this Covenant', could have come straight from George Buchanan's *De jure regni apud Scotos*.

However, the same can hardly be said of his emphasis on the principle of Romans 13 that 'A necessity to obey, is laid upon all'.[4] 'It is a great errour', he assured the king, 'to think that a Covenant diminisheth obedience'; on the contrary, 'it was ever thought Cumulative'. By renewing their covenant with God the Scots were pledging themselves to continue striving after fulfilment of His law, and since that law included the injunction in Romans 13, 'entring Covenant with GOD doth not lessen their obedience and allegiance to the King; but increaseth it, and maketh the obedience firmer'. The covenanters were the godly people who obeyed 'not only for wrath, but also for conscience sake', and they could be contrasted with the '*Anabaptists*, who deny there should be Kings in the New Testament', many of whom infested the ranks of the sectarian army approaching from the south. These men had 'not been content to oppose a king in an evill course, (as they might lawfully doe), but contrary to *Covenant, Vows*, many Declarations, have cast off kings, and kingly Government'.[5]

A not dissimilar charge might plausibly have been advanced against the more radical covenanters, many of whom were opposed to the coronation. For decades presbyterian writers had not only been encouraging people to disobey the laws of men when they conflicted with the laws of God, but had also been arguing that all human laws, even those designed to regulate things indifferent, ought to conform precisely with divine law; they had been arguing that human laws were only to be obeyed when they were found to require what the law of God already required.[6] Yet to argue that people were only to obey their rulers when they were already bound in conscience to do the thing commanded came close to saying that rulers as such were only to be obeyed for wrath's sake, and to denying that kings ruled by divine right. Episcopalian authors were used to responding that people were always bound in conscience to comply with their rulers' determinations in the area of indifferency, whatever they personally thought of the commands. No sooner had the National Covenant appeared than the celebrated Doctors of Aberdeen asked how it was possible to swear both to uphold the

---

[3] *Forme and order*, p. 10.   [4] *Ibid.*, p. 11.   [5] *Ibid.*, p. 6.

[6] John D. Ford, 'Conformity in conscience: the structure of the Perth Articles debate in Scotland, 1618–38', *Journal of Ecclesiastical History* (forthcoming) and 'The lawful bonds of Scottish society: the Five Articles of Perth, the Negative Confession and the National Covenant', *Historical Journal*, 37 (1994), 1–20.

king's authority and to withhold obedience from his laws on indifferent church ceremonies.[7] The Doctors suspected the covenanters of harbouring the subversive opinions of '*Buchanan, Knox,* and *Goodman*', opinions which seemed to accord with the teachings of the Jesuits.[8]

For the time being the covenanters declined the Doctors' invitation to enter into formal disputation on the question of disobedience and resistance: the authority of kings, they replied, was the sort of subject that could 'hardly be disputed and discussed except in a large *Treatise*'.[9] In the following year, however, Alexander Henderson, the 'best penman' in the presbyterian party, was charged with the task of producing a set of 'Instructions for defensive arms', and three further tracts were printed in the year after that, assembling arguments previously put forward by Buchanan, Knox and other Calvinist writers.[10] The accusations adumbrated by the Doctors were not long in being filled out. 'Is your doctrine so Jesuiticall and rebellious', asked John Corbet, 'to thinke that the Kings authority is of humane institution by positive lawes, and not from God?'[11] Elsewhere, writing under the pseudonym of Lysimachus Nicanor of the Society of Jesus, Corbet pretended to congratulate the covenanters 'for rejecting that former errour, to defend that Kings are of *Divine institution*', and for adopting instead the Jesuit position 'that they are of *humane institution by positive Lawes*'.[12] Walter Balcanquhal, writing on behalf of the king, likewise endeavoured to prove that all the covenanters' 'Maximes are the same with the Jesuites', that 'all the weapons wherewith they now fight' were purloined from 'the most rigid Jesuites Magazins'.[13]

It was in a similar vein that John Maxwell, the former bishop of Ross, set out in his *Sacro-sancta regum majestas* to undermine the 'Puritanicall, Jesuiticall, Antimonarchicall grounds' relied on by the covenanters and

---

[7] *Generall demands concerning the late Covenant* (Aberdeen, 1638), p. 24.   [8] *Ibid.*, p. 8.

[9] *Ibid.*, p. 26; *The answeres of some brethren of the ministerie to the replies of the ministers and professours of divinitie in Aberdene* (Aberdeen, 1638), p. 16.

[10] The 'Instructions' eventually appeared as *Some speciall arguments which warranted the Scottish subjects lawfully to take up armes in defence of their religion and liberty* (n.p., 1642). The circumstances surrounding their composition and publication are explained in *The letters and journals of Robert Baillie*, ed. David Laing (3 vols., Bannatyne Club, 1841–2), vol. I, pp. 189–90. It seems that Henderson may also have been responsible for *A remonstrance concerning the present troubles* (n.p., 1640); *The intentions of the army of the kingdome of Scotland* (n.p., 1640), and *The lawfulnesse of our expedition into England manifested* (Edinburgh, 1640). For commentary, see Ian M. Smart, 'The political ideas of the Scottish covenanters, 1638–88', *History of Political Thought*, 1 (1980), 167–93, at pp. 167–75.

[11] John Corbet, *The ungirding of the Scottish armour* (Dublin, 1639), p. 29.

[12] *The epistle congratulatorie of Lysimachus Nicanor of the Societie of Jesu, to the covenanters in Scotland* (n.p., 1640), p. 12.

[13] *A large declaration concerning the late tumults in Scotland* (London, 1639), pp. 3–4.

others,[14] and to defend instead the thesis that 'the King is onely and immediately dependent from Almighty God, the King of Kings, and Lord of Lords, and independent in his Soveraigntie and Power, from the Communitie'.[15] On the positive side it was Maxwell's contention that royal authority was derived immediately from God so that 'all the acts done by Kings are ascribed to God, and we finde them the immediate instruments by whom God worketh here'.[16] This did not mean, however, that the people played no part in the appointment of the monarch. To explain what he had in mind Maxwell turned to a scholastic distinction between three different senses in which a thing could be said to be immediately from God. The first was 'when it is so *soly from God*', and he conceded that only one or two biblical kings had been appointed in so direct a fashion. His own position was that kings received their authority immediately from God in the second sense, 'when the *collation of the power, and investing of the person in, and with such power, is from God*'. The third sense, when a power was conferred on someone by human right or title, 'and the *approbation or confirmation of this right is immediately from God*', came close to the second, but Maxwell felt that approbation was 'too flat an expression, and doth not sort well with the magnifick expressions of Holy Scripture'.[17]

The value of the distinction lay in enabling Maxwell to concede that the people chose the king while restricting their involvement 'to *the designation of the person*': the king might appear to be appointed by popular election, but 'the *reall constitution, the collation of soveraignty and Royalty* is immediately from God'. Maxwell proceeded to link this designation theory with the patriarchalist notion that 'Monarchie is founded in paternall Soveraignty', that the essence of political power could be discerned from a consideration of the natural power of fathers over their children. Originally, he believed, all the people of the earth had been governed by their common father, with the implication that Adam's heir, could he be found, would be the rightful monarch of the earth; but through sin men had lost sight of the natural order and had been dispersed into separate family units, until eventually it had become necessary for them to 'condescend that one shall have Soveraigne power over all, and so by consent shall be surrogated in the place of the common father'. The families had the *potestas designativa* to appoint a king, but the *potestas collativa* must have been in God: 'The reason is evident, the Substitute must have it by the same hand, by the same meanes he had it, in whose place he was

---

[14] (Oxford, 1644), long title. Robert Baillie, *An historicall vindication of the government of the church of Scotland* (London, 1646), pp. 2–3, suspected Maxwell of having had a hand in Corbet's *Epistle congratulatorie.*

[15] Maxwell, *Sacro-sancta regum majestas*, p. 6.   [16] *Ibid.*, p. 52.   [17] *Ibid.*, pp. 20–3.

substituted.' It could be taken for granted that 'the father's right is immediately from God, and of God'.[18]

On the negative side Maxwell insisted that the people could not possibly have had a power of government to devolve on the king.[19] For one thing, it was unthinkable that God should have invested anyone with 'a power which is idle and to no purpose': since no community had ever in fact governed itself it was offensive to suppose that God had endowed the people with a power of self-government. Furthermore, the idea that individual men might govern themselves was a logical absurdity since 'Government *intrinsecally, essentially,* includes in it a *specifick distinction* of *regentes* and *recti*, some to be governours, and some to be governed'. In reality, the power the people had was no more than 'a capacity or susceptibility to be governed', and that power was necessarily more passive than active. For given that submission to government was required by the law, and that fallen men could not satisfy the law without assistance, it followed that government had to be imposed on them by an act of divine providence. To argue otherwise, to suggest that men could institute government for themselves and so fashion the godly life from natural resources, would be to tend towards Pelagianism, and Maxwell feared that he also perceived a tendency towards the antinomian principle '*Nec Rex, nec Lex iusto posita*: No Superiour, No Law for the Saints, the holy ones, the perfect ones'.[20]

Within a few months of the appearance of Maxwell's book a response was published by Samuel Rutherford, professor of divinity at St Andrews.[21] If the short title of his *Lex, rex: the law and the prince* can be read as a forthright disclaimer of the antinomian principle, the long title suggests that his purpose was to supply at last the large treatise considered essential by the covenanters for an adequate treatment of royal authority. Where Maxwell had given his book the English title *The sacred and royall prerogative of Christian kings*, Rutherford gave his the subtitle *A dispute for the just prerogative of king and people*. He would try to show that both king and people had political power, that one prerogative could be reconciled with the other. Not only would he explain again 'the *Reasons* and *Causes* of the most necessary Defensive Wars of the Kingdom of SCOTLAND, and of their expedition for the ayd and help of their dear Brethren of ENGLAND', but he would also respond to Maxwell's 'Seditious Pamphlet', and would more generally provide 'a Scripturall Confutation of the ruinous Grounds' relied on in the works of some 'late *Anti-Magistratical Royalists*'.

---

[18] *Ibid.,* p. 85.   [19] *Ibid.,* pp. 90–1.   [20] *Ibid.,* p. 1.
[21] (London, 1644). Page references in the text are to this edition. For commentary, see W. M. Campbell, 'Lex rex and its author', *Records of the Scottish Church History Society*, 7 (1941), 204–28; and Smart, 'Political ideas', pp. 175–80.

What follows is an attempt to elucidate one aspect of Rutherford's political thought, and one aspect alone: the account of the origins of government which he developed in the earlier chapters of his book in response to Maxwell. Other aspects of his treatment of the prerogative powers of king and people will have to be neglected, nothing will be said of his bid to justify the defensive wars, and the views of opponents other than Maxwell will not be discussed. The limited aim will be to discover how Rutherford, 'the theorist of the radical presbyterians',[22] contrived to balance the notion of popular involvement in the establishment of government with the conviction of orthodox Calvinists that government was of necessity imposed on men by God. If that aim can be achieved it may help us to understand how the spokesman of the moderate presbyterians at Scone could have come to combine allusion to Buchanan's radical teaching with use of a language more familiar from the works of episcopalian royalists.[23]

II

Maxwell's positive contention was that God was the immediate author of sovereignty. But 'who denyeth that?', Rutherford asked (p. 16). He was happy to open his own book with an affirmation of the principle that 'All civill power is immediately from God in its root', as scriptural citations such as Romans 13. 1–7 and 1 Peter 2. 13–14 made clear (pp. 1–2). Since men were enjoined to obey their rulers not only for wrath but also for conscience' sake, and since only God could lay an obligation on the conscience, it followed that government must have been warranted by a divine law, which Rutherford identified as the law of nature. He accepted, moreover, that a distinction should be drawn between 'the institution of the Office, to wit, Government, and the designation of person, or persons to the Office', agreeing that the office came from God. Enough, he trusted, had already been said in these opening pages to show how ridiculous it was to impute the antinomian principle to the presbyterians.

Unlike Maxwell, however, Rutherford believed that when the people designated someone to fill the office of governor they actually made him governor: although God guided them in their selection,[24] it was still their

---

[22] Walter Makey, *The church of the covenant, 1637–1651* (Edinburgh, 1979), p. 59.

[23] Many of Douglas's remarks were reminiscent of comments made by William Struther, an associate of Maxwell, in *A looking glasse for princes and people* (Edinburgh, 1632), an expanded version of a sermon preached to mark 'the birth of the hopefull prince Charles'.

[24] Rutherford's position was that the selection of rulers could be shown to be determined in detail by God since submission to government was required by the moral law, and since 'no Morall acts in their exercises and use are left indifferent to us' (p. 8). See again, Ford, 'Conformity in conscience'.

choice that conferred authority on one man rather than on others. Furthermore, Rutherford insisted that a distinction should also be drawn between '*Government* in generall' and 'particular species of *Government*', such as monarchy, aristocracy and democracy. He believed that '*God* hath *immediately* by the law of nature appointed there should be a Government; and mediately defined by the dictate of natural light in a communitie, that there shall be one, or many Rulers to governe the Communitie' (p. 5). While the office of governor was immediately instituted by God, the choice of a person or persons to fill the office, and hence of a particular species of office, was made immediately by the people and only mediately by God.

The designation of particular persons to govern was therefore linked by Rutherford with the constitution of particular governments. Where Maxwell had contrasted the popular *potestas designativa* with the divine *potestas collativa*, and had identified the latter as the true power of constitution, Rutherford contrasted the immediate constitution of the people with the immediate institution of God, going so far as to describe the people's part as being performed '*Collative vel communicative*' (p. 10). Far from the people designating rulers on whom God then conferred authority, it was the people's choice that conveyed authority: 'we cannot here find two actions, one of God, another of the people; but in one, and the same action; God by the peoples free suffrages & voices createth such a man King, passing by many thousands' (p. 11). Again, if it was true that the 'power of Government is *immediately* from God', it could also be said that 'this or this definite power is *mediately* from *God*, proceeding from *God* by the mediation of the consent of a Communitie, which resigneth their power to one or moe Rulers' (p. 5).

In support of this claim that government was both immediately from God and immediately from the people, Rutherford cited the Jesuit Francisco Suárez (together with the canonist Diego Covarruvias and the Dominican Domingo de Soto). Suárez (who also cited Covarruvias and de Soto) taught that God was the immediate author of political power in the sense that He had created men who must by nature have had the power to form communities, which in turn must by nature have had the power to govern themselves.[25] Political power was therefore natural, and it was also natural – in a more permissive sense – for men to transfer political power from the community as a whole to particular governors, so that 'although the power in question is in an absolute sense an effect of the natural law, its specific application as a certain form of power and government is dependent upon human choice'.[26] It could thus be concluded on the one hand that 'this

---

[25] Francisco Suárez, *De legibus ac Deo legislatore*, III. 3, in *Selections from three works*, tr. G. L. Williams *et al.* (Oxford, 1944), p. 1. Rutherford referred to this passage at p. 2 of his book.
[26] Suárez, *De legibus*, III. 4. 1.

governing power, regarded from a political viewpoint and in its essence, is undoubtedly derived from God',[27] and on the other hand that 'the power in question may be received immediately from men, and mediately from God'.[28]

When towards the end of his book Rutherford devoted a short chapter to rebutting Maxwell's charge that the puritans had borrowed all their ideas from the Jesuits, he granted that the presbyterians and Jesuits did have a great deal in common, merely insisting that the views at issue were more widely held. All the same, he believed he had put his finger on one important point of divergence when he complained that it was 'a *Calumnie*, that we teach that the power of the *King* is from *God* mediatly, by *meere approbation*' (p. 416). To see what he was driving at we need to return to the earlier passage we have been examining, in which he went on to enumerate four senses in which royal authority could be said to come from God (pp. 5–6). Two could be passed over quickly as irrelevant to the ordinary case. Very occasionally God allowed tyrants to reign '*By way of permission*', and in Old Testament times he had installed one or two kings directly 'by *particular designation*'. But leaving aside such exceptional occurrences the question was whether kings usually received their authority from God 'by way of naked approbation' or 'by *divine institution*'.

It was Rutherford's impression that Maxwell's 'master Bellarmine, and other Jesuites'[29] adhered to the former opinion, conceiving 'Kingly power to be from *God* in the generall, but in the particular to be an invention of men, negatively lawfull, and not repugnant to the Word'. The Jesuits, he understood, were of the opinion that men were required to submit to government by the law of nature, but were left to devise particular forms of government for themselves under the ambit of the law of nations. 'But we', he insisted, 'teach no such thing' (pp. 7–8). On the contrary, the presbyterians regarded texts such as Romans 13 and 1 Peter 2 as proof that the 'Kingly or Royall office is from God by *divine institution* and not by naked approbation'. Monarchy, aristocracy and democracy were all forms of the power instituted by God, and were all instituted *in specie* by God.[30] In

---

[27] *Ibid.*, III. 4. 5.   [28] *Ibid.*, III. 4. 8.

[29] Suárez, *ibid.*, III. 4. 1, advised his readers to turn to Bellarmine for a lucid discussion of the different forms of government.

[30] Shortly before this, it should be said, Rutherford had contrasted domestic authority, 'warranted by natures law even in its species', with political authority, 'in its spece and kind warranted by a positive law, and in the generall only warranted by a law of nature' (p. 5). But elsewhere he pointed out that domestic authority was also dependent on human volition to the extent that the husband and wife had to designate each other, and that what made political authority distinctive was the need for the people to choose between monarchy, aristocracy or democracy by a 'politick constitution' (pp. 11 and 125). The contrast, in other words, was between two kinds of authority instituted immediately by God, only one of

selecting one form in preference to the others the people constituted a particular government, but they did not invent the authority of that government as if they 'had by an act of reason, devised and excogitated such a power' (p. 9). 'God ordained the power', and the people merely constituted it in specific rulers.

Rutherford returned to the same question a little later when he reviewed Maxwell's three senses in which a thing could be said to come immediately from God (pp. 17–20). The first, when it came solely from God, was equivalent to Rutherford's particular designation, which simply did not happen any more:

> we cannot conceive how *God* in our daies, when there are no extraordinary revelations, doth *immediatly* create this man a King, and immediatly tie the crown to this family rather then to this; this he doth by the people now, without any *Propheticall Unction*; and by this *medium*, to wit, by the free choice of the people.

As we have seen, Rutherford believed that the people's *potestas designativa* encompassed the *potestas collativa*, and he consequently took Maxwell's second sense to mean that 'God giveth Royall Power by moving the peoples hearts to confer royall power'. Of course, regarded in this way collation was no longer a means by which power could be said to come immediately from God; but Rutherford's point was that collation (as Maxwell seemed to agree) was a method of constituting, not of instituting, government. Of itself, he observed, popular election could no more confer royal authority than the waters of baptism could confer grace: both depended ultimately for their efficacy on divine institution, 'except you dream with your *Iesuits*'.

Turning to Maxwell's third sense of immediacy Rutherford declared that the divine approbation of government was indeed 'the Prelates dreame, not a *Tenet* of ours'. The presbyterians 'never said that soveraigntie in the King is *immediately* from God by approbation or *confirmation* only, as if the people first made the King, and God did only by a posterior and latter act say *Amen* to the deed done'. In another passage Rutherford tried to shed more light on the presbyterian position by explaining that the people's voluntary constitution of a government rested partly on 'the Law of nature, That men must have Governours, either many, or one supreme Ruler', and partly on 'a positive institution of God', 'the supervenient institution of God, ordaining, That there should be such Magistrates, both Kings, and other Iudges' (p. 44).[31] God's role in the institution of government was not confined to

which required human constitution, and not between one kind of authority instituted immediately by God and another instituted only mediately through the people.

[31] The distinction between natural law and positive institution performed a useful explanatory function here, though elsewhere, in reiterating that 'the Office of a King' was 'immediately instituted of God', Rutherford added: 'Whether the institution be naturall, or positive, it is no matter' (p. 409).

issuing a general decree that men should submit to authority, to warranting or approving the forms of government devised by men. Thus when Maxwell said that the king was no creature of the people's making, if he meant 'the King in *abstracto*, that is, *the royall dignity*', he was not speaking against the presbyterians 'but against his owne father *Bellarmine*' (p. 17).

His own father Bellarmine? Maxwell's failure to distinguish sharply between collation and approbation had left him open to the charge that he was himself advancing the same sort of theory as the Jesuits. In fact, he confessed at one point to sympathizing with the view that sovereignty was conferred on the king immediately by the people, mediately by God, 'who intending the good peace and safety of mankind, which cannot be obtained without preservation of order, hath commanded, and by an inviolable ordinance and institution, appointed all to submit and subject themselves to the lawes of Society'.[32] If he found this doctrine hard to reconcile with his reading of the Bible, in which God, not man, was described as the immediate author of sovereignty, he was not averse to distinguishing between the act of the people in setting up a government and the act of God in making the authority of the government real. Rutherford's complaint was that the true distinction lay not between the act of the people and the act of God, but between God's act of institution, and His act of constitution, the one immediate, the other mediate. The problem with the Jesuit theory, as he saw it, was that by limiting God's role to the issuing of a general decree it suggested that not only His act of constitution, but also His act of institution, was mediated through the rational decision making of the community.

Maxwell, however, was guilty of the opposite error: whereas the Jesuits seemed to understate God's involvement in the institution of government, Maxwell seemed to understate the people's involvement in the constitution of government. Yet the solution was the same in either case, and time and again we find Rutherford reiterating his insistence that the relevant distinction was not between the act of the people and the act of God:

When *God* doth apply the person to royall power, what? is this a different action from the peoples applying the person to royall dignitie? It is not imaginable: but the people by creating a *king*, applyeth the person to *royall dignitie*; and *God* by the peoples act of constituting the man *king*, doth by the mediation of this act convey royall authoritie to the man. (p. 20)

The constitution of a government was not like the ordination of a cleric when, it was said, 'God doth immediatly without any act of the Church, infuse from heaven supernaturall habilities on the man, without any active influence of the *Church*' (pp. 144–5). Nor was 'the heroick spirit of a Royall

---

[32] Maxwell, *Sacro-sancta regum majestas*, pp. 17–19.

facultie of governing', the 'gift or grace of Governing', to be confused with the 'Authority of governing'. While the 'Royall indowments' essential to effective monarchy were indeed bestowed immediately by God, the royal power or dignity was conferred on the king through the mediation of the people (pp. 14, 43 and 409).

III

So far we have focused on Rutherford's response to Maxwell's positive contention that God was the immediate author of sovereignty. Who denies that? he asked, and the answer might have been given: certainly not George Buchanan, who in his *De jure regni* expressly approved the view that 'God Himself in the beginning gathered people together' with the aid of 'neither orator nor law-maker'.[33] Buchanan believed that solitary individuals who at first 'had no laws or fixed abode, but roamed at large in a primitive condition' were drawn into civil society not so much by considerations of expediency as by natural instinct.[34] Natural instinct was another name for natural law, given to men by God in order that they might not only know how to defend themselves but might also have the capacity to distinguish good from evil. It was under the guidance of natural law that the people assembled together to form a body politic; but since the body politic was as prone to illness as any other body, the people were led to appoint a physician to maintain their healthy coexistence, a physician they called their king.[35] Having guarded against injustice in the community by appointing a king, the people then proceeded to guard against the danger of an unjust king by enacting civil laws.[36]

God could therefore be identified as the author of sovereignty because constitutional government was not so much an expedient devised by men as an institution grounded on natural law. Read like this, Buchanan's work might easily have been cited in support of Rutherford's attempt to reconcile the orthodox stress on divine institution with the more populist notion of human constitution. Yet Rutherford did not cite Buchanan in this context.[37] We may begin to see why not by noting the similarity between Buchanan's criticism of the classical dictum *utilitas iusti prope mater et aequi* and Hugo

---

[33] George Buchanan, *The art and science of government among the Scots*, tr. D. H. MacNeil (Glasgow, 1964), §. 11. Richard Tuck, *Natural rights theories* (Cambridge 1979), p. 43, cites this passage as evidence of close affinity between Buchanan and Rutherford.

[34] Buchanan, *De jure regni*, §§. 8–11.   [35] *Ibid.*, §. 12.   [36] *Ibid.*, §. 18.

[37] In true scholastic fashion Rutherford packed his treatise with learned citations, referring to over two hundred different authors. Buchanan was only cited twelve times.

Grotius's comments on the same dictum in his *De jure belli ac pacis*,[38] suggesting that Buchanan's individualist account of the origins of government may have taken him some distance towards the natural rights theories developed in the seventeenth century. In turn, Grotius's remark that just as contract was the mother of civil laws, so natural law was their grandmother, human nature their great-grandmother, should also remind us that this way of accounting for the origins of government involved God – to the extent that it involved Him at all – in instituting government through the mediation of human deliberation and consent. In other words, it involved the sort of dilution of the notion of divine institution which Rutherford went out of his way to repudiate. From this point of view, Buchanan's careful denial of the contemporary relevance of Romans 13 might be taken to show that he had travelled further from his Calvinist roots than Rutherford was prepared to go.[39]

Nevertheless, in opposition to Maxwell's negative contention that the people could not possibly have had a power of government to convey to the ruler, Rutherford did insist that the power was originally vested in the community from whom it passed immediately to the ruler; and in the opening pages of his book he seemed to suggest that this power of government was founded on a natural right of self-defence:

We are to distinguish betwixt a power of Government, and a power of Government by Magistracy. That we defend our selves from violence, is a consequent of unbroken and sin-lesse nature; but that we defend our selves by devolving our power over in the hands of one, or more Rulers, seemeth rather positively morall, then naturall. (p. 2)

Since God had created men with an instinct to live together and to defend themselves against attack, civil society could be considered natural to the extent that it resulted from man's innate sociability and defensiveness, from what Rutherford called 'that root of reasonable nature'. Yet if all men were 'born equally free', as he believed, there could be 'no reason in Nature, why one Man should be King and Lord over another'. It therefore followed that all civil government must be 'Artificiall and Positive', and that it must imply 'some servitude, whereof Nature from the womb hath freed us' (p. 3).

Admittedly, men were born in subjection to the rule of their parents; but Rutherford pointed out that domestic society was entirely natural, whereas civil society was only natural *'in radice*, in the root, and voluntary, *in modo*,

---

[38] Buchanan, *De jure regni*, §. 11; Hugo Grotius *De jure belli ac pacis*, tr. F. W. Kelsey (Oxford, 1925), Prolegomena 16. This is certainly the impression left by the treatment of Buchanan in Quentin Skinner, *The foundations of modern political thought* (2 vols., Cambridge, 1978), vol. II, pp. 338–45.

[39] Buchanan, *De jure regni*, §§. 63 and 69–70.

in the manner of coalescing'. Although men were naturally inclined to live together in families, civil society was both 'natural' and 'against Nature'. On the one hand, if all creatures had a power of self-defence, 'as we see Lyons have pawes, some beasts have hornes, some clawes', then surely men, 'being reasonable creatures, united in societie, must have power in a more reasonable and honorable way to put this power of warding off violence, in the hands of one or moe Rulers, to defend themselves by magistrates' (p. 10). At one level, it could be said, the formation of civil society was instinctive, and determined by natural law.[40]

On the other hand, however, that phrase 'united in societie' was vital. For although it could become necessary for fallen men to resign their native liberty to a ruler in order that they might live together and defend themselves, to concede that the ruler should punish them, should inflict violence on them, would be contrary to their natural instinct: 'reason may be necessitated to assent to the conclusion, being as it were forced by the prevalent power of the evidence of an insuperable and invincible light in the premises, yet from natural affections there resulteth an act of self-love, for self-preservation' (p. 4). Nonetheless, men united in society could agree in principle that offenders against the law should be punished, accepting only by implication that they might themselves be punished: 'I may by an antecedent will, agree to a Magistrate and a Law, that I may be ruled in a politick Society, and by a consequent will onely, yea and conditionally onely agree to the penalty and punishment of the Law' (p. 3; cf. pp. 156–7). Civil government was thus rooted in natural instinct yet dependent on volition, and it was in this sense, Rutherford believed, that jurists were justified in attributing government to a secondary law of nature or to the law of nations.

In the light of these remarks we need hardly wonder that Richard Tuck should describe Rutherford as having come as close as any presbyterian writer to promoting a natural-rights theory.[41] It might easily be imagined that Rutherford conceived of the power of government as a human construct, created when the people voluntarily imposed limitations on their

---

[40] Rutherford's association of natural instinct with natural law may to some extent have reflected his understanding of the way in which men discovered the law of God, but it also enabled him – and this will be important later – to explain how fallen men could perform lawful acts. In his *Divine right of church-government and excommunication* (London, 1646), pp. 79–80, he observed: 'there be some things that the Law of Nature commandeth, as to move, eat, sleepe; and here with leave I distinguish *Factum*, the common practise of men from the *jus*, what men in conscience ought to do'. The instinctive practice of 'morall and naturall' men could in fact be in conformity with the requirements of the law, but they would not be acting in obedience to the law. It was the error of 'Papists and Arminians to justifie the actions of the unregenerated, as simply Lawfull and good, though performed by them with no respect to God or his Commandment'.

[41] Tuck, *Natural rights theories*, p. 145.

natural power of self-defence, authorizing the ruler to exercise the power on their behalf. In this way the ruler's power could be claimed to be both natural (derived from God) and positive (derived from men). But in the light of what has already been said we need no more wonder that Tuck should only describe Rutherford as having *come close* to advancing a natural-rights theory; for we have seen that when Rutherford affirmed the principle that all civil power was immediately from God in its root, he meant more than that God had instructed men to submit to government, leaving them to work out for themselves how that could be done. To say that God enabled and impelled men to create the power of civil government would be to say that God, at least in part, instituted civil government mediately through men.

In fact, we find on closer inspection that Rutherford did not maintain that the power of government was the same thing as, or was derived from, the power of self-defence. 'To be tyed to a lawfull King', he remarked, 'is no making away of liberty, but a resigning of a power to be justly governed, protected and awed from active and passive violence' (p. 87). The people 'give to the King a politique power for their own safetie, and they keepe a naturall power to themselves, which they must conserve, and cannot give away' (p. 51). That they had a 'Politick power of Government' to devolve could be shown in two ways: firstly, it was surely inconceivable that God should have made man, as Aristotle taught, 'a sociall creature, and one who inclineth to be governed by man', without also putting the power of government in his nature; and secondly, it could be argued that if 'God and nature intendeth the policie and peace of mankinde, then must God and nature have given to mankinde, a power to compasse this end; and this must be a power of *Government*' (p. 2).

Thus although it was true that God directed men to establish government by making them sociable and defensive, and by so ordering circumstances that they could not live together safely without accepting restrictions on their liberty, He directed them to constitute particular governments and not to institute the power of government in any of its forms. Instead of suggesting that the people imposed limitations on their power of self-defence as a means to instituting government, Rutherford argued that they accepted restraint as a consequence of their constitution in a specific government of the power instituted by God. In any case, he felt that this talk of power and liberty could be misleading:

Individuall persons in creating a Magistrate, doth not properly surrender their right, which can be called a right; for they do but surrender their power of doing violence to these of their fellows in that same Communitie; so as they shall not now have Morall power to do injuries without punishment; and this is not right or libertie properly, but servitude; for a power to do violence and injuries, is not liberty, but servitude and bondage. (p. 44)

In Rutherford's opinion the 'right' of self-defence, a negative freedom to act without threat of punishment, was more *factum* than *ius*: it was a 'Morall' power available to 'naturall *Moralists*', an instinctive capacity common to all men without exception, as opposed to a gracious virtue available to the regenerate alone.[42] The only genuine right was the positive liberty to lead the godly life, and since it was only possible to exercise that liberty in a Christian polity, the rhetoric of liberty and servitude could be reversed: the establishment of government was, in a manner of speaking, a process of emancipation.

IV

Despite initial appearances, then, a closer reading confirms that Rutherford did not consider the power of government to emanate from the people in the sense that they created it by a transfer of their natural power of self-defence: quite simply, the power of government was distinct from the power of self-defence. But in what other sense could the power of government have been vested in the people? Is it possible that Rutherford subscribed to what John Locke was to call the 'very strange Doctrine' that all men were empowered by God to enforce the law of nature?[43] We may start to appreciate what Rutherford had in mind if we turn to the chapter of his book in which he dealt with Maxwell's argument that the people could not possibly have had a power to devolve.

As we have seen, Maxwell began by complaining that since 'God and nature hath not bestowed upon any thing in the universe a power which is idle and to no purpose, as certainly that power must be which is never actuated', and since the people had never in fact governed themselves, it could not be contended that God had bestowed a power of government on the people.[44] Rutherford responded by asserting that the power was 'not *formally* in the people, but only *vertually*', adding that it was meaningless to say that 'a vertuall power is idle, because it cannot be actuated by that same subject that it is in, for then it should not be a vertuall, but a formall power'. To explain what he was driving at he gave two illustrations: not all men procreated, and some were blind, yet the powers of generation and sight

---

[42] See again n. 40 above. More might profitably be said about Rutherford's use of the language of rights. Some further observations are made in John D. Ford, 'Stair's title "Of Liberty and Servitude"', in A. D. E. Lewis and D. Ibbetson (eds.), *The Roman law tradition* (Cambridge, 1994), pp. 135–58.

[43] John Locke, *Two treatises of government*, ed. Peter Laslett (Cambridge, 1967), II. 9.

[44] Maxwell, *Sacro-sancta regum majestas*, p. 90.

could be said to belong to all men virtually provided only that they were exercised by at least some men. By the same token, the power of government 'in the community is not idle, because it is not put forth in acts of the people, in which it is vertually'; it was enough for it to be 'put forth in action in some of them, whom they choose to be their Governours' (p. 50).

It is evident from Rutherford's response that he accepted not only that God had never given any idle power to man, but also that the people had never actually governed themselves, indeed could never actually have governed themselves. It was unreasonable, he observed, to demand that the power of government 'should be put forth in action by all the people, as if all should be *Kings* and *Governours*'. Here and elsewhere he endorsed the point made by Maxwell that it was absurd to talk of the same persons as both rulers and ruled: it could not be claimed that the power of government was exercised formally by the people, 'for they should then all have been *one King*, and so both above and superiour, and below and inferiour to themselves, which we cannot say' (p. 10; and also pp. 52–3). Rutherford preferred to make the more logical claim that the power was virtually in the people.

So much for the strange doctrine: the power of government belonged to the people only because the power that was formally vested in their governors was virtually vested in them, and not because they had originally governed themselves. Yet the purpose of the strange doctrine was to avoid the legal objection that *nemo dat quod non habet*. The problem remained: how could the power of government have been transferred from the people to the ruler when the people could only be said to have had the power when it was being exercised by the ruler? Rutherford did not address the issue directly, for it seemed to him that the current controversy was not so much concerned with 'the power of governing' – with the people's power 'of ruling and Monarchicall commanding of themselves' – as with 'the power of *Government*' – with the people's power 'of making Governours and Kings' (p. 50).[45] As he saw it, the gravamen of Maxwell's charge was that the people had only a passive power of submitting to government, to which the obvious rejoinder was that they must surely have exercised a 'free, voluntary, and active power' when they constituted monarchy in preference to aristocracy or democracy, and designated one man to be king in preference to others.

Behind Maxwell's objection, however, lay the persuasive theological argument that 'every singular and individuall person, by corruption and

---

[45] Rutherford felt that 'these two differ much': '*No man can give that which he hath not*, is true, but that people have no power to make their Governours, is that which is in question, and denied by us' (p. 52).

selfe love hath *naturalem repugnantiam,* a naturall aversenesse and repugnancy to submit to any'.[46] Rutherford countered by alluding to the distinction between gracious virtue and natural morality that underpinned the presbyterian theory of discipline:

> It is true that people through corruption of nature are averse to submit to Governours, *for conscience sake, and as to the Lord,* because the naturall man remaining in the state of nature can doe nothing that is truely good, but it is false that men have no active Morall power to submit to superiours, but only a passive capacity to be governed. (p. 51)

Although it went against the grain for men to consent to 'suffering ills of punishment', they still had a 'naturall moral active power' to submit to the rule of their superiors, 'though it be not Evangelically, or legally in *Gods* Court, good'. It was because men remaining in a state of nature could perform deeds in external conformity with the law, even though they lacked the inner strength available to those in a state of grace, that it was both possible and worthwhile for moral discipline to be maintained in the visible church.[47]

Rutherford felt that he had a strong card to play here since all over the world and throughout most of history communities of men had in fact submitted to government voluntarily, as Maxwell himself conceded. Now if Maxwell were to deny that unregenerate men had an active moral power of submission, he would surely be saying that the grace essential to faith and to the works that were the fruits of faith was available to all those who would receive it; he would be agreeing with the Jesuits and Arminians that the submission of the people was 'not naturall, but done by the helpe of universall grace' (p. 52). Yet to preach universal grace was tantamount, in the opinion of orthodox Calvinists, to preaching Pelagianism. On the other hand, if Maxwell seemed to be approaching Pelagianism circuitously by referring government entirely to divine grace, Rutherford was clearly alert to the more obvious danger of placing too much stress on the role of the people. Towards the end of the chapter he repeated that the community was moved to constitute a particular government by 'an eminent and singular act of Gods speciall providence', and that the chosen ruler could only be endowed with 'heroick and royall parts' by a further 'act of grace' (p. 57).

'But what is all this? doth it exclude the peoples consent? in no wayes'. We noted earlier how Rutherford used an analogy with baptism to emphasize that government was ultimately dependent on divine institution. Concerned now with the constitution of government he suggested that belief provided a more instructive parallel, for while baptism was entirely dependent on the

---

[46] Maxwell, *Sacro-sancta regum majestas,* p. 91.   [47] See again n. 40 above.

grace of God for effect, it could hardly be denied that the will and understanding of the believer, though insufficient on their own to effect conversion, were significant. Following this analogy it could be said that the people
did have an active moral power of submission, and Rutherford concluded
that they had

an active power of ruling and directing themselves toward the intrinsecall end of
humane policie, which is the externall safety and peace of a societie, in so far as there
are morall principles of the Second Table for this effect written in their heart, and
therefore that *royall authoritie*, which by *Gods* speciall providence, is united in one
King, and as it were overgilded and lustered with Princely grace and royall endow-
ments, is diffused in the people, for the people hath an after-approbative consent in
making a King, as Royalists confesse, water hath no such action in producing grace.
(p. 57)

The hand of God was certainly to be discerned behind the constitution of
particular governments, yet men were actively involved in the process. At
this point, however, Rutherford seems to have moved on from talking about
an active power of constituting governments to talk of an active power of
governing, of the diffusion in the people of the power instituted by God. To
add to the confusion, the power was said to be diffused in the people in that
they had 'an after-approbative consent in making a King', on the analogy
with belief. If there is some kind of solution to the *nemo dat* problem lurking
here we will have to look elsewhere for illumination.

We may begin with one or two passages in which Rutherford observed
that government, properly speaking, would not have been necessary without
the Fall. 'If all were innocent persons', he opined, 'and could doe no
violence one to another; the Law would rule all, and all men would put the
Law in execution, *agendo sponte*, by doing right of their own accord'
(p. 184). It was only because sin had entered the world that God had
'devised, as a remedy of violence and unjustice, a living, rationall, breathing
Law called a King, a Iudge, a Father' (p. 213). But the point was not so
much that men could have governed themselves had they remained in the
state of innocence, as that their instinctive obedience would then have
rendered government otiose. Although the people might have 'put the Law
in execution', what Rutherford was not prepared to say was that they had an
executive power over themselves. Instead he described the power in the
people as 'a legall and natural power to guide themselves in *peace and
godlinesse*, and save themselves from unjust violence, by the benefit of
Rulers' (p. 184).

He explained what he meant more clearly elsewhere. If it was true, as he had
already conceded, that individual men – 'consider them as men onely, and not
as associated' – could have no 'politicke power', it was not true that the
community could have no political power 'before Magistrates be established'

(p. 81). On the contrary, the people assembled together in a community 'have virtually a power *to lay on Commandments*, in that they have a power to appoint to themselves Rulers, who *may lay commandements on others*'. We have seen that the power the people had collectively but lacked individually was the ability to submit to the penal sanctions giving force to the law:

> though no man can take away his own life, or hath power over his own life formally; yet a man, and a body of men hath power over their own lives, *radically* and *virtually*; in respect that they may render themselves to a *Magistrate*, and to Lawes, which if they violate, they must be in hazard of their lives, by putting them under the power of good lawes for the peace and safety of the whole. (pp. 156–7)

The people could not rule themselves, but as a community they could appoint rulers over themselves, and in this way the active power of government, the power of constituting or submitting to government, could be identified with the virtual power of governing, and vice versa. On the one hand, by actively submitting to government the people would in effect be governing themselves, while on the other hand they would only be able to govern themselves by actively submitting to the government of others.

At a number of places in his book Rutherford developed this line of thought in relation to the Scottish constitution. The 'first, and ultimate, and native subject of all power', he declared, 'is the Communitie, as reasonable men inclining to a society', though 'the ethicall and politicall subject, or the legall and positive receptacle of this power is various, according to the various constitutions of the policie' (p. 58). Fundamentally, of course, men had the power as individuals to defend themselves and to combine for the purpose of self-defence; but it was only when they had combined that they could make laws, and especially constitutional laws, by agreement. Under the Scottish constitution the community manifested itself as 'the three Estates of Parliament', who shared 'the power of making Lawes' with the king, and who placed the king 'above them, *quoad potestatem legum executivam*, in regard of a power of executing lawes and actuall government, for their good and safetie' (pp. 148–9). In this way the people effectively governed themselves, not only by electing the king in the first place, but also by exercising an 'after-approbative consent'. Although the executive power was exercised exclusively by the king, the estates reserved the right to legislate alone when he became incapacitated, and the people reserved the right (or duty) 'to resist *tyrannical Lawes*' (pp. 60–1; and also pp. 68, 90–1, 145, 178–9, 208 and 377).

V

The subtlety of Rutherford's response to Maxwell now becomes apparent. By arguing that the people could constitute in a ruler the power of government instituted by God, and by arguing that in doing so they would effectively be governing themselves, he managed to maintain both that sovereignty came immediately from God and that the people had the power to transfer government to the ruler. The solution to the legal problem lay in recognizing that although the people did not formally have the power of government to transfer, their power of transfer was itself a virtual power of government. As Rutherford commented in typically biblical terms, 'Though not on [sic] single man in *Israel* be a Judge, or King by nature, nor have in them formally any ray of Royaltie, or of Magistraticall Authoritie; yet it followeth not, that *Israel* Parliamentarily convened, hath no such authoritie, as to make *Saul* King' (p. 43). When assembled together the people had the power to govern themselves because they had the power to establish a government over themselves.

Of course, their power was not to institute but to constitute government, a distinction Rutherford sometimes expressed by using the words 'formal' and 'virtual' in a rather different way, as when he wrote that the power flowed from the people 'by a virtuall emanation' and not 'by formall institution' (p. 9), and that the power was 'virtually in the people, formally from God' (p. 18). While the virtual power of the people was normally contrasted with the formal power of their chosen ruler, here it was contrasted with the divine power of institution. Likewise, confronted with the allegation that the 'people cannot produce so noble an effect as royalty, a beame of God', Rutherford replied, 'True, formally they cannot, but *virtually* it is in a society of reasonable men, in whom are left beames of authoritative Majesty, which by a divine institution they can give, Deut. 17. 14. to this man, to *David*, not to *Eliah*' (p. 19). Although royal power was devised by God rather than by men, it was in effect produced in a particular monarchy by popular constitution.

In the last passage quoted, however, Rutherford indicated that some rays or beams of authoritative majesty were left in the people. Could this hint at another sense in which the power of government might be said to belong to the people? Actually, when Rutherford remarked that the Israelites could have made Saul king even if none of them had formally exercised the power of government, he also remarked that in reality the power was in all men virtually since it was in some men formally: 'the Father, the Master, the Judge, have it by Gods institution in some measure, over son, servant, and subject, though it be more in the supreme Ruler: and for our purpose, it is not requisite that authoritative majestie should be in all' (p. 43). If the people could in principle have conveyed power to the king without any prior exercise of authority, the truth of the matter was that all men had lived in subjection to formal authority from the day they were born.

'Man by nature is under government Paternall' (p. 95). Rutherford concurred with the common opinion that '*God* and nature hath laid a necessity on all men to be under government, a natural necessity from the wombe to be under some government, to wit, a paternall government' (p. 94).[48] Children were naturally subject to the rule of their parents, servants to the rule of their masters, the young to the rule of the old, the ignorant to the rule of the wise, and so on (though these last were only 'improperly' examples of government) (p. 142; and also pp. 89–90). Since the family, 'the only naturall and first societie in the world' (p. 92), was warranted by the law of nature, the child might reasonably 'expect help against violence, from his father' (pp. 2–3), who in turn 'had a power of governing his own family, and of punishing malefactors' (p. 4). This 'power of punishing ill-doers' was bestowed on the father for the benefit of the family and not for his own sake: it was a power that God, in making men sociable, would have instituted in any society He formed, and that He had in fact decided to institute in the fathers of families, not as individuals but as heads of domestic societies.

In biblical terms, there had been no government apart from family rule until the time of Noah, or more strictly of his great-grandson Nimrod, and there was no trace of the formal institution of monarchy until the time of Moses (p. 93; and also pp. 48 and 223). At that stage God had forbidden His people from taking kings like other nations, apparently on the basis of the principle that 'Fatherly government being the first, and measure of the rest, must be the best; for it is better that my father governe me, then that a stranger governe me'. An obvious corollary was that the most natural choice when it came to constituting a civil government would be aristocracy:

when many families were on earth, every one independent within themselves, if a commune enemy should invade a tract of land governed by families, I conceive, by natures light they should incline to defend themselves, and to joyne in one politique body for their owne safety, as is most naturall; but in that case they having no *King*, and there were no reason of many fathers all alike loving their own families and self-preservation, why one should be *King* over all, rather then another, except by

---

[48] The prevalence of this sort of thinking is brought out in Gordon J. Schochet, *The authoritarian family and political attitudes in seventeenth century England* (New Brunswick, N.J., 1988). Campbell, 'Lex rex', p. 216, suggests that Rutherford was following Bodin here, a suggestion no doubt reinforced by the claim in David Stevenson, 'The "Letter on sovereign power" and the influence of Jean Bodin on political thought in Scotland', *SHR*, 61 (1982), 25–43, at pp. 35 and 43, that Rutherford's book was 'founded on the thought of Jean Bodin', though mediated through Johannes Althusius's *Politica methodice digesta*. Edward J. Cowan, 'The making of the National Covenant', in John S. Morrill (ed.), *The Scottish National Covenant in its British context, 1638–51* (Edinburgh, 1990), pp. 68–89, at p. 81, similarly remarks that 'Rutherford had clearly devoured the whole of Althaus'. That Rutherford was influenced by Althusius, cited eleven times in his book, is clear, but it is worth remarking that he would not have found in the *Politica* his key distinction between divine institution and human constitution, or his assimilation of the virtual power of governing and the active power of submitting to government.

voluntary compact; so it is cleare that Nature is nearer to *Aristocracy* before this contract, then a *Monarchy*. (p. 169)

Nearer to aristocracy than monarchy, but also than democracy. When Maxwell taunted his opponents with the paradox that if sovereignty came from the people rather than from God, democracy would be closer to nature than monarchy, contrary to the opinion of all the best authorities,[49] his shot went wide. According to Rutherford, the presbyterians believed that the power of government had been formally vested in the fathers of families, and not in individuals. Aristocracy was consequently the form of government closest to nature.

Nonetheless, the transition to aristocracy was no less voluntary than the transition to monarchy. If experience showed that people were inclined to appoint '*Aristocraticall* guides' (p. 145), it was still the case that when families first banded together for mutual defence they had no common government (pp. 238–9; and also pp. 52–3). Rutherford assured his readers that '*Politicians* agree to this as an undeniable truth, that as domestick society is naturall, being grounded upon Natures instinct; so Politique societie is voluntary, being grounded on the consent of men' (p. 93). For this reason alone the view could not be seriously entertained that 'the Kingly power is essentially and univocally that same with a paternall or fatherly power' (p. 111; and also pp. 112, 115, 125 and 183).[50] Fathers might become aristocrats, but not through paternity alone, and still less was the king *pater patriae* 'by generation and naturall propagation'. The king was only called a father '*Metaphorically*, and by a *borrowed speech*', and Rutherford believed it would be more illuminating to compare the king with a tutor, appointed voluntarily to perform the functions of a father under trust (p. 124). Yet even this more remote comparison could be misleading since domestic authority had never been as extensive as political power: Rutherford doubted whether fathers had really been authorized to impose the death penalty on their children (as Roman *patresfamilias* had done) under natural law (p. 89).[51]

The king was thus no surrogate father, inheriting authority from an

---

49 Maxwell, *Sacro-sancta regum majestas*, p. 95.
50 It would be easy to attribute more significance to this turn of phrase than it merits. Rutherford also argued that the king was only described as the head of the body politic '*metaphorically*, by a borrowed speech' (p. 128), and that God alone was '*univocally* and *essentially*' a judge or king, human rulers only '*equivocally* and *improperly*, Iudges or Kings' (p. 195).
51 Again, it would be easy to ascribe more importance to this point than it is due. Maxwell, *Sacro-sancta regum majestas*, p. 85, acknowledged that although it was possible to learn something of the nature of political power from the study of paternal power, 'because of mans corruption and untowardnesse by reason of sinne, it is like God hath allowed more to Soveraigne power to enable and secure it'. In *The ungirding of the Scottish armour*, p. 35, Corbet agreed explicitly that kings differed from fathers in exercising *ius vitae necisque*.

ancestor infused with power directly from above: although paternal power was purely natural, political power was partly conventional. So did the people fashion political power for themselves from paternal power? Clearly not. As we have seen, Rutherford maintained that all forms of government were instituted specifically by God: 'Gods Word hath not onely commanded that government should be, but that fathers and mothers should be. 2. and not only that politick Rulers should be, but also Kings by name, and other *Iudges Aristocraticall* should be' (p. 28). If texts such as Romans 13 and 1 Peter 2 confirmed that 'the fift Commandement layeth obedience to the *King* on us, no lesse then to our *parents*' (p. 6), that did not mean that kings and parents derived their authority from the same divine institution. Paternal power had been instituted in the Garden of Eden, whereas it was not until the children of Israel were crossing the wilderness that God had taught them – in Deuteronomy 17 – to convey those earlier beams of authoritative majesty to a king (pp. 19 and 409).

Yet the king was no more an artificial than a surrogate father: if he was not appointed by the people to exercise the authority of their lost common father, nor was he appointed to exercise an authority remodelled from the power vested in every father. Rather, in submitting to the royal authority separately instituted by God, the people anticipated that the functions hitherto performed by the fathers of families would in future be performed by the king, and accepted that the authority of fathers over their families would be correspondingly diminished. In this way it could be said that the power of governing, 'of ruling and Monarchicall commanding of themselves', was vested in the people, formally and virtually, and was surrendered by them to the king. Only now, thanks largely to the work of Jenny Wormald on the relationship between feuding and government in early modern Scotland, can we begin to appreciate how plausible this picture must have seemed.[52] For however dubious the historians' accounts of the

---

[52] Jenny Wormald, 'Bloodfeud, kindred and government in early modern Scotland', *Past and Present*, 87 (1980), 54–97, and *Lords and men in Scotland: bonds of manrent 1442–1603* (Edinburgh, 1985). A rather more pessimistic view of the old regime is taken in Keith M. Brown, *Bloodfeud in Scotland 1573–1625* (Edinburgh, 1986). Brown explains the kirk's involvement in the shift from private vengeance to public adjudication at pp. 184–207, a point already touched on in Arthur H. Williamson, *Scottish national consciousness in the age of James VI* (Edinburgh, 1979), pp. 48–63. Both books afford some credibility to Robert Baillie's boast, in *Historicall vindication*, pp. 27–8, that 'all the Kings in Christendome had never been able to have abolished these feuds without the helpe of the Ministry'. Baillie made it clear that it was not the kirk's primary intention to reduce the power of the nobility; indeed, to the extent that presbyterian government in the church was inclined to reinforce any one form of government in the state more than others he believed that it was inclined to back up aristocracy (pp. 64–5). It was independency, he maintained, that tended to encourage democracy.

What, though, of Rutherford, described in Campbell, 'Lex rex', p. 204, as 'the most

beginnings of Scottish kingship may have been, the century or so before Rutherford put pen to paper had witnessed a dramatic transformation in Scottish government, with central authority enhanced at the expense of the traditional authority of local magnates over their kin. Where once a Scotsman would have turned for protection to his father, real or surrogate, from now on he would turn instead to his king.

Whatever might have happened in principle, then, Rutherford believed that in practice God had first instituted authority in the heads of families and had only later directed men to submit to civil governors. Although he was clearly not a patriarchalist, holding neither that political power was identical with paternal power nor that political power was derived from paternal power, he did accept that the constitution of a civil government involved the people in devolving authority from family heads on political rulers. Moreover, while he was every bit as vigorous in opposing Maxwell's patriarchalism as Locke was to be in opposing Filmer's, he made no attempt, as Locke would do,[53] to ground all obligation – including the obligation of adult children to obey their parents – on consent. The father had authority 'before his children by an act of their free-will consent that he be their father, yea & whether the children consent or no, from a physical act of generation' (p. 407).

Civil authority was different from domestic authority precisely because it did depend on consent; yet Rutherford understood that it was the consent of the fathers that counted. Maxwell's aim had again been slack when he posed the following conundrum:

If this Soveraigntie be natively inherent in the multitude, it must be proper to every individuall of the community; if it be so, and must be so according to their Tenet, which is enforced by that other as groundlesse and false state-maxime which they hold and maintain, that *Quisque nascitur liber*, every one is borne a free man in the forrest; then it will necessarily follow that the generation and posteritie of those who

democratic of his contemporaries', and in Makey, *Church of the covenant*, p. 19, as intent on 'an assault on the feudal system'? Certainly, he could not see 'what priviledge Nobles have above Commons in a Court of Parliament, by Gods law' (p. 59), and he may have had the heritable jurisdictions in mind when he asserted: 'that our Nobles are borne Lords of Parliament, and Iudges by blood, is a positive Law' (p. 170). But David Stevenson, *Revolution and counter-revolution in Scotland, 1644–1651* (London, 1977), pp. 235–9, argues cogently that Rutherford was in favour of mixed monarchy: although he greatly admired the tempered aristocracy to be found in Holland and Venice (pp. 48, 168, 211–12, 238, 259, 350 and 376), and admitted that he found the choice between mixed aristocracy and mixed monarchy perplexing (p. 67), he never expressed support for democracy. He eventually concluded on an ostensibly conservative note: 'By experience it is knowne to be lesse obnoxious to change, except that some think the Venetian Common-wealth best; but with reverence, I see small difference betweene a King, and the Duke of *Venice* ... A limited and mixed Monarchy, such as is in *Scotland and England*, seeme to me the best government' (p. 387).

[53] Locke, *Two treatises*, II. 52–76.

have first contracted with their elected King are not bound to that covenant, but upon their native right and libertie may start aside, appoint another King, and that without breach of covenant, or any just title in the King of their fathers to force or reduce them to his obedience.[54]

A telling blow no doubt against those who wished to trace political power back to individual sovereignty; but there was nothing to hinder Rutherford from affirming that 'the lawfull Covenant of the Fathers in point of Government, if it be not broken, tieth the children' (p. 54; and also p. 87).[55] In the end, the power of constituting government, like the power of governing, was vested formally in fathers and only virtually in the rest of the community (p. 125).

VI

Rutherford's acknowledgement that God had actually vested the power of government in fathers may seem little more than a concession to the standard perception of human history, a practical gloss on a theory already clear in principle; but it should serve to remind us that his attempt to balance the prerogatives of king and people on the ground that the power of the people was to govern themselves through the king was not only subtle but also paradoxical. For although the involvement of the people in the process of government was at its most manifest when they found the king's demands inconsistent with the will of God, when they declined to obey him or in the last resort took up arms against him, those were not so much times at which they resumed their power of government as times at which they found themselves bereft of government. The moment of appointment of a governor, the crucial moment at which the people had to decide how God would have them govern themselves, was the moment at which they were least in possession of the power of government. Only once they were being governed, only once the power instituted by God had been constituted in a ruler, could they truly be said to be governing virtually and submitting to government actively by the exercise of an after-approbative consent. Far from ceasing to govern themselves when they appointed a ruler, it was then that they became involved in a process ideally envisaged as a collaborative enterprise between a godly ruler and his godly people.[56]

---

[54] Maxwell, *Sacro-sancta regum majestas*, p. 97.

[55] In 1649 the commissioners of the general assembly actually posed the same sort of conundrum for their English allies in *A solemn testimony against toleration* (Edinburgh, 1649), p. 9: 'If power be originally in the people, and all of them do equally share in the priviledge of Libertie and freedom, how comes it to passe that a few take upon them to impose this Agreement upon others'.

[56] Richard Tuck, '*Power* and *authority* in seventeenth-century England', *Historical Journal*, 17 (1974), 43–61, identifies here the emergence of 'a significantly new political theory'.

Moments of crisis when the balance of the constitution failed did occur, however, and it is in relation to these moments that Rutherford's acknowledgement of the role of fathers assumes significance. Basically, what we have been examining here was an attempt to show that a claim could be made for the involvement of the people in government without it being implied that men could lead godly lives without God first having to impose government on them from above. So long as the people ruled themselves through a ruler it made good sense, but what if ruled and ruler were at odds to the extent that there was no rule? Though Rutherford obviously could not have addressed the issue confronting the Scots after the execution of Charles I in 1649,[57] he did discuss the initial breakdown of authority in 1638 when the people took it upon themselves to 'set up Tables, and extraordinary judicatures of the three estates, seeing there could not be any other government for the time' (p. 153). He was suitably vague about who exactly set up the Tables, and more generally about the transition from paternal governors to '*Aristocraticall* guides', preferring to write loosely of the estates as 'the legall and positive receptacle' of the community's power, in opposition, as we noted at the outset, to '*Anti-Magistraticall Royalists*'. For all his advocacy of the power of the people Rutherford was clearly reluctant to conclude that they found themselves entirely devoid of government. Acknowledging that they would always be governed at least by their fathers, though not in that case by governors who derived authority from their consent, was a revealing facet of that reluctance.

The problem was that while Rutherford had shown that the people had the power to constitute government, he had not explained how they could be relied on to make a sound decision in accordance with the determinations of divine providence. On the contrary, his argument for the involvement of the people in government rested on the assumption that it would only be possible for men to follow the will of God, to build the godly polity, if the king and the people worked together in reasoning out solutions to the difficulties they faced. If the king needed the people, the people more evidently needed the king; so how could they hope to discover which ruler God would have them elect without the aid of a ruler?[58] An indication of the sort of strategy which might have been employed can be found in the remarks of the English republican J. H., quoted at the head of this chapter,

---

[57] Not, that is, in the *Lex, rex*. *The diary of Mr John Lamont of Newton, 1649–71*, ed. G. R. Kinloch (Edinburgh, 1830), p. 20, reveals that shortly after Charles arrived in Scotland, and some months before his coronation, he was taken to St Andrews where 'Mr Samuell Rutherfoorde had a spech to him in Latine, runing mutch upon what was the dewtie of kings'. Sadly, no record appears to exist.

[58] The classic analysis of this sort of problem appears of course in J. G. A. Pocock, *The Machiavellian moment* (Princeton, N.J., 1975).

who condemned the tendency of writers on monarchy to focus on 'generall and universall Notions' and to indulge in the assertive thrust and counter-thrust of scholastic disputation.[59] He felt it was misleading to talk of monarchy in abstract terms as if it could be assumed that subjects were 'under men virtuous'.[60] He would concentrate on 'Practicall things, and observations of King-ship', and would show by a review of the history of Scottish monarchy that subjects more often lived 'under lewd Kings and unsetled Laws'.

We might perhaps have expected Robert Douglas to put the opposite case in similar terms when he set out to persuade doubters of the providential necessity of the coronation of Charles II, especially given the theme of his sermon. He would admittedly have found it difficult to make much of the heroic virtues of the later Stewarts – indeed, Charles had to be warned to eschew the vices of his forbears – but Douglas might have recalled the legendary antiquity of the royal line in Scotland, the mere survival of which would surely have counted for something – it was after all the dynastic connection that enabled the Scots to crown a British king. Yet he did not pursue this line, nor did he make much of the imperial vision of a Scottish or British church. Of course, he made a great deal of the fact that the Scots, like Israel of old, were crowning a covenanted king and renewing their covenant with God, stressing that Charles was now committed to carrying forward the reformation of all his kingdoms, and observing that '*Scotland* hath a Preference in this before other Nations'.[61] But the point was not so much that the Scots had been singled out for special favour as that they were exemplifying a universal process. Instead of describing the particular past or future of the Scots and their kings, Douglas chose to talk in the universal terms condemned by J. H., affirming that the people had a 'necessary duty to Crown the King'.[62] Was this to concede that the king's enemies had the better of the argument? Was Douglas resorting to the level of abstract generalization because he feared to join issue with the radicals?

It appears from the *Lex, rex* that Douglas was in fact addressing the radicals in their own language. Although quotations can be assembled from Rutherford's letters and sermons as evidence of his millenarian incli-nations,[63] there is scarcely a hint of that strain of thought in the *Lex, rex*.

[59] J. H., *Grounds and reasons*, pp. 9–10.   [60] *Ibid.*, p. 53.
[61] Douglas, *Forme and order*, p. 7.
[62] *Ibid.*, p. 4.
[63] S. A. Burrell, 'The apocalyptic vision of the early covenanters', *SHR*, 43 (1964), 1–24, at pp. 15-16; Williamson, *Scottish national consciousness*, p. 143; 'Latter day Judah, latter day Israel: the millennium, the Jews, and the British future', *Pietismus und Neuzeit*, 14 (1988), 149–65, at pp. 159–60; and 'The Jewish dimension of the Scottish apocalypse: climate, covenant and world renewal', in Y. Kaplan *et al.* (eds.), *Menasseh Ben Israel and his world* (Leiden, 1989), pp. 7–30, at pp. 25–8.

Although some interest was shown there in the particular Scottish constitution, Rutherford was impatient with demands that the 'written authentick covenant' be produced, responding that his concern was with 'the generall covenant of nature' presupposed in any coronation, the terms of which could be found in Deuteronomy 17.15, Joshua 1.8–9 and 2 Chronicles 31, 32 (p. 106; and also p. 215). He did add that 'the standing law and practice of many hundreth acts of Parliament' was equivalent to a written covenant, and he did devote one chapter of his book to a review of Scottish constitutional procedure (pp. 433–54); but the striking thing is the contrast in style between that chapter and the other forty-three.[64] In a book arguing for a balanced constitution the presence of republican language may seem especially significant,[65] and Rutherford's comparisons between the king of Scotland, the doge of Venice and the stadholder of Holland would merit closer scrutiny; yet his claim was that God led each people to constitute either monarchy, aristocracy or democracy, and that '*God* having chosen the best government to bring men fallen in sinne to happinesse, must warrant in any one a mixture of all three' (p. 212). If examples could helpfully be drawn from history, sacred or secular, that was because Rutherford believed that 'neither civility, nor grace destroyeth, but perfitith nature' (p. 122; and also p. 327).

Douglas was relying on the same principle when he framed his sermon in terms of the universal language of law and necessity, comparing Scotland with ancient Israel. In his text (2 Kings 11. 12 and 17) Jehoiada the priest presented the king with the testimony, the law of God: 'kings read Books that they may learn to govern well', Douglas reflected, 'but all the books a king can read, will not make him govern to please GOD, as this Book'.[66] Rutherford would no doubt have agreed, adding only that 'the Scriptures arguments may well be drawn out of the school of nature' (p. 5). If Douglas's sermon in the end owed as much to the scholastic natural law tradition as to the mirror for princes tradition and its early modern offshoots that was because the presbyterians, radical and moderate alike, were as committed to the former tradition by the mid-seventeenth century as their episcopalian and royalist opponents.[67] Far from evading the issue, Douglas was exploit-

---

[64] Campbell, 'Lex rex', p. 211, suggests that Archibald Johnston of Wariston may have had a hand in its composition.

[65] See again, n. 52 above.   [66] Douglas, *Forme and order*, p. 5.

[67] To some extent this was a revival of the language examined in Roger A. Mason, 'Knox, resistance and the moral imperative', *History of Political Thought*, 1 (1980), 411–36, and also in J. R. Gray, 'The political theory of John Knox', *Church History*, 8 (1939), 132–47; J. H. Burns, 'The political ideas of the Scottish Reformation', *Aberdeen University Review*, 36 (1955–6), 251–68; and Richard L. Greaves, 'John Knox and the covenant tradition', *Journal of Ecclesiastical History*, 24 (1973), 23–32. The earlier emergence and decline of the language is considered in Roger A. Mason, 'Kingship and commonweal', pp. 291–357, and

ing the fundamental tension in radical presbyterianism: either the Scots recognized their covenanted king, laid claim to the status of a covenanted nation and got on with building the godly polity, or they accepted that they were without government, had returned to the chaos of feuding families and so had scarcely started to become a godly people.[68] The way of the covenant could only be followed by fallen men within the polity, and if that meant that humanism had more appropriate vocabularies to offer, the surprising fact is that the presbyterians continued to use the language of natural law.

'Covenant and commonweal: the language of politics in Reformation Scotland', in Norman Macdougall (ed.), *Church, politics and society: Scotland 1408–1929* (Edinburgh, 1983), pp. 97–126.

[68] That a similar tension was felt in relation to church government is apparent from David Stevenson, 'Conventicles in the kirk, 1619–37: the emergence of a radical party', *Records of the Scottish Church History Society*, 18 (1973), 99–114.

Postscript

Two kingdoms and three histories? Political thought in British contexts

J. G. A. Pocock

A Centre for the History of British Political Thought, such as sponsored the seminar out of which this volume has grown, must sooner or later pay attention to its own title. The enterprise which Roger Mason was asked to initiate was that of examining and if possible establishing the distinctive characteristics of Scottish political discourse – meaning a discourse including among its concerns those of a kingdom and nation of Scotland – and proceeding to enquire into the nature of 'British' political thought, meaning by that term not just the aggregate of 'political thought' conducted in the several nations and sub-nations composing modern 'Britain', but a discourse directed at the 'matter of Britain', that is at the problematics of conceiving and realizing a political entity to be known by that name. The length of the sentence just concluded is an index of the complexity of the problems arising once one asks what 'British political thought' really signifies, or (to be more daring) really is.

The volume which has emerged is both nationalist and unionist. It has as one of its themes the shaping of a political discourse concerned with a nation and kingdom to be known as 'Scotland', and as another the shaping of a discourse concerned with the union of this entity with another, described and self-described as 'England', to form a third entity to be known as 'Britain' and perhaps (or perhaps not) to furnish this last with a self capable of setting about shaping and describing itself. Whether 'Britain' is to be a nation, possessing a locus in which a self is to be invented and self-invented, or an association of such nations and a conversation between such selves, is a problem at the outset of the seventeenth century and looks likely to be a problem at the outset of the twenty-first; though in stating that there is a question, one must be careful to avoid suggesting that one already knows the answer.[1]

[1] Among recent publications, Linda Colley's *Britons: forging the nation 1707–1837* (New Haven, Conn., 1992) examines the creation of a 'British' national identity and concludes (pp. 4–9, 374–5) by acknowledging that its future is problematic. Jenny Wormald's 'The creation of Britain: multiple kingdoms or core and colonies?', *TRHS*, sixth series 2 (1992),

Dr Mason has edited, and powerfully helped in writing, a series of essays which in the first place examine the political discourse concerned with a 'matter of Scotland'. The period is the sixteenth century and the medium of discourse is print. We are therefore looking at an age in which historians once conventionally located the emergence of 'national monarchies', and indeed 'nation' and 'monarchy' are organizing concepts in the discourse before us. In such an age it would be reasonable also to look for the emergence of canons of authoritative literature, invented either by contemporaries or in retrospect by subsequent authors and authorities. Canons are to be mistrusted, lest they come to control our minds as they may have controlled those of others; nevertheless, in organizing a new field of study – and we are still exploring 'the unknown subject'[2] – it can be of experimental value to construct a canon and then enquire if it needs to be deconstructed. Let it be suggested, then, that scholars are now in a position to organize (should they decide to do so) a 'history of Scottish political thought' around a canon or succession of prominent authors, minimally consisting of John Mair, Hector Boece, John Knox, George Buchanan, James VI (and I), Sir Thomas Craig and (if we reach as far as the covenanting period) Samuel Rutherford. There are figures who might be added – Arthur Williamson speaks strongly for David Hume of Godscroft, Robert Pont and John Napier – and absences that may be felt: it is an inconvenience that neither Andrew Melville nor any of his colleagues is known to have expounded in full folio his view of kirk and kingship. But we have a canon; it sets paradigms which endure until, and even after, they are challenged – Craig's statement of Scottish law's historic distinctiveness lasts into the age of Stair and the age of Kames, George Buchanan's mythic history endures until it is deconstructed after 1707[3] – and it would be possible to construct a history around these major figures and then to look critically at our own construction. However organized, a 'history of Scottish political thought' would be a valuable addition to our resources, and Dr Mason and his collaborators have taken long strides towards providing us with one.

Faced with a canon, and in consequence a tradition, which we have invented – that is, which we have both constructed and discovered – we ask with what image of the political culture surrounding it we are now furnished. There appears a 'Scotland' and a 'kingdom' – in Buchanan's phrase a *jus regni apud Scotos* – constituting a nation, a monarchy, and a 'European'

175–94, concludes (p. 194) by acknowledging its counter-logical strength and persistence. Both scholars wisely avoid making fashionable and premature assumptions.

[2] J. G. A. Pocock, 'The limits and divisions of British history: in search of the unknown subject', *American Historical Review*, 87 (1982), 311–36.

[3] Colin Kidd, *Subverting Scotland's past: Scottish Whig historiography and the creation of an Anglo-British identity* (Cambridge, 1993).

cultural province: one, that is to say (since 'Europe', too, is a construct and not a given) built out of interacting Latin, Roman–British, Gaelic, Norman, Norse and Anglian (since we had better not say English) cultural components in an archipelagic province of the Latin West. The connotations of 'province' are cultural and not political; the *rex Scottorum* is not a *subregulus* but wears a closed imperial crown, though he has had to fight for it against the endeavours of his powerful southern neighbour to reduce it and him to vassal or tributary status. He can be the contested focus of loyalties and images of community capable of stating themselves in national terms, and histories of kingdom and nation can be written in ways which affirm their autonomy. At the same time, however, our canon arrestingly begins with an affirmation that Scottish history can only be written within the context of a *Historia Maioris Britanniae*.

This is an Anglo-oriented if not an Anglocentric proposition, but at the same time it is to be observed that 'Scotland', nearly if not quite alone among the kingdoms of Latin 'Europe', believes itself to possess a cultural and even a barbarian frontier. Mair's 'wild Scots', speaking a Gaelic or Irish tongue from which the very name they share with their civilized neighbours may be derived, form part of the cumulative European image of 'savage' or feral man,[4] and Lowlanders entertain an image of them as ethnically 'other' no less vivid than that which English entertain of Scots in general. In this volume, aside from Edward Cowan's brief exploration of the possible Gaelic roots of the marquis of Argyll's political ideas, we do not hear much of any political discourse which the *Gaidhealtachd* may have practised or possessed, and it is a question whether any such existed in scribal or typographic form. Gaeldom was not an illiterate culture, and the idea that its discourse must have been oral and bardic in character is part of an Anglo-Scottish stereotype which perhaps ought to be challenged; but while there may be no reason in principle why an ecclesiastic or humanist Latin–Gaelic discourse should not have existed, the reader of this volume is left ignorant whether one in fact did. Is it an unfair assumption that Gaelic units of government were not of a size or a sort to have been held together by systems of practising law both written and unwritten, or by courtly centres where lay as well as sacerdotal clerisies might form themselves? Ecclesiastics, lawyers and humanists furnish the three professions which originate the literate and literary discourse helping to hold together the monarchies and commonwealths of early modern Europe and generating their 'political thought'; in this respect Anglian-speaking 'Scotland' is not an exception, and we are left asking whether Gaelic-speaking 'Scotland' is. Both 'wild' and 'civilized' Scots are 'Scots' to John Mair.

---

[4] John Mair, *History of Greater Britain* ed. and trans. A. Constable (SHS, 1892), pp. 48–50.

England – we enter here on the dangerous but useful course of defining Scotland by the non-presence of English characteristics – was a highly if imperfectly unified *communitas regni* or *corpus misticum* held together by (*inter alia*) a common law or common custom of the realm, administered by a hierarchy of courts in all of which the crown was mystically present (*coram rege*), and by a polity of counsel which humanists were engaged in partially transforming into a literary and rhetorical culture. A discourse of common law, common lawyers and law students therefore entered into a series of complex interactions with a discourse of courtly humanism, proliferating in increasingly sophisticated poetical forms and an increasingly populous print culture with its centre at Paul's Churchyard, to develop and disseminate an image of the realm as mystical body with the crown as its mystical head, the laws as its nerves or ligaments and counsel as its spirit or intelligence.[5] The great discourse of 'the king's two bodies' was certainly not unknown in Edinburgh; James VI was its accomplished exponent before he became James I; but it does seem possible to say that it was not supported and disseminated by so thick and widespread an integument of institutions and language as can be detected in England. There was no Scottish institution closely resembling the English common law or the political culture of the shires; the marriage of court and country was not the intimate and ubiquitous love–hate relationship to be found in England; there was less of a parliamentary or court-seeking gentry; and for all these reasons Scottish humanism had less to lay hold on in its incessant struggle to convert baronial counsel into a counsel of rhetoric, and the baron into God's and the king's good servant in a culture at once courtly and civic. Consequently the practice and the discourse of Scottish politics remained conspicuously baronial. The greatest of Scottish civic humanists, George Buchanan, developed a historical myth in which noble rebellion and regicide formed the ultimate check on royal misgovernment, and even his sophisticated and scholarly pupil and enemy, James VI, liked to affect a rough and genial informality when chatting with his nobles – though one wonders how well he did it, and he lost no time in re-educating some of them at the English court when he had the chance.

Behind the baron stood a more ancient figure, the chief of a clan or kindred. Blood ties and the honour of the name formed part of the image of

---

[5] For all this see, among many monographs: Arthur B. Ferguson, *The articulate citizen and the English Renaissance* (Durham, N.C., 1965) and *Clio unbound: perception of the social and cultural past in Renaissance England* (Durham, N.C., 1979); J. G. A. Pocock, *The ancient constitution and the feudal law* (2nd edn, Cambridge, 1987); Ernst H. Kantorowicz, *The king's two bodies: a study in medieval political theology* (Princeton, 1957); Richard Helgerson, *Forms of nationhood: the Elizabethan writing of England* (Chicago, 1992); Paul A. Fideler and T. F.

the 'wild Scot' or Gaelic barbarian, but could not be excluded from even the revered and legitimate values of the Lowland kingdom. The 'kindly Scot' practised the 'lovable' ('allowable', 'laudable') customs of obligation to his kindred, not exclusive of manrent and deadly feud; and it is possible to see that French- or English-trained humanists and jurists were less than happy about this. We must not be tempted – even though contemporaries were sometimes tempted – into dismissing the kin culture as backward by civilized standards. Jenny Wormald has argued strongly that manrent and deadly feud formed a workable and self-moderating system,[6] and it can also be argued that if the level of private violence was high in Scotland, that of public violence, dynastic and civil war was low. There were feuds and forays, Rizzio murders and Gowrie conspiracies, but no Scottish Towson Moor or Tewkesbury, Marston Moor or Naseby. But humanists propounding the religion of counsel found Scottish blood and name[7] even harder to deal with than English hunting and hawking, and some areas of Scots political discourse are haunted by a sense of backwardness. Their attitudes towards the Auld Enemy and the Auld Ally are marked by ambivalence, and the union of kingdoms which came to be known as 'Britain' was more a Scottish invention and agendum than an English.

We have next to ask a question whose premisses are partly, but by no means wholly, counter-factual. Blessed or cursed with hindsight, we know that an autonomous Scottish discourse did not develop over the next two centuries; there was not, that is to say, a continuum of publication and debate concerned with the character of an autonomous Scottish polity. The union of the crowns diverted Scottish self-fashioning into a British context; it became engrossed with establishing the character of a 'Britain', with maintaining Scottish autonomy as that of a province or partner in that 'empire', and with resisting the incapacity of an intensely self-centred English discourse to conceive of 'Britain' as anything but an enlargement of 'England'. Yet throughout the reigns of Mary Stewart and James VI (until his metamorphosis into James VI and I became a certainty) there was such a discourse centred on 'Scotland', its character and its problems; and we can ask, factually, what its character and parameters were, and counter-factually, how they might have developed had they continued to do so in autonomy (never, of course, in isolation).

Mayer (eds.), *Political thought and the Tudor commonwealth: deep structure, discourse and disguise* (London and New York, 1992).

[6] See in particular her 'Bloodfeud, kindred and government in early modern Scotland', *Past and Present*, 87 (1980), 54–97.

[7] For studies of how far this ethos was overcome in English northern and highland regions, see Mervyn James, *Family, lineage and civil society: a study of society, politics and mentality in the*

We can isolate major figures as dominating the last phase of Scottish historical discourse before it became part of the discourse of Britain. There is George Buchanan, enemy of Mary and tutor of James; there is James himself, developing a theoretical intelligence rare among kings in rebellion against his detested preceptor; there is Andrew Melville, James's second and perhaps principal opponent, from whom unfortunately we have no major text, so that we are obliged to reconstruct the Melvillian challenge of kirk to crown from a variety of sources, including James's by no means always direct rebuttals. The king's response to the challenge of Melvillian presbyterianism is of vast consequence in Scottish, English and British history all three; but it is often subordinated or disguised. Catholics as well as Calvinists employed populist arguments, and royalist attacks on Genevan or Melvillian claims to the independence of presbyterial authority are often concealed within attacks on Catholic and Jesuit claims that the pope may depose kings because the people has elected them. Rightly or wrongly, we do not think these claims as great a practical danger to kings as contemporaries did; our hindsight urges us to bring the danger from presbyterian claims to the foreground, reversing the monarchical strategy of situating them within the paradigm formed by the popish menace. This is not necessarily how James VI, or Thomas Hobbes, perceived matters.

In the second place, James's response to what was assuredly a Melvillian challenge was often directed against George Buchanan, both because he lacked a Melvillian opponent text and because he was obsessed by Buchanan's role and personality; yet when we look at Buchanan we may discern less a classic Genevan or Knoxian Calvinist than a Protestant–Stoic humanist of the same stamp as François Hotman or Duplessis-Mornay – with whom Buchanan was grouped by the circle of Sir Philip Sidney in England[8] and of whom, it has recently been argued, Algernon Sidney may have been a late and eccentric descendant.[9] There was a west European international of Protestant noblemen and theorists, and Buchanan is a figure European enough to rank among them – just as his principal Scottish opponents, other than James himself, were Catholics living abroad, in France, Lorraine and Germany.[10] To characterize Scottish debate as that between Buchanan at one pole and James at the other may be to depict it as one between

---

Durham region, 1500–1640 (Oxford, 1974) and *Society, politics and culture: studies in early modern England* (Cambridge, 1986).

[8] See J. E. Phillips, 'George Buchanan and the Sidney circle', *Huntington Library Quarterly*, 12 (1948–9), 23–55.

[9] Jonathan Scott, *Algernon Sidney and the English Republic* (Cambridge, 1989).

[10] J. H. Burns, 'George Buchanan and the anti-monarchomachs', in Nicholas Phillipson and Quentin Skinner (eds.), *Political discourse in early modern Britain* (Cambridge, 1993), pp. 3–22; see also above ch. 6.

monarchomachs and monarchists of a classic if confusing European pattern; yet to do so may be to ignore problems about the specific character of Scottish history which refuse to go away.

To our eyes it may seem evident that both the king and the baronial nobility of Lowland Scotland were in large measure products of Norman expansion; in search of a unifying model for 'British history' we may orchestrate the diversities of Norman organizing power in England, Wales, Ireland and, more independently, Scotland. However, neither Buchanan nor James takes an exclusively Norman route; both focus on the kingdom of Dalriada and the Irish origins of the 'Scots' themselves, and the debate comes to turn on the question whether 'Scotland' is a monarchy ruled by the descendants of Fergus the Conqueror, or an aristocracy ruled by the noble and baronial heirs of his companions. For Buchanan it is the one tempered by the other. Malcolm Canmore, his English queen and the incoming Normans after him are brought in by various writers to mitigate the unalterable Anglo-Scottish conviction that Gaelic forms of rule, whether Irish, Hebridean or Highland, were less baronial than barbaric, and the argument turns back towards the European themes of the association between kingly power and the noble commonwealth – the *jus regni apud Scotos*. A cultural frontier ran through the kingdoms of *Britannia major* and the seas which linked and divided them; it inhibits us in reducing – but never in relating – Scottish debate to the Franco-Burgundian model which is meant by 'Europe' in this context.

The Scottish monarchy faced a turbulent partly Protestant nobility as did other princely rulers from Languedoc to Transylvania; but if we state – or stage – the opposition between the views of Buchanan and James on the character of Fergusian kingship, we perceive them as debating a Scottish prehistory in terms Gaelic and archipelagic enough to have included some vision of Ireland. What effect the Dalriadic thesis had on Scottish perceptions of pre-Norman (or pre-Norse) Ireland may be a question worth asking; the debate over the Irish origins of the *Scoti* re-emerged in the late eighteenth century, somewhat to the dismay of Edward Gibbon, who found himself caught up in a bitter exchange between James Macpherson and the Englishman John Whitaker.[11] So much for the Gaelic and archipelagic – it would be inappropriate to call them 'British' – aspects of the matter of Scotland. As James VI moved towards – when did he begin? – perceiving himself as James I, his thought and writings began to move into the dominating (perhaps we should say domineering) contexts provided by

---

[11] Edward Gibbon, *History of the decline and fall of the Roman empire*, ed. J. B. Bury (7 vols., London, 1909), vol. III, pp. 42–5 and footnotes. Gibbon was surprised by Whitaker's revival of the Irish thesis, and held that the *Scoti* were originally nomadic highlanders.

English self-fashioning, and his Scottish concerns began to incur the perils (*traduttore traditore*) of translation into English. It used to be a commonplace that James I understood little of the people he had come to rule; it needs to be added that he can hardly be blamed for that – the English were an idiosyncratic people – and perhaps further, that he possessed his own means of understanding them and they did not always like it.

We may make it a point of first instance that in England he did not meet with a dangerous baronage claiming descent, and inheriting rusty swords, from the companions of some conqueror. Historians are rightly re-emphasizing the power of the peerage in English politics, and the extent to which their notions of counsel were still as much baronial as humanist;[12] but their actions were conducted within an intensely articulated corporate unity or community of the realm as body with the crown as head, conducted through the intimate associations of king with counsel and court with country. This was not simply a union of king and nobility; when all is said and done, there existed in England a parliament and a house of commons, serving alongside the court to associate, in the mechanisms of counsel, the king with the communities of shire gentry, as well placed to assimilate the boroughs as to be assimilated to them. The Scottish realm in council may or may not have consisted of the 'thrie estaitis' of Sir David Lindsay's *Satyre* (1552); but two houses differ from three estates. This parliament already possessed a discourse of its own, which was increasingly becoming a discourse of the common law. We no longer believe as unhesitatingly as we once did that to depict James as ignorant of his new subjects means that in his bookish ignorance he did not know that the English were inveterate ancient-constitutionalists and long had been; the proposition that they were has not been falsified so much as joined by others, providing a context in which it must be read.[13] What was perhaps new to him was that he was coming to rule a kingdom in which head and body were so tightly bound in one by ties of law, counsel and religion that the body had its own voice and could accuse the head of breaking away from it. James understood the vocabulary of the Two Bodies very well, and could deal not unacceptably with the great ambivalences of a prince both above the law and subject to it. His English subjects were in no imaginable circumstances likely to tell him that his kingship was elective or conditioned by the principle that all power originated in the people. What could not be anticipated was that they would find themselves telling his son that he was laying claim to his divinely

---

[12] J. A. Guy, 'The Henrician age', in J. G. A. Pocock (ed.), *The varieties of British political thought, 1500–1800* (Cambridge, 1994), pp. 13–46.

[13] See the revisionary material added to the 2nd edition of my *The ancient constitution and the feudal law* (Cambridge, 1987).

sanctioned monarchy in ways that were fatal to it, with the result that the
unimaginable happened and they were compelled to enunciate principles in
which they fundamentally did not believe. This was not the predicament of
the Scots, who spoke other languages to other ends.

It is now a commonplace that to understand this process we do better to
begin with church than with constitution. The proposition that James's
English kingdom affirmed its unity of head and body with a more passionate
and dangerous intensity than did his Scottish now rests less on its supposedly ancient unification by a common law, and its more recent unification by a discourse of counsel, than on an exegesis of the sovereignty
proclaimed in the preamble to the Act in Restraint of Appeals (1533). Here a
parliamentary statute declared and enacted, but denied that it was inventing
in the sense of creating, the crown's imperial headship of a body both
political and ecclesiastical, so that its duality of person became a duality of
spiritual and temporal and a king's failure to accept counsel in his realm
might come to seem its betrayal as a church of Christ. Such – vastly
complicated by contingencies – was the fate of Charles I as king of England,
but not as king of Scotland. In the latter kingdom there was no such statute,
no such imperial duality-in-unity, and James VI's perception of his Two
Bodies and his role as a vicegerent to God must have been shaped less
directly. Here we must look for the origins of his Scottish conviction that
Buchanan and Melville together threatened him with a populist presbyterianism, which grew into his more English (and Anglican) conviction that
his crown was menaced by Jesuits and puritans in an unholy alliance.

If it is uncertain how far George Buchanan shaped his political thought as
a Calvinist, let alone as a Melvillian, it is less certain still that he envisaged
his baronial populism as conducive to the independence of Christ's people,
under their presbyters, from 'God's sillie vassal'. Similarly, it is uncertain
how far Andrew Melville relied on Buchanan's histories of justified baronial
rebellion; he may have shared the strong convictions of Geneva and Sedan
on the subject of civil order. What is clear is that the two themes came
powerfully together in the mind of James VI, and doubtless in the minds of
many others; a further question which may be asked is how far this con-
vergence contributed to shaping the mind of James I, and on the contrary to
shaping a Buchananite and covenanting synthesis which would be the
Scottish equivalent of English parliamentary Protestantism. By the time he
wrote the *Trew lawe of free monarchies* (1598), King James was conscious of
the difference between the English Reformation as an act of state, king and
parliament, and the Scottish as unfortunately achieved by noble and
popular rebellion.[14] It seems safe to infer that he was thinking about his

14 See above, ch. 5.

succession to the crown of England, directly challenged by Catholic assertions of the illegitimacy of both Elizabeth's rule and his own and less directly, but more far reachingly, by Jesuit and Dominican theses of the popular origins of power. No doubt his counter-theses of the indefeasible and absolute authority of kings, proof by divine right against popes, presbyters and peoples all together, could have taken shape around his fury at Melvillian impudences; but once he found, or as soon as he imagined, himself king of England and supreme governor or head of its church, he possessed a kingship, and a sacred, royal and imperial self, which must be asserted by means of richer and more potent discourse against dangers more universal and far reaching. The Gowrie conspiracy might have threatened James VI, but the Gunpowder plot which threatened James I was of incomparably greater symbolic significance. The better stabilized the polity, the more terrible the threat to it.

The political thought of James VI therefore reached full flowering as the political thought of James I, wearer of one sacred and two imperial crowns and in every way but the papist lawful inheritor of Henry VIII and Elizabeth I. In a great many ways he understood his English subjects very well and was telling them exactly what they wanted to hear. If he lectured them too much, and said things which made them uncomfortable, about his relation to the privileges, customs and laws of parliament, we now see these matters as capable of being handled and James himself as quite capable of handling them. But this image of a not unsuccessful or unconsensual reign applies least well to its closing years, overshadowed by a mighty favourite and bedevilled by the calamitous wars touched off by James's son-in-law on the continent, and to its opening, if characterized by the great abortive act of state with which so much of this book has been concerned: his attempt to make the union of the crowns a union of Great Britain.

This enterprise placed the 'matter of Britain' on the agenda of both kingdoms. Foreshadowed by John Mair and others, it used 'Britain' as a term denoting a Scottish initiative aimed at a union of the poorer with the richer kingdom, and in choosing the name of the Roman province for its planned merger, it annexed Arthurian and Galfridian traditions to Scottish uses, much to the indignation of the by now partly Anglicized Welsh, who declared that they and not the upstart descendants of Irish freebooters were entitled to glory in the name of 'Britons'. So saying, they enlisted on the side of the English in the dispute over the priority of title to the imperial crown, and any full study of the discourse of 'Britain' must allow the Welsh their voice. Since King James inaugurated the union debate, however, it has normally been the Scots who have insisted on using and clarifying the term, and the English who have refused to pay attention to it beyond employing it as a simple extension of 'England'. Such was James's achievement and the measure of his failure.

It helps in understanding the character – if not necessarily the causation[15] – of the union enterprise and its failure if we think of it as originating in the king's clear and vivid perception of the demands of his Two Bodies. He was the husband, he said, and the whole island was his wife; he could not be the husband of two wives, or the head of two bodies.[16] (It was George III, a century and two-thirds later, who found himself briefly faced with the demand that he keep a harem of twenty or more independent legislatures; this role as a British Solomon was rejected even before it was clearly expressed.[17]) But James was not to escape the beast with two backs; he rightly understood that to wear a single crown he must make his two kingdoms a single corporate body, but he underrated the challenge of the few means then existing of uniting head and body to make a corporation. If in England he wore a closed imperial crown, that of Scotland had been closed and imperial since the reign of James III, though there was no Act in Restraint of Appeals to give Scottish empire the terrible specificity the term possessed in England. James united his crowns by a single proclamation, but by so doing incurred the obligation of making two bodies one body, two wives one wife; and it was not clear that there existed anywhere the power to do that.

The Nimrodic or conquering king ruling *regaliter tantum* could give his subjects laws, but this was not to form them into a single corporate body; Fortescue's king ruling *politice* owes his being as head of a mystical body to an act of self-incorporation in which the *populus* appears to have played some part.[18] The aetiology of the body politic, however, matters less than its ontology; when it exists, head and body are unified by a network of law and counsel, and the laws are multiple in their origin so that it is needless to decide which lawgiver came first. 'Kings were the authors and makers of the laws, and not the laws of the kings', James had declared, alluding not improperly to Fergus and William the conquerors;[19] but to say that the king made laws was not quite to say that his laws made his kingdom (or in consequence that the laws he had made he could unmake at will). To make the king author, begetter or creator of the body of which he was head was to

---

[15] No doubt some high-politics explanation is already forthcoming.

[16] McIlwain, *Works*, p. 272.

[17] For this see Richard Koebner, *Empire* (Cambridge, 1961); Jack P. Greene, *Peripheries and center: constitutional development in the extended polities of the British empire and the United States, 1607–1788* (Athens, Ga., 1986); J. C. Robertson (ed.), *A union for empire: the political identities of Britain, 1688–1750* (Cambridge, forthcoming).

[18] S. B. Chrimes (ed.), *Sir John Fortescue: De laudibus legum Angliae* (Cambridge, 1949), cap. XIII, pp. 30–3.

[19] McIlwain, *Works*, pp. 62–3.

make him more divine even than godlike; to say that he could abolish or unmake his own kingdom and merge it in another was to make his *patria potestas* a *potestas vitae et necis*. James claimed no such power; his proclamation did not abolish and unify his kingdoms, but directed them to set about abolishing and unifying themselves by counsel and consent. It did not, and James could not, furnish them with the means of doing so.

The judgment in the case of the *post-nati* resolved that allegiance was due the king in his natural, not his political person; a conclusion dangerous in Fortescuean terms, since it ascribed an indefinite power to command obedience to the Nimrodic ruler *regaliter tantum*, and might threaten to separate the king as conqueror from the king as head of his people – the charge to be brought against Roger Manwaring by Pym's impeachment in 1628.[20] The unsuccessful argument in the same case, however, pointed to dreadful difficulties when it seemed to argue that, allegiance being due the political person, Scotsmen and Englishmen could never be subjects of one another's crowns: 'Scotland is of itself an absolute kingdom, an absolute government, and hath absolute laws whereunto they are subjects, and are not subject to the crown, government and laws of England ... The politic body of a kingdom consisteth of a head, which is the king, of a body, which are the subjects, of a life [? lief], which is the laws, of a soul, which is the execution of them...'[21] The central assertion was that only laws united a head and body and formed them into a *corpus politicum*; consequently two such bodies could become one only if their laws were homogenized. Yet neither kingdom contained the authority to annul the whole body of its laws, which would be to abolish itself, and any such authority if it existed must be extra-legal and extra-regnal. To effect his more perfect union, James must not only rule both his kingdoms by an authority derived from conquest; he would have to reconquer them both, and there was a sense in which his original proclamation could be read as an attempt to do just that. But James disclaimed any such authority, and sought to persuade his two political persons to become one, in virtue of their union in his natural person. As king of England and as king of Scotland, unhappily, he was not merely the husband of two wives; he was two husbands.

The premiss that law was the essence of union between a political head and body was insuperable, both because in England there existed a common law, or common custom of the realm, which defined the realm and was held to be coeval with it, and because James's long and successful reign in

---

[20] Robert C. Johnson *et al.*, *Commons debates, 1628* (4 vols., New Haven, Conn., 1978), vol. III, pp. 261–2; Glenn Burgess, *The politics of the ancient constitution: an introduction to English political thought, 1603–1642* (London, 1992), pp. 173–8.

[21] Quoted in Wormald, 'Creation of Britain,' p. 183, n. 16. Spelling and punctuation here modernized.

Scotland had witnessed an expansion of the practice, the concept and the profession of the law to the point where the expression 'common law' could form part of Scottish discourse. Sir Thomas Craig, James's active supporter in promoting the union, figures in our canonical history of Scottish political thought as the first great Scottish jurist. He was far removed from what we used to miscall the 'insularity' of the English 'common-law mind', he had studied the interactions of Roman law, *droit coutumier* and feudal law, and emerged with a sophisticated grasp of their complex history which he was as prepared to apply to English law as to Scottish.[22] The opponents of the *post-nati* in England might observe that the more 'absolutely' Scotsmen possessed their own laws, government and kingdom the more 'absolute' became the authority of these over them, and the less were they capable of escaping, renouncing or abolishing the second nature and political personality which was now of their essence. But Craig's understanding of law and nationality was both Roman and feudal, imperial and provincial; he saw Scotland as one province of a Roman and feudal cosmopolis in which the interactions of the historical patterns of law had worked out in one way, as in other nations they had worked out in others. He therefore saw Scottish political personality less as 'absolute' than as historically contingent, and was unafraid of the task of adapting it to the new contingencies of a 'British' history.

In *Jus feudale*, he told the English that the same was true of them, but could by no means get them to listen. We reach the point at which historians customarily observe that Scottish culture was highly cosmopolitan, but English provincial to the point of 'insularity'. King James's phrase 'the whole island' should be enough to warn us that 'insular' is the wrong adjective; his English subjects were engaged in denying that their part of the island had anything in common with the part he had ruled, while Lowland Scots were little less resolute in denying kinship with the Highlands and Islands north of them in the archipelago. Even the term 'provincial' may prove two edged. Scots were more 'cosmopolitan', more willing to admit that Roman and French (if not Gaelic and Irish) components had gone to make them what they were, precisely because their kingdom was more 'provincial' in the sense of less autonomous. Englishmen were more 'insular', more 'ethnocentric', more 'provincial' in their refusal to admit 'cosmopolitan' components in their national life and history, because they could and they did assert that they possessed 'sovereign' and 'absolute' power over themselves in the two vital respects of law and ecclesiastical

---

[22] J. G. A. Pocock, *The ancient constitution and the feudal law* (Cambridge, 1957; 1987), pp. 79–90. For this capacity re-emerging in eighteenth-century Scottish jurisprudence, see David Lieberman, *The province of legislation determined* (Cambridge, 1990).

structure. It was this passionately – one could add desperately – preserved sense of sovereign autonomy, traceable back to the Act in Restraint of Appeals by one route, to Fortescue's *De laudibus legum Angliae* by another, and to time whereof the memory of man runneth not to the contrary by a third, which James VI and I's proclamation of union had seemed to threaten; one of the first in a long series of steps by which the Stewart monarchy came to be perceived as a menace to the unity of its English realm; probably the first which we may ascribe to the exigencies of 'multiple monarchy' and the 'British problem', and which ended in the imposition of English upon 'British' history.

The immediate problem was that there existed two political bodies (and persons), defined by two apparently incommensurable systems of royal and national law. Craig was prepared to set about the long task of assimilating Scots and English law by means of precedent, judgments and legal reason in Scottish courts, and in this foreshadows such figures as Kames and Mansfield late in the next century. Among English jurists, Francis Bacon could entertain philosophically exciting visions of a codification which should reduce both systems to one, and in this (if in little else) he resembles Jeremy Bentham two hundred years after him. But the mind of Lord Ellesmere did not reach quite so far, and the alarmingly powerful intelligence of Sir Edward Coke was trained in quite other directions. Dr Wormald provides reason to suppose that the effect of the union debate was to intensify, not mitigate, the English sense of the autonomy and uniqueness of both their law and their sovereignty. The Virgilian tag *divisos ab orbe Britannos*, once used to enjoin the union of Scots and English under a common name, was by 1628 employed by Coke in declaring that English law was autochthonous, self-sustaining, and admitted no law within the realm that it had not itself approved.[23] *Divisos ab orbe Britannos*; *divisos ab insulis Anglos*. In a sense which could well be termed anti-historical, English history was to be written in exclusively English terms – 'like a silkworm which formeth all her web out of her self only'[24] – and could acknowledge no 'British history' which was not its own. It was a reaction as much defensive as expansive; a question of maintaining sovereignty over one's own laws and customs, one's own identity and history.

The union of head and body, which constituted a political kingdom, was thus formed by laws which were nationally and culturally specific; the more 'absolute' (and less relative or contingent) each kingdom's laws, the harder it was to merge its personality with another's. The same union could also be conceptualized in religious and ecclesiological terms; the sovereign must be

[23] Johnson *et al.*, *Commons debates, 1628*, vol. II, pp. 101, 550, 555.
[24] Pocock, *Ancient constitution*, p. 34.

head of his realm in its spiritual capacity, and the way in which he was so was another determinant of its personality. In England this had been written into law in 1533, to a point where it was definitive of the Two Bodies and the political person. The king's headship of his temporal realm was inseparable from his headship of the church coextensive with it. In Scotland, as James was uneasily aware, the separation of the realm from Rome had not been effected by unalloyed royal authority, and those who had effected it might claim ecclesiastical independence of him. Hence 'no bishop, no king'; once he found himself supreme head of the church of England, James would be far from unwilling to assimilate Scotland to the English model. Even after his defeat and elimination of Melville, however, James acted cautiously; but the English must decide how much responsibility they wanted for the recalcitrant presbyterians of the north. It was hard enough work accustoming the Scots to the authority of bishops *jure humano*; the disasters of the next reign followed when a section of the English clergy began insisting on them *jure divino*. Ecclesiology was less salient than law in the debates which derailed James's union policy, but the two differences in structure have together ensured that Britain has never been the single political culture which James desired, but lacked the means, to make it. Brian Levack's title, *The formation of the British state*,[25] therefore, contains an ambiguity; is there a single state, or is 'state' distinct from 'civil society'?

It is, in the older language of historiography, instructive as well as amusing to speculate on what might have happened had James carried out two intentions which figure briefly in his inscribed and spoken discourse: those of taking the style of 'Emperor of the whole island of Britain', which appears on a medal struck at his accession to the English throne,[26] and of setting up his seat at York, leaving both his Scottish and his English subjects *procul a numine, procul a fulmine*[27] – to quote the witty and menacing phrase he used to parliament in 1607.[28] There was the well-established, though rather Scottish than English, language of Constantinian empire, which Arthur Williamson has memorably brought to light,[29] and York was a city of late-antique Constantinian associations. If James wished to be the Protestant emperor of reformed apocalyptic, as his son-in-law Frederick so disastrously attempted a decade later, he had the symbolic means of assuming the role at York, more safely than at Prague. But as Williamson has also

[25] (Oxford, 1987).
[26] J. R. S. Whiting, *Commemorative medals: a medallic history of Britain from Tudor times to the present day* (Newton Abbot, 1972), p. 36.
[27] 'Far from the god, far from his thunderbolt'.
[28] Wormald, 'Creation of Britain', p. 175.
[29] *Scottish national consciousness in the age of James VI* (Edinburgh, 1979).

shown, Constantine was a dangerously ambiguous figure – the founder of the Christian empire, the author of fatal concessions to the papal Antichrist – and apart from the effects on the English hierarchy of such an exaltation of York at the expense of Canterbury, the English already possessed their own image of the 'godly prince', defined in the royal and parliamentary language of the Act in Restraint of Appeals, which made the legend of King Lucius more native to the symbolism than that of the Emperor Constantine.

The reasons why James retained the royal and did not adopt the imperial style are complex if evanescent, since in fact the move was never debated in detail; but it is possible to render them of some significance. As Adam Blackwood, one of Buchanan's opponents, observed,[30] an emperor was something other (and perhaps less) than a king further magnified; he ruled over many bodies politic and was not necessarily the incarnate head of any one. James might have taken the style of emperor of Great Britain while retaining those of king of Scots and king of England, France and Ireland; but this would have entailed admitting the plurality of his empire and the multiplicity of his political persons. He set out to make Britain a single body politic and reign as its head and king; the style of emperor would have entailed resignation of the duality-in-unity of the Two Bodies, which appears to have been what rendered him kingly and godlike in his own sight. We have already found two reasons why he failed to reach his goal; law and ecclesiastical authority, two principal ligaments uniting the head and body of the political person, differentiated England and Scotland to the point where they resembled Judah and Israel – two kingdoms ruled by the same divine law – less than Judaea and Samaria, between whom there were now dealings, and so could not be reduced to one. The phrase *procul a numine, procul a fulmine* provides us with a third, to which the clue may be found in the word *procul*. What united head and body, in this third perspective, was counsel; counsel depended upon access, and access depended upon court. When James proposed setting up his seat at York, or becoming peripatetic between Holyrood, York and Westminster, he was making a threat; he was warning his subjects north and south that they might find themselves *procul a numine*, far from the focus of service and counsel, the fount of office and honour (the seats of justice were already fixed). They might be obliged to travel greater distances in search of access to their king, or to take turns in having that access conveniently at hand. It all sounds very reasonable, but in fact the threat was two edged; kings everywhere, and kings of multiple monarchies in particular, were having to decide between rendering themselves accessible or remote, stationary or peripatetic – the problem confronted by Deioces the Mede in the imaginary history

---

[30] See above, pp. 149–50.

by Herodotus.[31] The Escorial and Versailles were palaces designed to make the subject seek out the king, and hopefully to exploit distance to the latter's advantage. Would the court and palace of a British Constantine at York have proved a British Milan, a British Byzantium, a British Kyoto? We cannot answer, because the experiment was never made. James in 1607 was threatening the English with something he knew they would not like, but implicitly and surely unconsciously they called his bluff. He remained stationary at Whitehall and went once (though more often than his successors) to Holyrood; that is, he chose to situate himself as head in a body larger and more richly textured than Scotland, united by a more complex integument in all three modes of counsel, law and religion – though a price to be paid was that the challenges with which the head-and-body union faced a king of England in all three modes were greater in proportion as the union was more intense. Meanwhile, it was a lesser price that Scots (and Irish) notables would have to journey to Whitehall in search of their king, and that the English would have to get used to seeing them there. James kept his promise that he would not rule Scotland through a viceroy (like Naples) or a deputy (like Ireland), though his reported words 'here I sit and govern it by my pen'[32] indicate that this kingdom had not quite escaped provincial status; and it was the judgement of William Robertson that the departure of a court culture in 1603 had condemned it to be a provincial culture,[33] until Union and Enlightenment had made possible a *translatio studii* to Modern Athens.

With the abandonment of James VI and I's vision of reducing two imperial crowns and two bodies politic to one, the principle of multiple monarchy triumphed; we enter the age of the ambiguities of 'Britain', and at the same time the age of the Three Kingdoms. These consisted of the two bodies politic of England and Scotland – the latter easily imagined as possessing unincorporated barbarian marchlands to the north and west – and the conquered kingdom of Ireland, whose ruler was not the head of a mystical body and which resembled a captive concubine rather than a wife. Wales, which had been conquered, was now incorporated; Ireland was conquered but not incorporated until 1780 (in one sense) or 1801 (in another). The American colonies which now began their existence were neither conquered nor properly incorporated as bodies politic; to declare themselves such, as 'independent states', was to be a revolutionary act in 1776.[34] This political typology at once provides a framework for 'British

---

[31] Herodotus, *History of the Persian War*, I, 96ff.   [32] McIlwain, *Works*, p. 301.

[33] William Robertson, *History of Scotland during the reigns of Queen Mary and King James VI* (1759) in *The works of William Robertson, D.D.* (8 vols., London, 1824), vol. II, pp. 245–8.

[34] J. G. A. Pocock, 'Empire and confederation: the American Revolution as a problem in multiple monarchy', in Robertson (ed.), *A union for empire* (forthcoming).

history' and raises the question whether, or in what sense, there can be said to have been such a thing. Of the two bodies politic properly so called, one – England – claimed to be so tightly and intensely incorporated that it contained its own history (which was principally that of the ancient constitution) and could recognize 'British history' only as contained within, or a simple extension of, the history of England – a propensity which has survived so stubbornly that it is not even yet eliminated. The other – Scotland – contained authors capable of seeing its history as that of a province of western European culture, whose autonomy consisted in the recognition and management of its own marginality – a history of Scottish interdependence with Roman and French jurisprudence, Norman and English feudalism, Pictish and Gaelic kin systems, Scandinavian and Flemish commerce. In Craig we are entitled to see foreshadowed the capacity of Scottish Enlightened historians to present both Scottish and English – and therefore 'British' – history as that of provinces locally manifesting the principles of a general 'history of mankind', convinced that they were writing English history better than the English could write it themselves.[35]

But there was another side to the medal. The Scottish capacity to see their history as marginal and contingent was the product of their conviction that their body politic was not (as the English believed theirs was) so intensely unified as to contain its own history; and consequently what George Buchanan supplied was the history, not of an 'ancient constitution' in the English sense,[36] but of a turbulent baronial polity in which monarchical misgovernment was tempered by noble rebellion. It took major collapses of government, such as that occurring on either side of the year 1649, to force the English to admit that their history had once been baronial in this sense; and even this they contained within the paradigm of an 'ancient constitution' in every way they could imagine. Buchanan depicted a primeval politics in sophisticated language; perhaps there is room for regarding him as a Gaelic–Latin humanist after all;[37] and his image of the Scottish past had to be overthrown before the philosophical history of the Scottish Enlightenment could be developed.[38] Scottish sophistication and a Scottish sense of backwardness went together, as they had for John Mair himself. Scots might

---

[35] David Hume, *The history of Great Britain*, in later volumes *The history of England* (London, 1754–62); Robertson, *History of Scotland*; Robert Henry, *The history of Great Britain ... written on a new plan* (London, 1771–93); John Millar, *A historical view of the English constitution* (London, 1787–1803).

[36] H. R. Trevor-Roper, 'George Buchanan and the ancient Scottish constitution', *EHR*, supplement 3 (1966).

[37] George Buchanan, *History of Scotland*, trans. James Aikman (4 vols., Glasgow, 1827), vol. I, p. 9.

[38] Kidd, *Subverting Scotland's past*.

write English history better than the English wrote it, but when the English wrote history they seldom admitted the Scots to it.

It follows that there was, and still is, no 'British history' in the sense of the self-authenticated history of a self-perpetuating polity or culture. The term must be used to denote a multiplicity of histories, written by or (more probably) written about a multiplicity of kingdoms and other provinces, which have interacted to produce intelligible narratives, or the need and capacity to write intelligible narratives, of their interactions to produce 'Britain' and 'British history'. In very recent work, such as Linda Colley's, the possibility has re-emerged that there may have been produced a 'British' culture, politics and nationality more durable than it has been fashionable to suppose; but it does not seem likely that this culture will provide itself, as the English once did, with a unified and monostructural history. More probably there will continue to be written a multiple history of what was once (and perhaps still is) a multiple monarchy, whose unity is contingent upon its multiplicity and may not persist, though equally it may.

This should be good news for historians, since it enables them to write 'British history' with the sophisticated attention to the shifting balance between provincial and universal perspectives that characterized their great Scottish and English predecessors. In the history of political discourse, however, it is particularly evident that 'British history' can be written only when there is dialogue between the several national discourses, when there can be found a perspective in which they can be viewed as coexisting, or when there is a history of discourse 'of Britain' – one concerning the possibility that such an entity can be created, invented, said to exist or to have existed. Such moments occur with some frequency in Scottish history from Mair to Craig and beyond; when there is debate over union, as in 1603 or 1707, they seek with varying success to establish themselves within the obdurately self-sufficient structures of English discourse. The present volume has explored the history of Scottish political discourse, down to and after the time at which it sought to enlarge itself into a 'discourse of Britain' and even a 'British discourse' at the time of the union of the crowns. Another volume, edited by John Robertson, performs the same office with respect to the union of the parliaments in 1707. Perhaps there is room for an intercalary third, which would take the rise and decline of the covenants, and more incidentally the abortive Cromwellian union, as its central theme, and would explore the interactions of Scottish, English and other regional discourses in the period from 1637 to 1690, describable as that of the Wars (the plural seems expedient) of the Three Kingdoms. In such a history Anglo-Irish, Old English and Old Irish discourses must play their part, and one might look beyond it to a history which would reconstitute the patterns of Irish political discourse as their work has reconstituted those of Scottish, and could be conducted to a climax in the fateful third union of 1801. With the completion of a series such as here imagined, a Centre for the History of British Political Thought would have completed the task of delineating the early modern period; an ambition easier to project than to fulfil.

Index

For EU product safety concerns, contact us at Calle de José Abascal, 56–1°,
28003 Madrid, Spain or eugpsr@cambridge.org.

www.ingramcontent.com/pod-product-compliance
Ingram Content Group UK Ltd.
Pitfield, Milton Keynes, MK11 3LW, UK
UKHW042147130625

459647UK00011B/1227